SURFER SAFARI

Other Books by Jim Toomey

Sherman's Lagoon: Ate That, What's Next?

Poodle: The Other White Meat

An Illustrated Guide to Shark Etiquette

Another Day in Paradise

Greetings from Sherman's Lagoon

Surf's Up!

The Shark Diaries

Catch of the Day

A Day at the Beach

Treasury

Sherman's Lagoon 1991 to 2001:
Greatest Hits and Near Misses

SURFER SAFARI

The Tenth *Sherman's Lagoon* Collection
by JiM TOOMEY

**Andrews McMeel
Publishing**

Kansas City

Sherman's Lagoon is distributed internationally by King Features Syndicate, Inc. For information, write King Features Syndicate, Inc., 888 Seventh Avenue, New York, New York 10019.

06 07 08 09 BBG 10 9 8 7 6 5 4 3

ISBN-13: 978-0-7407-5452-4
ISBN-10: 0-7407-5452-1

Library of Congress Control Number: 2005925666

www.andrewsmcmeel.com

Sherman's Lagoon may be viewed on the Internet at
www.shermanslagoon.com.

To Stephanie

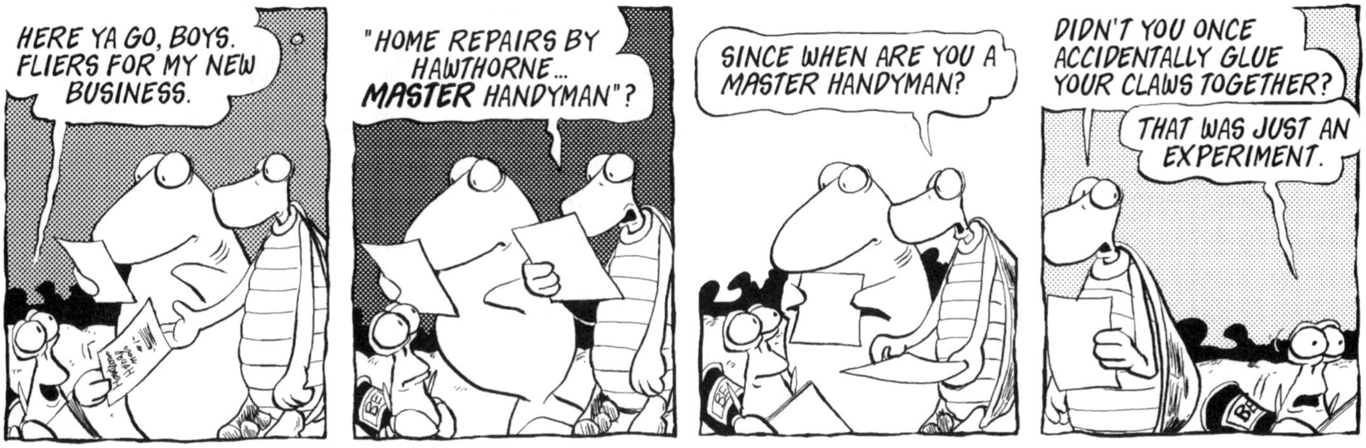
HERE YA GO, BOYS. FLIERS FOR MY NEW BUSINESS.
"HOME REPAIRS BY HAWTHORNE... **MASTER** HANDYMAN"?
SINCE WHEN ARE YOU A MASTER HANDYMAN?
DIDN'T YOU ONCE ACCIDENTALLY GLUE YOUR CLAWS TOGETHER?
THAT WAS JUST AN EXPERIMENT.

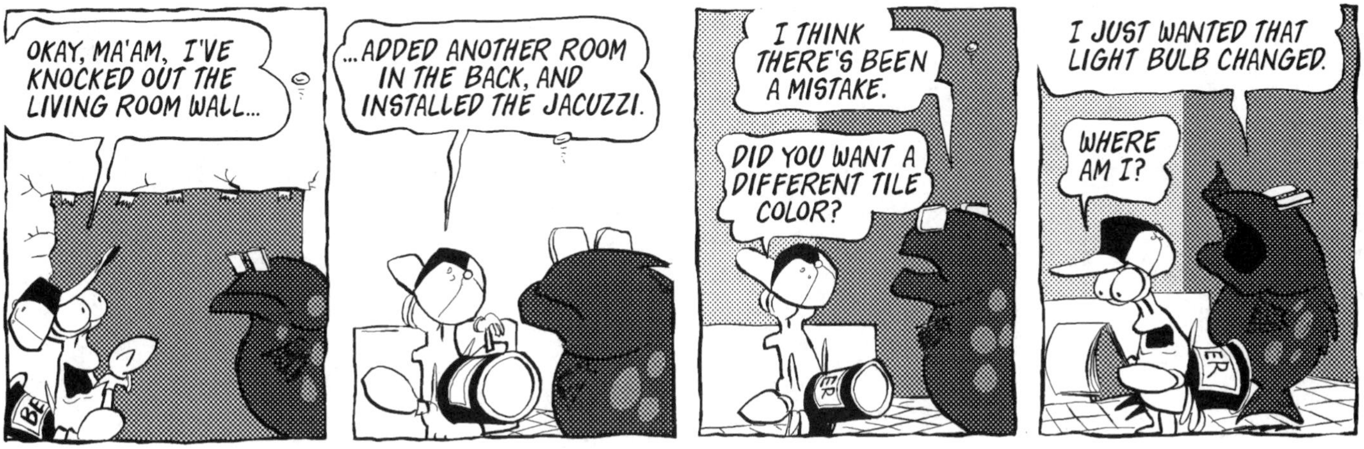
OKAY, MA'AM, I'VE KNOCKED OUT THE LIVING ROOM WALL...
...ADDED ANOTHER ROOM IN THE BACK, AND INSTALLED THE JACUZZI.
I THINK THERE'S BEEN A MISTAKE.
DID YOU WANT A DIFFERENT TILE COLOR?
I JUST WANTED THAT LIGHT BULB CHANGED.
WHERE AM I?

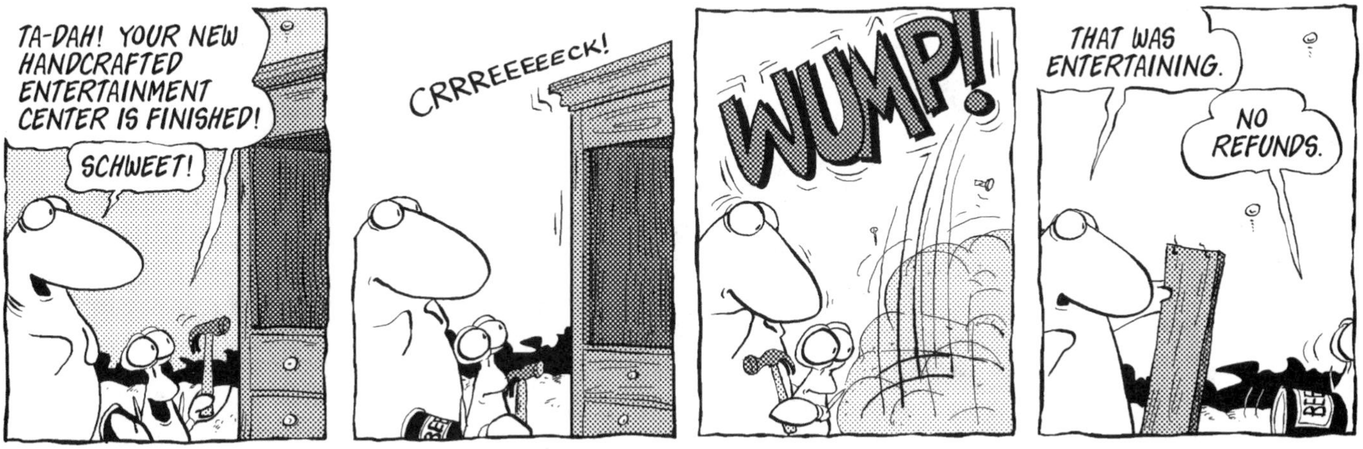
TA-DAH! YOUR NEW HANDCRAFTED ENTERTAINMENT CENTER IS FINISHED!
SCHWEET!
CRRREEEEECK!
WUMP!
THAT WAS ENTERTAINING.
NO REFUNDS.

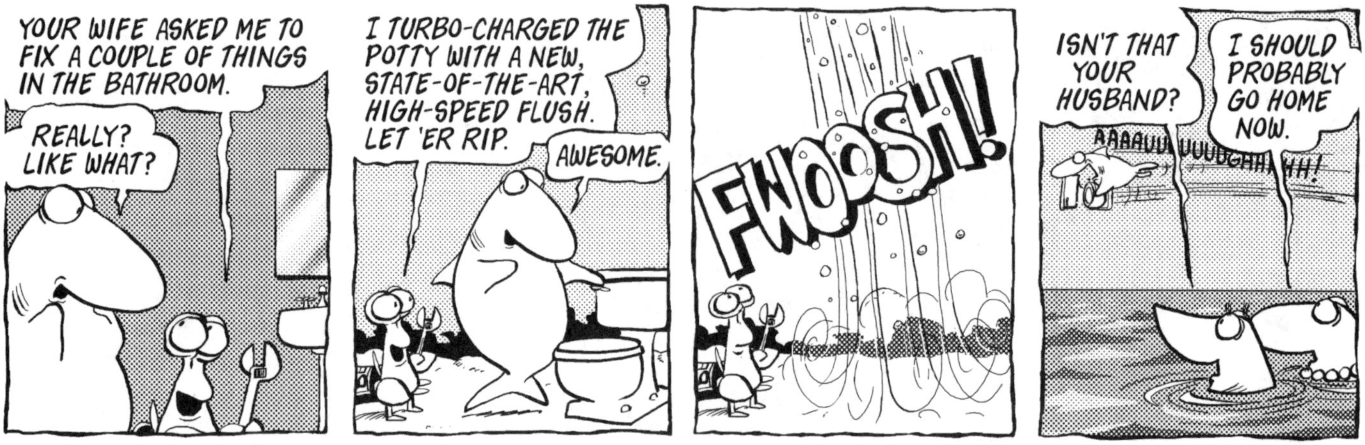
YOUR WIFE ASKED ME TO FIX A COUPLE OF THINGS IN THE BATHROOM.
REALLY? LIKE WHAT?
I TURBO-CHARGED THE POTTY WITH A NEW, STATE-OF-THE-ART, HIGH-SPEED FLUSH. LET 'ER RIP.
AWESOME.
FWOOSH!
ISN'T THAT YOUR HUSBAND?
I SHOULD PROBABLY GO HOME NOW.
AAAAUUUUUUUGHHHHH!

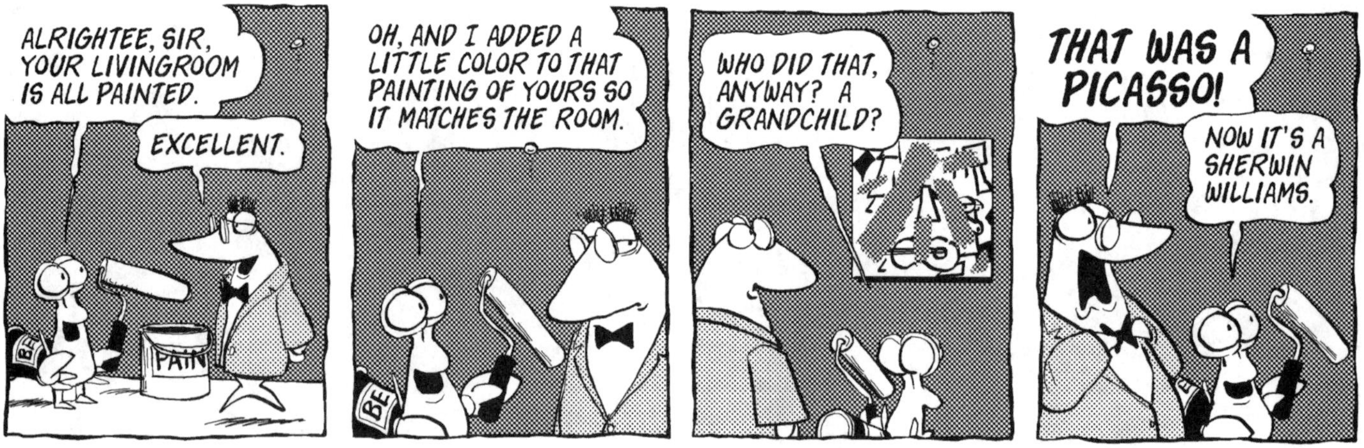
ALRIGHTEE, SIR, YOUR LIVINGROOM IS ALL PAINTED.
EXCELLENT.
OH, AND I ADDED A LITTLE COLOR TO THAT PAINTING OF YOURS SO IT MATCHES THE ROOM.
WHO DID THAT, ANYWAY? A GRANDCHILD?
THAT WAS A PICASSO!
NOW IT'S A SHERWIN WILLIAMS.

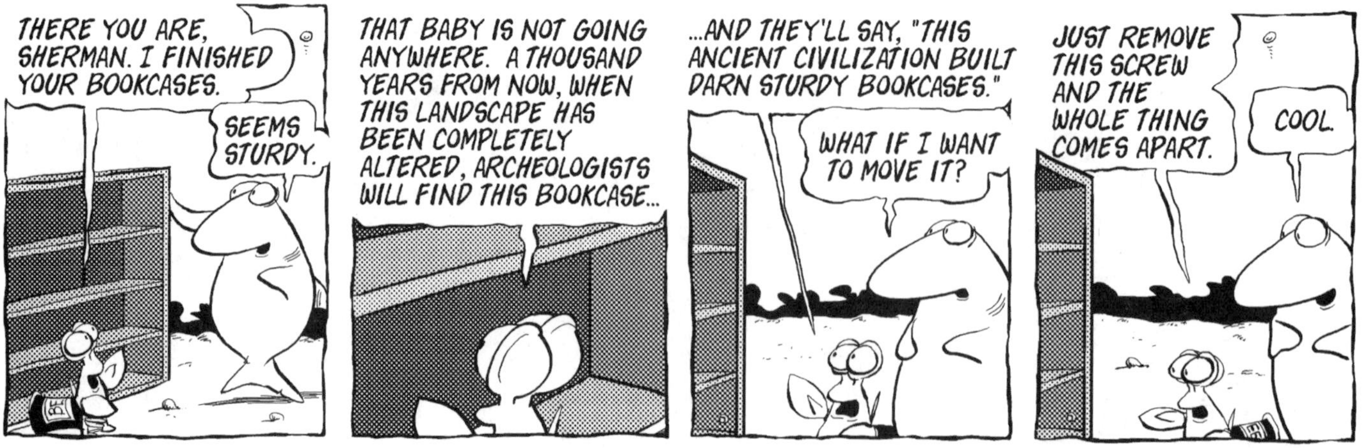
THERE YOU ARE, SHERMAN. I FINISHED YOUR BOOKCASES.
SEEMS STURDY.
THAT BABY IS NOT GOING ANYWHERE. A THOUSAND YEARS FROM NOW, WHEN THIS LANDSCAPE HAS BEEN COMPLETELY ALTERED, ARCHEOLOGISTS WILL FIND THIS BOOKCASE...
...AND THEY'LL SAY, "THIS ANCIENT CIVILIZATION BUILT DARN STURDY BOOKCASES."
WHAT IF I WANT TO MOVE IT?
JUST REMOVE THIS SCREW AND THE WHOLE THING COMES APART.
COOL.

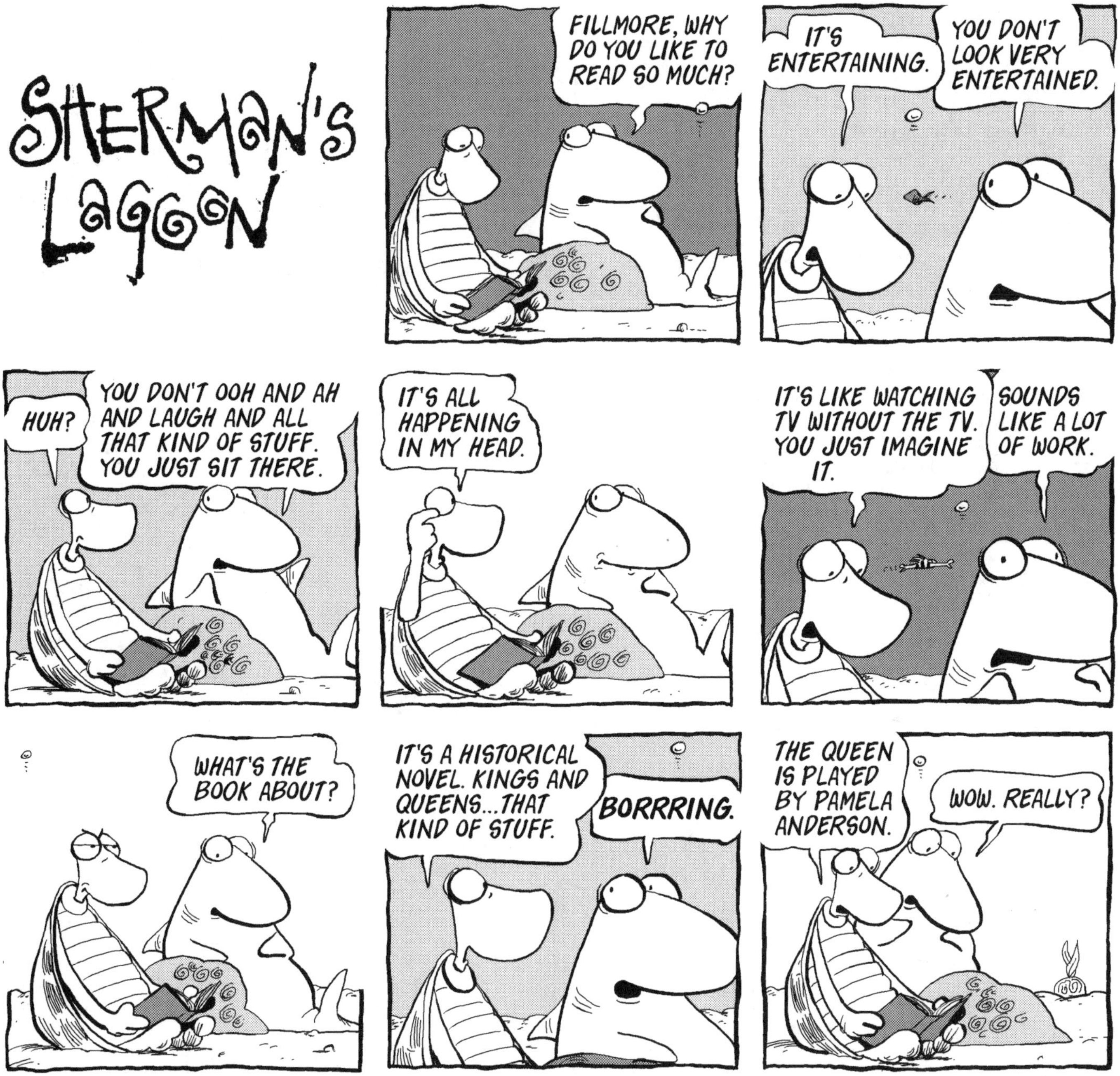
SHERMAN'S LAGOON
FILLMORE, WHY DO YOU LIKE TO READ SO MUCH?
IT'S ENTERTAINING.
YOU DON'T LOOK VERY ENTERTAINED.
HUH?
YOU DON'T OOH AND AH AND LAUGH AND ALL THAT KIND OF STUFF. YOU JUST SIT THERE.
IT'S ALL HAPPENING IN MY HEAD.
IT'S LIKE WATCHING TV WITHOUT THE TV. YOU JUST IMAGINE IT.
SOUNDS LIKE A LOT OF WORK.
WHAT'S THE BOOK ABOUT?
IT'S A HISTORICAL NOVEL. KINGS AND QUEENS...THAT KIND OF STUFF.
BORRRING.
THE QUEEN IS PLAYED BY PAMELA ANDERSON.
WOW. REALLY?

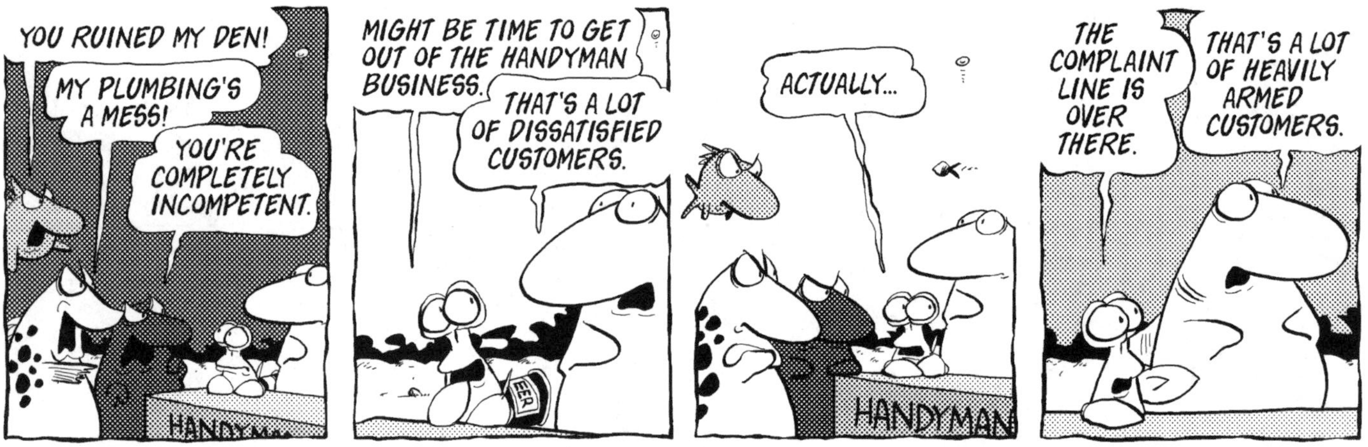
YOU RUINED MY DEN!
MY PLUMBING'S A MESS!
YOU'RE COMPLETELY INCOMPETENT.
MIGHT BE TIME TO GET OUT OF THE HANDYMAN BUSINESS.
THAT'S A LOT OF DISSATISFIED CUSTOMERS.
ACTUALLY...
HANDYMAN
THE COMPLAINT LINE IS OVER THERE.
THAT'S A LOT OF HEAVILY ARMED CUSTOMERS.

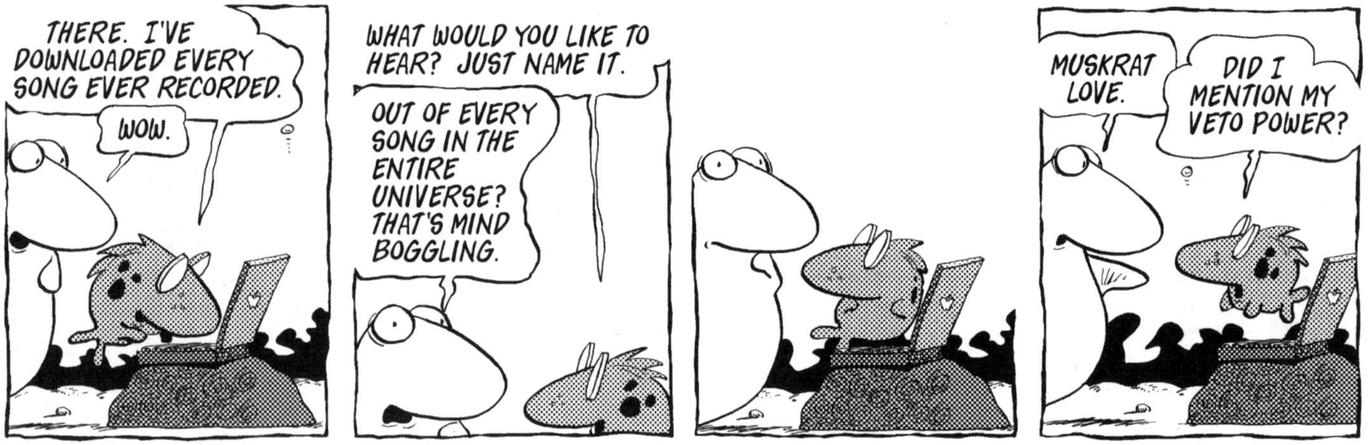
THERE. I'VE DOWNLOADED EVERY SONG EVER RECORDED.
WOW.
WHAT WOULD YOU LIKE TO HEAR? JUST NAME IT.
OUT OF EVERY SONG IN THE ENTIRE UNIVERSE? THAT'S MIND BOGGLING.
MUSKRAT LOVE.
DID I MENTION MY VETO POWER?

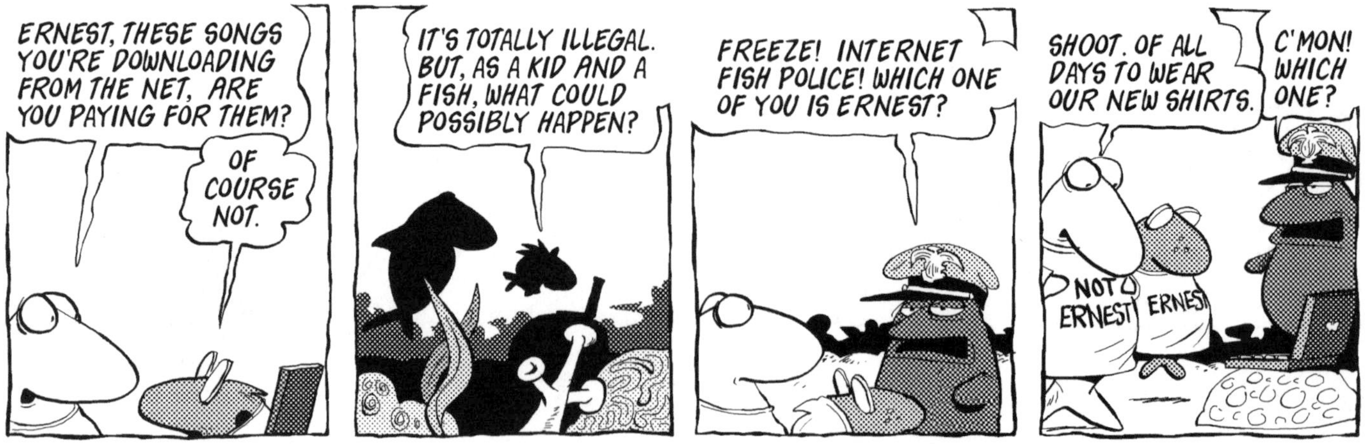
ERNEST, THESE SONGS YOU'RE DOWNLOADING FROM THE NET, ARE YOU PAYING FOR THEM?
OF COURSE NOT.
IT'S TOTALLY ILLEGAL. BUT, AS A KID AND A FISH, WHAT COULD POSSIBLY HAPPEN?
FREEZE! INTERNET FISH POLICE! WHICH ONE OF YOU IS ERNEST?
SHOOT. OF ALL DAYS TO WEAR OUR NEW SHIRTS.
C'MON! WHICH ONE?
NOT ERNEST

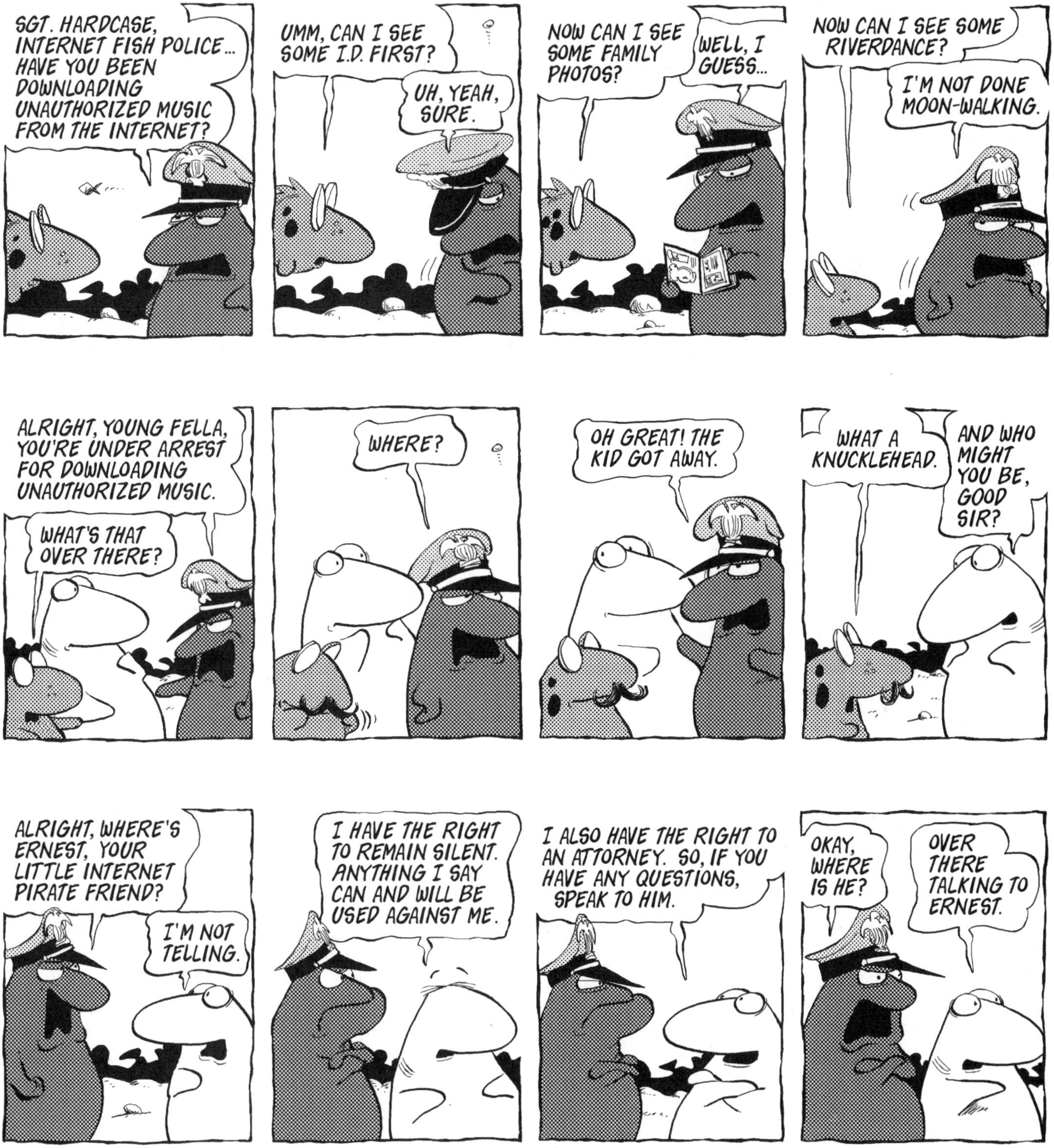
SGT. HARDCASE, INTERNET FISH POLICE... HAVE YOU BEEN DOWNLOADING UNAUTHORIZED MUSIC FROM THE INTERNET?
UMM, CAN I SEE SOME I.D. FIRST?
UH, YEAH, SURE.
NOW CAN I SEE SOME FAMILY PHOTOS?
WELL, I GUESS...
NOW CAN I SEE SOME RIVERDANCE?
I'M NOT DONE MOON-WALKING.
ALRIGHT, YOUNG FELLA, YOU'RE UNDER ARREST FOR DOWNLOADING UNAUTHORIZED MUSIC.
WHAT'S THAT OVER THERE?
WHERE?
OH GREAT! THE KID GOT AWAY.
WHAT A KNUCKLEHEAD.
AND WHO MIGHT YOU BE, GOOD SIR?
ALRIGHT, WHERE'S ERNEST, YOUR LITTLE INTERNET PIRATE FRIEND?
I'M NOT TELLING.
I HAVE THE RIGHT TO REMAIN SILENT. ANYTHING I SAY CAN AND WILL BE USED AGAINST ME.
I ALSO HAVE THE RIGHT TO AN ATTORNEY. SO, IF YOU HAVE ANY QUESTIONS, SPEAK TO HIM.
OKAY, WHERE IS HE?
OVER THERE TALKING TO ERNEST.

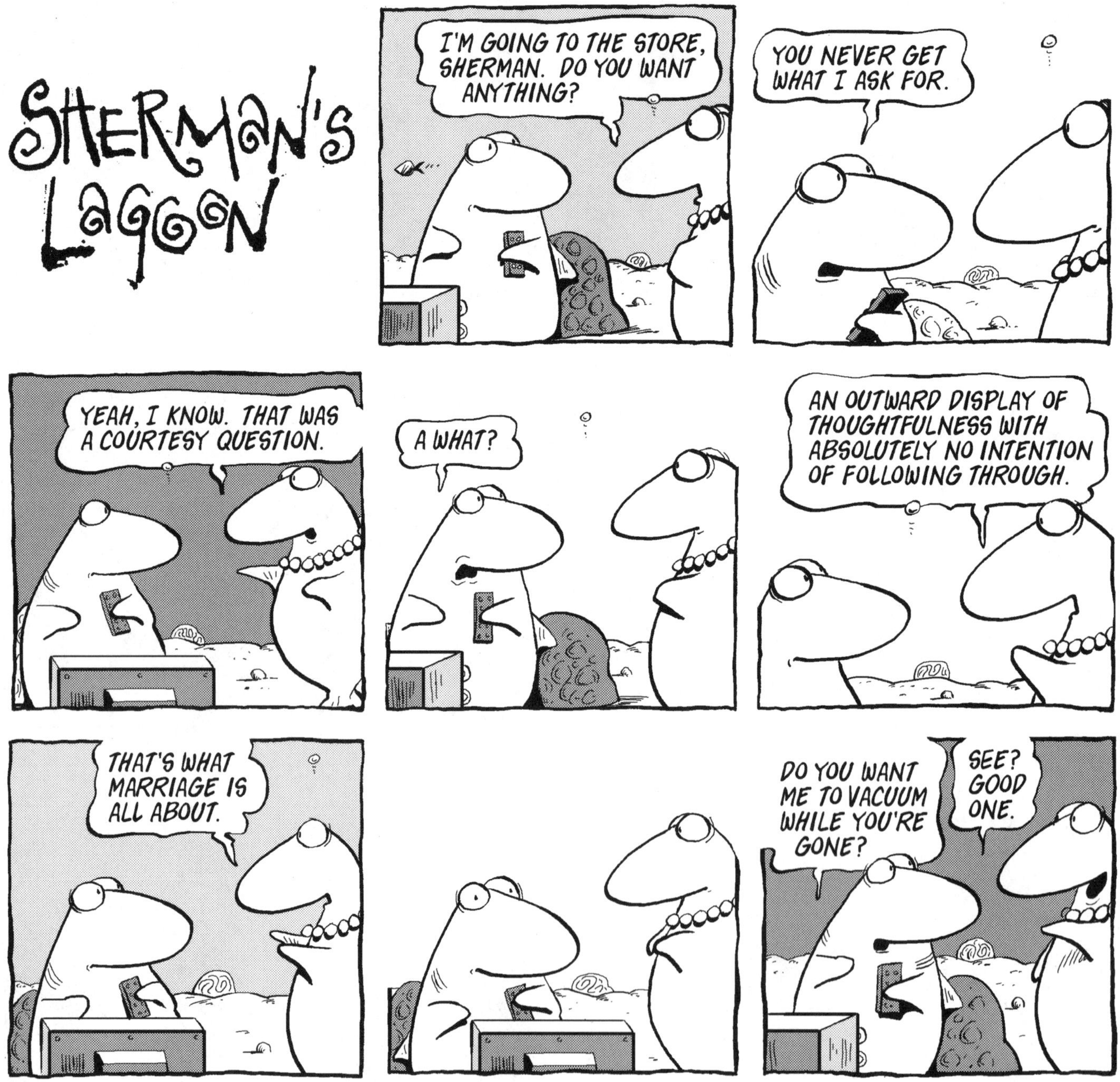
SHERMAN'S LAGOON
I'M GOING TO THE STORE, SHERMAN. DO YOU WANT ANYTHING?
YOU NEVER GET WHAT I ASK FOR.
YEAH, I KNOW. THAT WAS A COURTESY QUESTION.
A WHAT?
AN OUTWARD DISPLAY OF THOUGHTFULNESS WITH ABSOLUTELY NO INTENTION OF FOLLOWING THROUGH.
THAT'S WHAT MARRIAGE IS ALL ABOUT.
DO YOU WANT ME TO VACUUM WHILE YOU'RE GONE?
SEE? GOOD ONE.

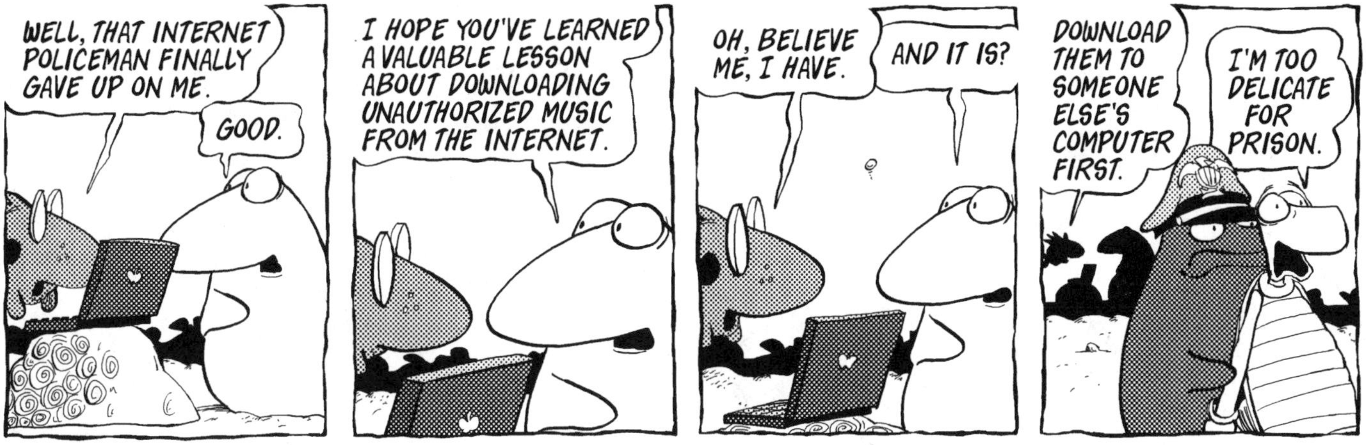
WELL, THAT INTERNET POLICEMAN FINALLY GAVE UP ON ME.
GOOD.
I HOPE YOU'VE LEARNED A VALUABLE LESSON ABOUT DOWNLOADING UNAUTHORIZED MUSIC FROM THE INTERNET.
OH, BELIEVE ME, I HAVE.
AND IT IS?
DOWNLOAD THEM TO SOMEONE ELSE'S COMPUTER FIRST.
I'M TOO DELICATE FOR PRISON.

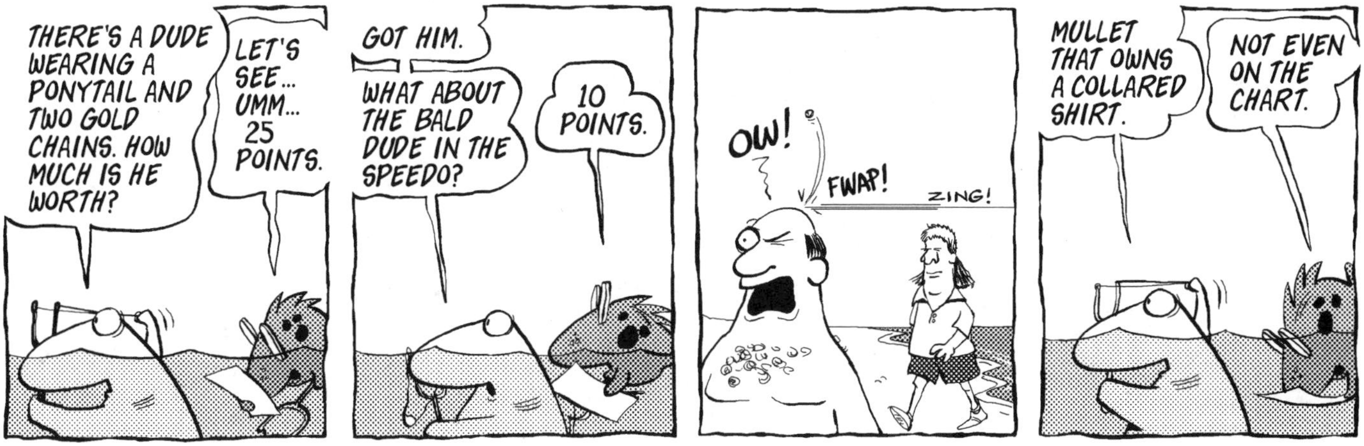
THERE'S A DUDE WEARING A PONYTAIL AND TWO GOLD CHAINS. HOW MUCH IS HE WORTH?
LET'S SEE... UMM... 25 POINTS.
GOT HIM.
WHAT ABOUT THE BALD DUDE IN THE SPEEDO?
10 POINTS.
OW!
FWAP!
ZING!
MULLET THAT OWNS A COLLARED SHIRT.
NOT EVEN ON THE CHART.

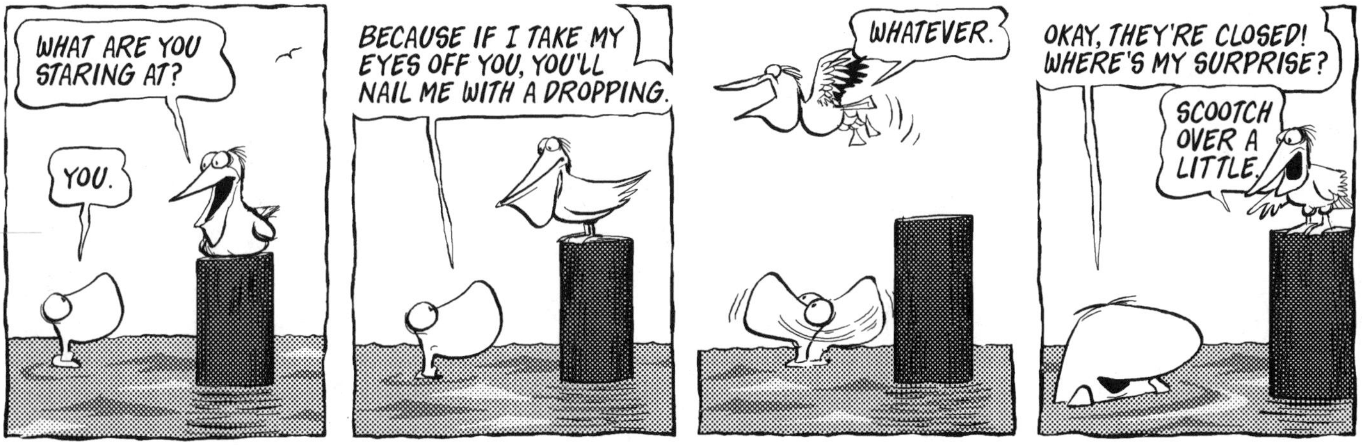
WHAT ARE YOU STARING AT?
YOU.
BECAUSE IF I TAKE MY EYES OFF YOU, YOU'LL NAIL ME WITH A DROPPING.
WHATEVER.
OKAY, THEY'RE CLOSED! WHERE'S MY SURPRISE?
SCOOTCH OVER A LITTLE.

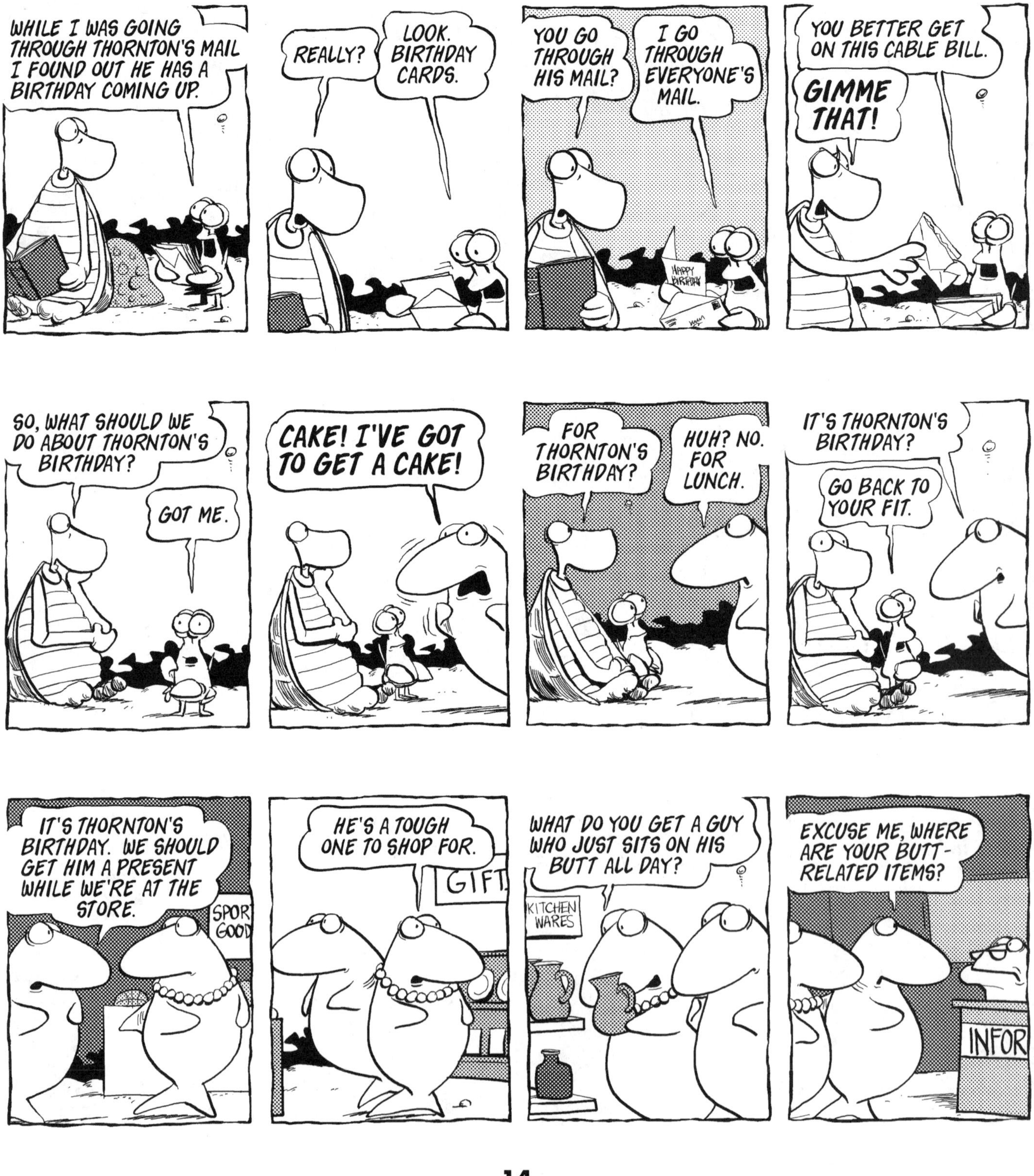
WHILE I WAS GOING THROUGH THORNTON'S MAIL I FOUND OUT HE HAS A BIRTHDAY COMING UP.
REALLY?
LOOK. BIRTHDAY CARDS.
YOU GO THROUGH HIS MAIL?
I GO THROUGH EVERYONE'S MAIL.
HAPPY BIRTHDAY
YOU BETTER GET ON THIS CABLE BILL.
GIMME THAT!
SO, WHAT SHOULD WE DO ABOUT THORNTON'S BIRTHDAY?
GOT ME.
CAKE! I'VE GOT TO GET A CAKE!
FOR THORNTON'S BIRTHDAY?
HUH? NO. FOR LUNCH.
IT'S THORNTON'S BIRTHDAY?
GO BACK TO YOUR FIT.
IT'S THORNTON'S BIRTHDAY. WE SHOULD GET HIM A PRESENT WHILE WE'RE AT THE STORE.
SPORT GOOD
HE'S A TOUGH ONE TO SHOP FOR.
GIFT
WHAT DO YOU GET A GUY WHO JUST SITS ON HIS BUTT ALL DAY?
KITCHEN WARES
EXCUSE ME, WHERE ARE YOUR BUTT-RELATED ITEMS?
INFOR

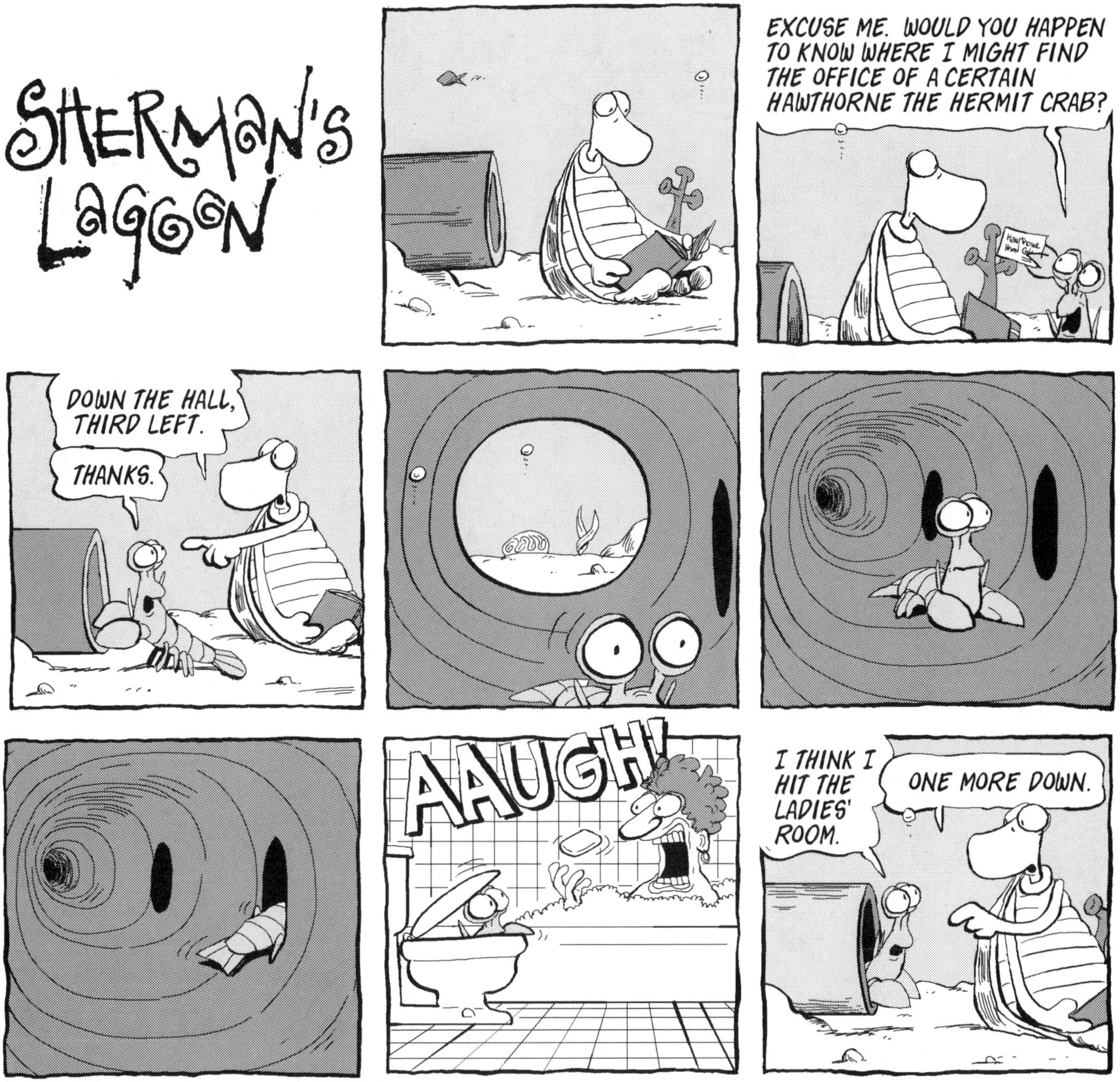
SHERMAN'S LAGOON
EXCUSE ME. WOULD YOU HAPPEN TO KNOW WHERE I MIGHT FIND THE OFFICE OF A CERTAIN HAWTHORNE THE HERMIT CRAB?
DOWN THE HALL, THIRD LEFT.
THANKS.
AAUGH!
I THINK I HIT THE LADIES' ROOM.
ONE MORE DOWN.

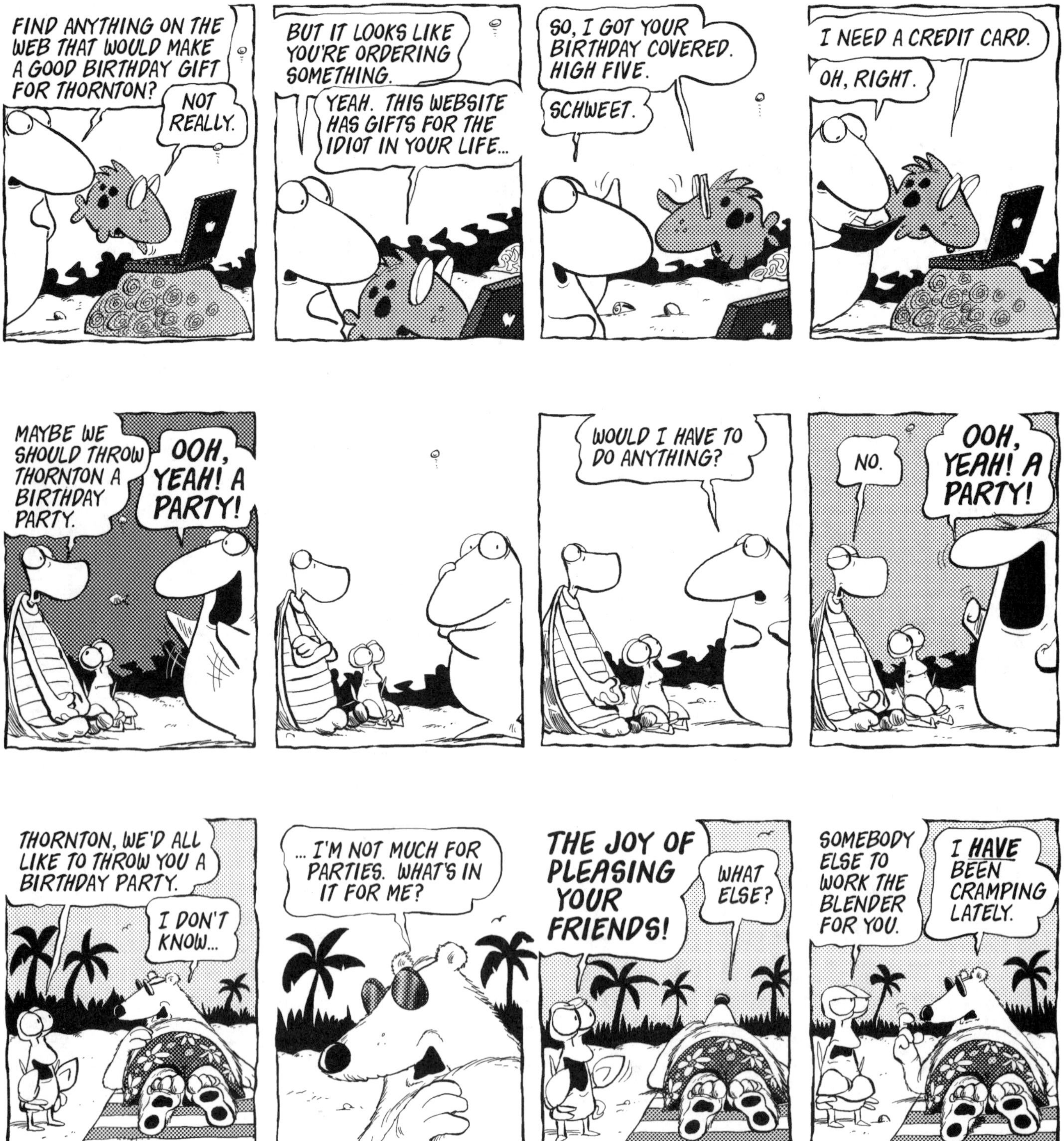
FIND ANYTHING ON THE WEB THAT WOULD MAKE A GOOD BIRTHDAY GIFT FOR THORNTON?
NOT REALLY.
BUT IT LOOKS LIKE YOU'RE ORDERING SOMETHING.
YEAH. THIS WEBSITE HAS GIFTS FOR THE IDIOT IN YOUR LIFE...
SO, I GOT YOUR BIRTHDAY COVERED. HIGH FIVE.
SCHWEET.
I NEED A CREDIT CARD.
OH, RIGHT.
MAYBE WE SHOULD THROW THORNTON A BIRTHDAY PARTY.
OOH, YEAH! A PARTY!
WOULD I HAVE TO DO ANYTHING?
NO.
OOH, YEAH! A PARTY!
THORNTON, WE'D ALL LIKE TO THROW YOU A BIRTHDAY PARTY.
I DON'T KNOW...
... I'M NOT MUCH FOR PARTIES. WHAT'S IN IT FOR ME?
THE JOY OF PLEASING YOUR FRIENDS!
WHAT ELSE?
SOMEBODY ELSE TO WORK THE BLENDER FOR YOU.
I HAVE BEEN CRAMPING LATELY.

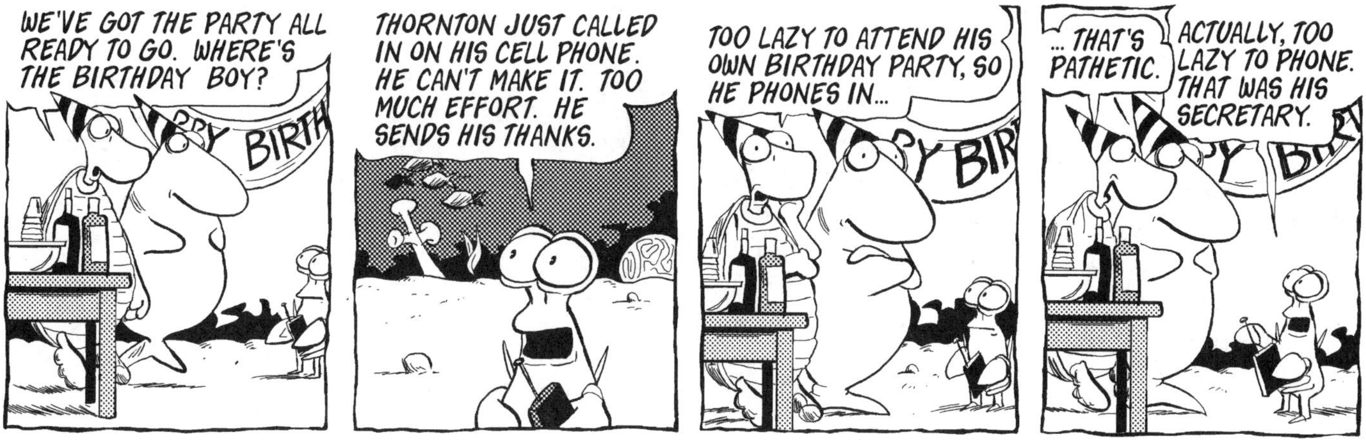
WE'VE GOT THE PARTY ALL READY TO GO. WHERE'S THE BIRTHDAY BOY?
THORNTON JUST CALLED IN ON HIS CELL PHONE. HE CAN'T MAKE IT. TOO MUCH EFFORT. HE SENDS HIS THANKS.
TOO LAZY TO ATTEND HIS OWN BIRTHDAY PARTY, SO HE PHONES IN...
... THAT'S PATHETIC.
ACTUALLY, TOO LAZY TO PHONE. THAT WAS HIS SECRETARY.

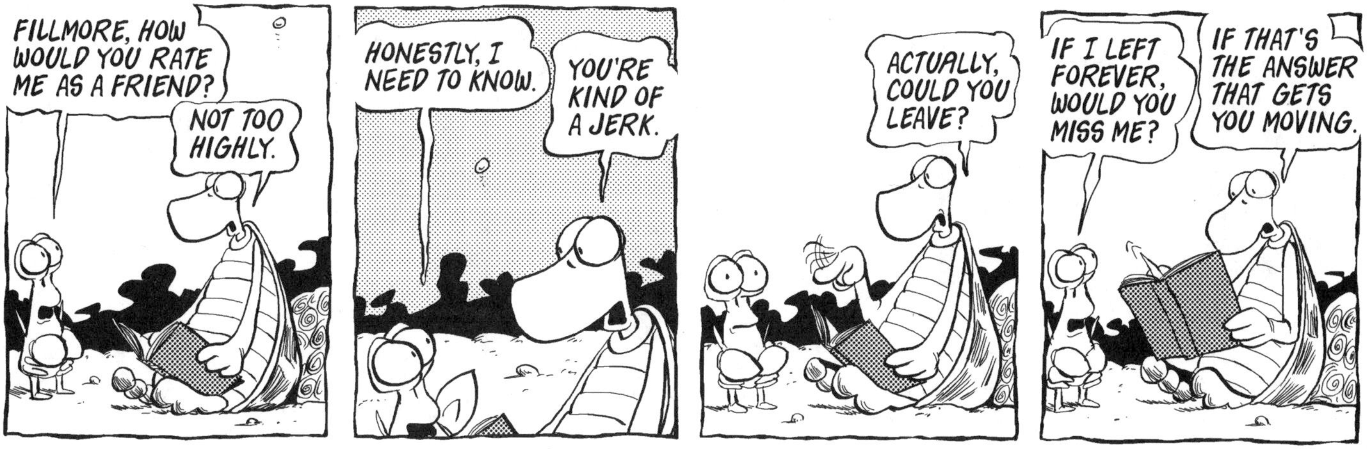
FILLMORE, HOW WOULD YOU RATE ME AS A FRIEND?
NOT TOO HIGHLY.
HONESTLY, I NEED TO KNOW.
YOU'RE KIND OF A JERK.
ACTUALLY, COULD YOU LEAVE?
IF I LEFT FOREVER, WOULD YOU MISS ME?
IF THAT'S THE ANSWER THAT GETS YOU MOVING.

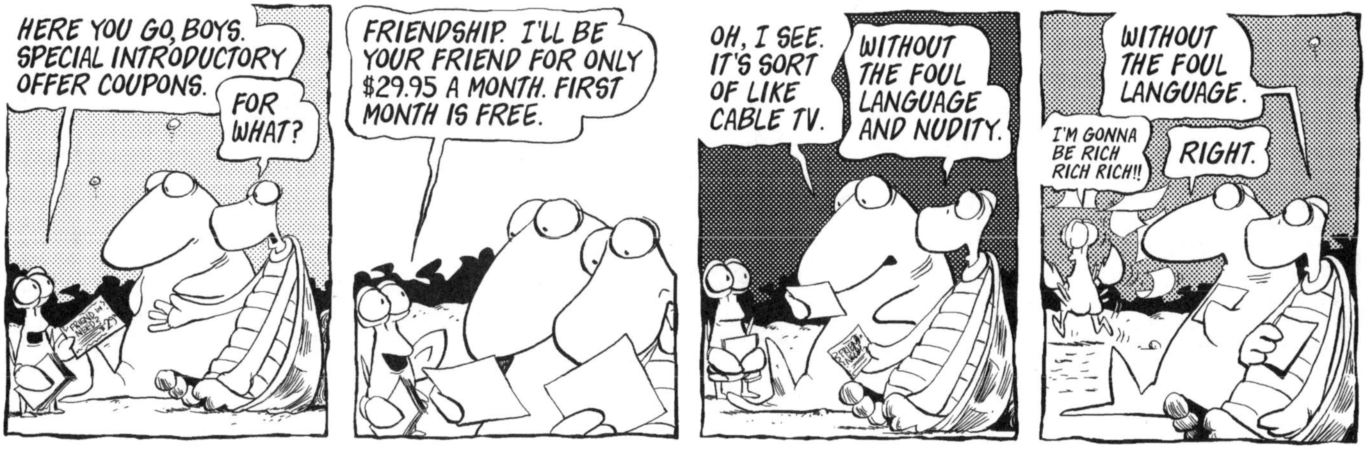
HERE YOU GO, BOYS. SPECIAL INTRODUCTORY OFFER COUPONS.
FOR WHAT?
FRIENDSHIP. I'LL BE YOUR FRIEND FOR ONLY $29.95 A MONTH. FIRST MONTH IS FREE.
OH, I SEE. IT'S SORT OF LIKE CABLE TV.
WITHOUT THE FOUL LANGUAGE AND NUDITY.
WITHOUT THE FOUL LANGUAGE.
I'M GONNA BE RICH RICH RICH!!
RIGHT.

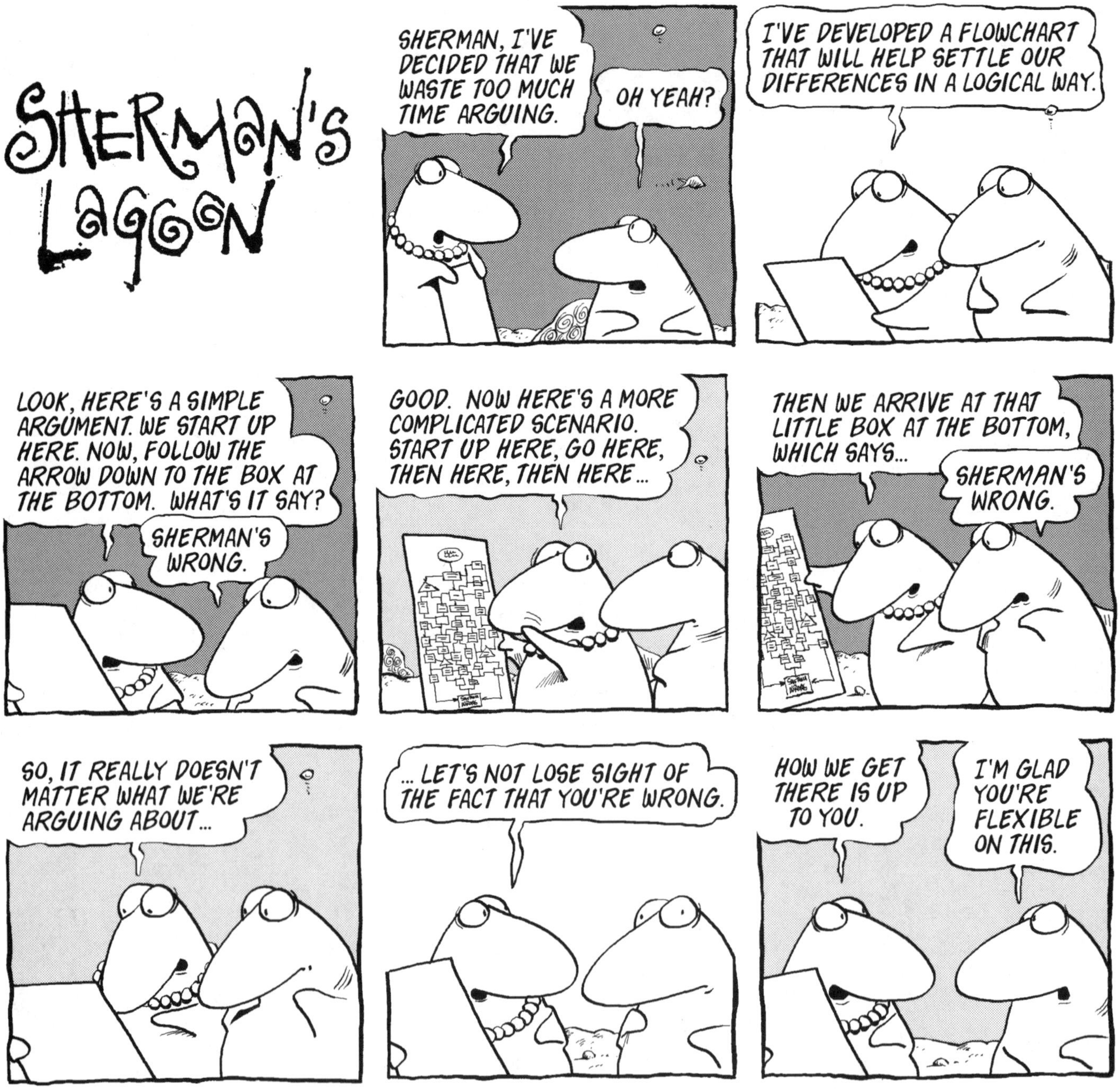
SHERMAN'S LAGOON
SHERMAN, I'VE DECIDED THAT WE WASTE TOO MUCH TIME ARGUING.
OH YEAH?
I'VE DEVELOPED A FLOWCHART THAT WILL HELP SETTLE OUR DIFFERENCES IN A LOGICAL WAY.
LOOK, HERE'S A SIMPLE ARGUMENT. WE START UP HERE. NOW, FOLLOW THE ARROW DOWN TO THE BOX AT THE BOTTOM. WHAT'S IT SAY?
SHERMAN'S WRONG.
GOOD. NOW HERE'S A MORE COMPLICATED SCENARIO. START UP HERE, GO HERE, THEN HERE, THEN HERE...
THEN WE ARRIVE AT THAT LITTLE BOX AT THE BOTTOM, WHICH SAYS...
SHERMAN'S WRONG.
SO, IT REALLY DOESN'T MATTER WHAT WE'RE ARGUING ABOUT...
... LET'S NOT LOSE SIGHT OF THE FACT THAT YOU'RE WRONG.
HOW WE GET THERE IS UP TO YOU.
I'M GLAD YOU'RE FLEXIBLE ON THIS.

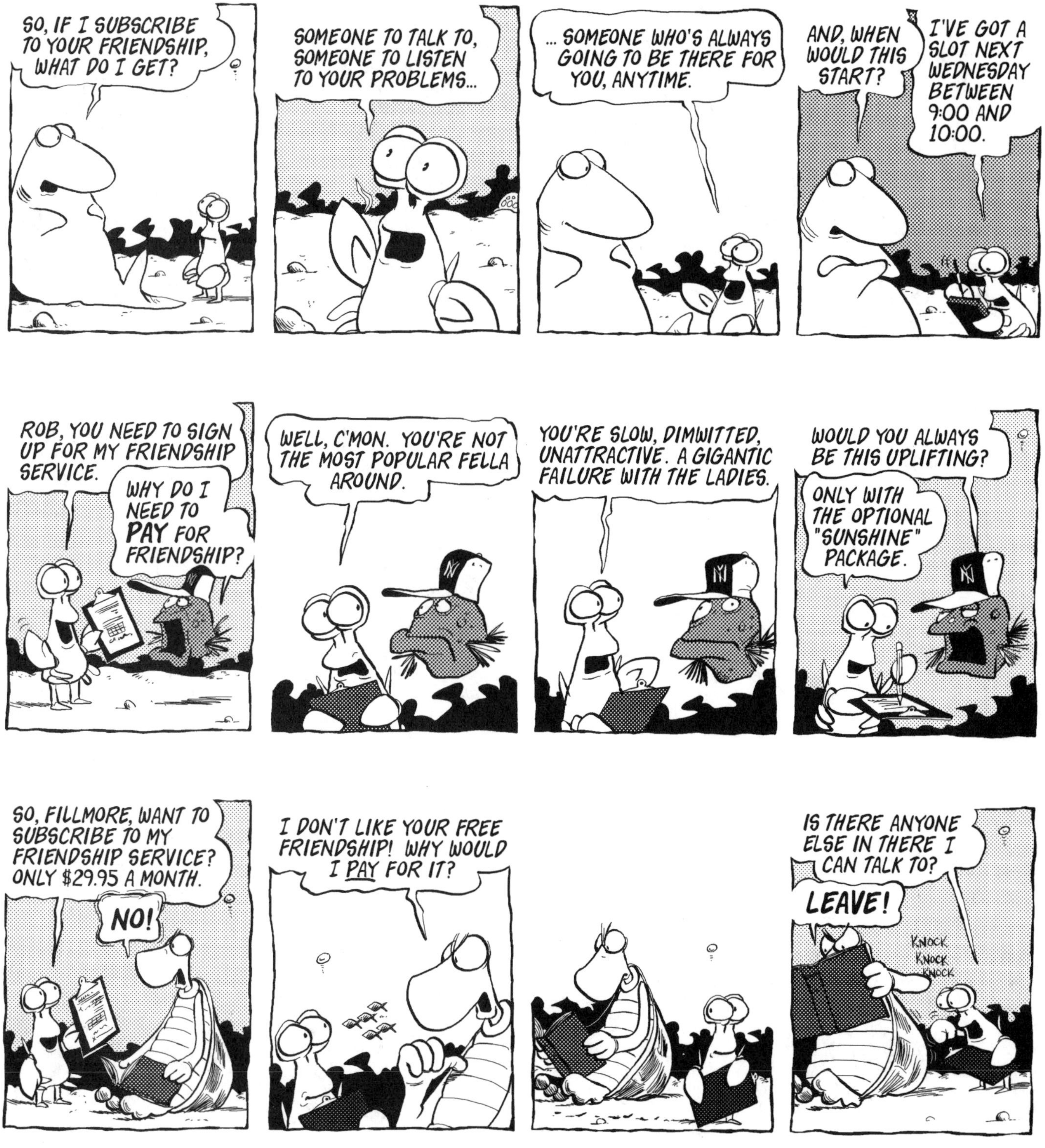
SO, IF I SUBSCRIBE TO YOUR FRIENDSHIP, WHAT DO I GET?
SOMEONE TO TALK TO, SOMEONE TO LISTEN TO YOUR PROBLEMS...
... SOMEONE WHO'S ALWAYS GOING TO BE THERE FOR YOU, ANYTIME.
AND, WHEN WOULD THIS START?
I'VE GOT A SLOT NEXT WEDNESDAY BETWEEN 9:00 AND 10:00.
ROB, YOU NEED TO SIGN UP FOR MY FRIENDSHIP SERVICE.
WHY DO I NEED TO PAY FOR FRIENDSHIP?
WELL, C'MON. YOU'RE NOT THE MOST POPULAR FELLA AROUND.
YOU'RE SLOW, DIMWITTED, UNATTRACTIVE. A GIGANTIC FAILURE WITH THE LADIES.
WOULD YOU ALWAYS BE THIS UPLIFTING?
ONLY WITH THE OPTIONAL "SUNSHINE" PACKAGE.
SO, FILLMORE, WANT TO SUBSCRIBE TO MY FRIENDSHIP SERVICE? ONLY $29.95 A MONTH.
NO!
I DON'T LIKE YOUR FREE FRIENDSHIP! WHY WOULD I PAY FOR IT?
IS THERE ANYONE ELSE IN THERE I CAN TALK TO?
LEAVE!
KNOCK KNOCK KNOCK

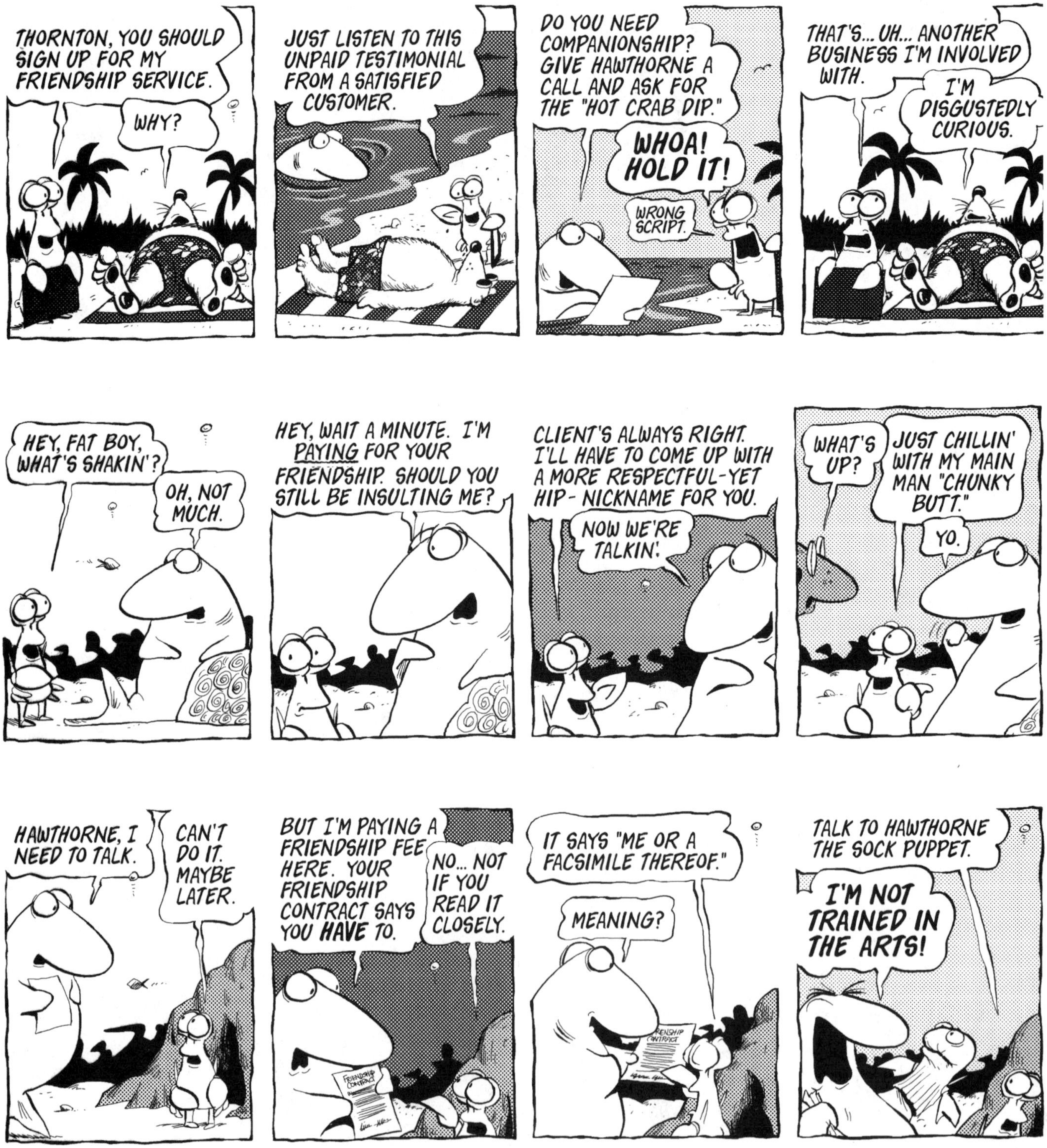
THORNTON, YOU SHOULD SIGN UP FOR MY FRIENDSHIP SERVICE.
WHY?
JUST LISTEN TO THIS UNPAID TESTIMONIAL FROM A SATISFIED CUSTOMER.
DO YOU NEED COMPANIONSHIP? GIVE HAWTHORNE A CALL AND ASK FOR THE "HOT CRAB DIP."
WHOA! HOLD IT!
WRONG SCRIPT.
THAT'S... UH... ANOTHER BUSINESS I'M INVOLVED WITH.
I'M DISGUSTEDLY CURIOUS.
HEY, FAT BOY, WHAT'S SHAKIN'?
OH, NOT MUCH.
HEY, WAIT A MINUTE. I'M PAYING FOR YOUR FRIENDSHIP. SHOULD YOU STILL BE INSULTING ME?
CLIENT'S ALWAYS RIGHT. I'LL HAVE TO COME UP WITH A MORE RESPECTFUL-YET HIP- NICKNAME FOR YOU.
NOW WE'RE TALKIN'.
WHAT'S UP?
JUST CHILLIN' WITH MY MAIN MAN "CHUNKY BUTT."
YO.
HAWTHORNE, I NEED TO TALK.
CAN'T DO IT. MAYBE LATER.
BUT I'M PAYING A FRIENDSHIP FEE HERE. YOUR FRIENDSHIP CONTRACT SAYS YOU HAVE TO.
NO... NOT IF YOU READ IT CLOSELY.
FRIENDSHIP CONTRACT
IT SAYS "ME OR A FACSIMILE THEREOF."
MEANING?
TALK TO HAWTHORNE THE SOCK PUPPET.
I'M NOT TRAINED IN THE ARTS!

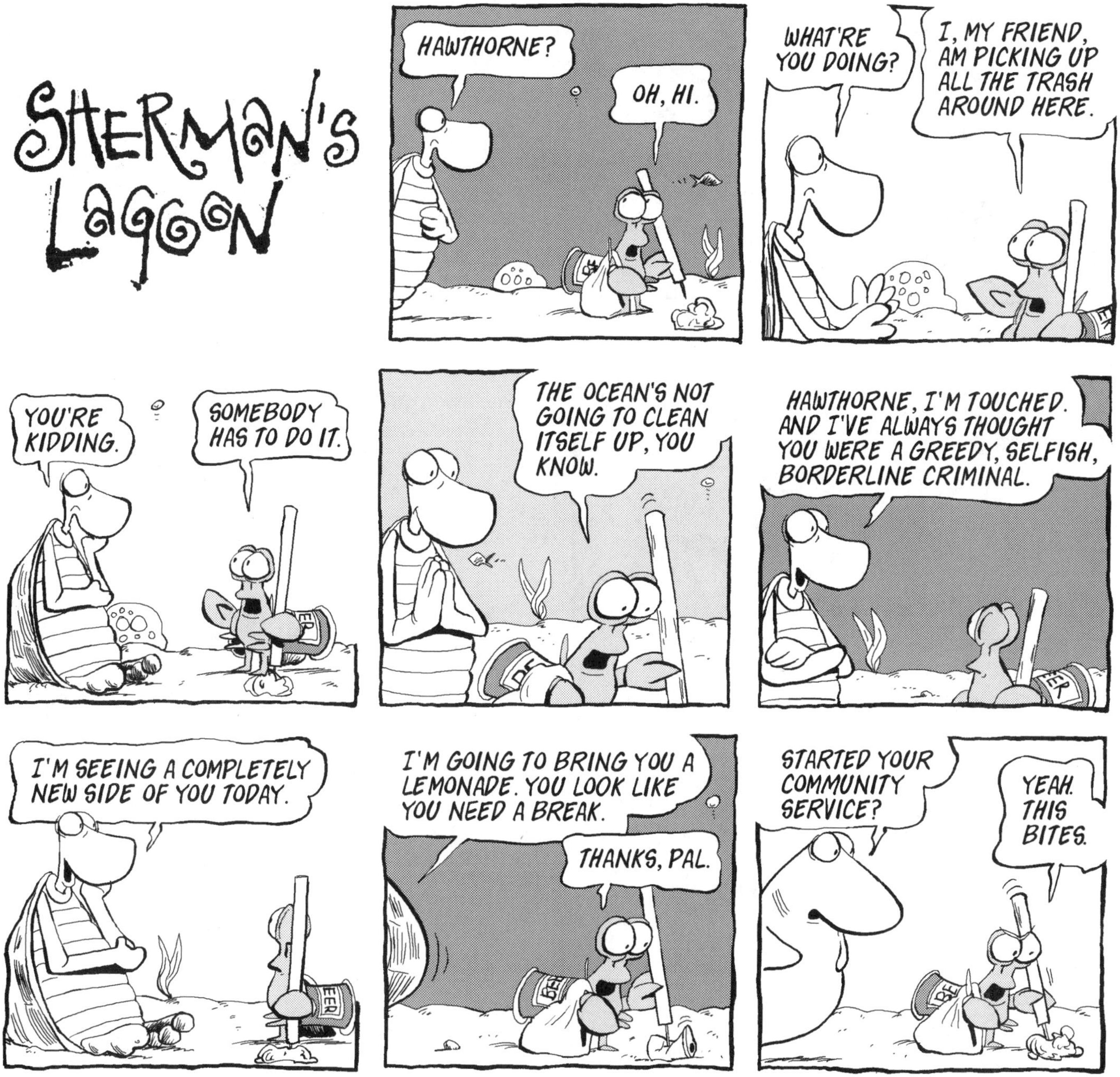
SHERMAN'S LAGOON
HAWTHORNE?
OH, HI.
WHAT'RE YOU DOING?
I, MY FRIEND, AM PICKING UP ALL THE TRASH AROUND HERE.
YOU'RE KIDDING.
SOMEBODY HAS TO DO IT.
THE OCEAN'S NOT GOING TO CLEAN ITSELF UP, YOU KNOW.
HAWTHORNE, I'M TOUCHED. AND I'VE ALWAYS THOUGHT YOU WERE A GREEDY, SELFISH, BORDERLINE CRIMINAL.
I'M SEEING A COMPLETELY NEW SIDE OF YOU TODAY.
I'M GOING TO BRING YOU A LEMONADE. YOU LOOK LIKE YOU NEED A BREAK.
THANKS, PAL.
STARTED YOUR COMMUNITY SERVICE?
YEAH. THIS BITES.

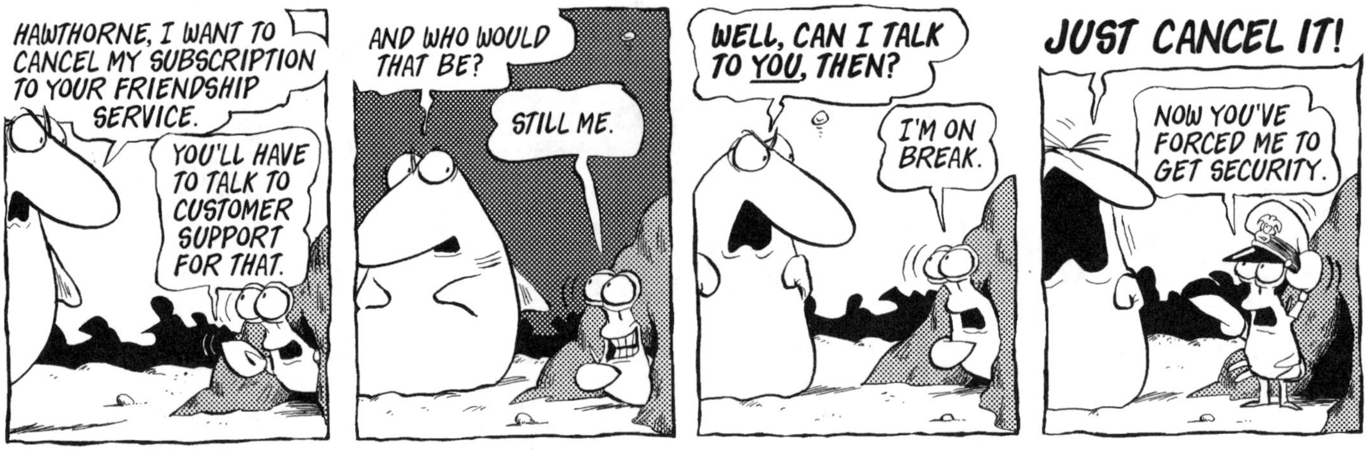
HAWTHORNE, I WANT TO CANCEL MY SUBSCRIPTION TO YOUR FRIENDSHIP SERVICE.
YOU'LL HAVE TO TALK TO CUSTOMER SUPPORT FOR THAT.
AND WHO WOULD THAT BE?
STILL ME.
WELL, CAN I TALK TO YOU, THEN?
I'M ON BREAK.
JUST CANCEL IT!
NOW YOU'VE FORCED ME TO GET SECURITY.

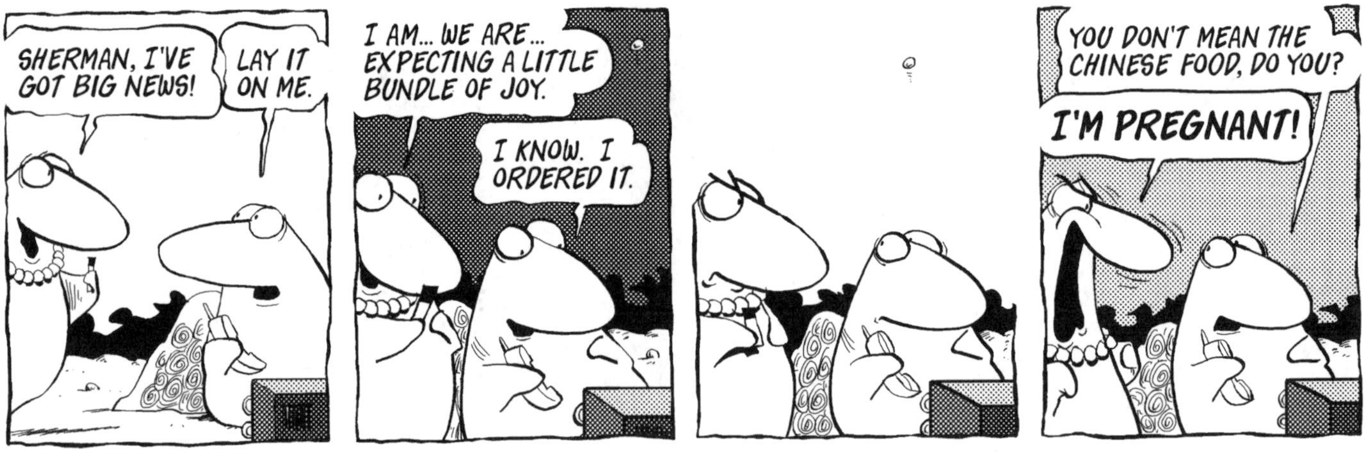
SHERMAN, I'VE GOT BIG NEWS!
LAY IT ON ME.
I AM... WE ARE... EXPECTING A LITTLE BUNDLE OF JOY.
I KNOW. I ORDERED IT.
YOU DON'T MEAN THE CHINESE FOOD, DO YOU?
I'M PREGNANT!

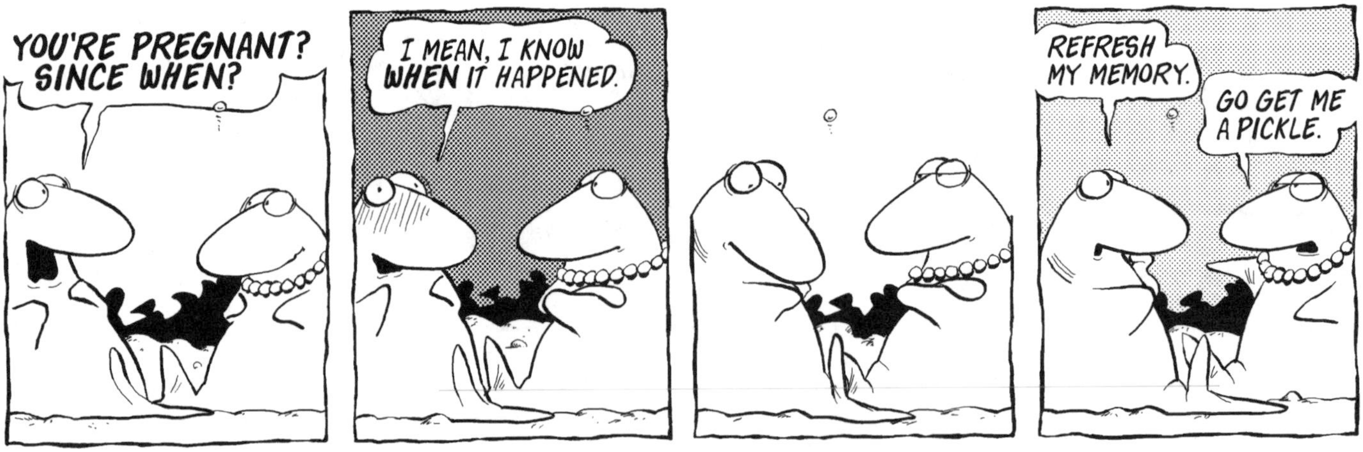
YOU'RE PREGNANT? SINCE WHEN?
I MEAN, I KNOW WHEN IT HAPPENED.
REFRESH MY MEMORY.
GO GET ME A PICKLE.

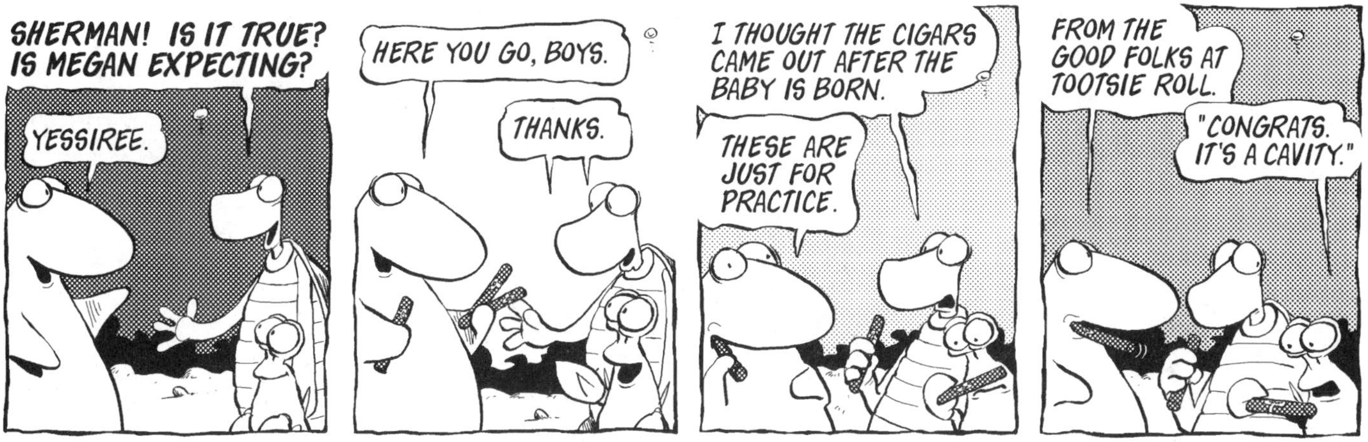
SHERMAN! IS IT TRUE? IS MEGAN EXPECTING?
YESSIREE.
HERE YOU GO, BOYS.
THANKS.
I THOUGHT THE CIGARS CAME OUT AFTER THE BABY IS BORN.
THESE ARE JUST FOR PRACTICE.
FROM THE GOOD FOLKS AT TOOTSIE ROLL.
"CONGRATS. IT'S A CAVITY."

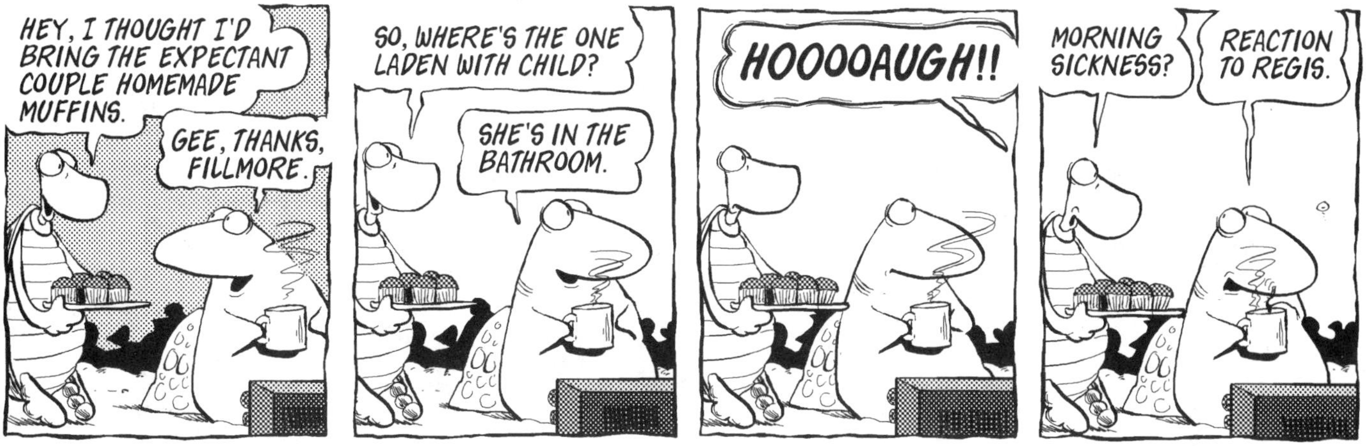
HEY, I THOUGHT I'D BRING THE EXPECTANT COUPLE HOMEMADE MUFFINS.
GEE, THANKS, FILLMORE.
SO, WHERE'S THE ONE LADEN WITH CHILD?
SHE'S IN THE BATHROOM.
HOOOOAUGH!!
MORNING SICKNESS?
REACTION TO REGIS.

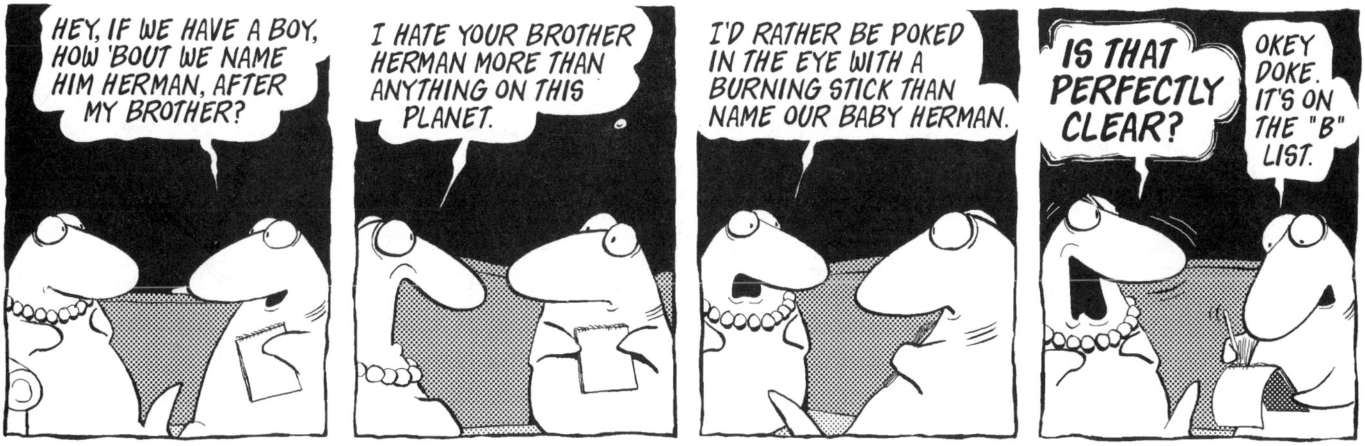
HEY, IF WE HAVE A BOY, HOW 'BOUT WE NAME HIM HERMAN, AFTER MY BROTHER?
I HATE YOUR BROTHER HERMAN MORE THAN ANYTHING ON THIS PLANET.
I'D RATHER BE POKED IN THE EYE WITH A BURNING STICK THAN NAME OUR BABY HERMAN.
IS THAT PERFECTLY CLEAR?
OKEY DOKE. IT'S ON THE "B" LIST.

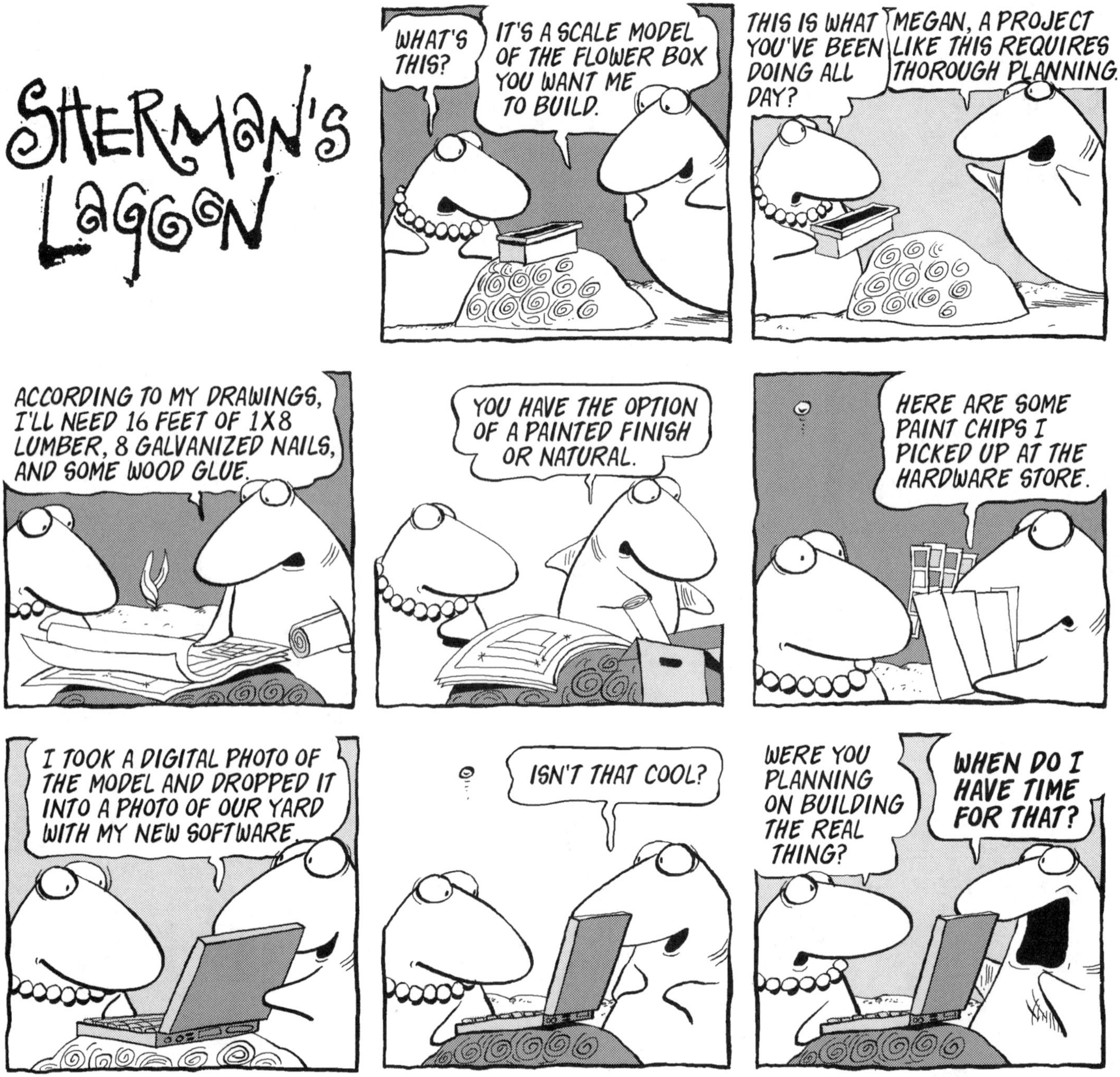
SHERMAN'S LAGOON
WHAT'S THIS?
IT'S A SCALE MODEL OF THE FLOWER BOX YOU WANT ME TO BUILD.
THIS IS WHAT YOU'VE BEEN DOING ALL DAY?
MEGAN, A PROJECT LIKE THIS REQUIRES THOROUGH PLANNING.
ACCORDING TO MY DRAWINGS, I'LL NEED 16 FEET OF 1X8 LUMBER, 8 GALVANIZED NAILS, AND SOME WOOD GLUE.
YOU HAVE THE OPTION OF A PAINTED FINISH OR NATURAL.
HERE ARE SOME PAINT CHIPS I PICKED UP AT THE HARDWARE STORE.
I TOOK A DIGITAL PHOTO OF THE MODEL AND DROPPED IT INTO A PHOTO OF OUR YARD WITH MY NEW SOFTWARE.
ISN'T THAT COOL?
WERE YOU PLANNING ON BUILDING THE REAL THING?
WHEN DO I HAVE TIME FOR THAT?

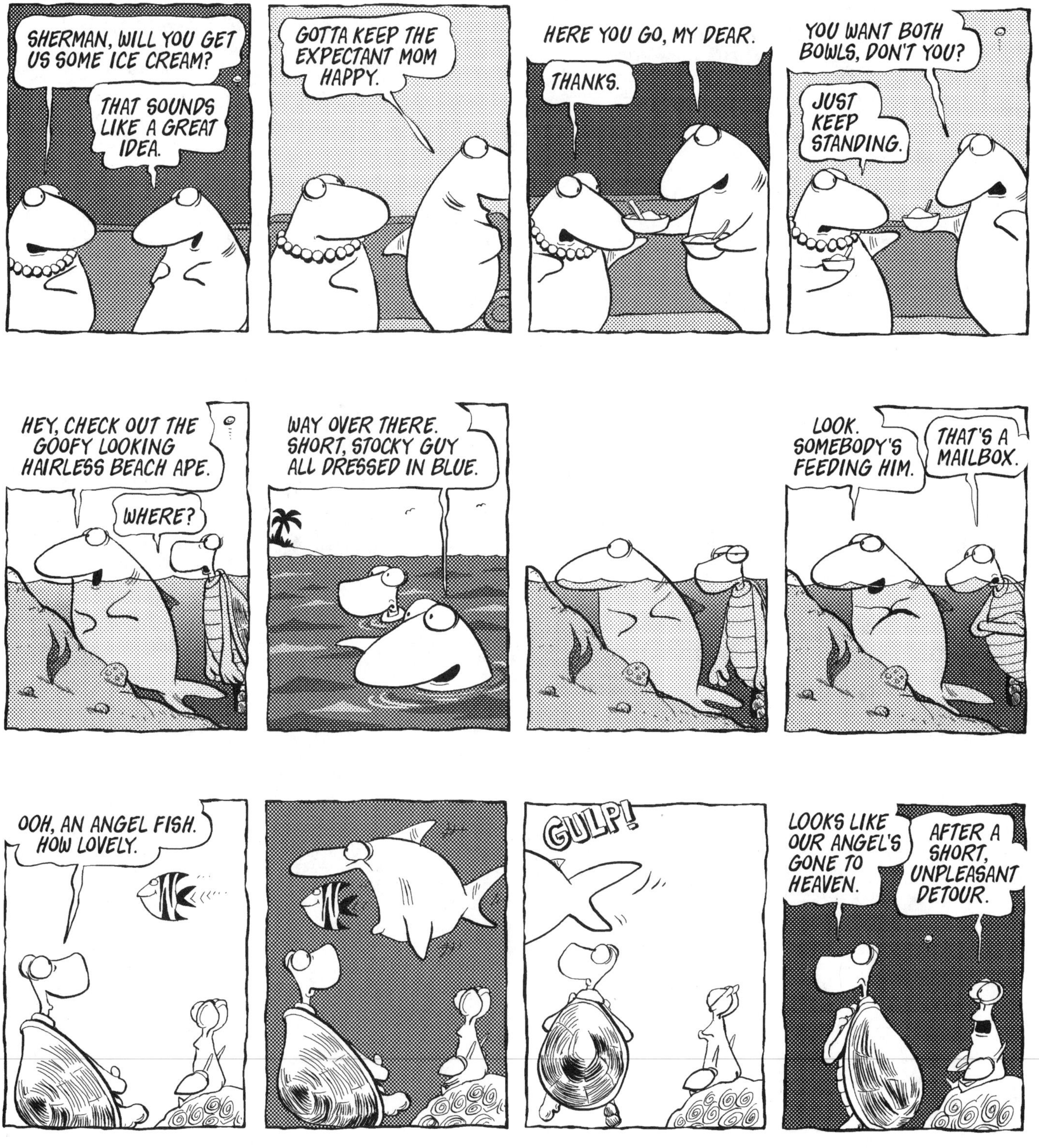
SHERMAN, WILL YOU GET US SOME ICE CREAM?
THAT SOUNDS LIKE A GREAT IDEA.
GOTTA KEEP THE EXPECTANT MOM HAPPY.
HERE YOU GO, MY DEAR.
THANKS.
YOU WANT BOTH BOWLS, DON'T YOU?
JUST KEEP STANDING.
HEY, CHECK OUT THE GOOFY LOOKING HAIRLESS BEACH APE.
WHERE?
WAY OVER THERE. SHORT, STOCKY GUY ALL DRESSED IN BLUE.
LOOK. SOMEBODY'S FEEDING HIM.
THAT'S A MAILBOX.
OOH, AN ANGEL FISH. HOW LOVELY.
GULP!
LOOKS LIKE OUR ANGEL'S GONE TO HEAVEN.
AFTER A SHORT, UNPLEASANT DETOUR.

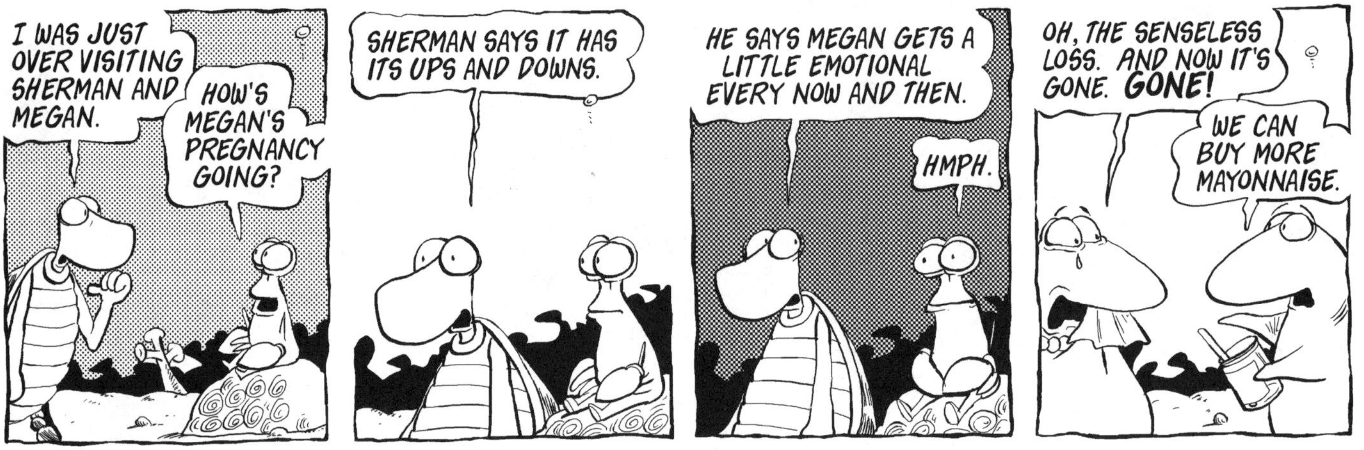
I WAS JUST OVER VISITING SHERMAN AND MEGAN.
HOW'S MEGAN'S PREGNANCY GOING?
SHERMAN SAYS IT HAS ITS UPS AND DOWNS.
HE SAYS MEGAN GETS A LITTLE EMOTIONAL EVERY NOW AND THEN.
HMPH.
OH, THE SENSELESS LOSS. AND NOW IT'S GONE. GONE!
WE CAN BUY MORE MAYONNAISE.

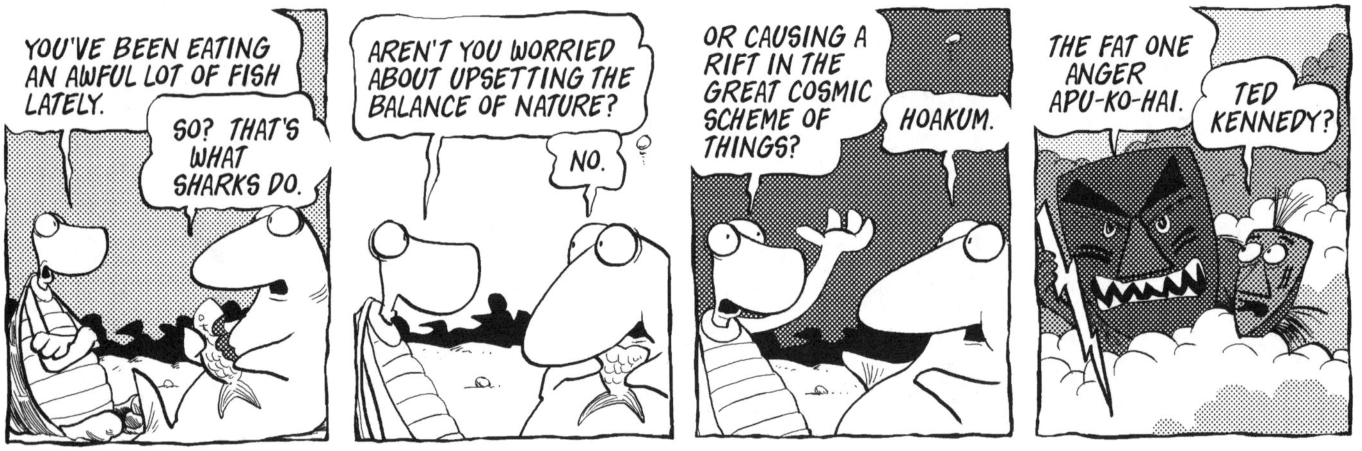
YOU'VE BEEN EATING AN AWFUL LOT OF FISH LATELY.
SO? THAT'S WHAT SHARKS DO.
AREN'T YOU WORRIED ABOUT UPSETTING THE BALANCE OF NATURE?
NO.
OR CAUSING A RIFT IN THE GREAT COSMIC SCHEME OF THINGS?
HOAKUM.
THE FAT ONE ANGER APU-KO-HAI.
TED KENNEDY?

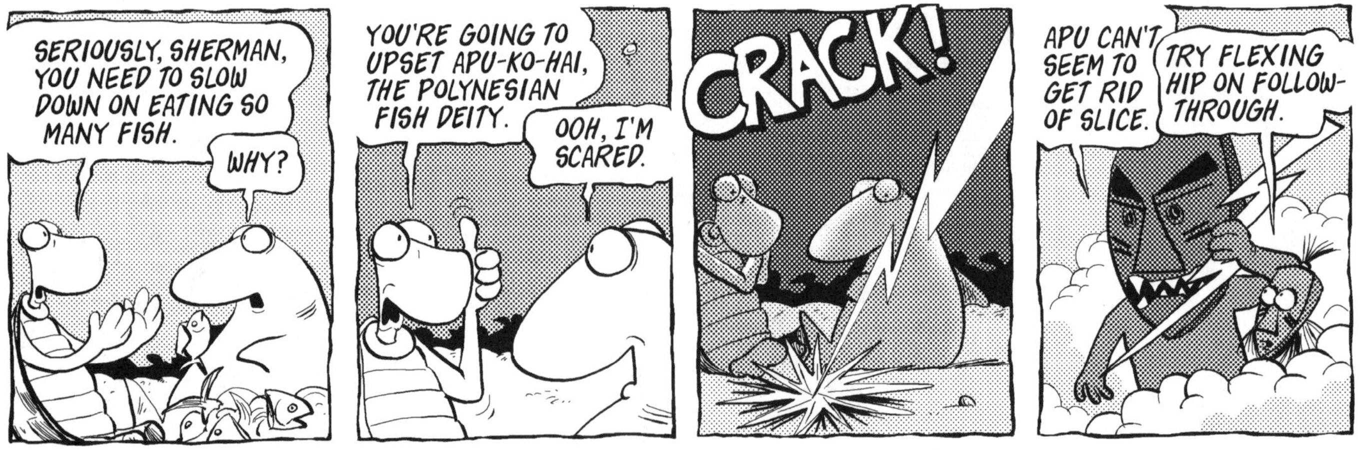
SERIOUSLY, SHERMAN, YOU NEED TO SLOW DOWN ON EATING SO MANY FISH.
WHY?
YOU'RE GOING TO UPSET APU-KO-HAI, THE POLYNESIAN FISH DEITY.
OOH, I'M SCARED.
CRACK!
APU CAN'T SEEM TO GET RID OF SLICE.
TRY FLEXING HIP ON FOLLOW-THROUGH.

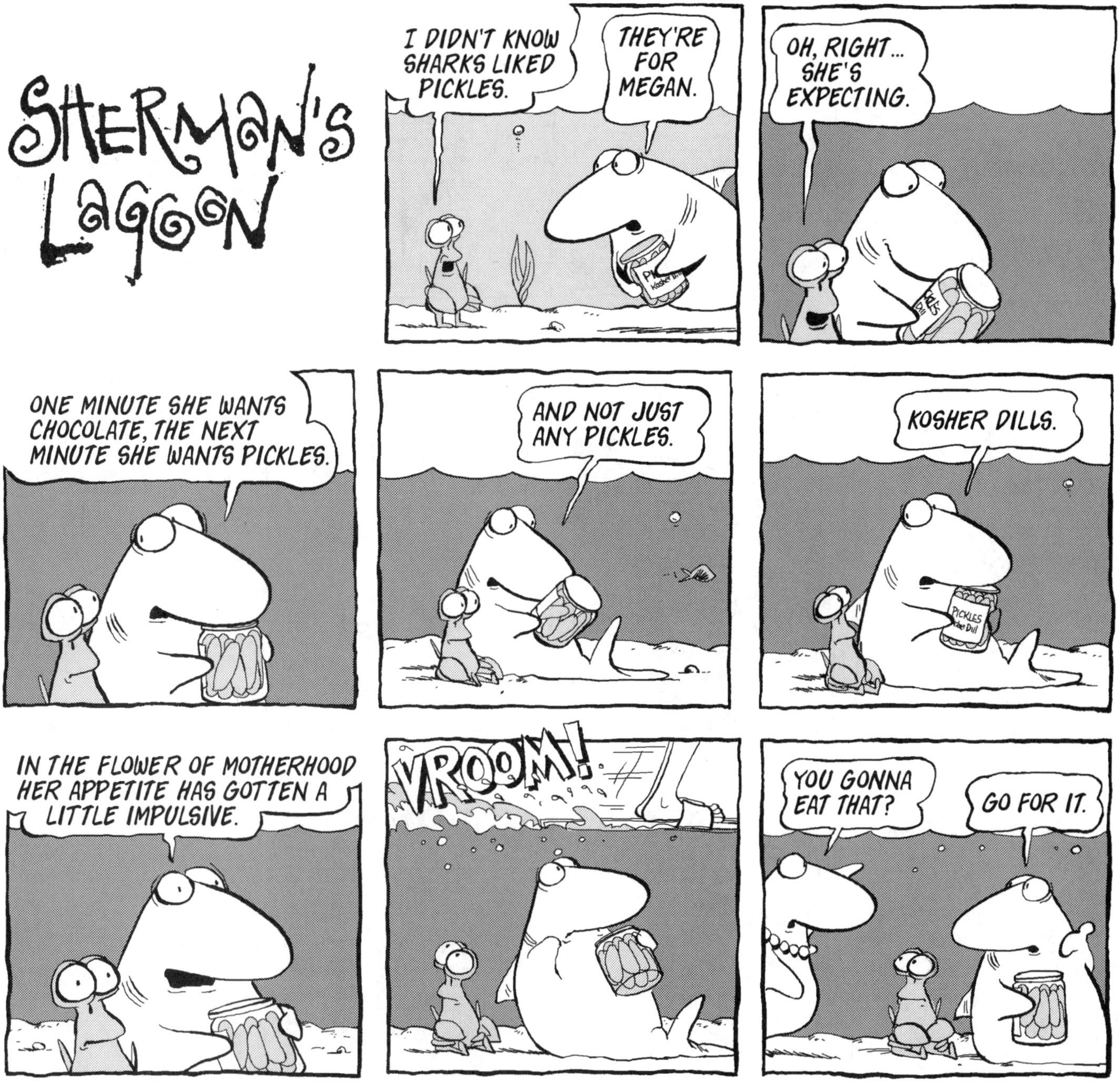
SHERMAN'S LAGOON
I DIDN'T KNOW SHARKS LIKED PICKLES.
THEY'RE FOR MEGAN.
OH, RIGHT... SHE'S EXPECTING.
ONE MINUTE SHE WANTS CHOCOLATE, THE NEXT MINUTE SHE WANTS PICKLES.
AND NOT JUST ANY PICKLES.
KOSHER DILLS.
PICKLES Kosher Dill
IN THE FLOWER OF MOTHERHOOD HER APPETITE HAS GOTTEN A LITTLE IMPULSIVE.
VROOOM!
YOU GONNA EAT THAT?
GO FOR IT.

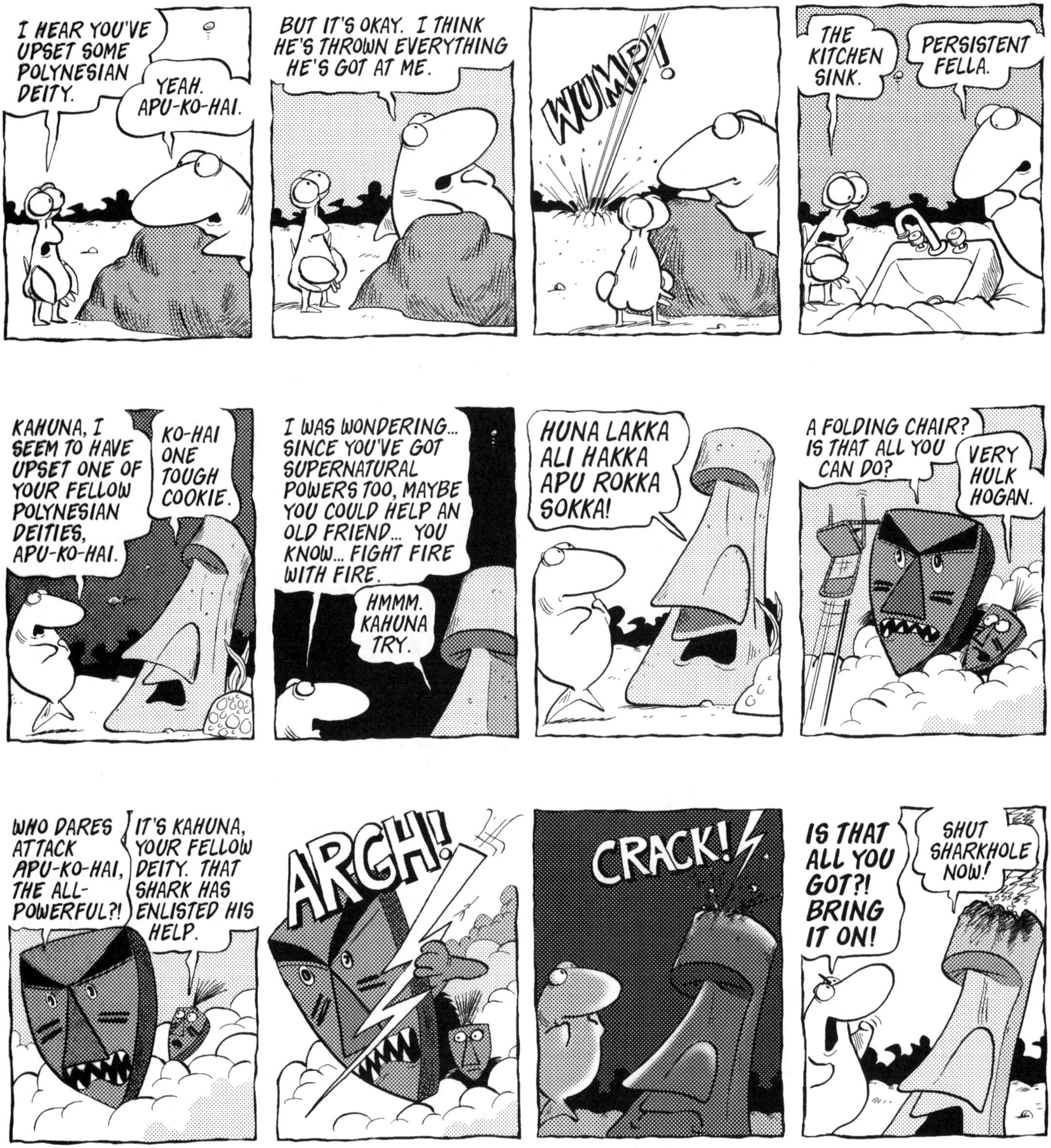
I HEAR YOU'VE UPSET SOME POLYNESIAN DEITY.
YEAH. APU-KO-HAI.
BUT IT'S OKAY. I THINK HE'S THROWN EVERYTHING HE'S GOT AT ME.
WUMP!
THE KITCHEN SINK.
PERSISTENT FELLA.
KAHUNA, I SEEM TO HAVE UPSET ONE OF YOUR FELLOW POLYNESIAN DEITIES, APU-KO-HAI.
KO-HAI ONE TOUGH COOKIE.
I WAS WONDERING... SINCE YOU'VE GOT SUPERNATURAL POWERS TOO, MAYBE YOU COULD HELP AN OLD FRIEND... YOU KNOW... FIGHT FIRE WITH FIRE.
HMMM. KAHUNA TRY.
HUNA LAKKA ALI HAKKA APU ROKKA SOKKA!
A FOLDING CHAIR? IS THAT ALL YOU CAN DO?
VERY HULK HOGAN.
WHO DARES ATTACK APU-KO-HAI, THE ALL-POWERFUL?!
IT'S KAHUNA, YOUR FELLOW DEITY. THAT SHARK HAS ENLISTED HIS HELP.
ARGH!
CRACK!
IS THAT ALL YOU GOT?! BRING IT ON!
SHUT SHARKHOLE NOW!

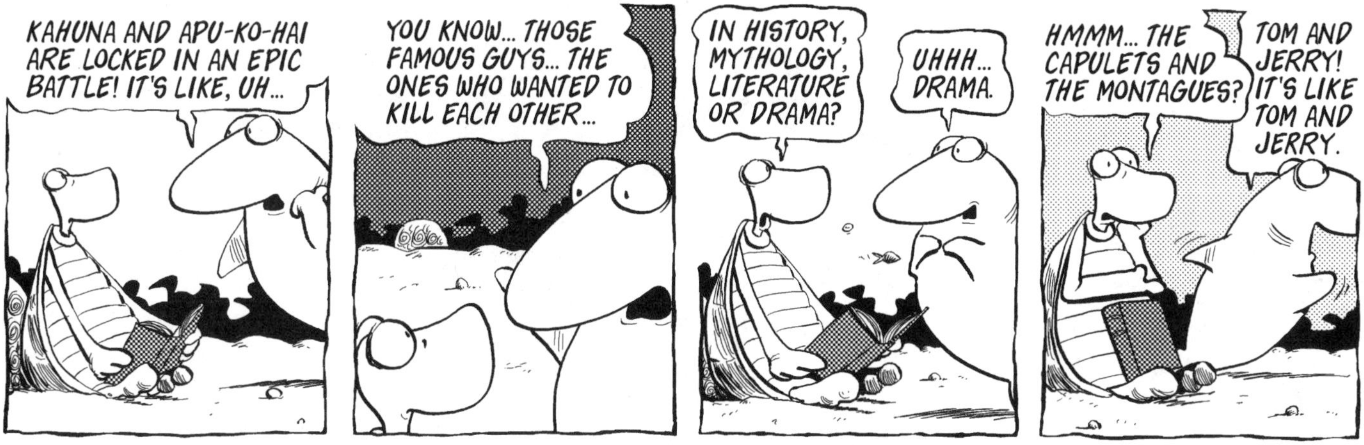
KAHUNA AND APU-KO-HAI ARE LOCKED IN AN EPIC BATTLE! IT'S LIKE, UH...
YOU KNOW... THOSE FAMOUS GUYS... THE ONES WHO WANTED TO KILL EACH OTHER...
IN HISTORY, MYTHOLOGY, LITERATURE OR DRAMA?
UHHH... DRAMA.
HMMM... THE CAPULETS AND THE MONTAGUES?
TOM AND JERRY! IT'S LIKE TOM AND JERRY.

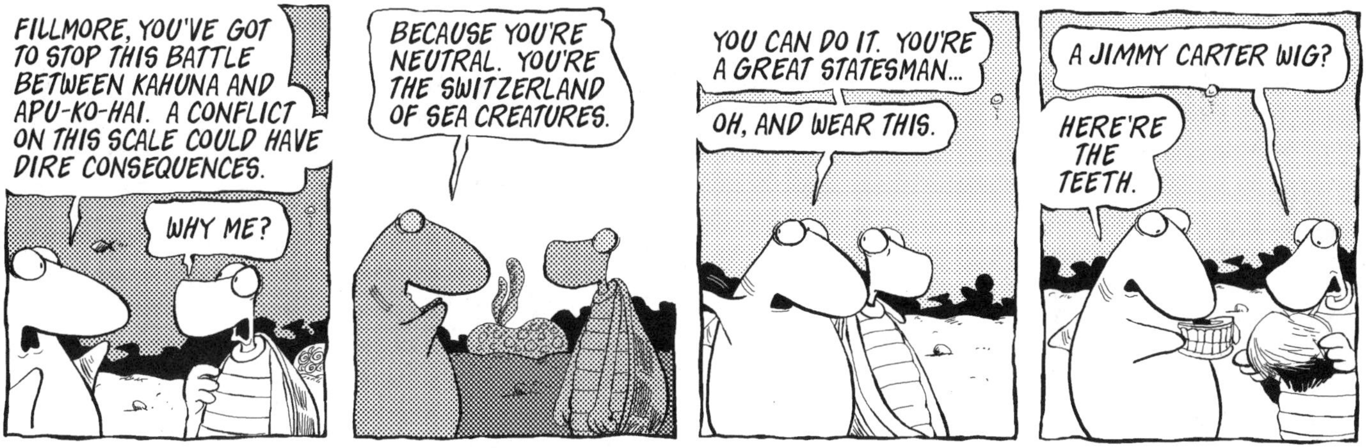
FILLMORE, YOU'VE GOT TO STOP THIS BATTLE BETWEEN KAHUNA AND APU-KO-HAI. A CONFLICT ON THIS SCALE COULD HAVE DIRE CONSEQUENCES.
WHY ME?
BECAUSE YOU'RE NEUTRAL. YOU'RE THE SWITZERLAND OF SEA CREATURES.
YOU CAN DO IT. YOU'RE A GREAT STATESMAN...
OH, AND WEAR THIS.
A JIMMY CARTER WIG?
HERE'RE THE TEETH.

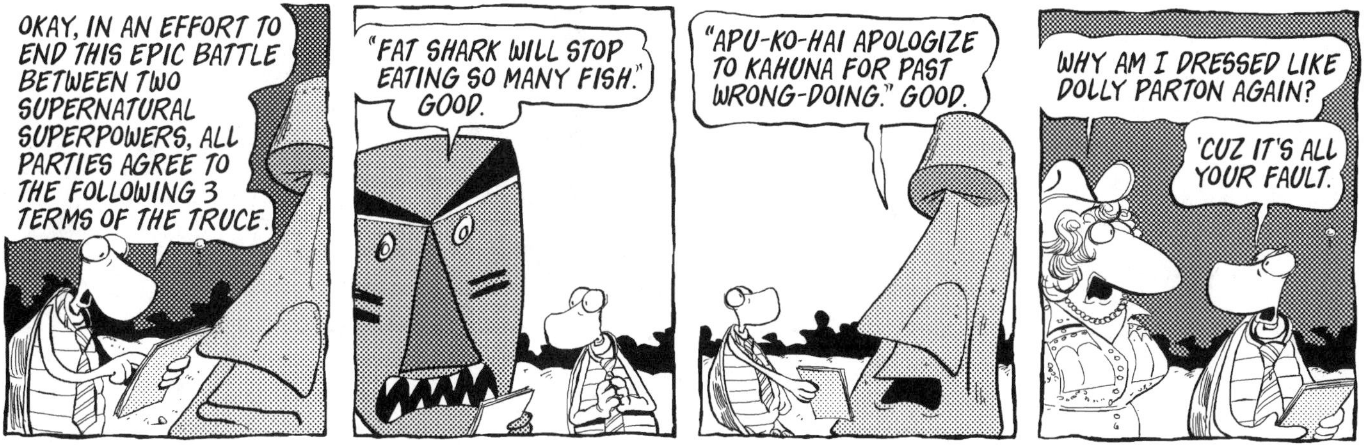
OKAY, IN AN EFFORT TO END THIS EPIC BATTLE BETWEEN TWO SUPERNATURAL SUPERPOWERS, ALL PARTIES AGREE TO THE FOLLOWING 3 TERMS OF THE TRUCE.
"FAT SHARK WILL STOP EATING SO MANY FISH." GOOD.
"APU-KO-HAI APOLOGIZE TO KAHUNA FOR PAST WRONG-DOING." GOOD.
WHY AM I DRESSED LIKE DOLLY PARTON AGAIN?
'CUZ IT'S ALL YOUR FAULT.

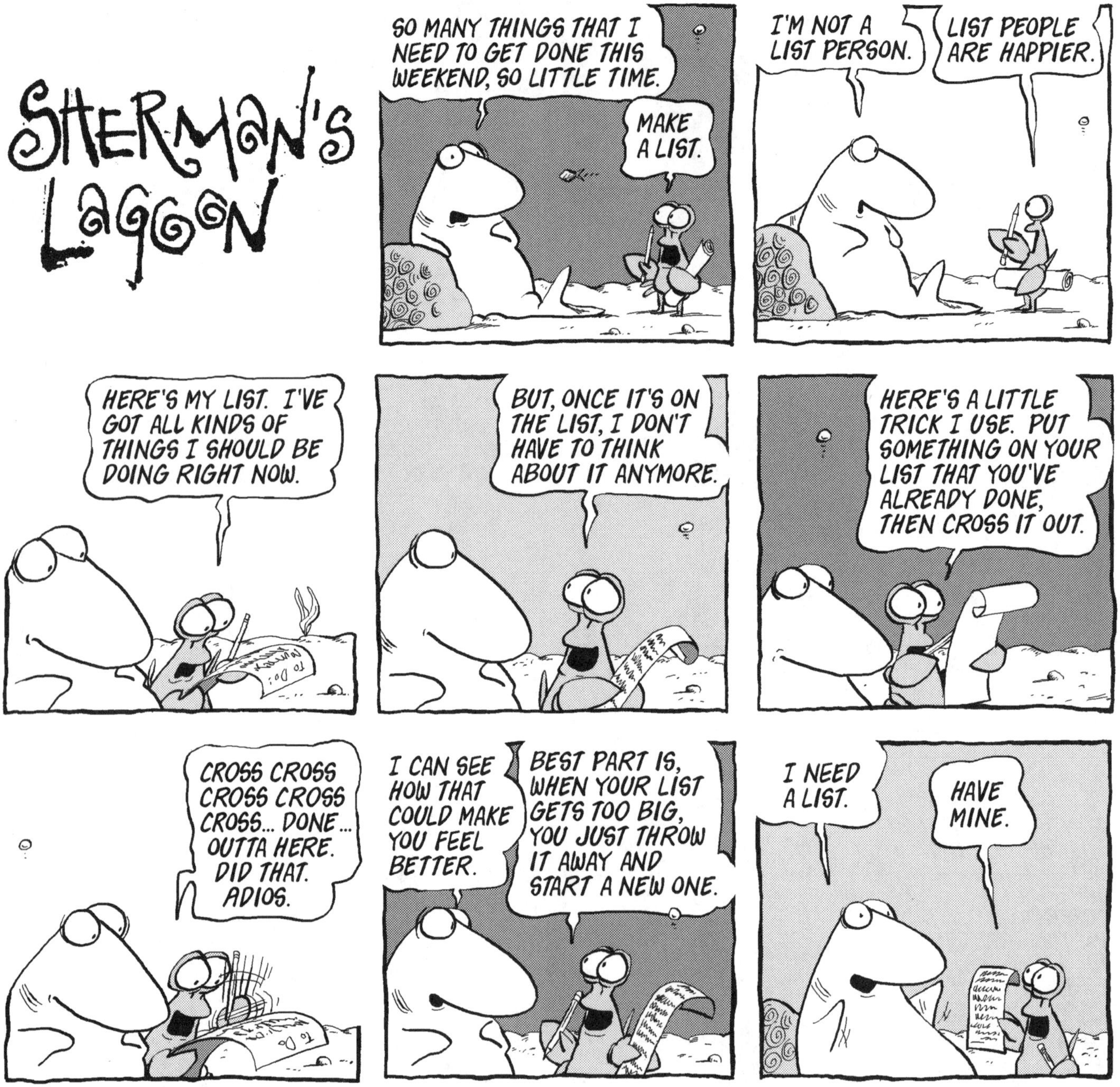
SHERMAN'S LAGOON
SO MANY THINGS THAT I NEED TO GET DONE THIS WEEKEND, SO LITTLE TIME.
MAKE A LIST.
I'M NOT A LIST PERSON.
LIST PEOPLE ARE HAPPIER.
HERE'S MY LIST. I'VE GOT ALL KINDS OF THINGS I SHOULD BE DOING RIGHT NOW.
BUT, ONCE IT'S ON THE LIST, I DON'T HAVE TO THINK ABOUT IT ANYMORE.
HERE'S A LITTLE TRICK I USE. PUT SOMETHING ON YOUR LIST THAT YOU'VE ALREADY DONE, THEN CROSS IT OUT.
CROSS CROSS CROSS CROSS CROSS... DONE... OUTTA HERE. DID THAT. ADIOS.
I CAN SEE HOW THAT COULD MAKE YOU FEEL BETTER.
BEST PART IS, WHEN YOUR LIST GETS TOO BIG, YOU JUST THROW IT AWAY AND START A NEW ONE.
I NEED A LIST.
HAVE MINE.

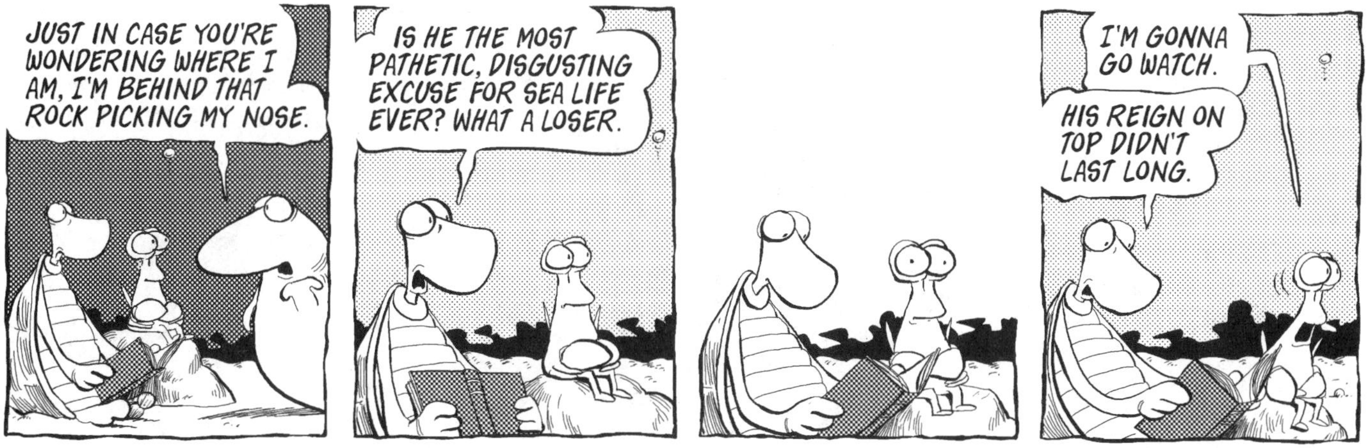
JUST IN CASE YOU'RE WONDERING WHERE I AM, I'M BEHIND THAT ROCK PICKING MY NOSE.
IS HE THE MOST PATHETIC, DISGUSTING EXCUSE FOR SEA LIFE EVER? WHAT A LOSER.
I'M GONNA GO WATCH.
HIS REIGN ON TOP DIDN'T LAST LONG.

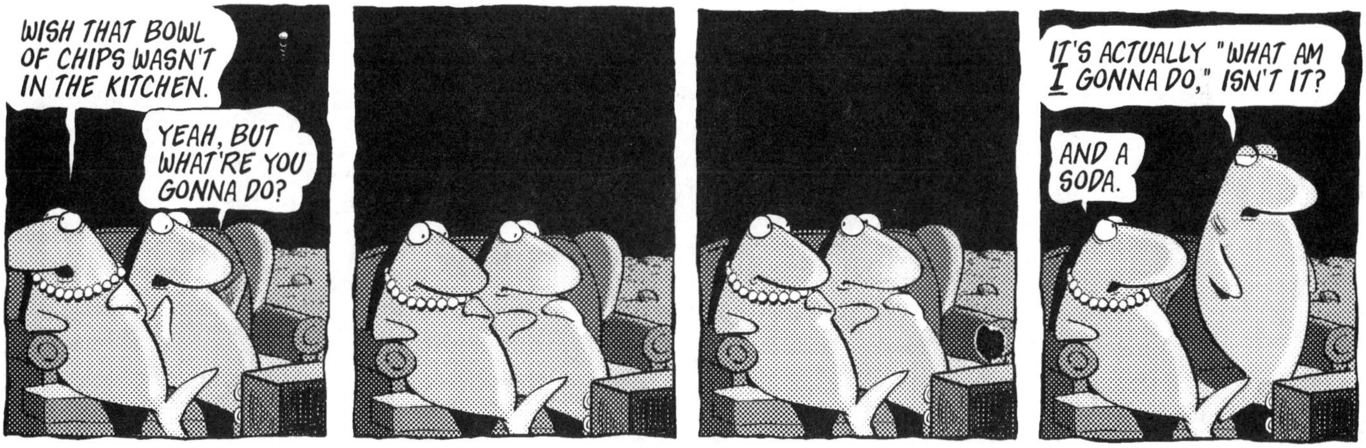
WISH THAT BOWL OF CHIPS WASN'T IN THE KITCHEN.
YEAH, BUT WHAT'RE YOU GONNA DO?
IT'S ACTUALLY "WHAT AM I GONNA DO," ISN'T IT?
AND A SODA.

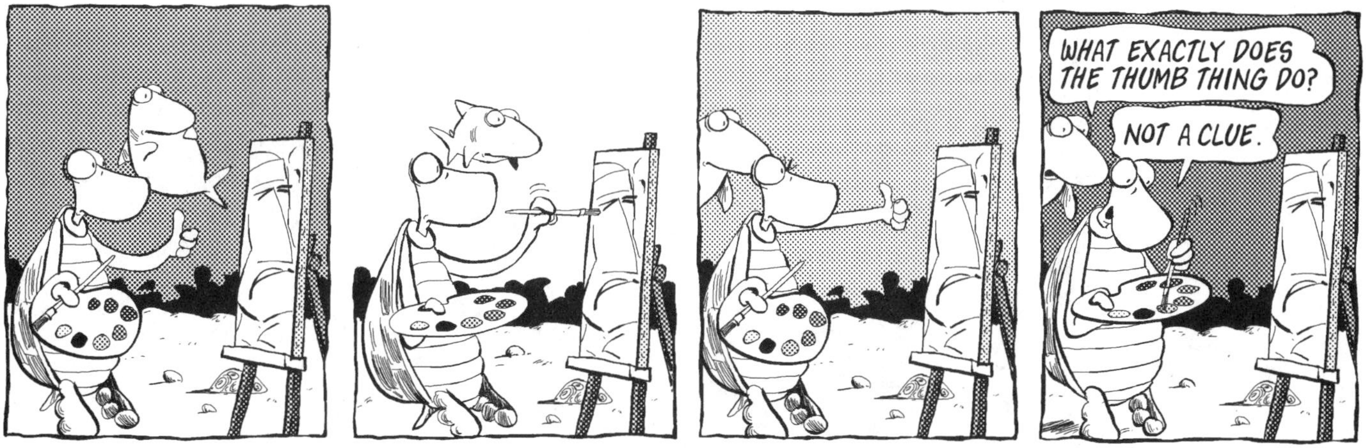
WHAT EXACTLY DOES THE THUMB THING DO?
NOT A CLUE.

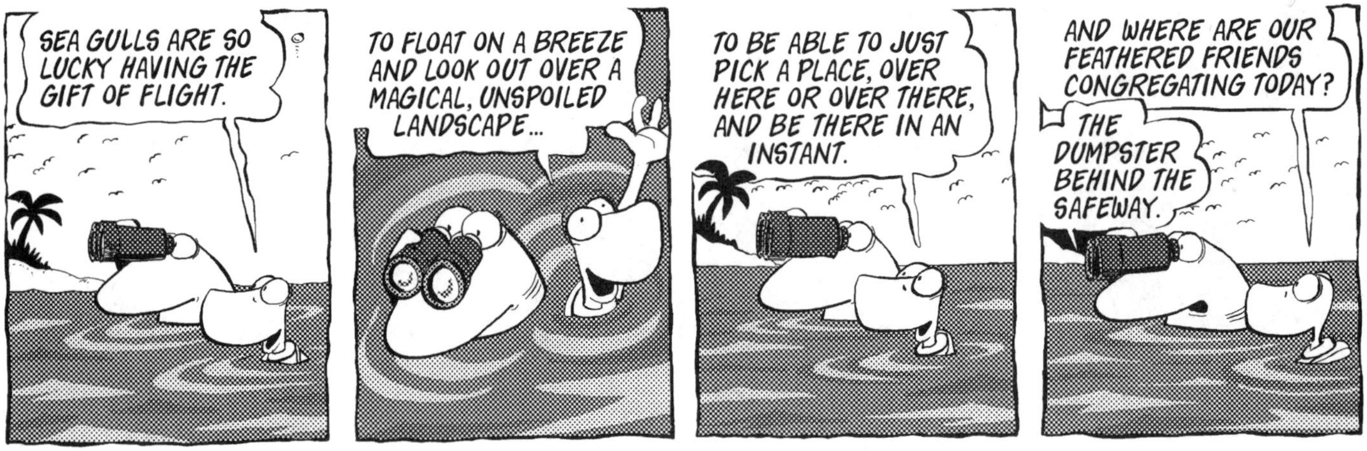
SEA GULLS ARE SO LUCKY HAVING THE GIFT OF FLIGHT.
TO FLOAT ON A BREEZE AND LOOK OUT OVER A MAGICAL, UNSPOILED LANDSCAPE...
TO BE ABLE TO JUST PICK A PLACE, OVER HERE OR OVER THERE, AND BE THERE IN AN INSTANT.
AND WHERE ARE OUR FEATHERED FRIENDS CONGREGATING TODAY?
THE DUMPSTER BEHIND THE SAFEWAY.

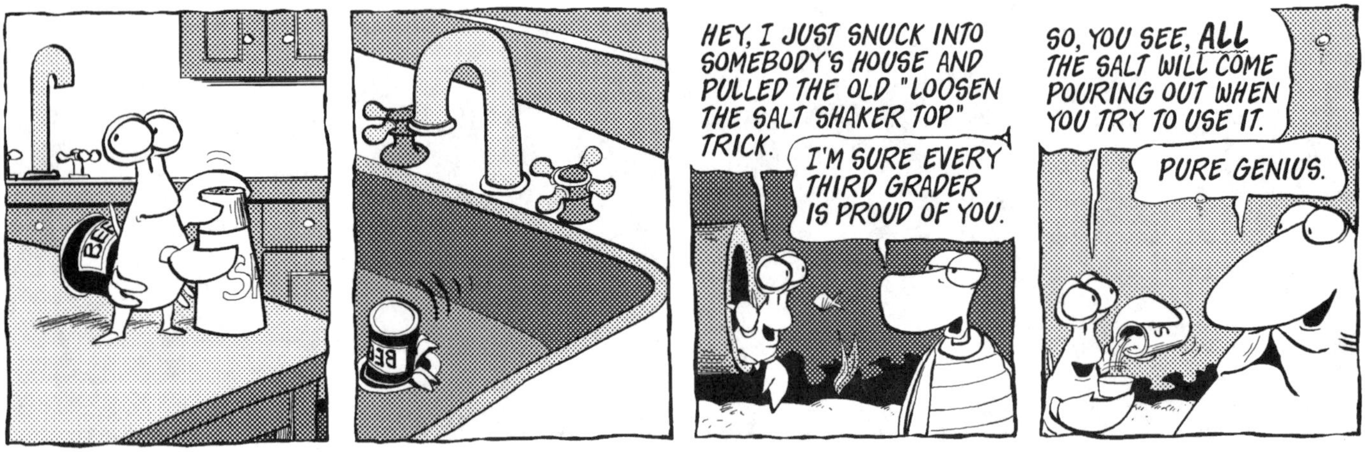
HEY, I JUST SNUCK INTO SOMEBODY'S HOUSE AND PULLED THE OLD "LOOSEN THE SALT SHAKER TOP" TRICK.
I'M SURE EVERY THIRD GRADER IS PROUD OF YOU.
SO, YOU SEE, ALL THE SALT WILL COME POURING OUT WHEN YOU TRY TO USE IT.
PURE GENIUS.

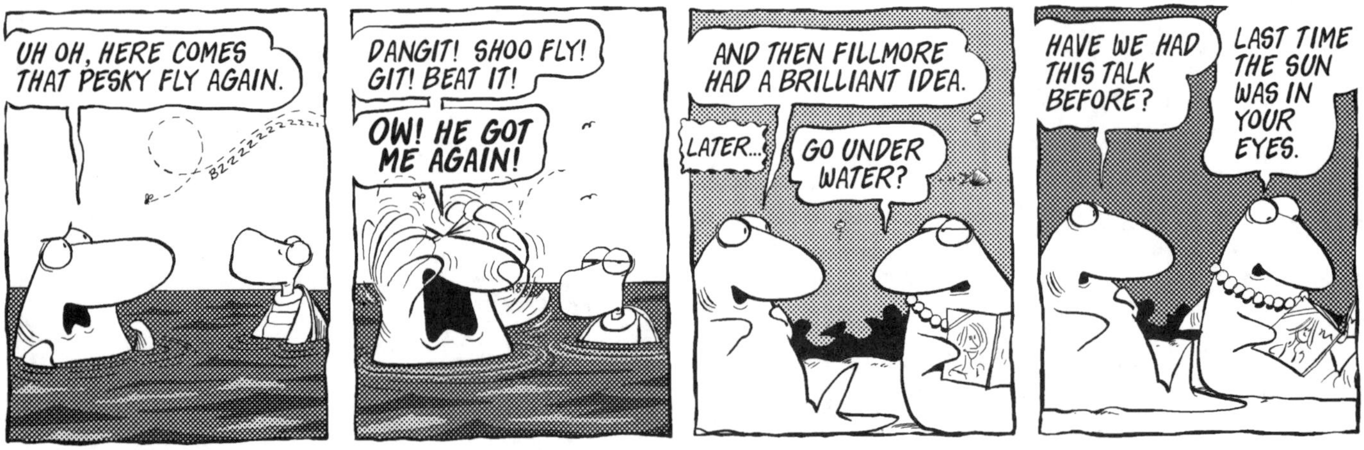
UH OH, HERE COMES THAT PESKY FLY AGAIN.
BZZZZZZZZZZ
DANGIT! SHOO FLY! GIT! BEAT IT!
OW! HE GOT ME AGAIN!
AND THEN FILLMORE HAD A BRILLIANT IDEA.
LATER...
GO UNDER WATER?
HAVE WE HAD THIS TALK BEFORE?
LAST TIME THE SUN WAS IN YOUR EYES.

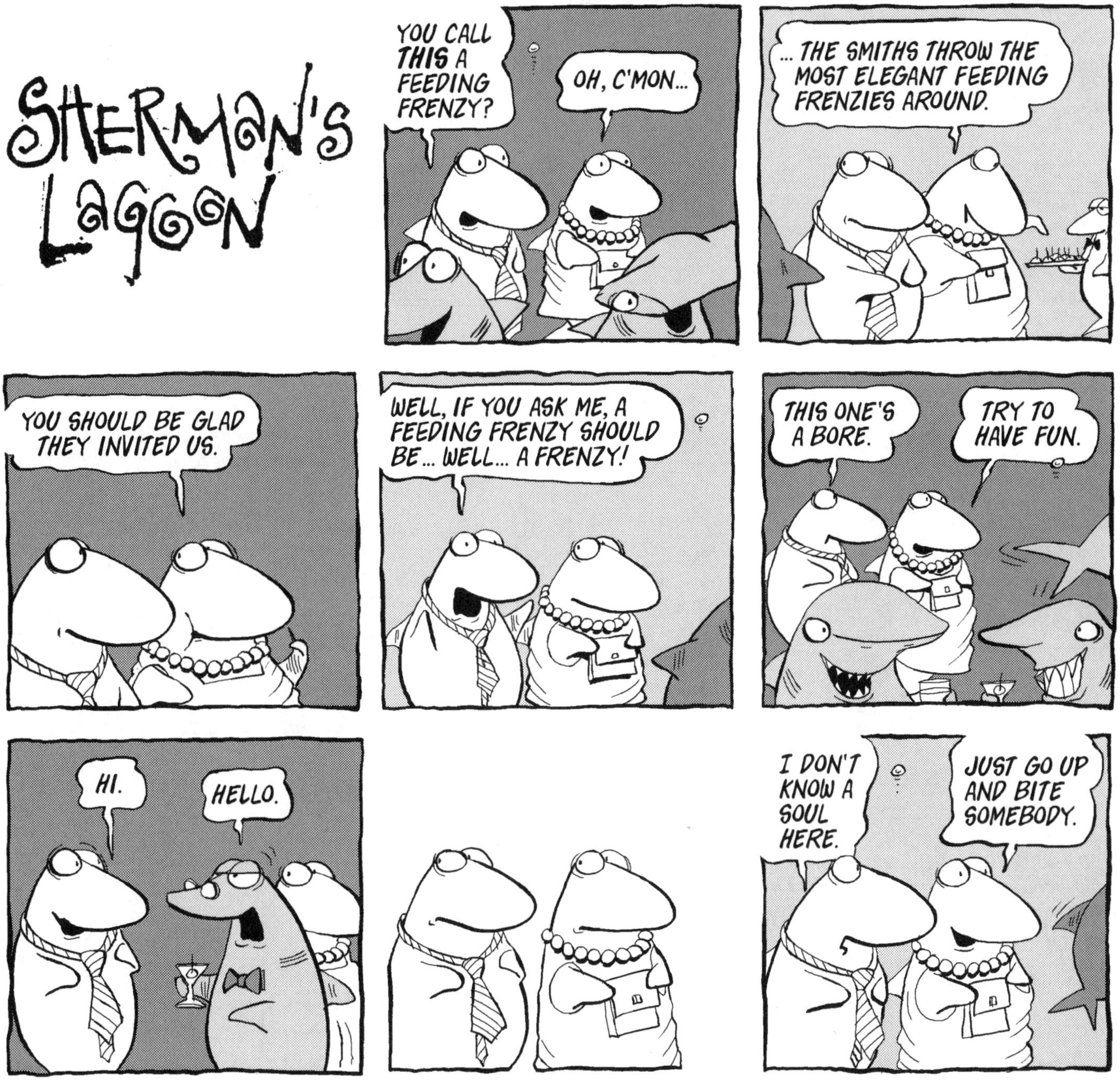
SHERMAN'S LAGOON
YOU CALL THIS A FEEDING FRENZY?
OH, C'MON...
... THE SMITHS THROW THE MOST ELEGANT FEEDING FRENZIES AROUND.
YOU SHOULD BE GLAD THEY INVITED US.
WELL, IF YOU ASK ME, A FEEDING FRENZY SHOULD BE... WELL... A FRENZY!
THIS ONE'S A BORE.
TRY TO HAVE FUN.
HI.
HELLO.
I DON'T KNOW A SOUL HERE.
JUST GO UP AND BITE SOMEBODY.

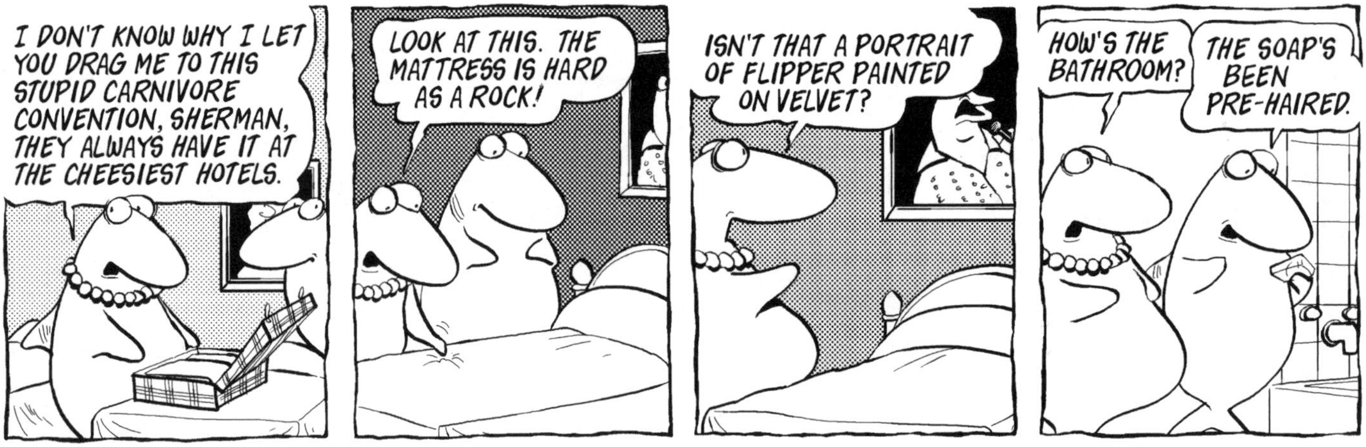
I DON'T KNOW WHY I LET YOU DRAG ME TO THIS STUPID CARNIVORE CONVENTION, SHERMAN. THEY ALWAYS HAVE IT AT THE CHEESIEST HOTELS.
LOOK AT THIS. THE MATTRESS IS HARD AS A ROCK!
ISN'T THAT A PORTRAIT OF FLIPPER PAINTED ON VELVET?
HOW'S THE BATHROOM?
THE SOAP'S BEEN PRE-HAIRED.

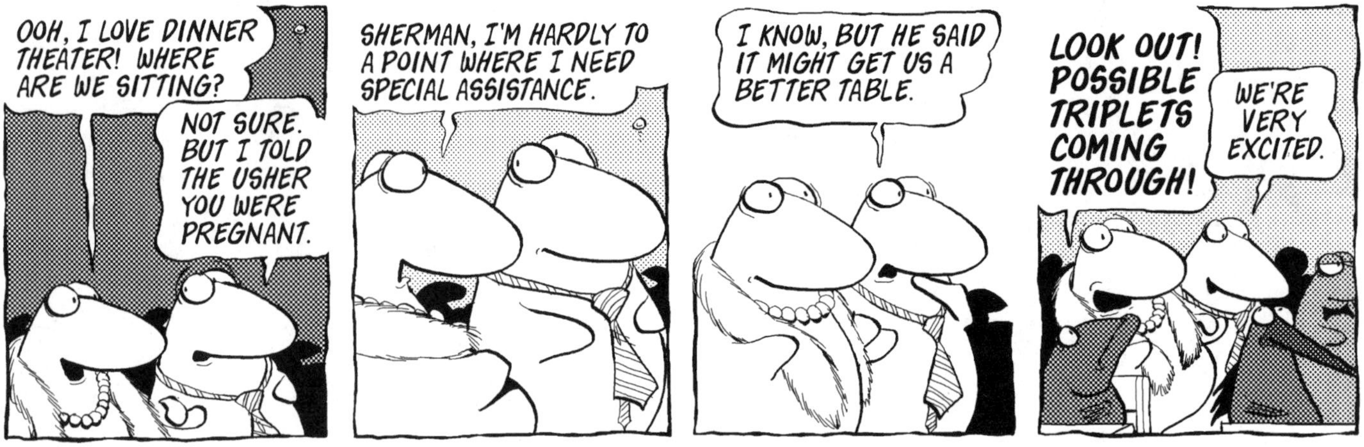
OOH, I LOVE DINNER THEATER! WHERE ARE WE SITTING?
NOT SURE. BUT I TOLD THE USHER YOU WERE PREGNANT.
SHERMAN, I'M HARDLY TO A POINT WHERE I NEED SPECIAL ASSISTANCE.
I KNOW, BUT HE SAID IT MIGHT GET US A BETTER TABLE.
LOOK OUT! POSSIBLE TRIPLETS COMING THROUGH!
WE'RE VERY EXCITED.

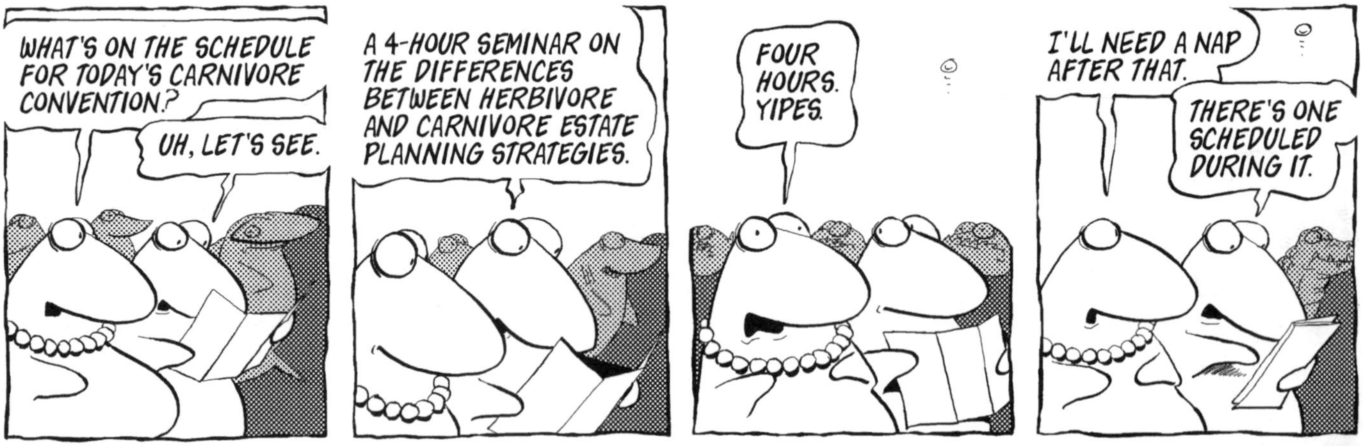
WHAT'S ON THE SCHEDULE FOR TODAY'S CARNIVORE CONVENTION?
UH, LET'S SEE.
A 4-HOUR SEMINAR ON THE DIFFERENCES BETWEEN HERBIVORE AND CARNIVORE ESTATE PLANNING STRATEGIES.
FOUR HOURS. YIPES.
I'LL NEED A NAP AFTER THAT.
THERE'S ONE SCHEDULED DURING IT.

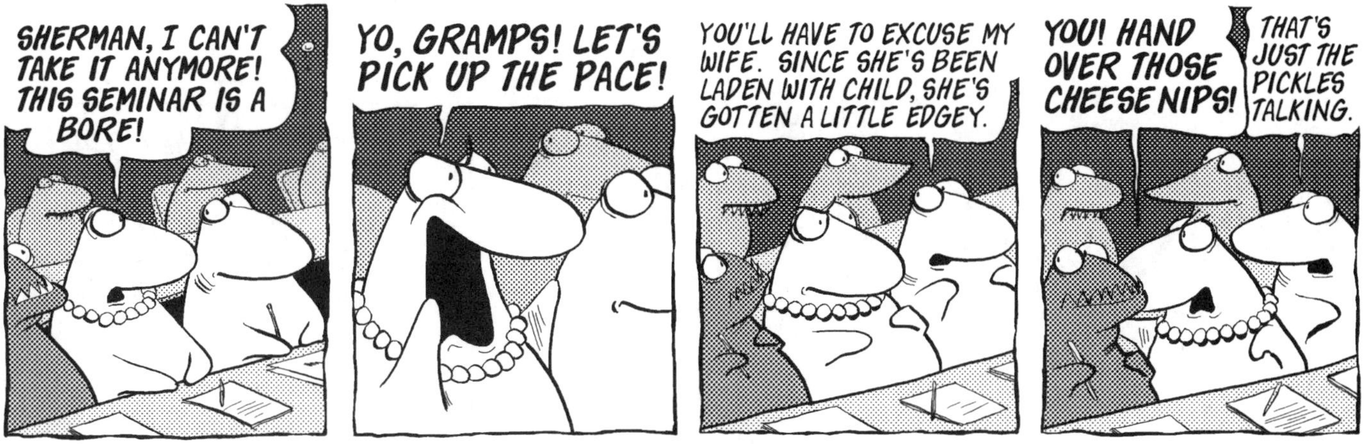
SHERMAN, I CAN'T TAKE IT ANYMORE! THIS SEMINAR IS A BORE!
YO, GRAMPS! LET'S PICK UP THE PACE!
YOU'LL HAVE TO EXCUSE MY WIFE. SINCE SHE'S BEEN LADEN WITH CHILD, SHE'S GOTTEN A LITTLE EDGEY.
YOU! HAND OVER THOSE CHEESE NIPS!
THAT'S JUST THE PICKLES TALKING.

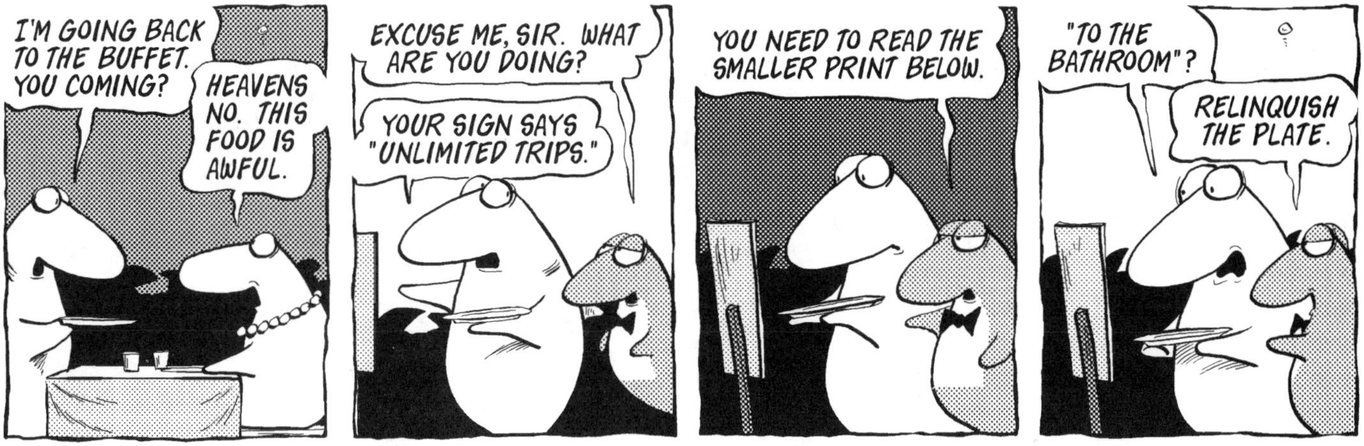
I'M GOING BACK TO THE BUFFET. YOU COMING?
HEAVENS NO. THIS FOOD IS AWFUL.
EXCUSE ME, SIR. WHAT ARE YOU DOING?
YOUR SIGN SAYS "UNLIMITED TRIPS."
YOU NEED TO READ THE SMALLER PRINT BELOW.
"TO THE BATHROOM"?
RELINQUISH THE PLATE.

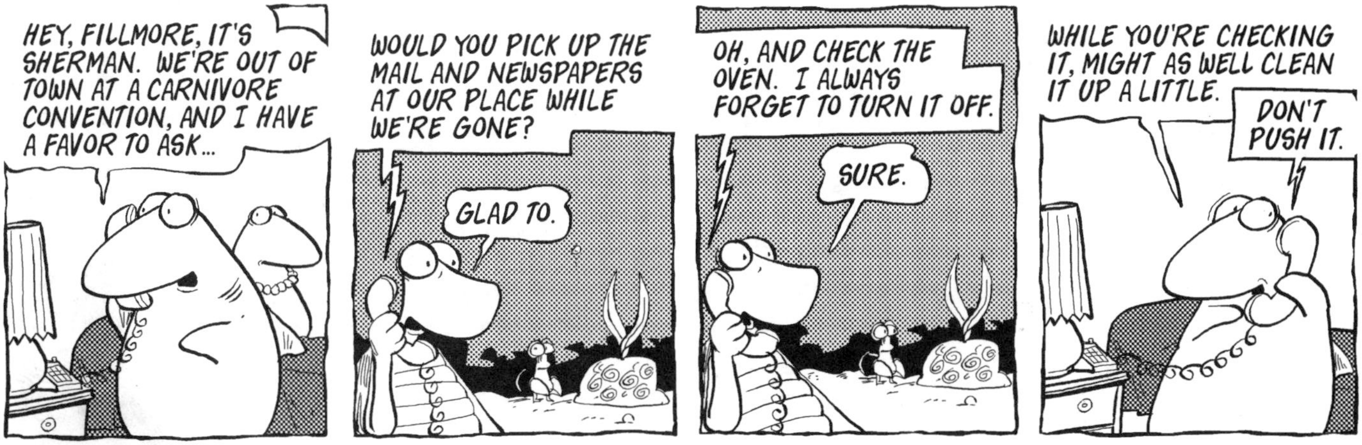
HEY, FILLMORE, IT'S SHERMAN. WE'RE OUT OF TOWN AT A CARNIVORE CONVENTION, AND I HAVE A FAVOR TO ASK...
WOULD YOU PICK UP THE MAIL AND NEWSPAPERS AT OUR PLACE WHILE WE'RE GONE?
GLAD TO.
OH, AND CHECK THE OVEN. I ALWAYS FORGET TO TURN IT OFF.
SURE.
WHILE YOU'RE CHECKING IT, MIGHT AS WELL CLEAN IT UP A LITTLE.
DON'T PUSH IT.

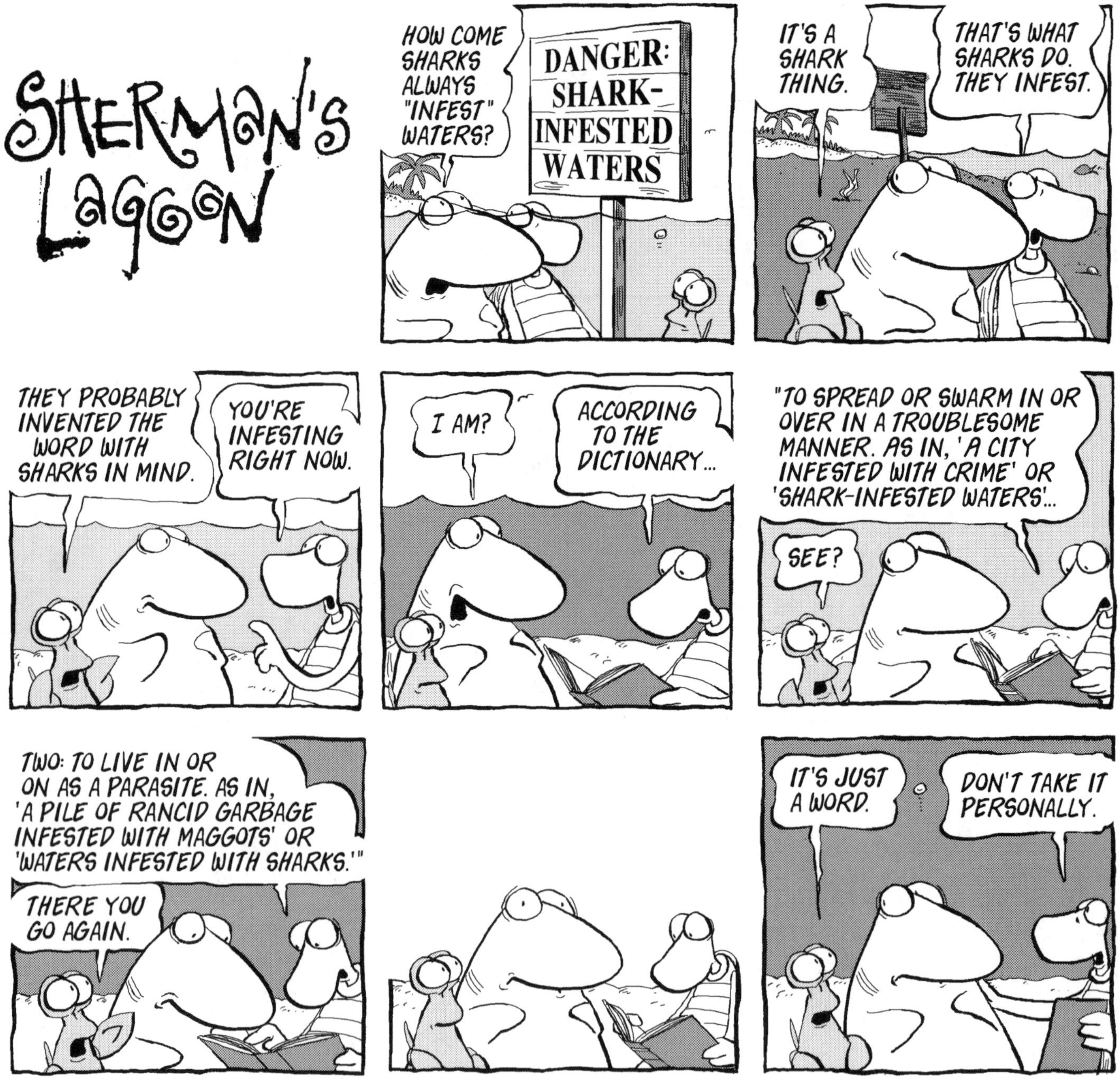
SHERMAN'S LAGOON
HOW COME SHARKS ALWAYS "INFEST" WATERS?
DANGER: SHARK-INFESTED WATERS
IT'S A SHARK THING.
THAT'S WHAT SHARKS DO. THEY INFEST.
THEY PROBABLY INVENTED THE WORD WITH SHARKS IN MIND.
YOU'RE INFESTING RIGHT NOW.
I AM?
ACCORDING TO THE DICTIONARY...
"TO SPREAD OR SWARM IN OR OVER IN A TROUBLESOME MANNER. AS IN, 'A CITY INFESTED WITH CRIME' OR 'SHARK-INFESTED WATERS'...
SEE?
TWO: TO LIVE IN OR ON AS A PARASITE. AS IN, 'A PILE OF RANCID GARBAGE INFESTED WITH MAGGOTS' OR 'WATERS INFESTED WITH SHARKS.'"
THERE YOU GO AGAIN.
IT'S JUST A WORD.
DON'T TAKE IT PERSONALLY.

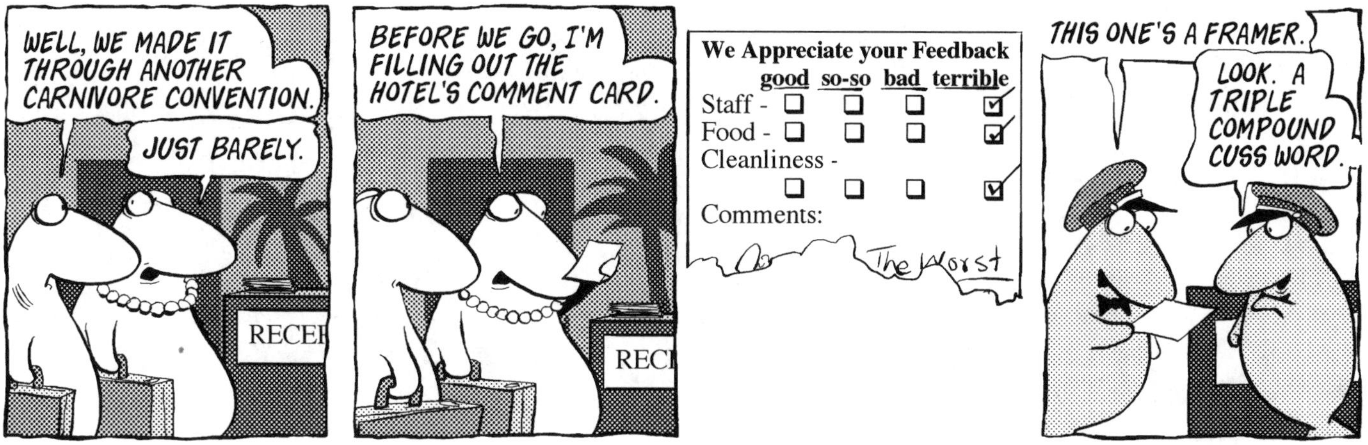
WELL, WE MADE IT THROUGH ANOTHER CARNIVORE CONVENTION.
JUST BARELY.
BEFORE WE GO, I'M FILLING OUT THE HOTEL'S COMMENT CARD.
We Appreciate your Feedback
good so-so bad terrible
Staff -
Food -
Cleanliness -
Comments:
The Worst
THIS ONE'S A FRAMER.
LOOK. A TRIPLE COMPOUND CUSS WORD.

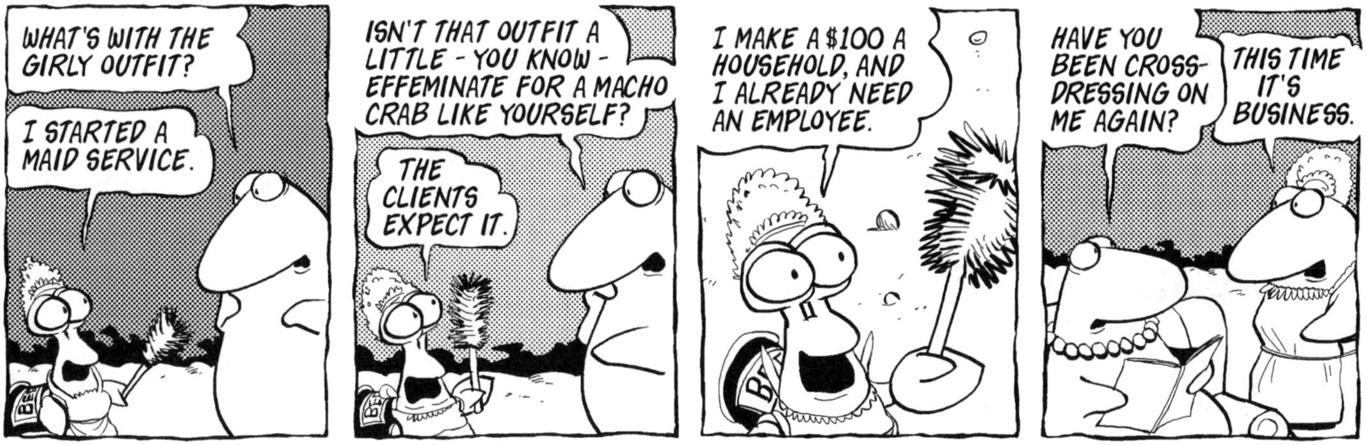
WHAT'S WITH THE GIRLY OUTFIT?
I STARTED A MAID SERVICE.
ISN'T THAT OUTFIT A LITTLE - YOU KNOW - EFFEMINATE FOR A MACHO CRAB LIKE YOURSELF?
THE CLIENTS EXPECT IT.
I MAKE A $100 A HOUSEHOLD, AND I ALREADY NEED AN EMPLOYEE.
HAVE YOU BEEN CROSS-DRESSING ON ME AGAIN?
THIS TIME IT'S BUSINESS.

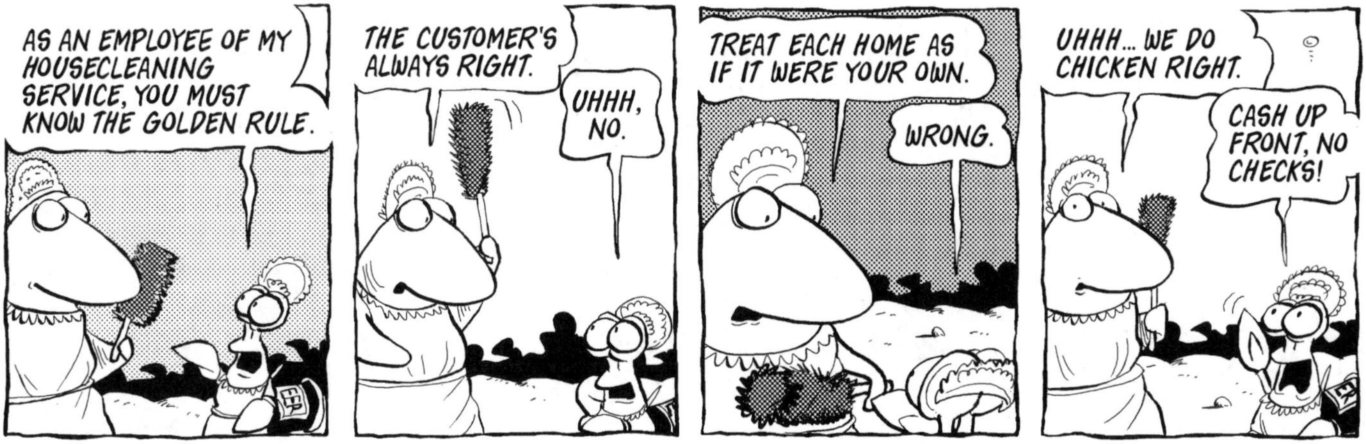
AS AN EMPLOYEE OF MY HOUSECLEANING SERVICE, YOU MUST KNOW THE GOLDEN RULE.
THE CUSTOMER'S ALWAYS RIGHT.
UHHH, NO.
TREAT EACH HOME AS IF IT WERE YOUR OWN.
WRONG.
UHHH... WE DO CHICKEN RIGHT.
CASH UP FRONT, NO CHECKS!

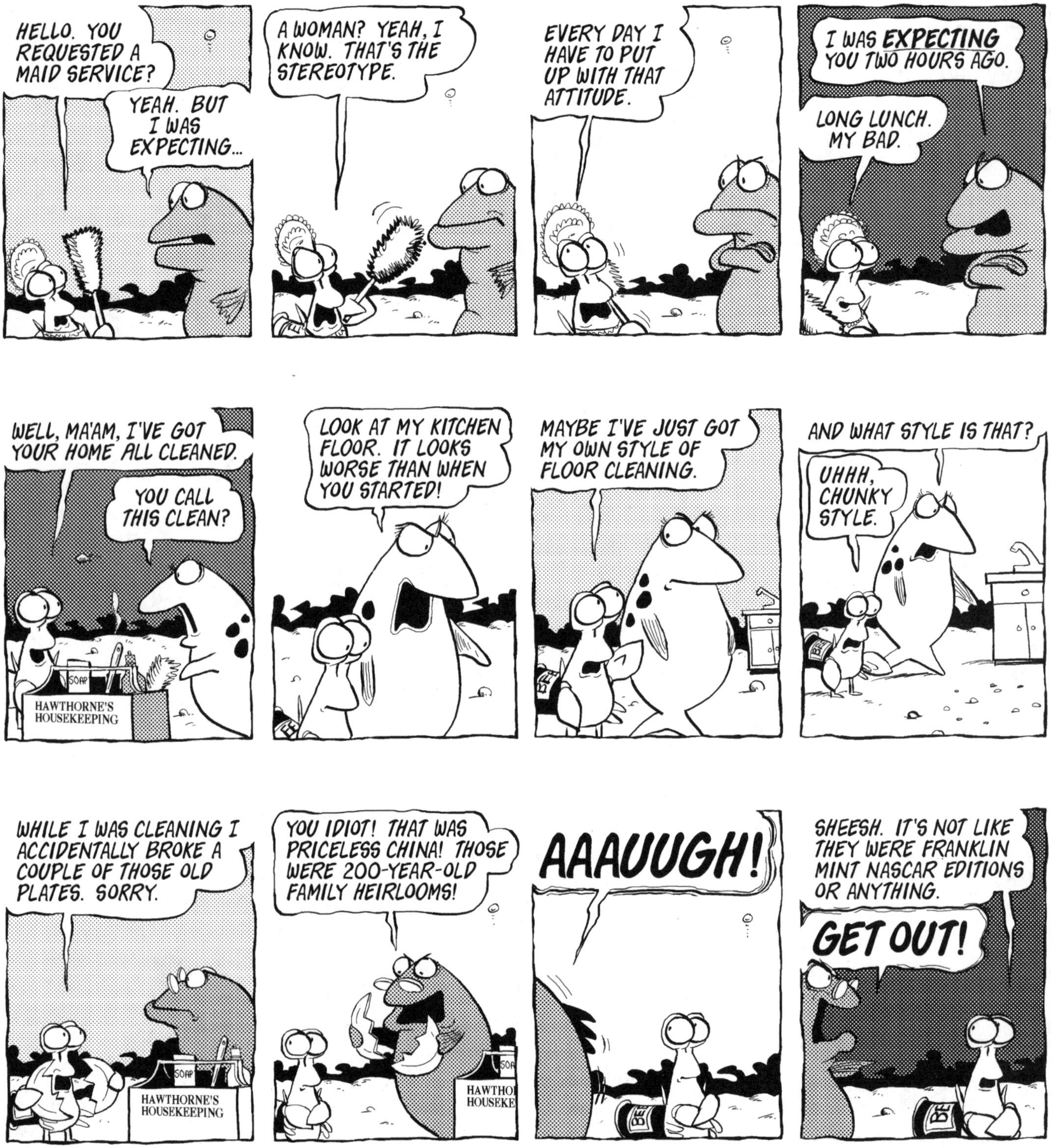
HELLO. YOU REQUESTED A MAID SERVICE?
YEAH. BUT I WAS EXPECTING...
A WOMAN? YEAH, I KNOW. THAT'S THE STEREOTYPE.
EVERY DAY I HAVE TO PUT UP WITH THAT ATTITUDE.
I WAS **EXPECTING** YOU TWO HOURS AGO.
LONG LUNCH. MY BAD.
WELL, MA'AM, I'VE GOT YOUR HOME ALL CLEANED.
YOU CALL THIS CLEAN?
SOAP
HAWTHORNE'S HOUSEKEEPING
LOOK AT MY KITCHEN FLOOR. IT LOOKS WORSE THAN WHEN YOU STARTED!
MAYBE I'VE JUST GOT MY OWN STYLE OF FLOOR CLEANING.
AND WHAT STYLE IS THAT?
UHHH, CHUNKY STYLE.
WHILE I WAS CLEANING I ACCIDENTALLY BROKE A COUPLE OF THOSE OLD PLATES. SORRY.
SOAP
HAWTHORNE'S HOUSEKEEPING
YOU IDIOT! THAT WAS PRICELESS CHINA! THOSE WERE 200-YEAR-OLD FAMILY HEIRLOOMS!
AAAUUGH!
SHEESH. IT'S NOT LIKE THEY WERE FRANKLIN MINT NASCAR EDITIONS OR ANYTHING.
GET OUT!

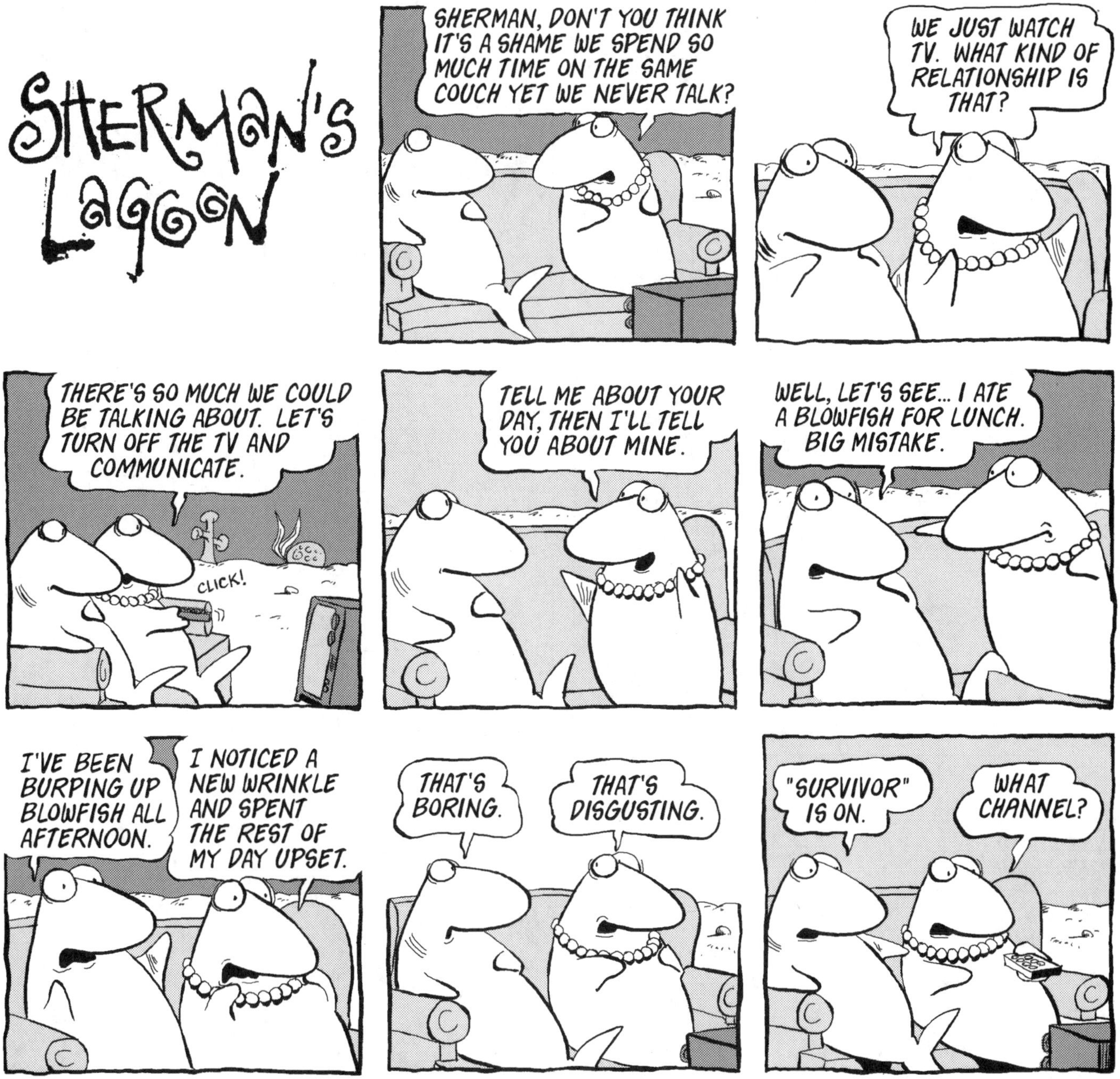
SHERMAN'S LAGOON
SHERMAN, DON'T YOU THINK IT'S A SHAME WE SPEND SO MUCH TIME ON THE SAME COUCH YET WE NEVER TALK?
WE JUST WATCH TV. WHAT KIND OF RELATIONSHIP IS THAT?
THERE'S SO MUCH WE COULD BE TALKING ABOUT. LET'S TURN OFF THE TV AND COMMUNICATE.
CLICK!
TELL ME ABOUT YOUR DAY, THEN I'LL TELL YOU ABOUT MINE.
WELL, LET'S SEE... I ATE A BLOWFISH FOR LUNCH. BIG MISTAKE.
I'VE BEEN BURPING UP BLOWFISH ALL AFTERNOON.
I NOTICED A NEW WRINKLE AND SPENT THE REST OF MY DAY UPSET.
THAT'S BORING.
THAT'S DISGUSTING.
"SURVIVOR" IS ON.
WHAT CHANNEL?

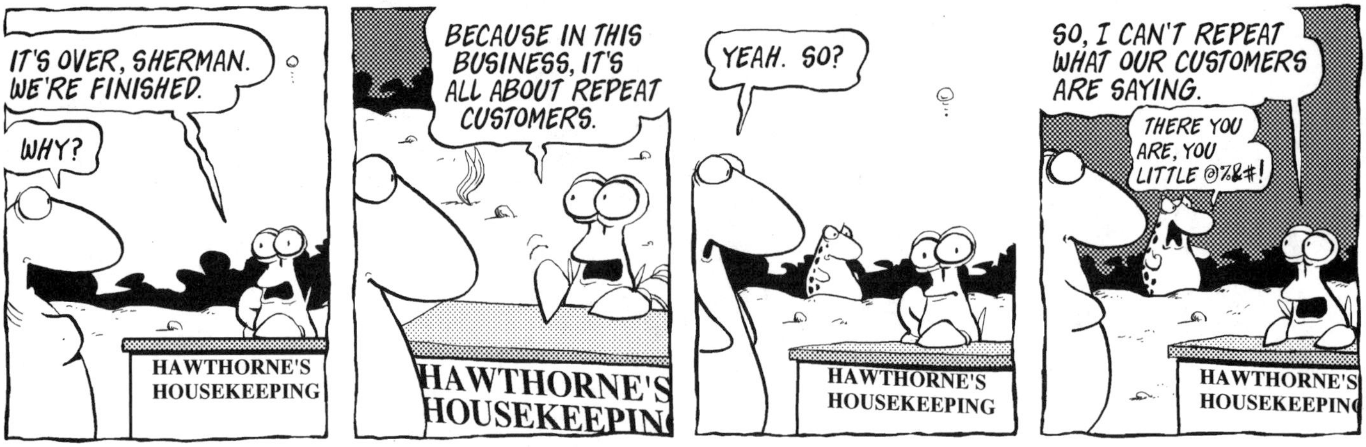
IT'S OVER, SHERMAN. WE'RE FINISHED.
WHY?
HAWTHORNE'S HOUSEKEEPING
BECAUSE IN THIS BUSINESS, IT'S ALL ABOUT REPEAT CUSTOMERS.
HAWTHORNE'S HOUSEKEEPIN
YEAH. SO?
HAWTHORNE'S HOUSEKEEPING
SO, I CAN'T REPEAT WHAT OUR CUSTOMERS ARE SAYING.
THERE YOU ARE, YOU LITTLE @%&#!
HAWTHORNE'S HOUSEKEEPIN

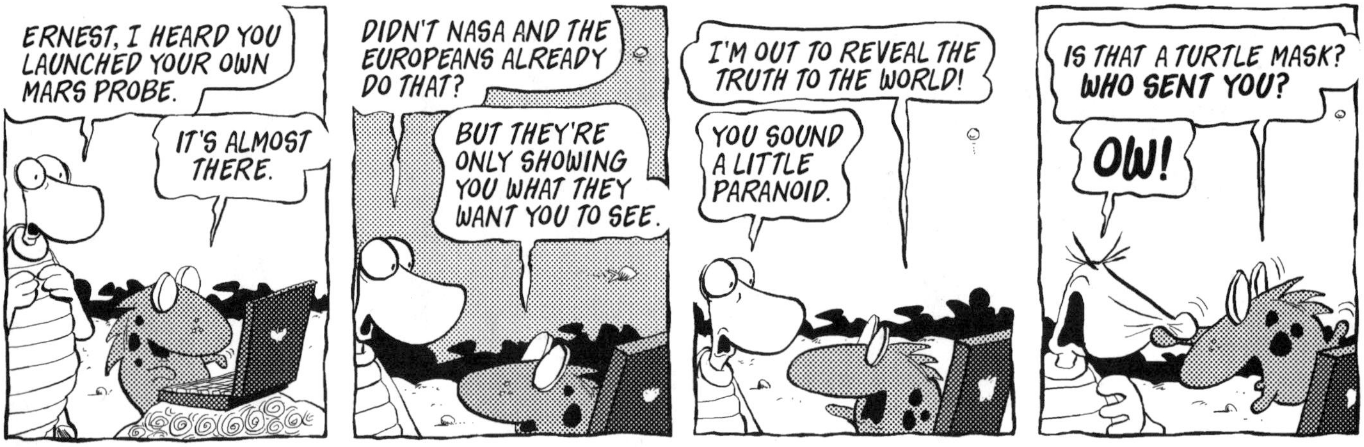
ERNEST, I HEARD YOU LAUNCHED YOUR OWN MARS PROBE.
IT'S ALMOST THERE.
DIDN'T NASA AND THE EUROPEANS ALREADY DO THAT?
BUT THEY'RE ONLY SHOWING YOU WHAT THEY WANT YOU TO SEE.
I'M OUT TO REVEAL THE TRUTH TO THE WORLD!
YOU SOUND A LITTLE PARANOID.
IS THAT A TURTLE MASK? **WHO SENT YOU?**
OW!

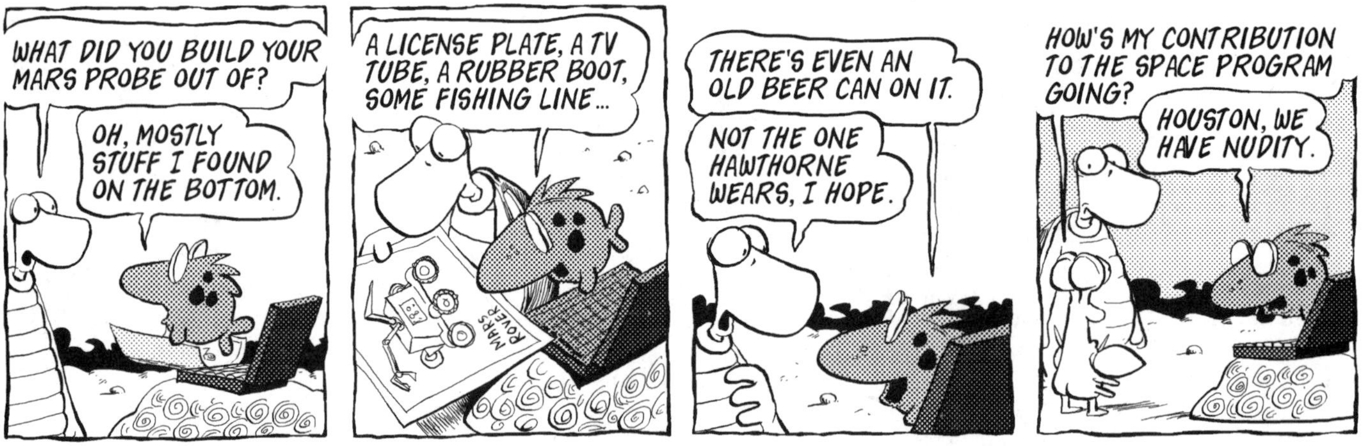
WHAT DID YOU BUILD YOUR MARS PROBE OUT OF?
OH, MOSTLY STUFF I FOUND ON THE BOTTOM.
A LICENSE PLATE, A TV TUBE, A RUBBER BOOT, SOME FISHING LINE...
MARS ROVER
THERE'S EVEN AN OLD BEER CAN ON IT.
NOT THE ONE HAWTHORNE WEARS, I HOPE.
HOW'S MY CONTRIBUTION TO THE SPACE PROGRAM GOING?
HOUSTON, WE HAVE NUDITY.

ERNEST, WHAT POSSESSED YOU TO SEND A PROBE TO MARS?

I'M ON A QUEST TO FIND LIQUID WATER. IT'S THE HOLY GRAIL OF MODERN SCIENCE.

THAT'S EASY.

YEAH?

SEND HIM TO MARS WITH A SET OF GOLF CLUBS AND A BALL.

IF THERE'S WATER, I'LL FIND IT.

YOU'VE LANDED YOUR PROBE SAFELY ON MARS. NOW WHAT HAPPENS?

I SWITCH IT OVER TO MANUAL CONTROL.

NOW I CAN GUIDE THIS DELICATE, HIGH-TECH INSTRUMENT ACROSS THE MARTIAN SURFACE.

WHAT ARE YOU GONNA DO FIRST?

SOME WHEELIES.

COOL.

WHAT HAS YOUR MARS ROVER DISCOVERED TODAY, ERNEST?

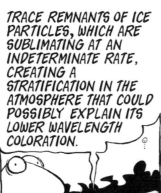

TRACE REMNANTS OF ICE PARTICLES, WHICH ARE SUBLIMATING AT AN INDETERMINATE RATE, CREATING A STRATIFICATION IN THE ATMOSPHERE THAT COULD POSSIBLY EXPLAIN ITS LOWER WAVELENGTH COLORATION.

DID YOU GET ANY OF THAT?

IF I'M NOT MISTAKEN, ICE IS FROZEN WATER.

GIVE HIM A COOKIE.

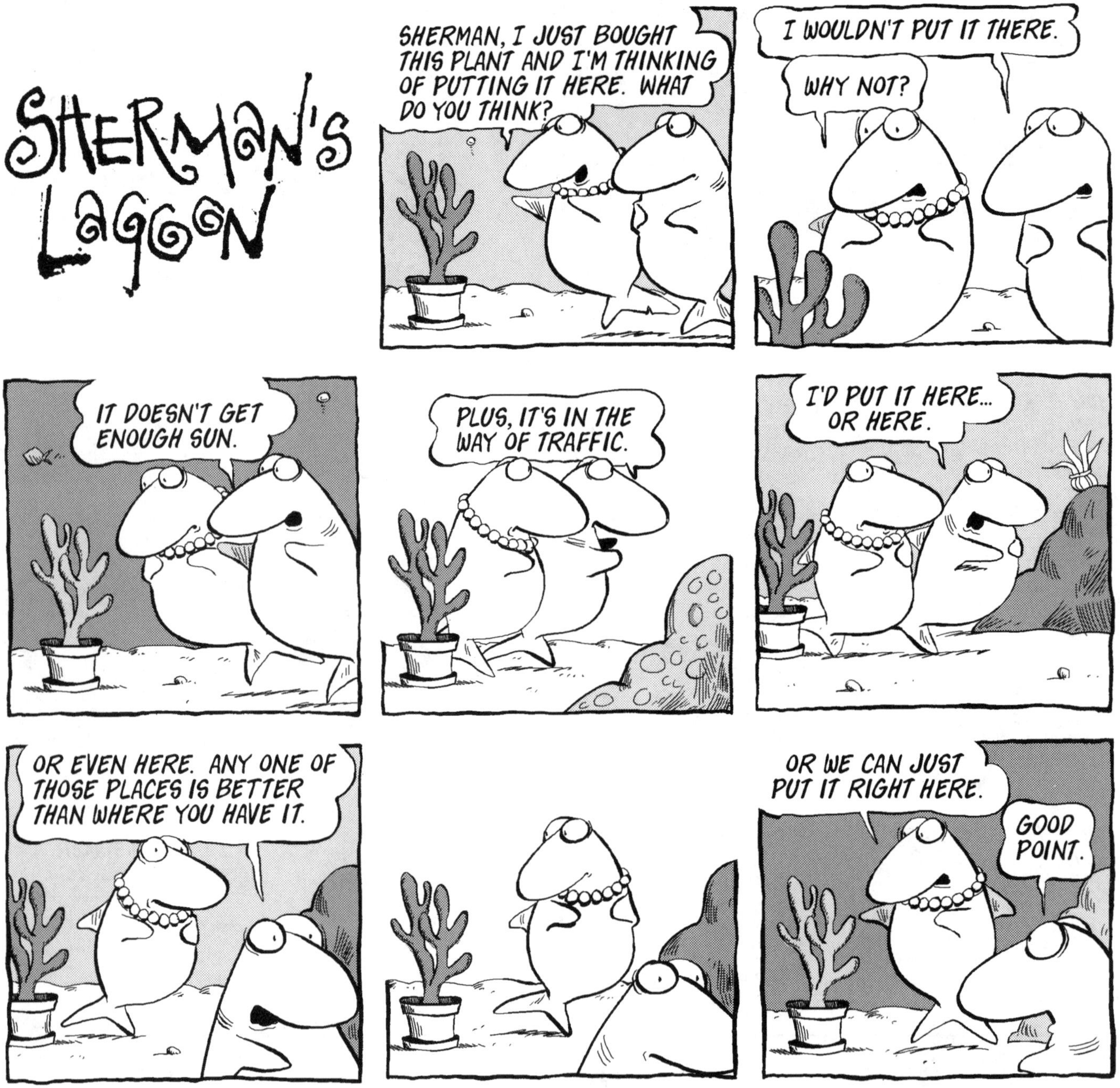
SHERMAN'S LAGOON
SHERMAN, I JUST BOUGHT THIS PLANT AND I'M THINKING OF PUTTING IT HERE. WHAT DO YOU THINK?
I WOULDN'T PUT IT THERE.
WHY NOT?
IT DOESN'T GET ENOUGH SUN.
PLUS, IT'S IN THE WAY OF TRAFFIC.
I'D PUT IT HERE... OR HERE.
OR EVEN HERE. ANY ONE OF THOSE PLACES IS BETTER THAN WHERE YOU HAVE IT.
OR WE CAN JUST PUT IT RIGHT HERE.
GOOD POINT.

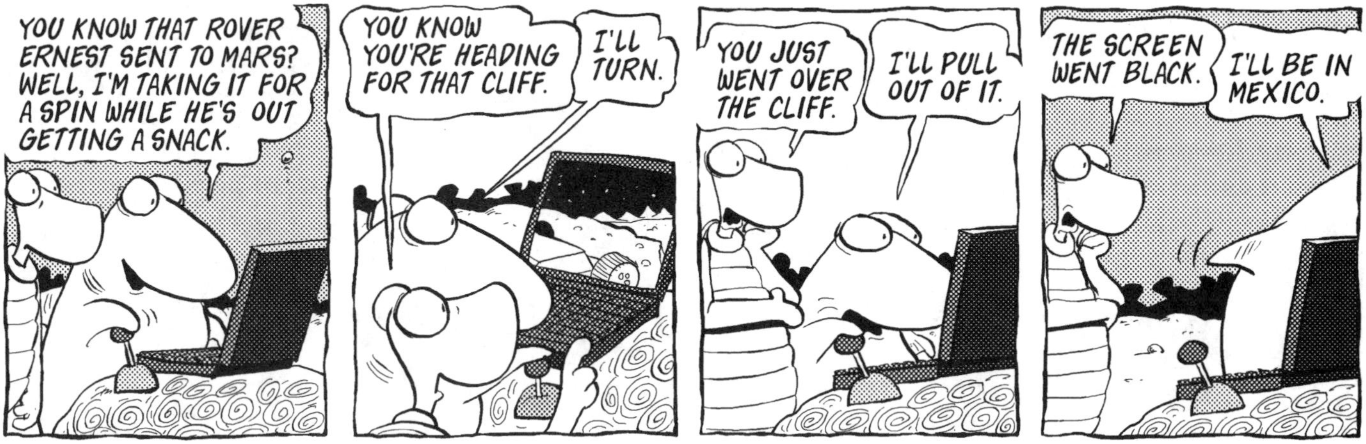
YOU KNOW THAT ROVER ERNEST SENT TO MARS? WELL, I'M TAKING IT FOR A SPIN WHILE HE'S OUT GETTING A SNACK.
YOU KNOW YOU'RE HEADING FOR THAT CLIFF.
I'LL TURN.
YOU JUST WENT OVER THE CLIFF.
I'LL PULL OUT OF IT.
THE SCREEN WENT BLACK.
I'LL BE IN MEXICO.

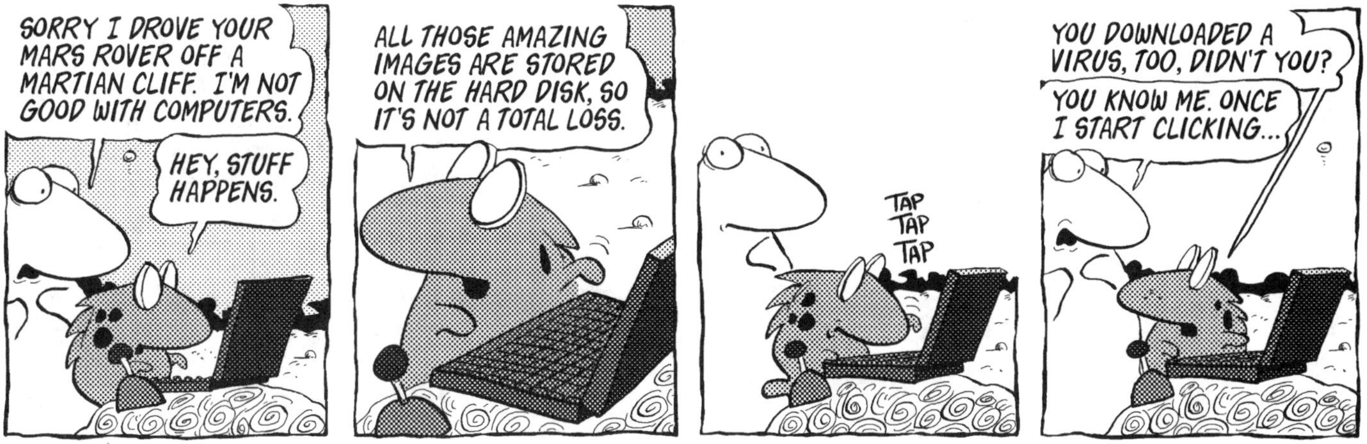
SORRY I DROVE YOUR MARS ROVER OFF A MARTIAN CLIFF. I'M NOT GOOD WITH COMPUTERS.
HEY, STUFF HAPPENS.
ALL THOSE AMAZING IMAGES ARE STORED ON THE HARD DISK, SO IT'S NOT A TOTAL LOSS.
TAP TAP TAP
YOU DOWNLOADED A VIRUS, TOO, DIDN'T YOU?
YOU KNOW ME. ONCE I START CLICKING...

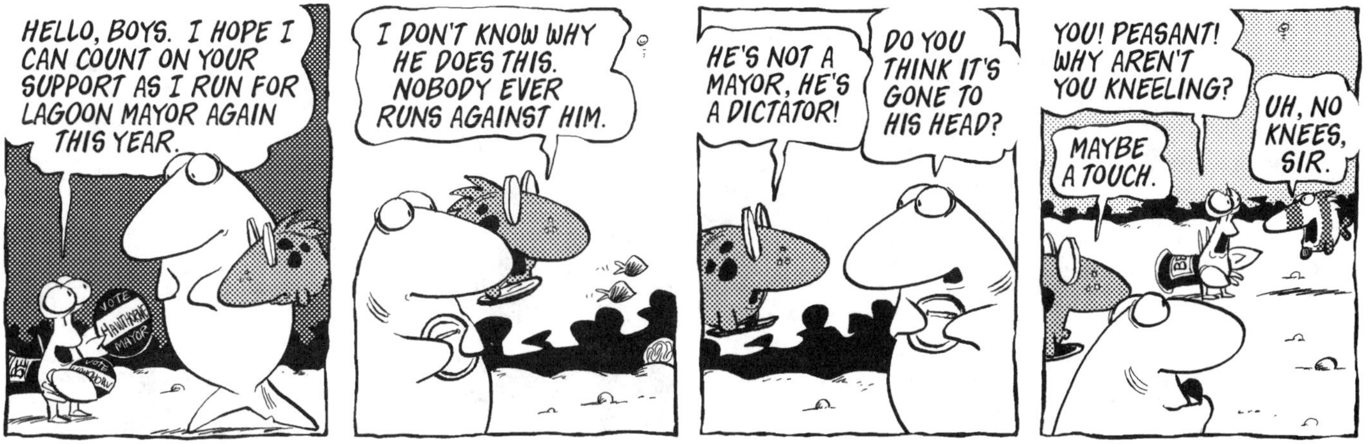
HELLO, BOYS. I HOPE I CAN COUNT ON YOUR SUPPORT AS I RUN FOR LAGOON MAYOR AGAIN THIS YEAR.
I DON'T KNOW WHY HE DOES THIS. NOBODY EVER RUNS AGAINST HIM.
HE'S NOT A MAYOR, HE'S A DICTATOR!
DO YOU THINK IT'S GONE TO HIS HEAD?
YOU! PEASANT! WHY AREN'T YOU KNEELING?
MAYBE A TOUCH.
UH, NO KNEES, SIR.

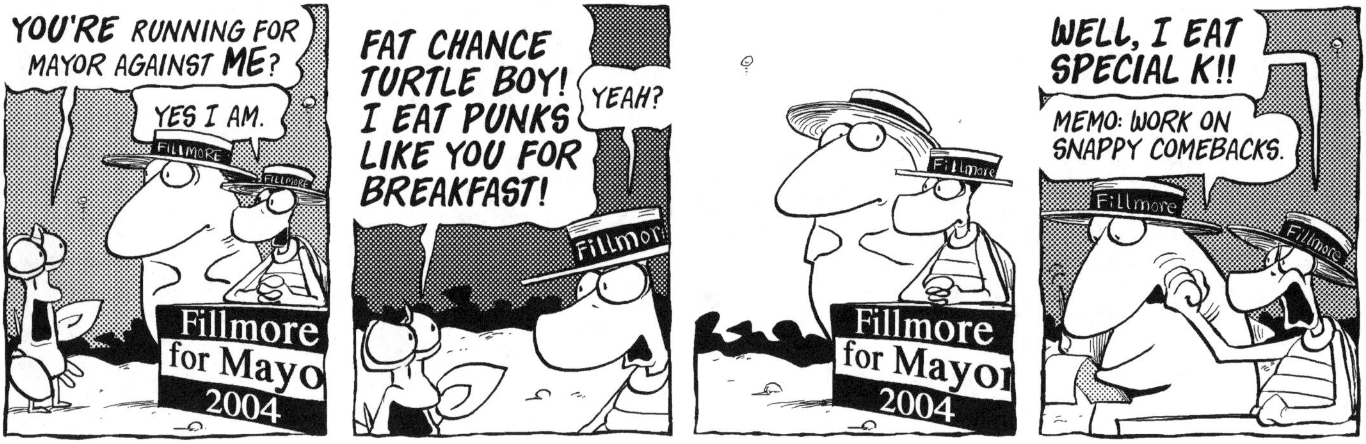
YOU'RE RUNNING FOR MAYOR AGAINST ME?
YES I AM.
FILLMORE
Fillmore for Mayor 2004
FAT CHANCE TURTLE BOY! I EAT PUNKS LIKE YOU FOR BREAKFAST!
YEAH?
Fillmore
Fillmore for Mayor 2004
WELL, I EAT SPECIAL K!!
MEMO: WORK ON SNAPPY COMEBACKS.
Fillmore

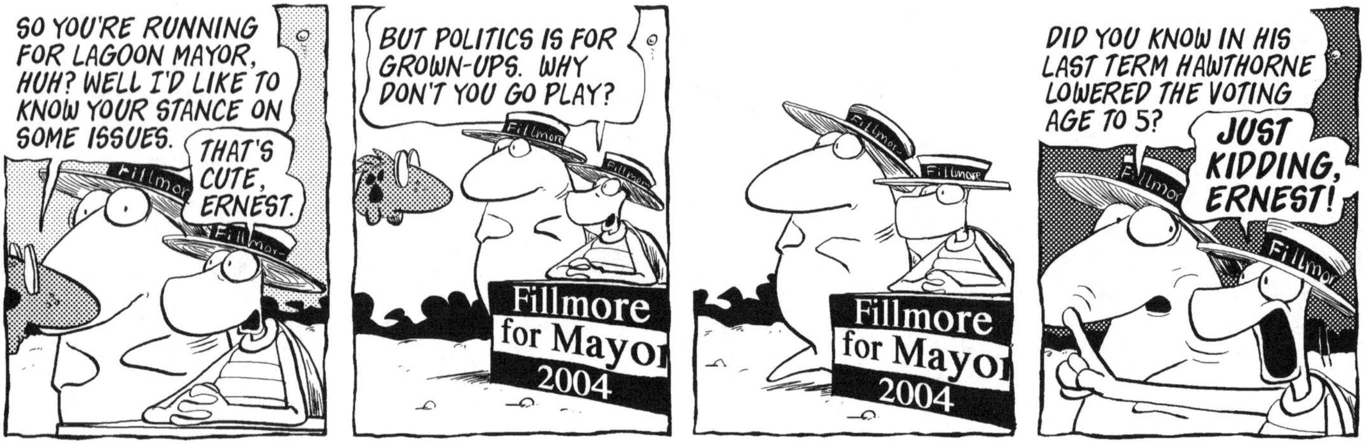
SO YOU'RE RUNNING FOR LAGOON MAYOR, HUH? WELL I'D LIKE TO KNOW YOUR STANCE ON SOME ISSUES.
THAT'S CUTE, ERNEST.
BUT POLITICS IS FOR GROWN-UPS. WHY DON'T YOU GO PLAY?
Fillmore for Mayor 2004
Fillmore for Mayor 2004
DID YOU KNOW IN HIS LAST TERM HAWTHORNE LOWERED THE VOTING AGE TO 5?
JUST KIDDING, ERNEST!

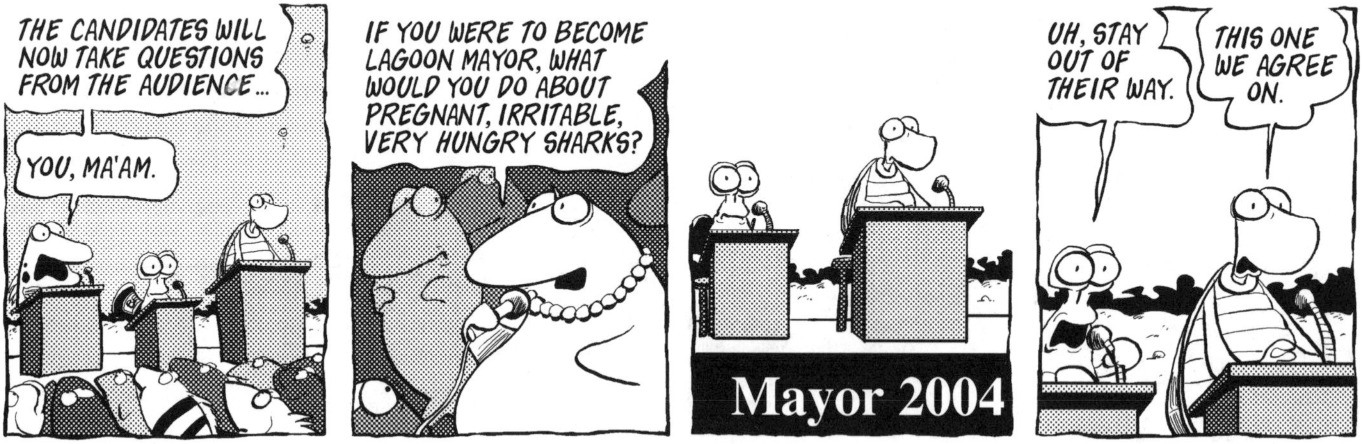
THE CANDIDATES WILL NOW TAKE QUESTIONS FROM THE AUDIENCE...
YOU, MA'AM.
IF YOU WERE TO BECOME LAGOON MAYOR, WHAT WOULD YOU DO ABOUT PREGNANT, IRRITABLE, VERY HUNGRY SHARKS?
Mayor 2004
UH, STAY OUT OF THEIR WAY.
THIS ONE WE AGREE ON.

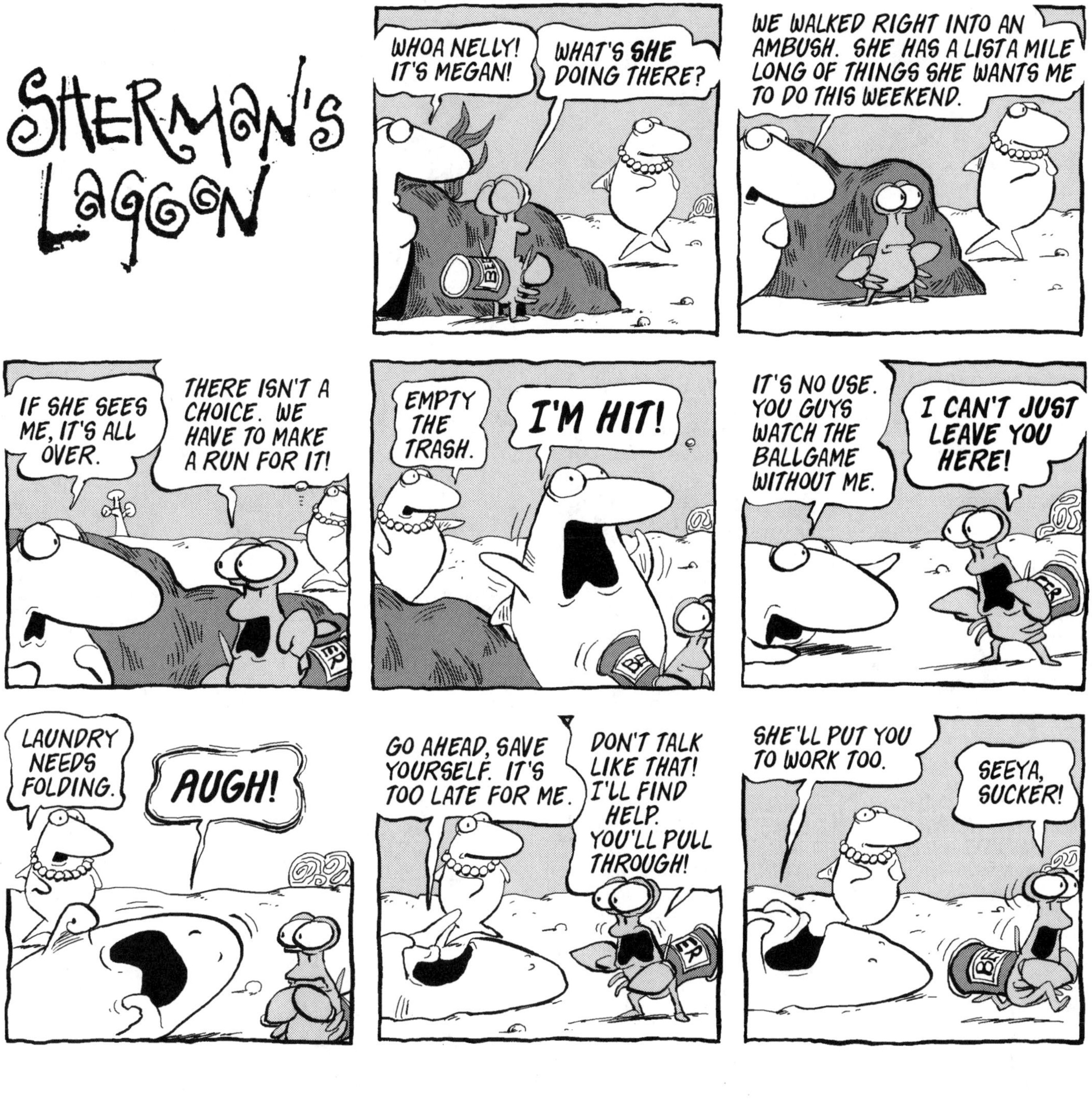
SHERMAN'S LAGOON
WHOA NELLY! IT'S MEGAN!
WHAT'S SHE DOING THERE?
WE WALKED RIGHT INTO AN AMBUSH. SHE HAS A LIST A MILE LONG OF THINGS SHE WANTS ME TO DO THIS WEEKEND.
IF SHE SEES ME, IT'S ALL OVER.
THERE ISN'T A CHOICE. WE HAVE TO MAKE A RUN FOR IT!
EMPTY THE TRASH.
I'M HIT!
IT'S NO USE. YOU GUYS WATCH THE BALLGAME WITHOUT ME.
I CAN'T JUST LEAVE YOU HERE!
LAUNDRY NEEDS FOLDING.
AUGH!
GO AHEAD, SAVE YOURSELF. IT'S TOO LATE FOR ME.
DON'T TALK LIKE THAT! I'LL FIND HELP. YOU'LL PULL THROUGH!
SHE'LL PUT YOU TO WORK TOO.
SEEYA, SUCKER!

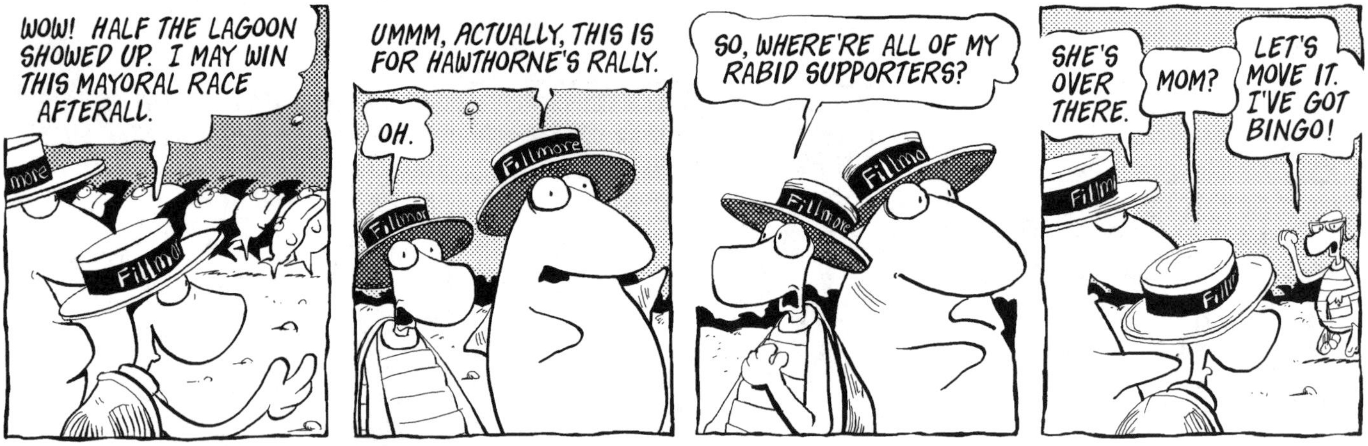
WOW! HALF THE LAGOON SHOWED UP. I MAY WIN THIS MAYORAL RACE AFTERALL.
UMMM, ACTUALLY, THIS IS FOR HAWTHORNE'S RALLY.
OH.
SO, WHERE'RE ALL OF MY RABID SUPPORTERS?
SHE'S OVER THERE.
MOM?
LET'S MOVE IT. I'VE GOT BINGO!

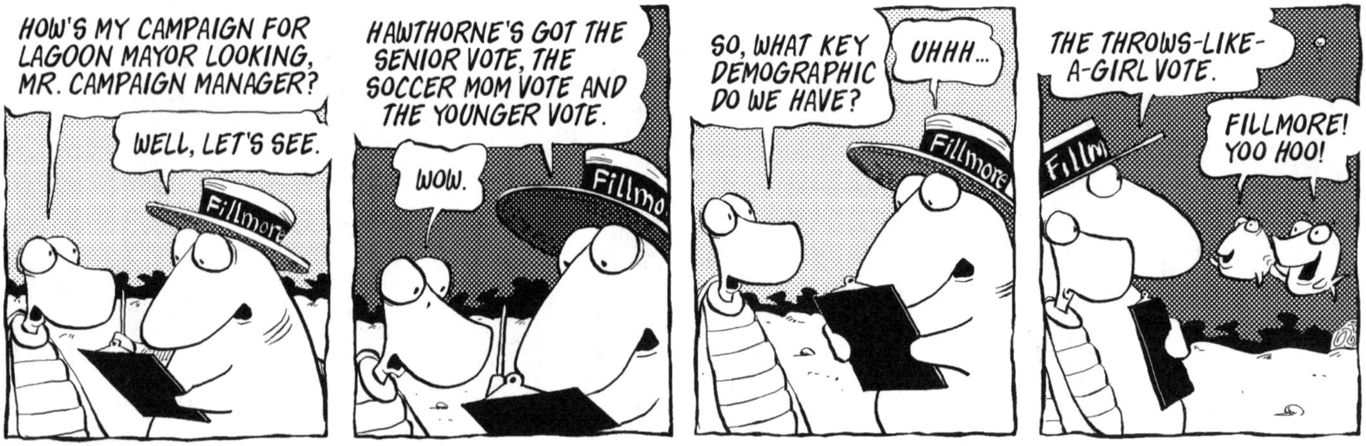
HOW'S MY CAMPAIGN FOR LAGOON MAYOR LOOKING, MR. CAMPAIGN MANAGER?
WELL, LET'S SEE.
HAWTHORNE'S GOT THE SENIOR VOTE, THE SOCCER MOM VOTE AND THE YOUNGER VOTE.
WOW.
SO, WHAT KEY DEMOGRAPHIC DO WE HAVE?
UHHH...
THE THROWS-LIKE-A-GIRL VOTE.
FILLMORE! YOO HOO!

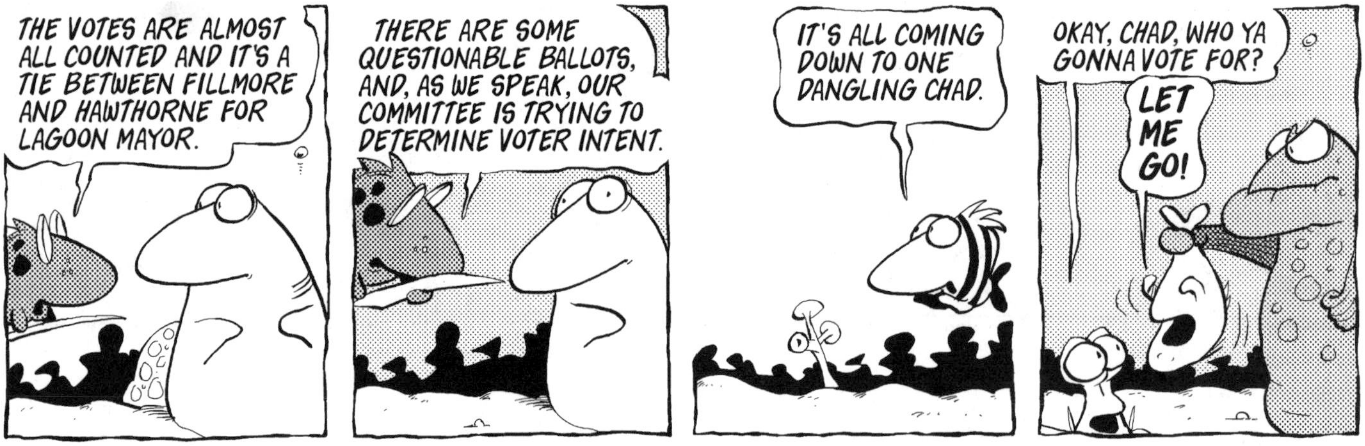
THE VOTES ARE ALMOST ALL COUNTED AND IT'S A TIE BETWEEN FILLMORE AND HAWTHORNE FOR LAGOON MAYOR.
THERE ARE SOME QUESTIONABLE BALLOTS, AND, AS WE SPEAK, OUR COMMITTEE IS TRYING TO DETERMINE VOTER INTENT.
IT'S ALL COMING DOWN TO ONE DANGLING CHAD.
OKAY, CHAD, WHO YA GONNA VOTE FOR?
LET ME GO!

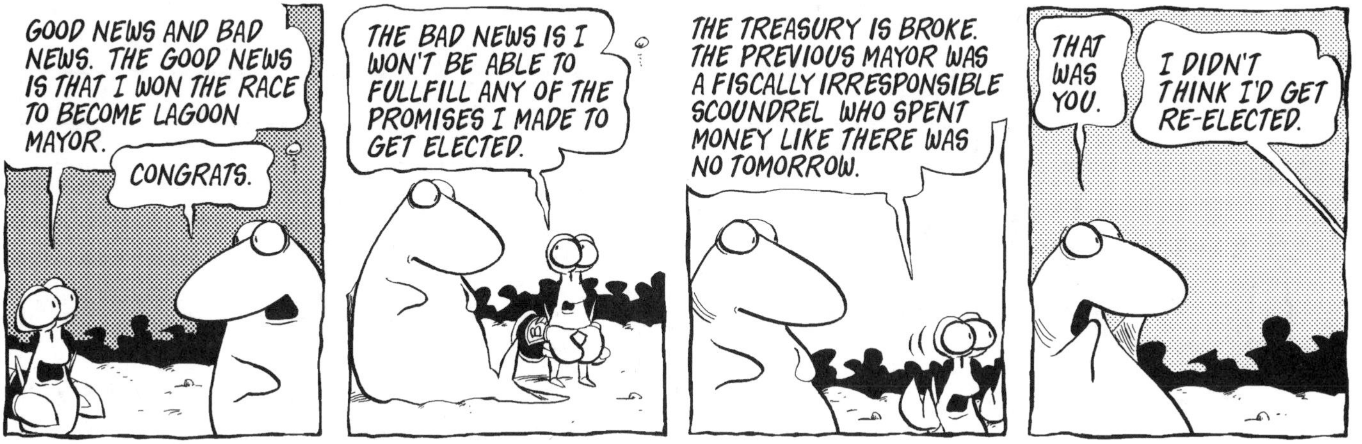
GOOD NEWS AND BAD NEWS. THE GOOD NEWS IS THAT I WON THE RACE TO BECOME LAGOON MAYOR.
CONGRATS.
THE BAD NEWS IS I WON'T BE ABLE TO FULLFILL ANY OF THE PROMISES I MADE TO GET ELECTED.
THE TREASURY IS BROKE. THE PREVIOUS MAYOR WAS A FISCALLY IRRESPONSIBLE SCOUNDREL WHO SPENT MONEY LIKE THERE WAS NO TOMORROW.
THAT WAS YOU.
I DIDN'T THINK I'D GET RE-ELECTED.

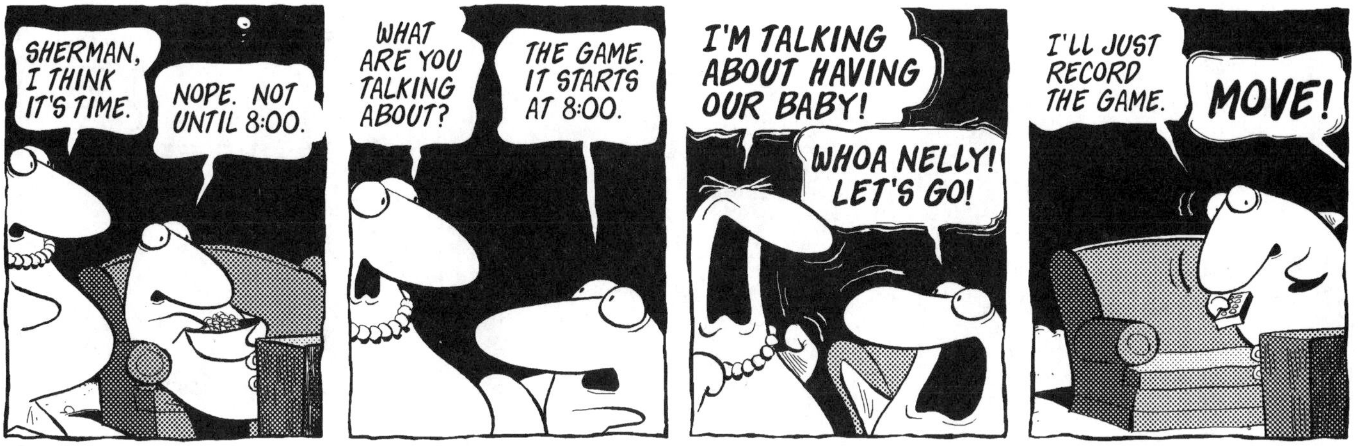
SHERMAN, I THINK IT'S TIME.
NOPE. NOT UNTIL 8:00.
WHAT ARE YOU TALKING ABOUT?
THE GAME. IT STARTS AT 8:00.
I'M TALKING ABOUT HAVING OUR BABY!
WHOA NELLY! LET'S GO!
I'LL JUST RECORD THE GAME.
MOVE!

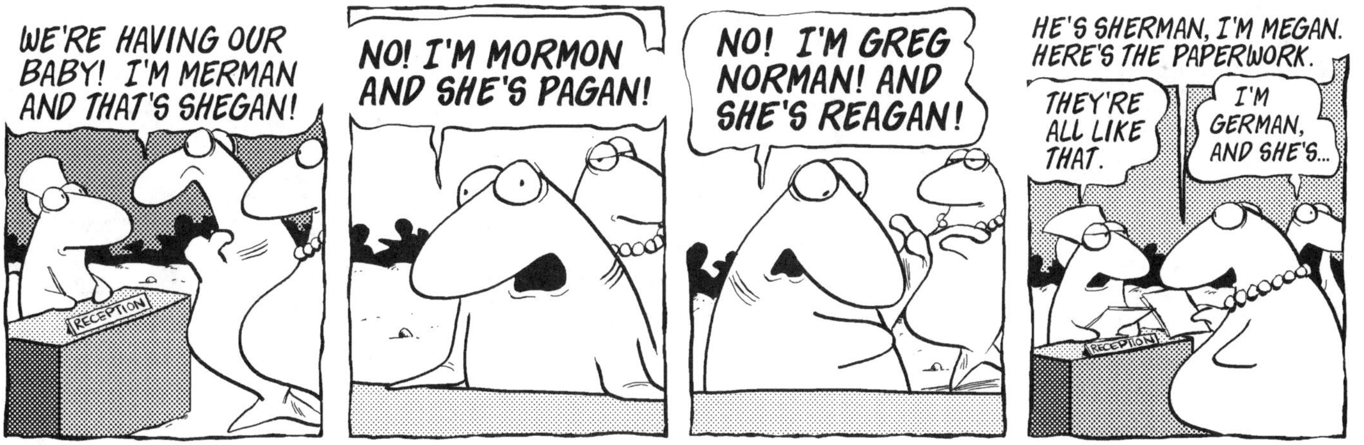
WE'RE HAVING OUR BABY! I'M MERMAN AND THAT'S SHEGAN!
RECEPTION
NO! I'M MORMON AND SHE'S PAGAN!
NO! I'M GREG NORMAN! AND SHE'S REAGAN!
HE'S SHERMAN, I'M MEGAN. HERE'S THE PAPERWORK.
THEY'RE ALL LIKE THAT.
I'M GERMAN, AND SHE'S...
RECEPTION

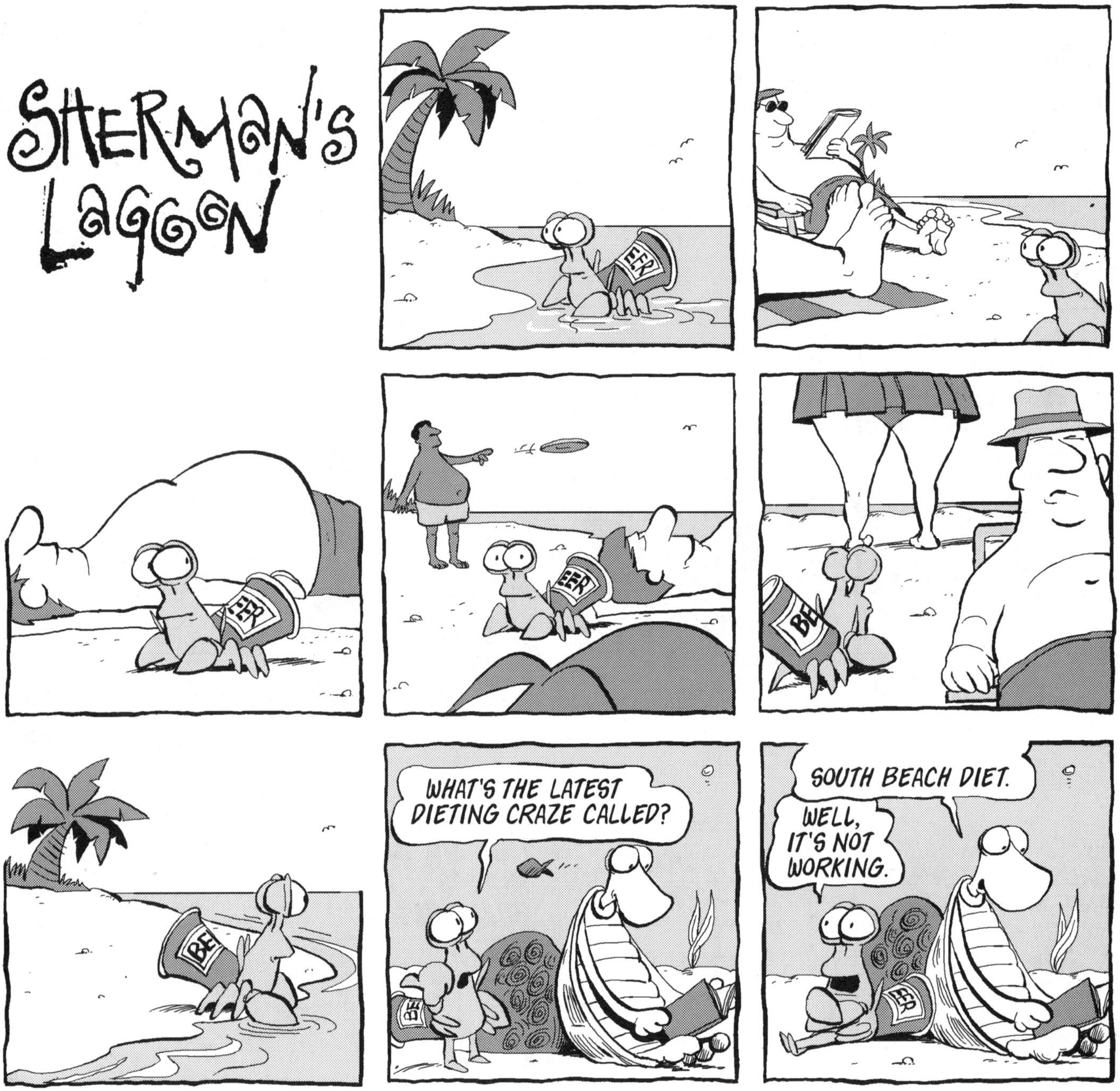
SHERMAN'S LAGOON
BEER
EER
EER
EER
BE
BE
WHAT'S THE LATEST DIETING CRAZE CALLED?
BE
SOUTH BEACH DIET.
WELL, IT'S NOT WORKING.
EER

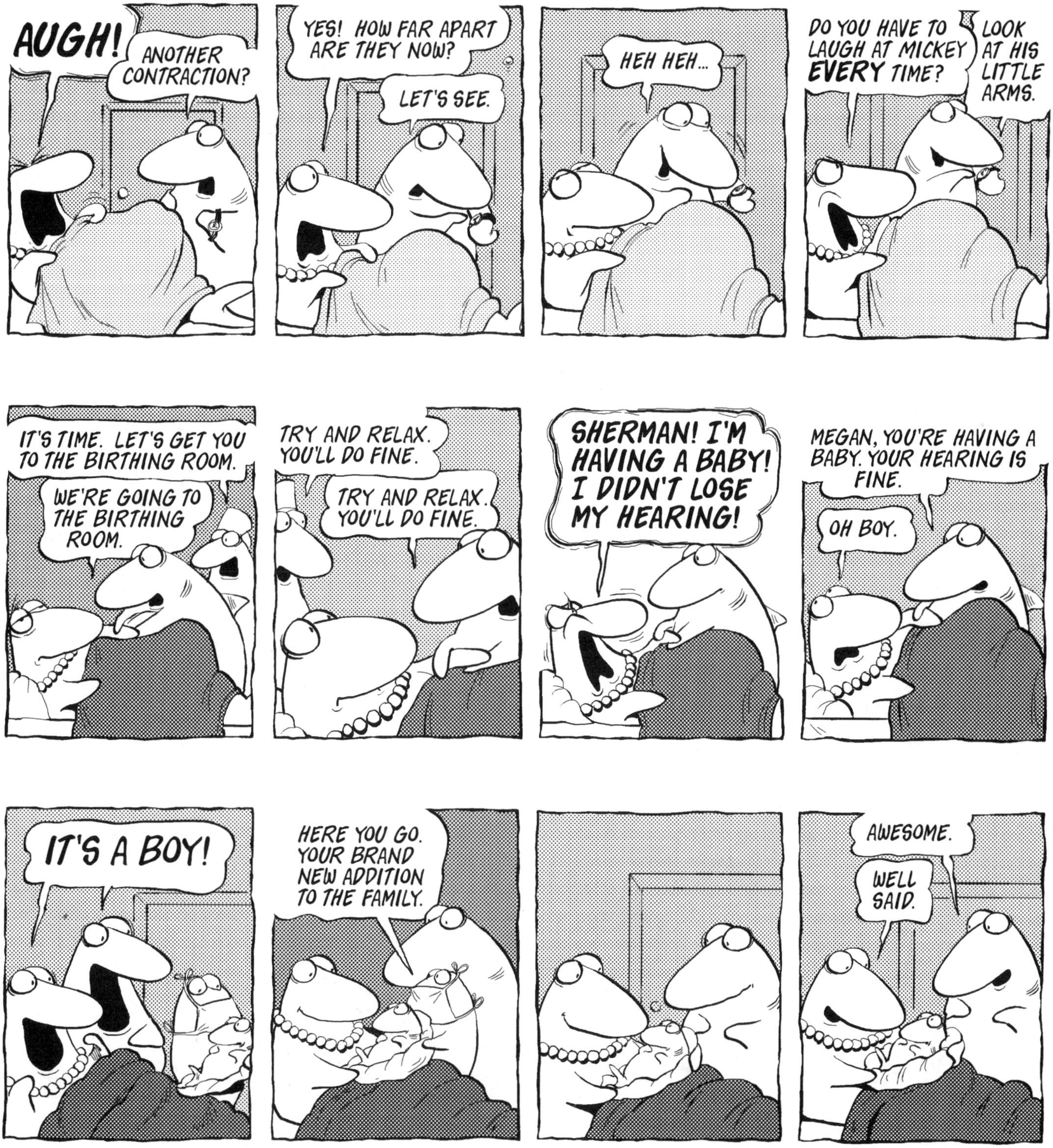
AUGH!
ANOTHER CONTRACTION?
YES! HOW FAR APART ARE THEY NOW?
LET'S SEE.
HEH HEH...
DO YOU HAVE TO LAUGH AT MICKEY EVERY TIME?
LOOK AT HIS LITTLE ARMS.
IT'S TIME. LET'S GET YOU TO THE BIRTHING ROOM.
WE'RE GOING TO THE BIRTHING ROOM.
TRY AND RELAX. YOU'LL DO FINE.
TRY AND RELAX. YOU'LL DO FINE.
SHERMAN! I'M HAVING A BABY! I DIDN'T LOSE MY HEARING!
MEGAN, YOU'RE HAVING A BABY. YOUR HEARING IS FINE.
OH BOY.
IT'S A BOY!
HERE YOU GO. YOUR BRAND NEW ADDITION TO THE FAMILY.
AWESOME.
WELL SAID.

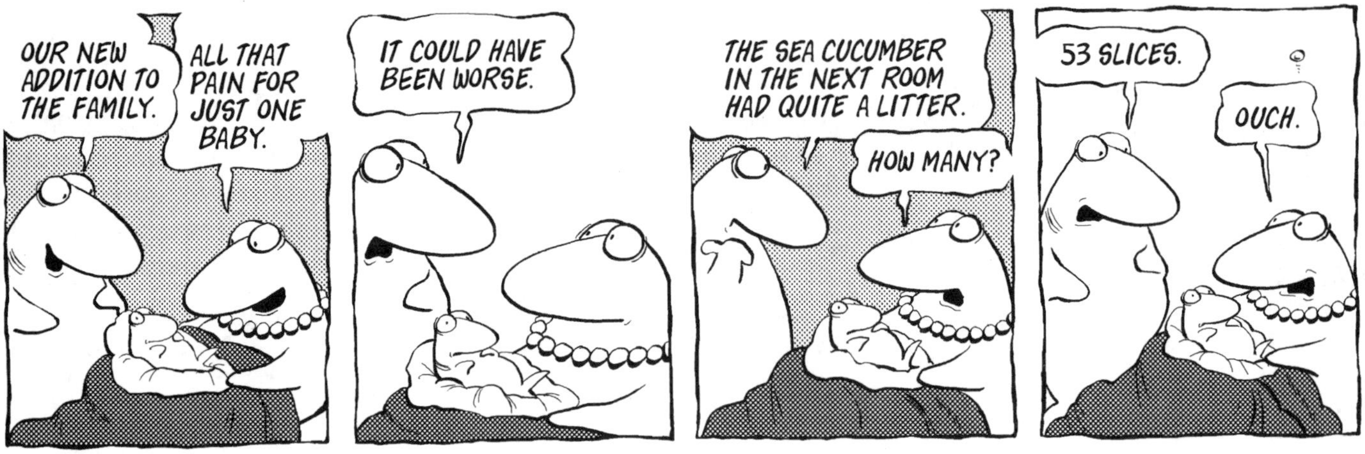
OUR NEW ADDITION TO THE FAMILY.
ALL THAT PAIN FOR JUST ONE BABY.
IT COULD HAVE BEEN WORSE.
THE SEA CUCUMBER IN THE NEXT ROOM HAD QUITE A LITTER.
HOW MANY?
53 SLICES.
OUCH.

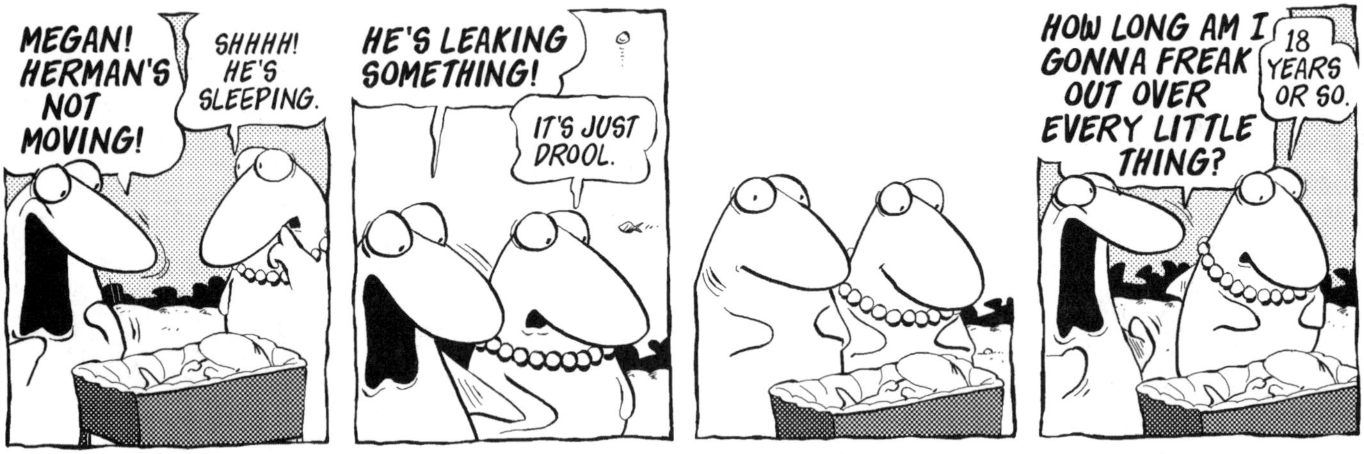
MEGAN! HERMAN'S NOT MOVING!
SHHHH! HE'S SLEEPING.
HE'S LEAKING SOMETHING!
IT'S JUST DROOL.
HOW LONG AM I GONNA FREAK OUT OVER EVERY LITTLE THING?
18 YEARS OR SO.

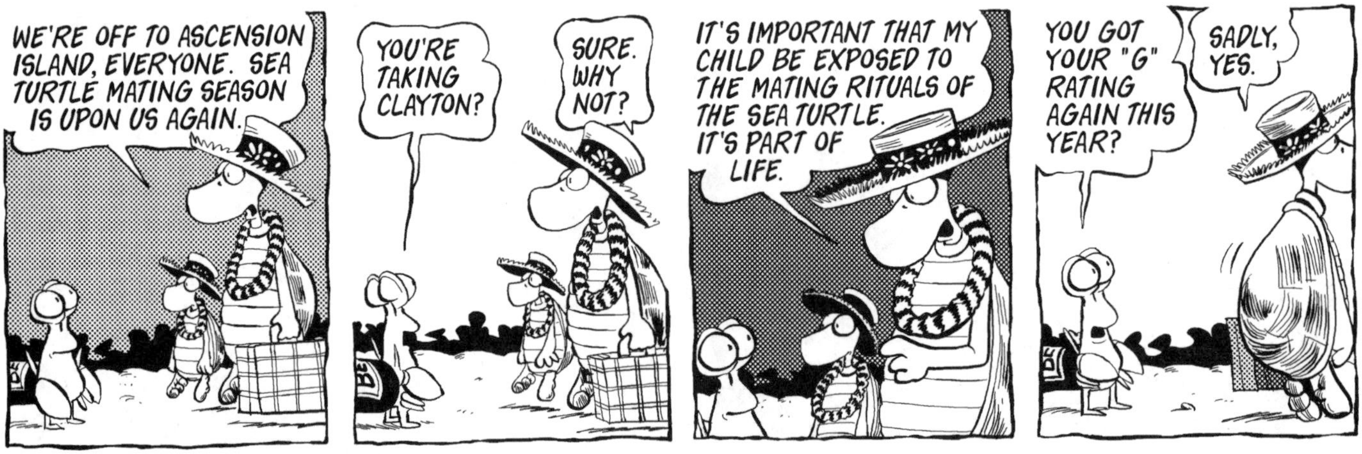
WE'RE OFF TO ASCENSION ISLAND, EVERYONE. SEA TURTLE MATING SEASON IS UPON US AGAIN.
YOU'RE TAKING CLAYTON?
SURE. WHY NOT?
IT'S IMPORTANT THAT MY CHILD BE EXPOSED TO THE MATING RITUALS OF THE SEA TURTLE. IT'S PART OF LIFE.
YOU GOT YOUR "G" RATING AGAIN THIS YEAR?
SADLY, YES.

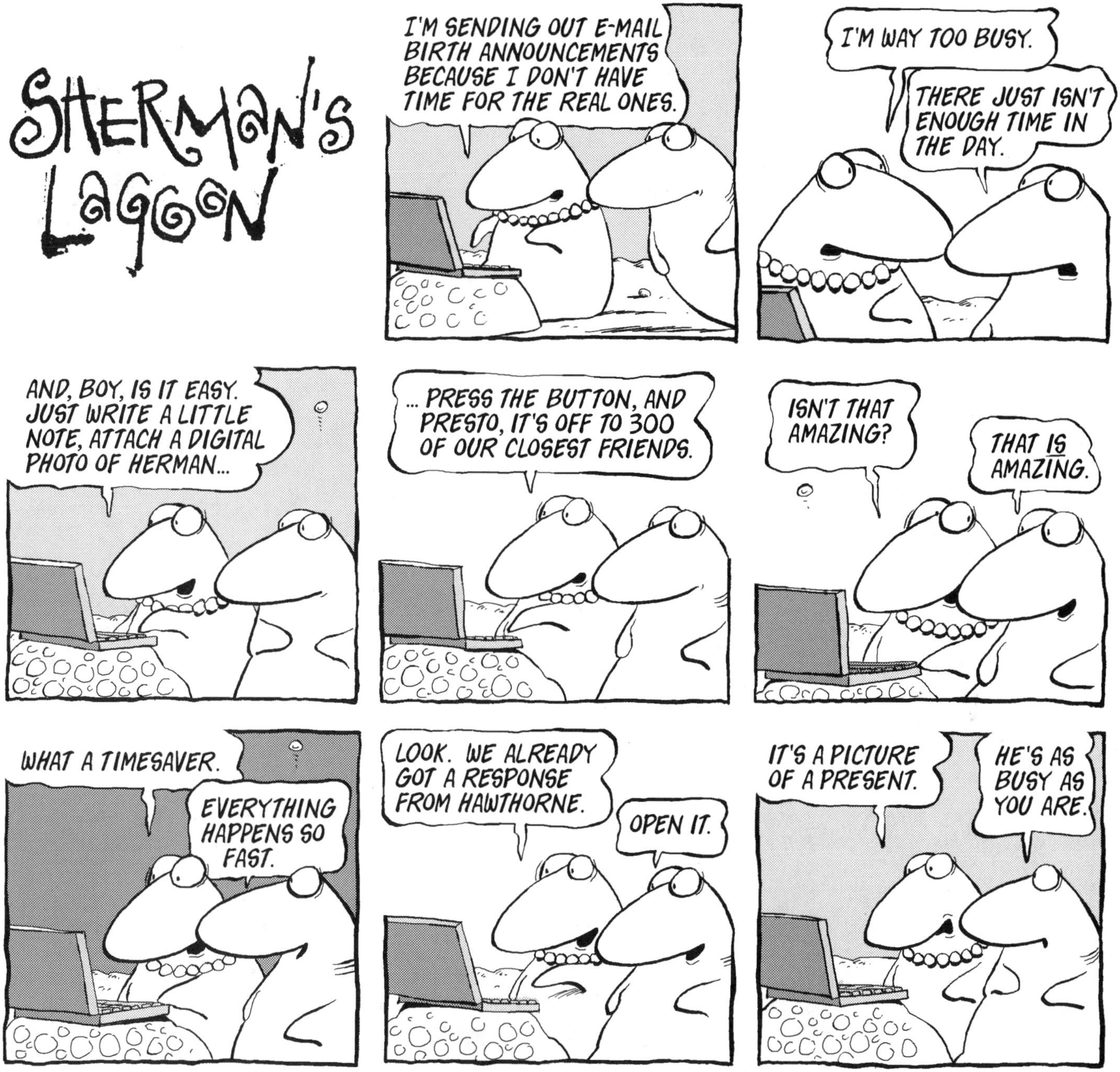
SHERMAN'S LAGOON
I'M SENDING OUT E-MAIL BIRTH ANNOUNCEMENTS BECAUSE I DON'T HAVE TIME FOR THE REAL ONES.
I'M WAY TOO BUSY.
THERE JUST ISN'T ENOUGH TIME IN THE DAY.
AND, BOY, IS IT EASY. JUST WRITE A LITTLE NOTE, ATTACH A DIGITAL PHOTO OF HERMAN...
... PRESS THE BUTTON, AND PRESTO, IT'S OFF TO 300 OF OUR CLOSEST FRIENDS.
ISN'T THAT AMAZING?
THAT IS AMAZING.
WHAT A TIMESAVER.
EVERYTHING HAPPENS SO FAST.
LOOK. WE ALREADY GOT A RESPONSE FROM HAWTHORNE.
OPEN IT.
IT'S A PICTURE OF A PRESENT.
HE'S AS BUSY AS YOU ARE.

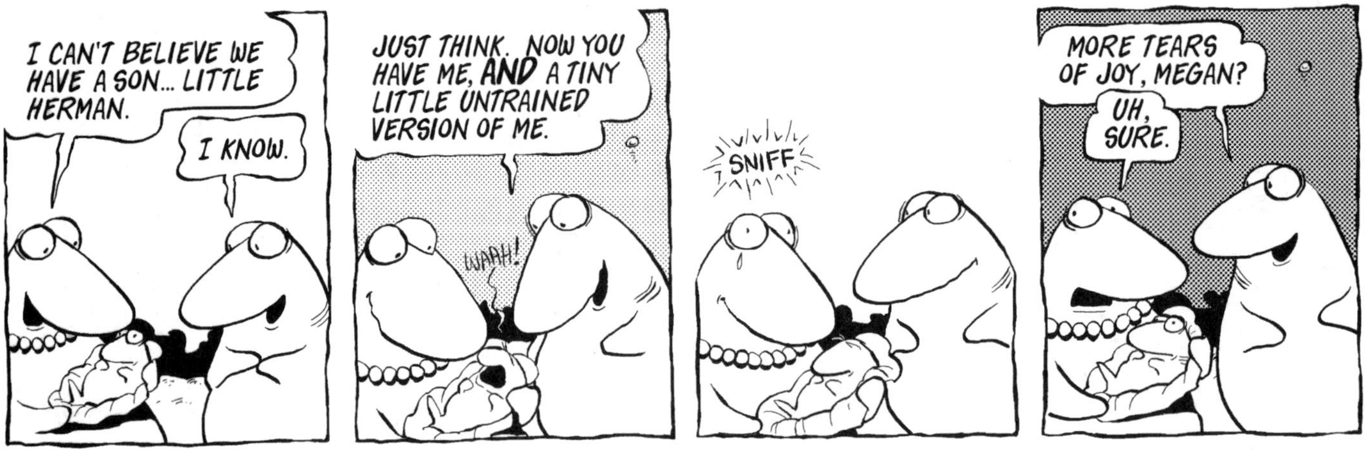
I CAN'T BELIEVE WE HAVE A SON... LITTLE HERMAN.
I KNOW.
JUST THINK. NOW YOU HAVE ME, AND A TINY LITTLE UNTRAINED VERSION OF ME.
WAAH!
SNIFF
MORE TEARS OF JOY, MEGAN?
UH, SURE.

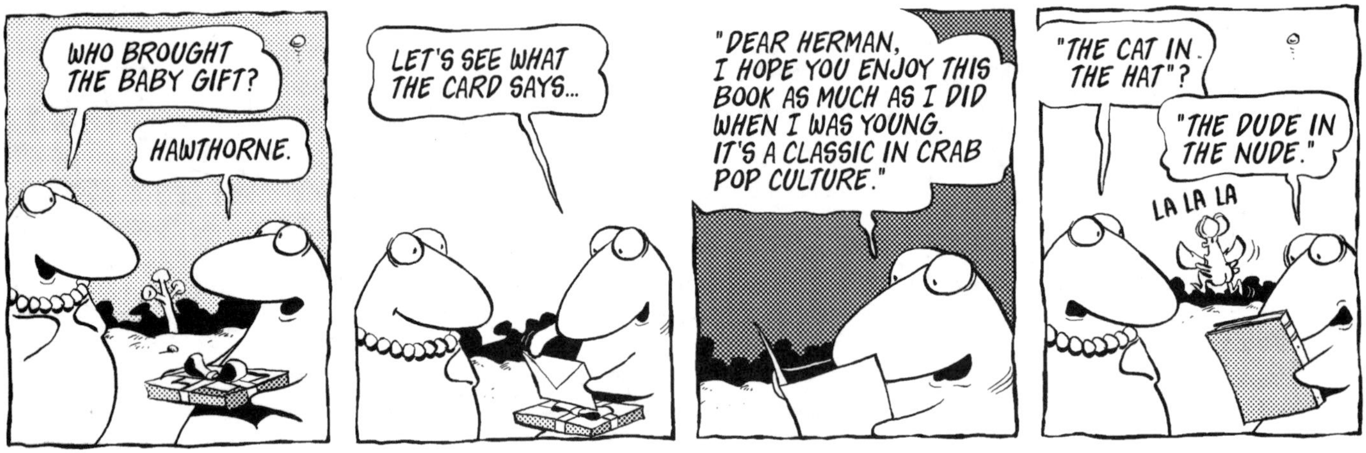
WHO BROUGHT THE BABY GIFT?
HAWTHORNE.
LET'S SEE WHAT THE CARD SAYS...
"DEAR HERMAN, I HOPE YOU ENJOY THIS BOOK AS MUCH AS I DID WHEN I WAS YOUNG. IT'S A CLASSIC IN CRAB POP CULTURE."
"THE CAT IN THE HAT"?
"THE DUDE IN THE NUDE."
LA LA LA

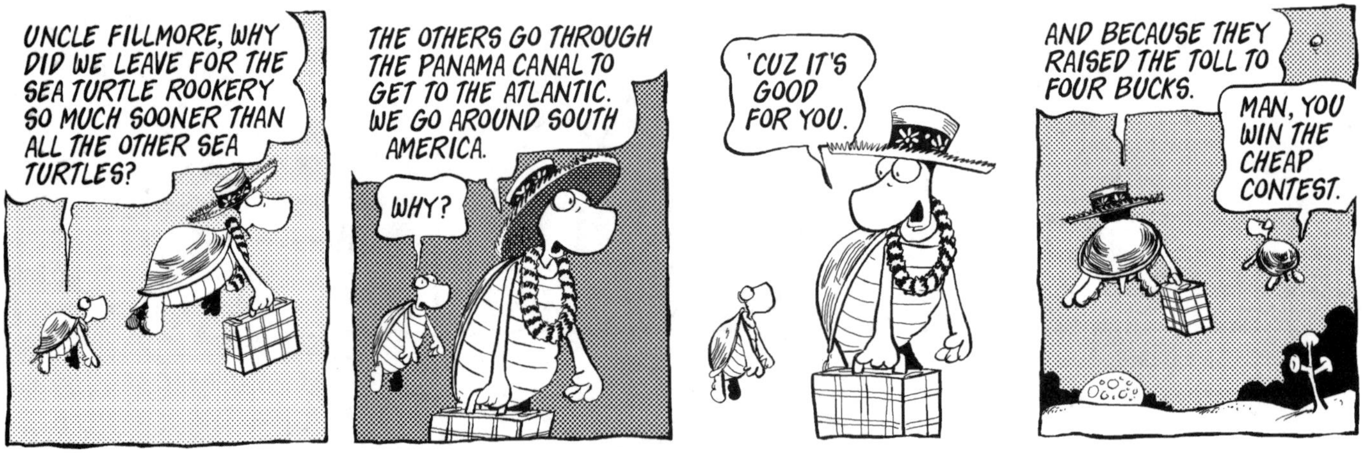
UNCLE FILLMORE, WHY DID WE LEAVE FOR THE SEA TURTLE ROOKERY SO MUCH SOONER THAN ALL THE OTHER SEA TURTLES?
THE OTHERS GO THROUGH THE PANAMA CANAL TO GET TO THE ATLANTIC. WE GO AROUND SOUTH AMERICA.
WHY?
'CUZ IT'S GOOD FOR YOU.
AND BECAUSE THEY RAISED THE TOLL TO FOUR BUCKS.
MAN, YOU WIN THE CHEAP CONTEST.

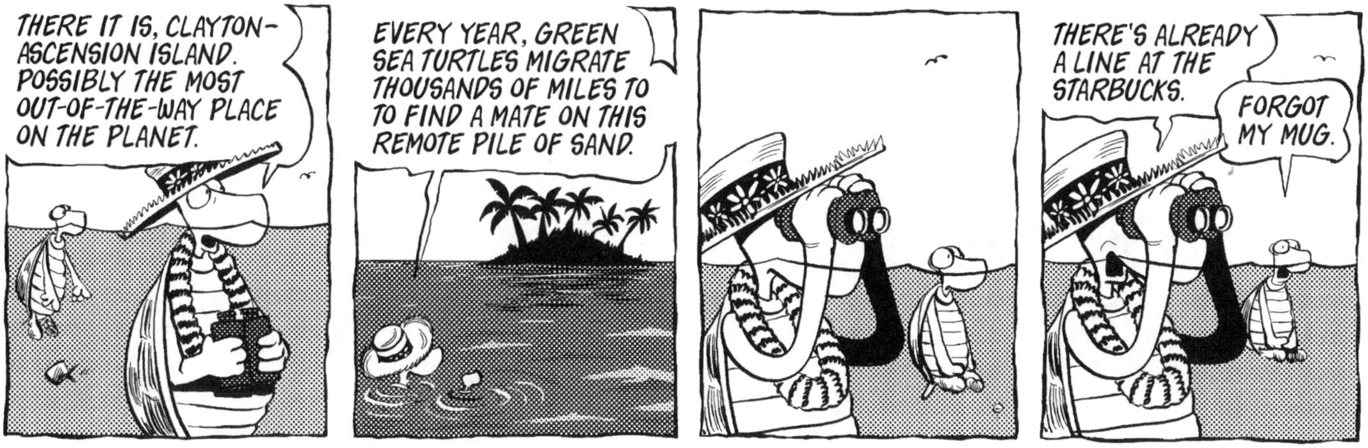
THERE IT IS, CLAYTON- ASCENSION ISLAND. POSSIBLY THE MOST OUT-OF-THE-WAY PLACE ON THE PLANET.
EVERY YEAR, GREEN SEA TURTLES MIGRATE THOUSANDS OF MILES TO TO FIND A MATE ON THIS REMOTE PILE OF SAND.
THERE'S ALREADY A LINE AT THE STARBUCKS.
FORGOT MY MUG.

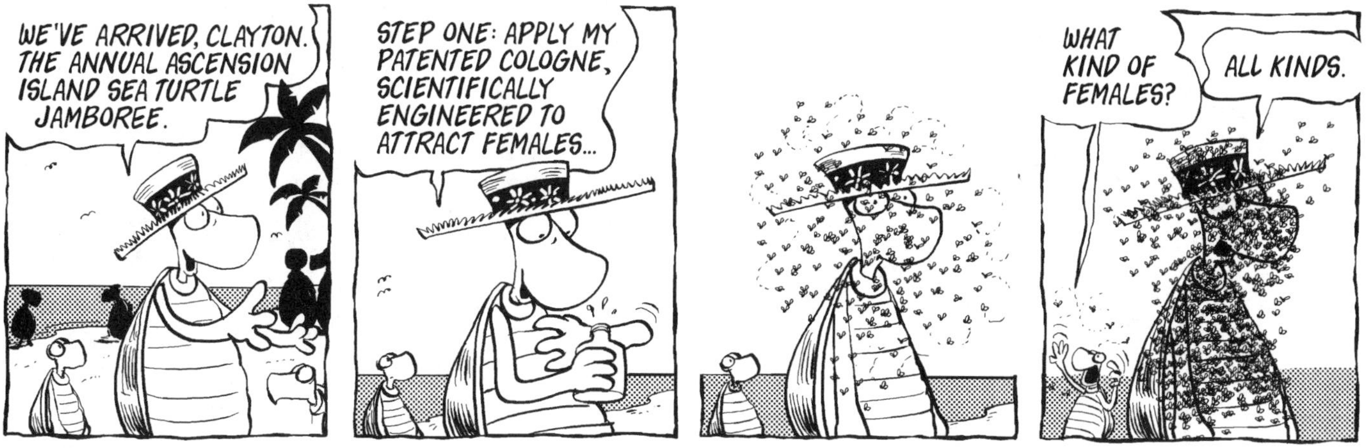
WE'VE ARRIVED, CLAYTON. THE ANNUAL ASCENSION ISLAND SEA TURTLE JAMBOREE.
STEP ONE: APPLY MY PATENTED COLOGNE, SCIENTIFICALLY ENGINEERED TO ATTRACT FEMALES...
WHAT KIND OF FEMALES?
ALL KINDS.

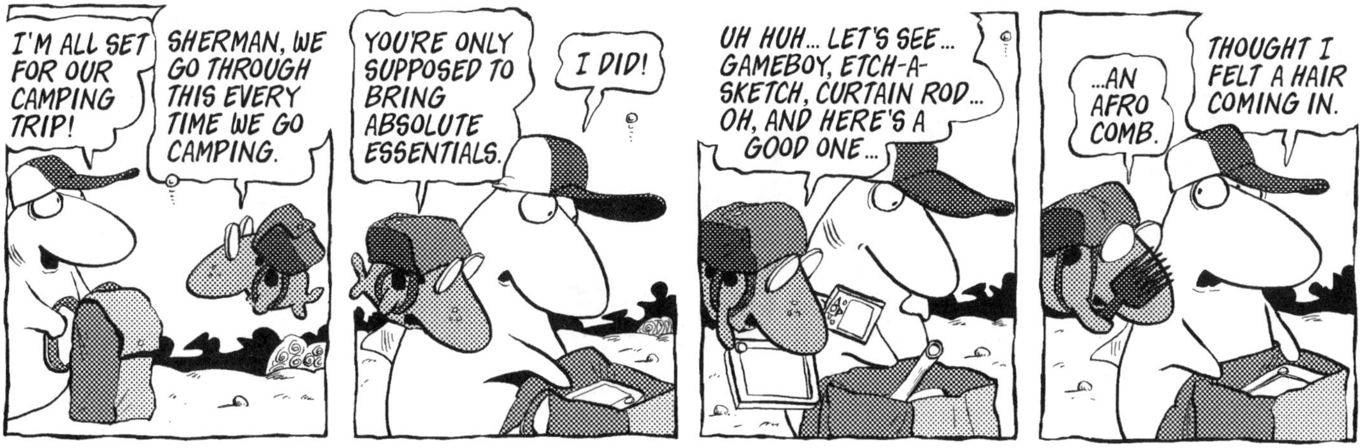
I'M ALL SET FOR OUR CAMPING TRIP!
SHERMAN, WE GO THROUGH THIS EVERY TIME WE GO CAMPING.
YOU'RE ONLY SUPPOSED TO BRING ABSOLUTE ESSENTIALS.
I DID!
UH HUH... LET'S SEE... GAMEBOY, ETCH-A-SKETCH, CURTAIN ROD... OH, AND HERE'S A GOOD ONE...
...AN AFRO COMB.
THOUGHT I FELT A HAIR COMING IN.

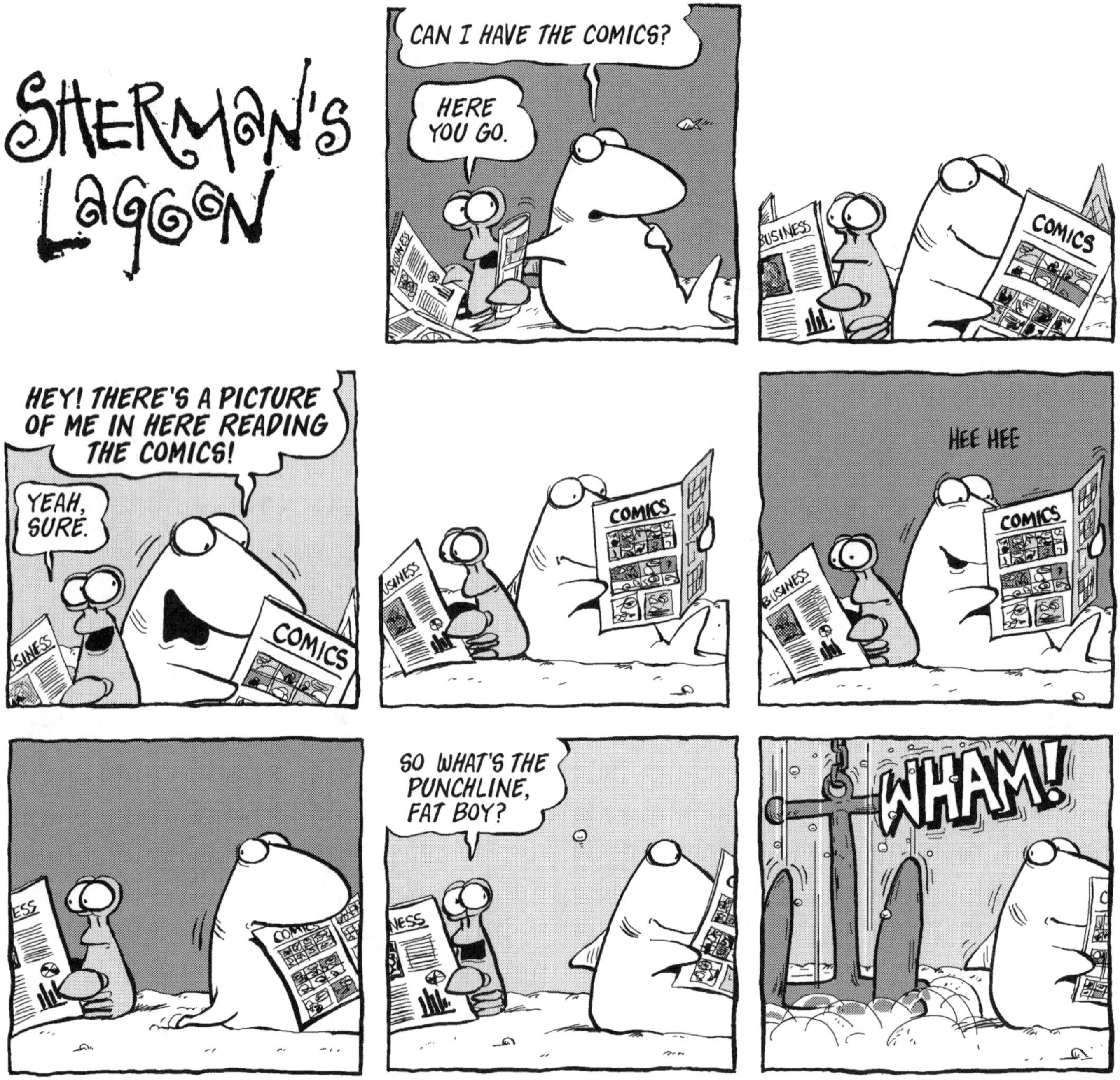
SHERMAN'S LAGOON
CAN I HAVE THE COMICS?
HERE YOU GO.
BUSINESS
COMICS
HEY! THERE'S A PICTURE OF ME IN HERE READING THE COMICS!
YEAH, SURE.
HEE HEE
SO WHAT'S THE PUNCHLINE, FAT BOY?
WHAM!

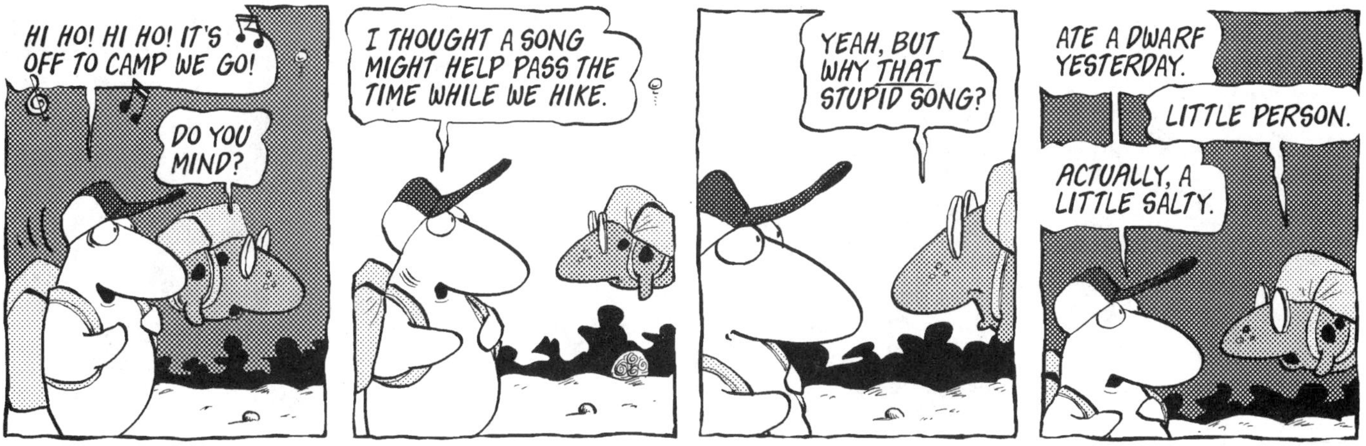
HI HO! HI HO! IT'S OFF TO CAMP WE GO!
DO YOU MIND?
I THOUGHT A SONG MIGHT HELP PASS THE TIME WHILE WE HIKE.
YEAH, BUT WHY THAT STUPID SONG?
ATE A DWARF YESTERDAY.
LITTLE PERSON.
ACTUALLY, A LITTLE SALTY.

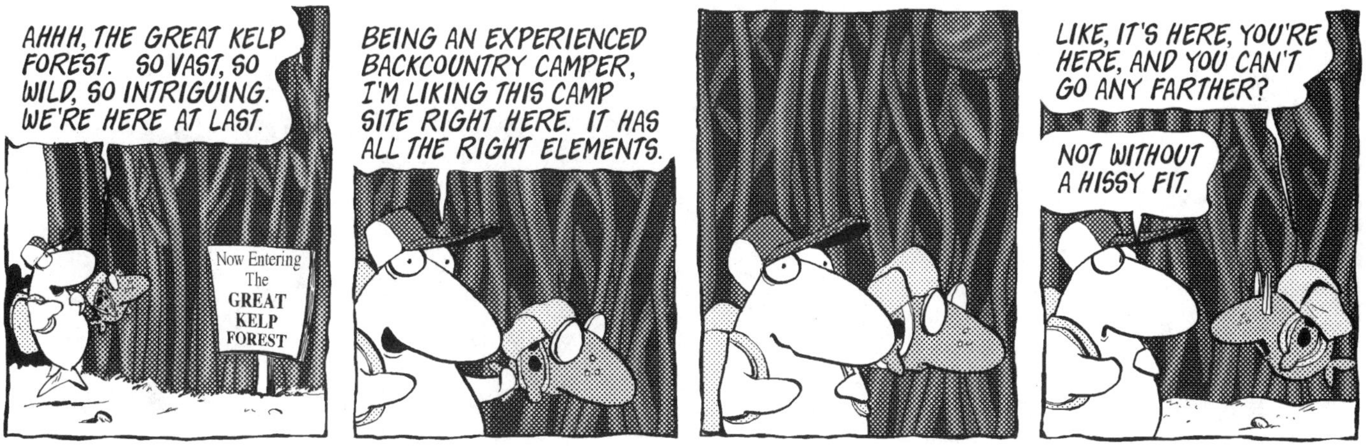
AHHH, THE GREAT KELP FOREST. SO VAST, SO WILD, SO INTRIGUING. WE'RE HERE AT LAST.
Now Entering The GREAT KELP FOREST
BEING AN EXPERIENCED BACKCOUNTRY CAMPER, I'M LIKING THIS CAMP SITE RIGHT HERE. IT HAS ALL THE RIGHT ELEMENTS.
LIKE, IT'S HERE, YOU'RE HERE, AND YOU CAN'T GO ANY FARTHER?
NOT WITHOUT A HISSY FIT.

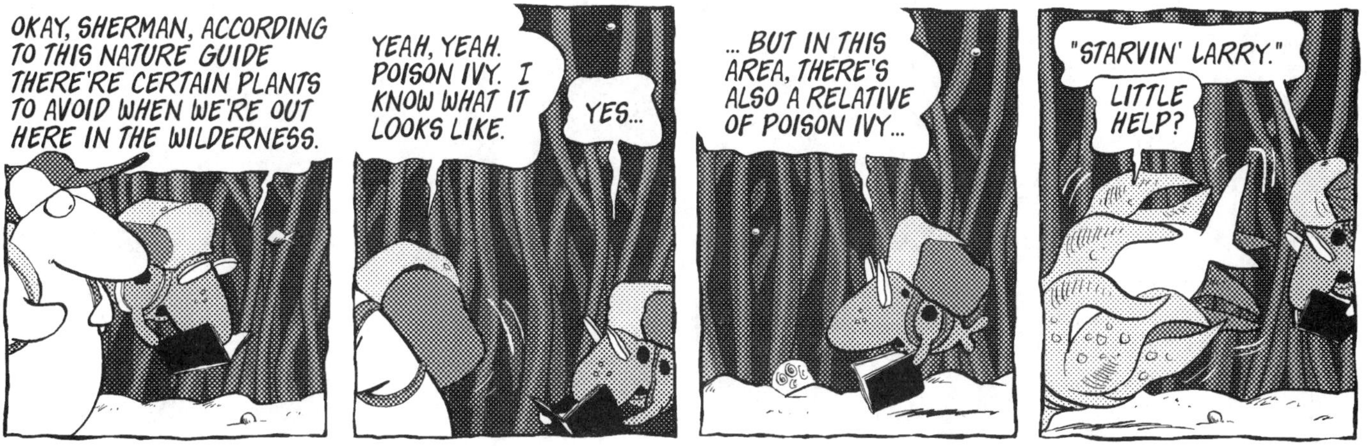
OKAY, SHERMAN, ACCORDING TO THIS NATURE GUIDE THERE'RE CERTAIN PLANTS TO AVOID WHEN WE'RE OUT HERE IN THE WILDERNESS.
YEAH, YEAH. POISON IVY. I KNOW WHAT IT LOOKS LIKE.
YES...
... BUT IN THIS AREA, THERE'S ALSO A RELATIVE OF POISON IVY...
"STARVIN' LARRY."
LITTLE HELP?

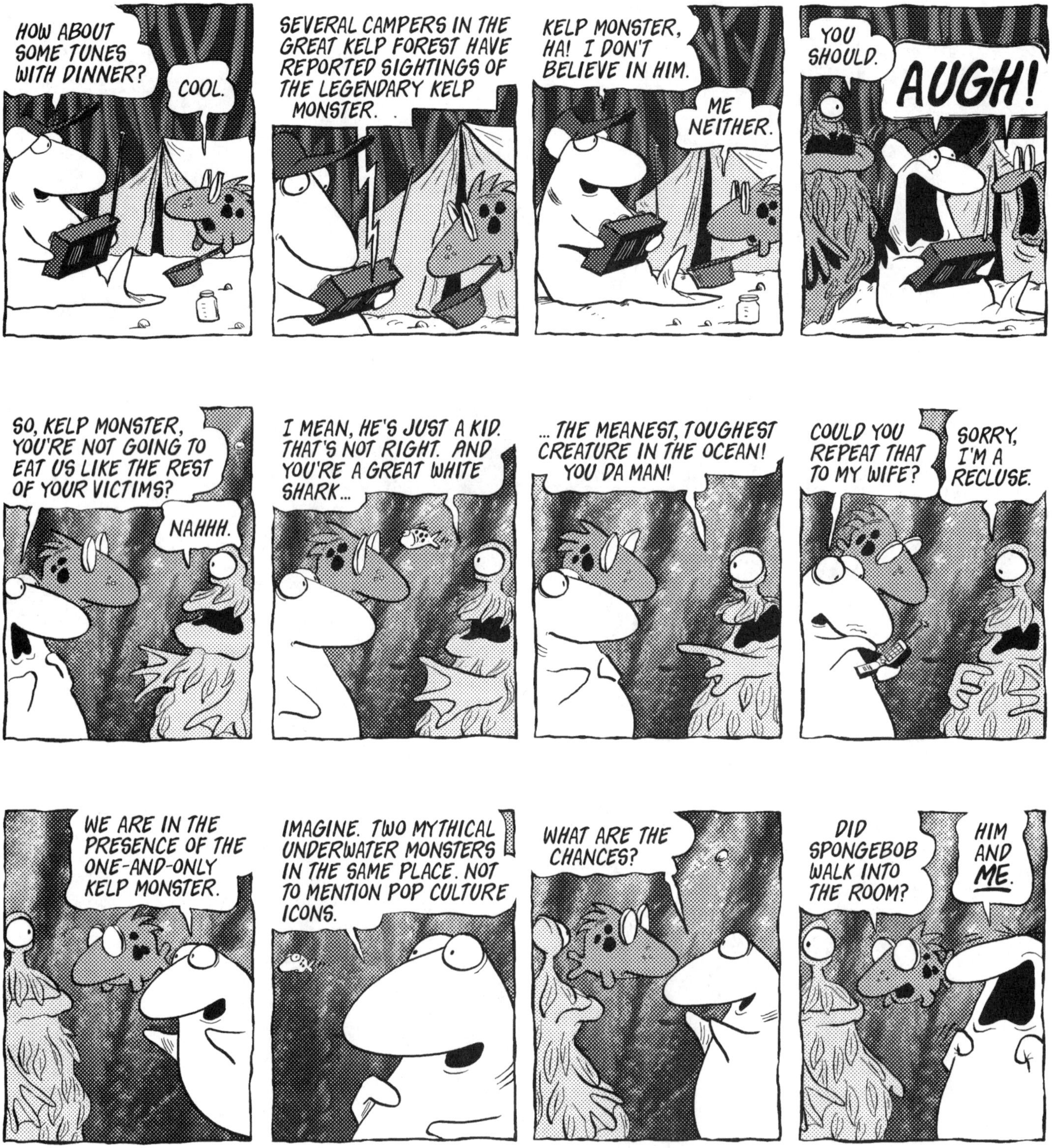

HOW ABOUT SOME TUNES WITH DINNER?
COOL.
SEVERAL CAMPERS IN THE GREAT KELP FOREST HAVE REPORTED SIGHTINGS OF THE LEGENDARY KELP MONSTER.
KELP MONSTER, HA! I DON'T BELIEVE IN HIM.
ME NEITHER.
YOU SHOULD.
AUGH!
SO, KELP MONSTER, YOU'RE NOT GOING TO EAT US LIKE THE REST OF YOUR VICTIMS?
NAHHH.
I MEAN, HE'S JUST A KID. THAT'S NOT RIGHT. AND YOU'RE A GREAT WHITE SHARK...
... THE MEANEST, TOUGHEST CREATURE IN THE OCEAN! YOU DA MAN!
COULD YOU REPEAT THAT TO MY WIFE?
SORRY, I'M A RECLUSE.
WE ARE IN THE PRESENCE OF THE ONE-AND-ONLY KELP MONSTER.
IMAGINE. TWO MYTHICAL UNDERWATER MONSTERS IN THE SAME PLACE. NOT TO MENTION POP CULTURE ICONS.
WHAT ARE THE CHANCES?
DID SPONGEBOB WALK INTO THE ROOM?
HIM AND ME.

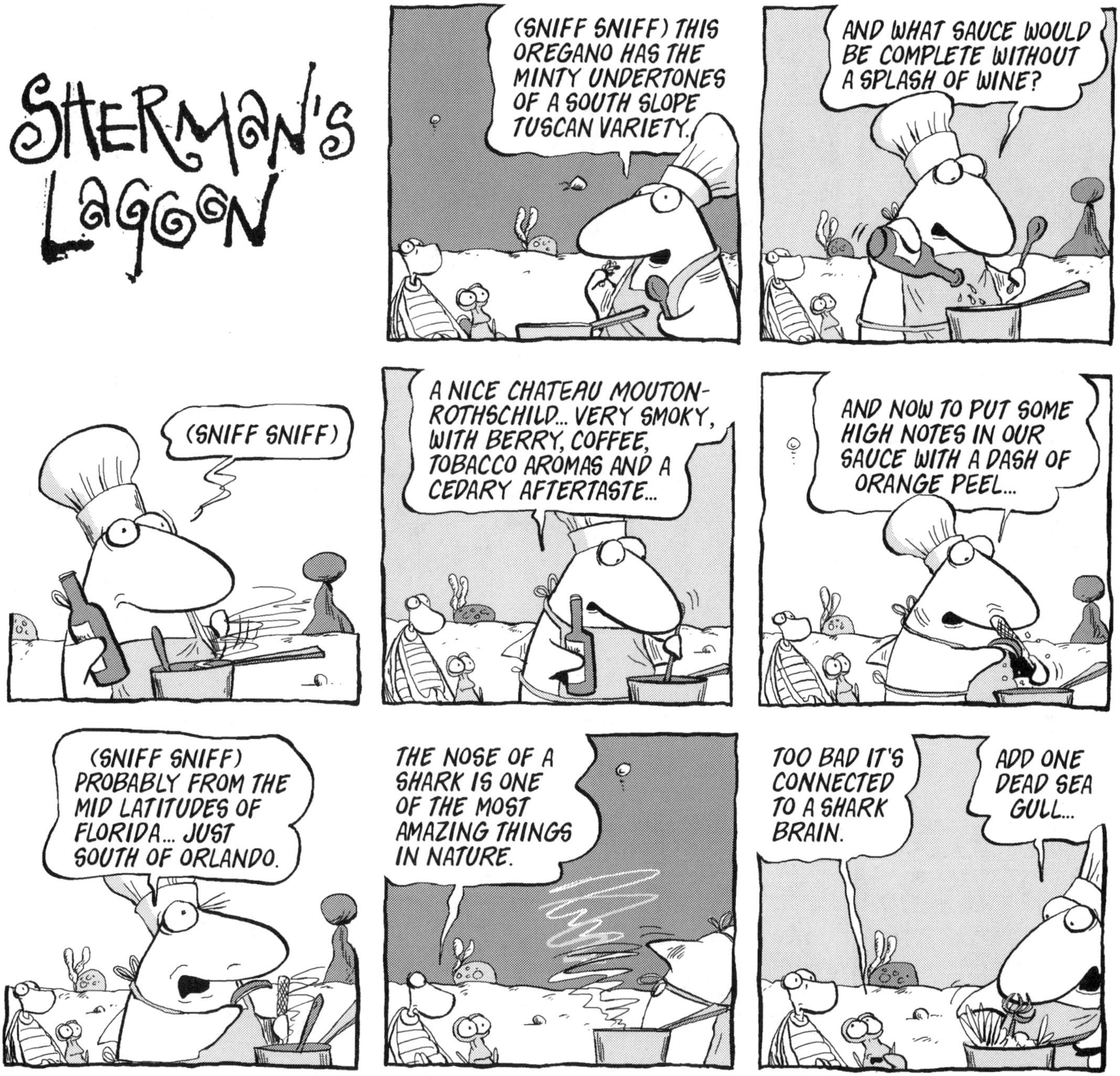
SHERMAN'S LAGOON
(SNIFF SNIFF) THIS OREGANO HAS THE MINTY UNDERTONES OF A SOUTH SLOPE TUSCAN VARIETY.
AND WHAT SAUCE WOULD BE COMPLETE WITHOUT A SPLASH OF WINE?
(SNIFF SNIFF)
A NICE CHATEAU MOUTON-ROTHSCHILD... VERY SMOKY, WITH BERRY, COFFEE, TOBACCO AROMAS AND A CEDARY AFTERTASTE...
AND NOW TO PUT SOME HIGH NOTES IN OUR SAUCE WITH A DASH OF ORANGE PEEL...
(SNIFF SNIFF) PROBABLY FROM THE MID LATITUDES OF FLORIDA... JUST SOUTH OF ORLANDO.
THE NOSE OF A SHARK IS ONE OF THE MOST AMAZING THINGS IN NATURE.
TOO BAD IT'S CONNECTED TO A SHARK BRAIN.
ADD ONE DEAD SEA GULL...

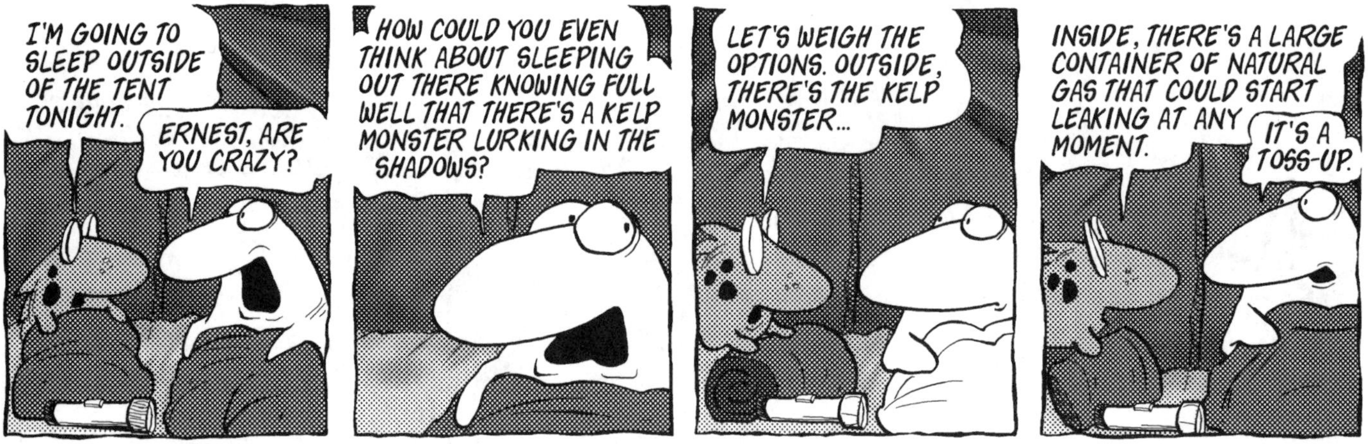
I'M GOING TO SLEEP OUTSIDE OF THE TENT TONIGHT.
ERNEST, ARE YOU CRAZY?
HOW COULD YOU EVEN THINK ABOUT SLEEPING OUT THERE KNOWING FULL WELL THAT THERE'S A KELP MONSTER LURKING IN THE SHADOWS?
LET'S WEIGH THE OPTIONS. OUTSIDE, THERE'S THE KELP MONSTER...
INSIDE, THERE'S A LARGE CONTAINER OF NATURAL GAS THAT COULD START LEAKING AT ANY MOMENT.
IT'S A TOSS-UP.

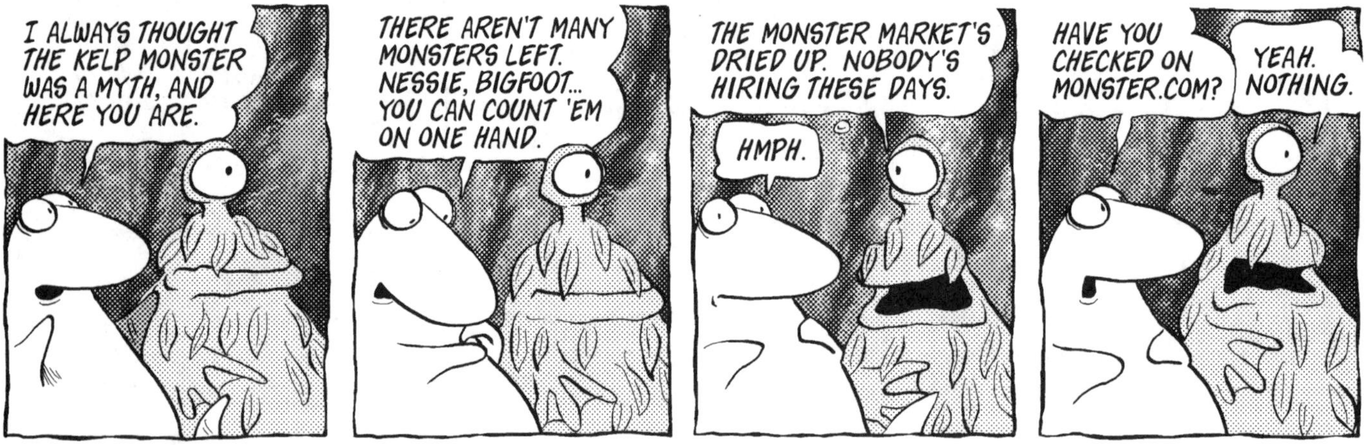
I ALWAYS THOUGHT THE KELP MONSTER WAS A MYTH, AND HERE YOU ARE.
THERE AREN'T MANY MONSTERS LEFT. NESSIE, BIGFOOT... YOU CAN COUNT 'EM ON ONE HAND.
THE MONSTER MARKET'S DRIED UP. NOBODY'S HIRING THESE DAYS.
HMPH.
HAVE YOU CHECKED ON MONSTER.COM?
YEAH. NOTHING.

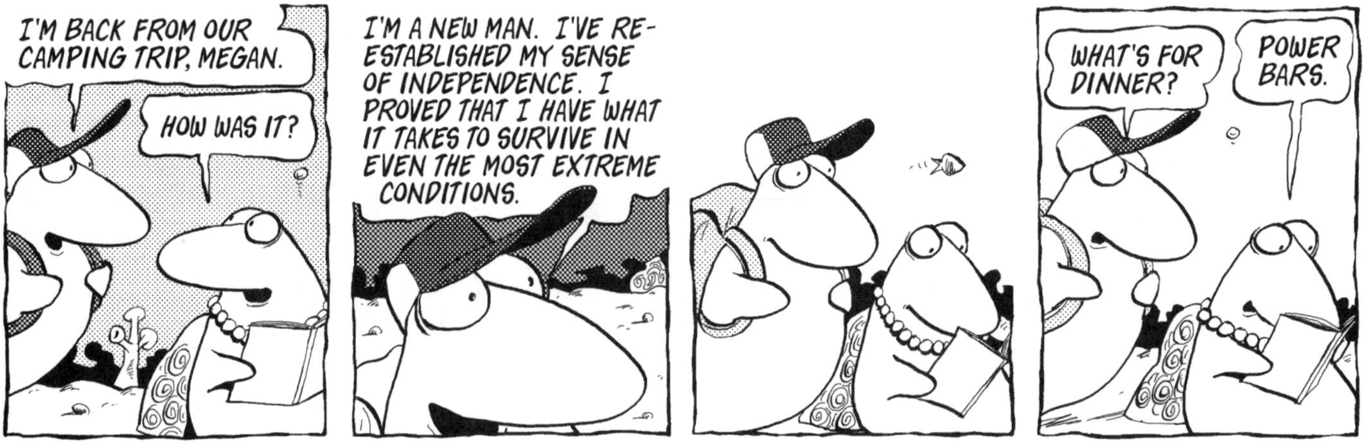
I'M BACK FROM OUR CAMPING TRIP, MEGAN.
HOW WAS IT?
I'M A NEW MAN. I'VE RE-ESTABLISHED MY SENSE OF INDEPENDENCE. I PROVED THAT I HAVE WHAT IT TAKES TO SURVIVE IN EVEN THE MOST EXTREME CONDITIONS.
WHAT'S FOR DINNER?
POWER BARS.

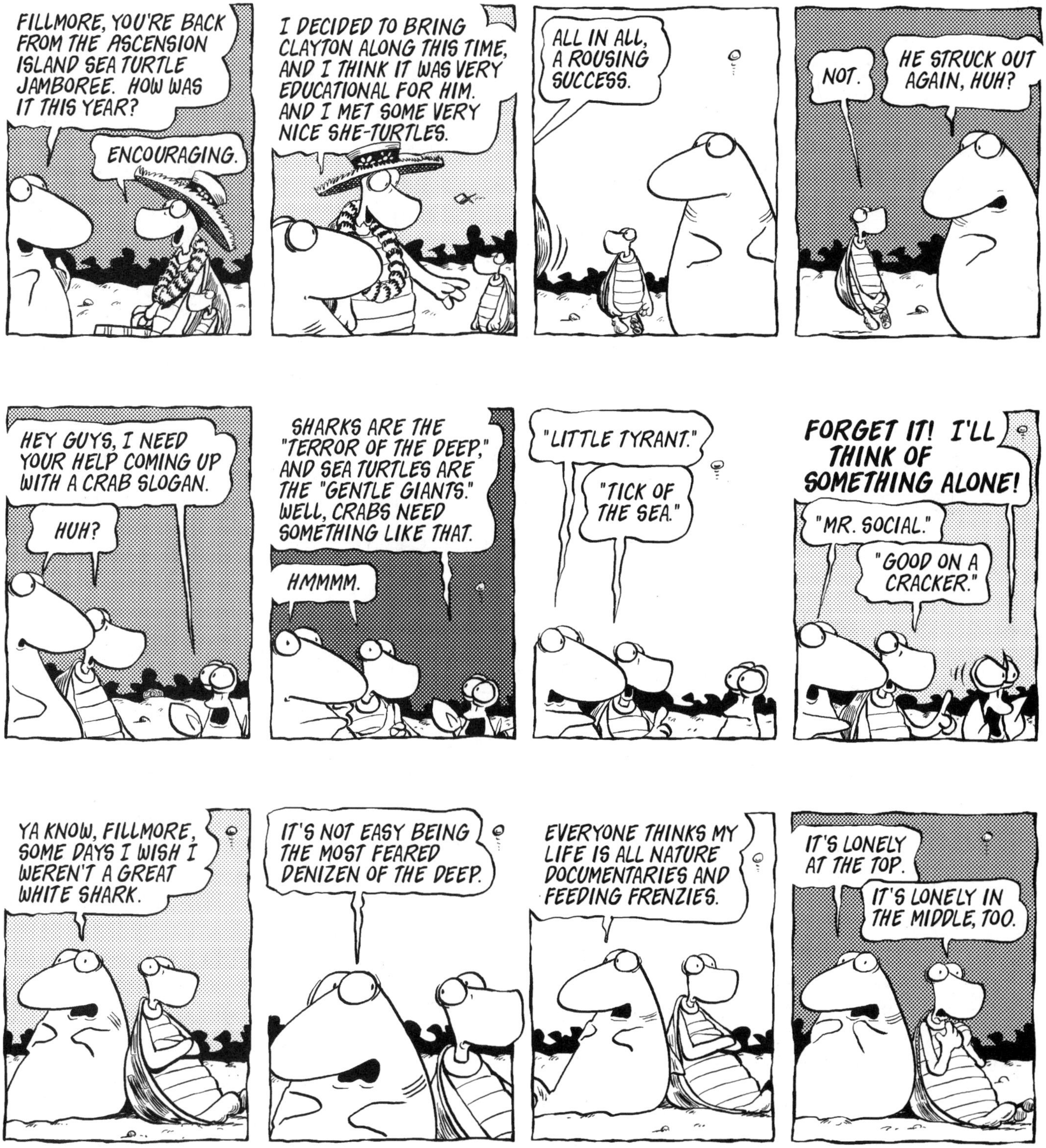
FILLMORE, YOU'RE BACK FROM THE ASCENSION ISLAND SEA TURTLE JAMBOREE. HOW WAS IT THIS YEAR?
ENCOURAGING.
I DECIDED TO BRING CLAYTON ALONG THIS TIME, AND I THINK IT WAS VERY EDUCATIONAL FOR HIM. AND I MET SOME VERY NICE SHE-TURTLES.
ALL IN ALL, A ROUSING SUCCESS.
NOT.
HE STRUCK OUT AGAIN, HUH?
HEY GUYS, I NEED YOUR HELP COMING UP WITH A CRAB SLOGAN.
HUH?
SHARKS ARE THE "TERROR OF THE DEEP," AND SEA TURTLES ARE THE "GENTLE GIANTS." WELL, CRABS NEED SOMETHING LIKE THAT.
HMMMM.
"LITTLE TYRANT."
"TICK OF THE SEA."
FORGET IT! I'LL THINK OF SOMETHING ALONE!
"MR. SOCIAL."
"GOOD ON A CRACKER."
YA KNOW, FILLMORE, SOME DAYS I WISH I WEREN'T A GREAT WHITE SHARK.
IT'S NOT EASY BEING THE MOST FEARED DENIZEN OF THE DEEP.
EVERYONE THINKS MY LIFE IS ALL NATURE DOCUMENTARIES AND FEEDING FRENZIES.
IT'S LONELY AT THE TOP.
IT'S LONELY IN THE MIDDLE, TOO.

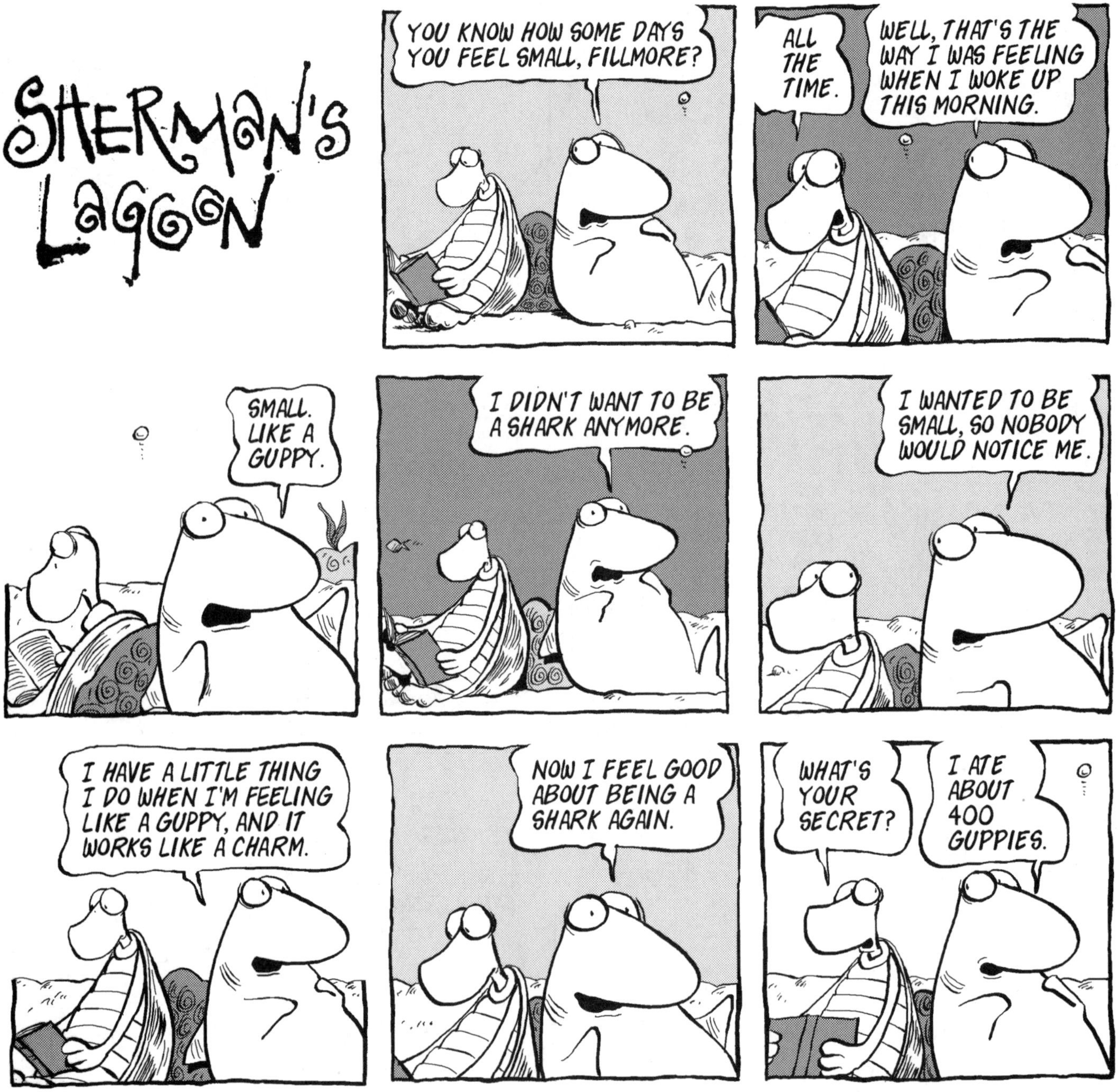
SHERMAN'S LAGOON
YOU KNOW HOW SOME DAYS YOU FEEL SMALL, FILLMORE?
ALL THE TIME.
WELL, THAT'S THE WAY I WAS FEELING WHEN I WOKE UP THIS MORNING.
SMALL. LIKE A GUPPY.
I DIDN'T WANT TO BE A SHARK ANYMORE.
I WANTED TO BE SMALL, SO NOBODY WOULD NOTICE ME.
I HAVE A LITTLE THING I DO WHEN I'M FEELING LIKE A GUPPY, AND IT WORKS LIKE A CHARM.
NOW I FEEL GOOD ABOUT BEING A SHARK AGAIN.
WHAT'S YOUR SECRET?
I ATE ABOUT 400 GUPPIES.

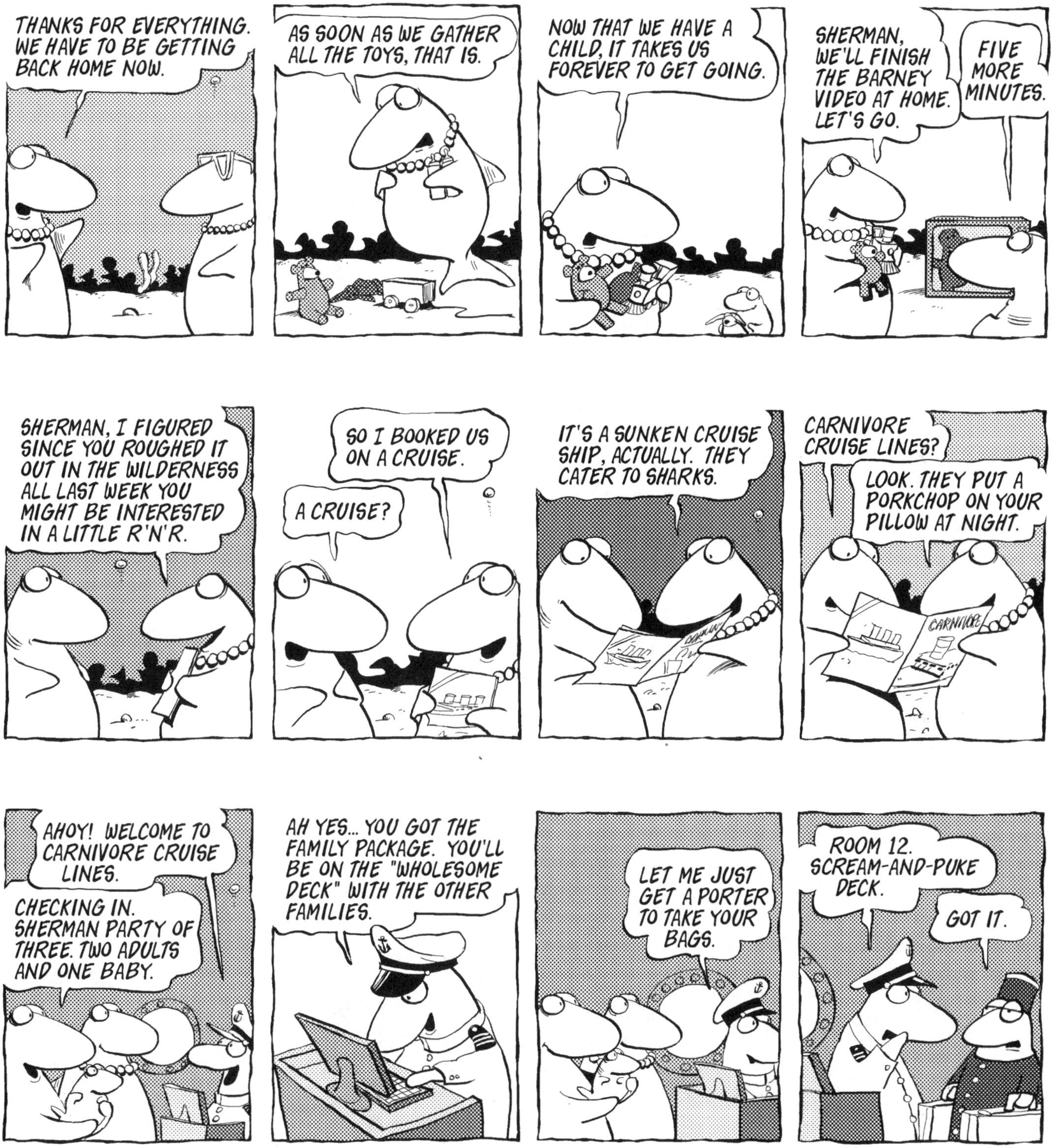
THANKS FOR EVERYTHING. WE HAVE TO BE GETTING BACK HOME NOW.
AS SOON AS WE GATHER ALL THE TOYS, THAT IS.
NOW THAT WE HAVE A CHILD, IT TAKES US FOREVER TO GET GOING.
SHERMAN, WE'LL FINISH THE BARNEY VIDEO AT HOME. LET'S GO.
FIVE MORE MINUTES.
SHERMAN, I FIGURED SINCE YOU ROUGHED IT OUT IN THE WILDERNESS ALL LAST WEEK YOU MIGHT BE INTERESTED IN A LITTLE R'N'R.
SO I BOOKED US ON A CRUISE.
A CRUISE?
IT'S A SUNKEN CRUISE SHIP, ACTUALLY. THEY CATER TO SHARKS.
CARNIVORE CRUISE LINES?
LOOK. THEY PUT A PORKCHOP ON YOUR PILLOW AT NIGHT.
AHOY! WELCOME TO CARNIVORE CRUISE LINES.
CHECKING IN. SHERMAN PARTY OF THREE. TWO ADULTS AND ONE BABY.
AH YES... YOU GOT THE FAMILY PACKAGE. YOU'LL BE ON THE "WHOLESOME DECK" WITH THE OTHER FAMILIES.
LET ME JUST GET A PORTER TO TAKE YOUR BAGS.
ROOM 12. SCREAM-AND-PUKE DECK.
GOT IT.

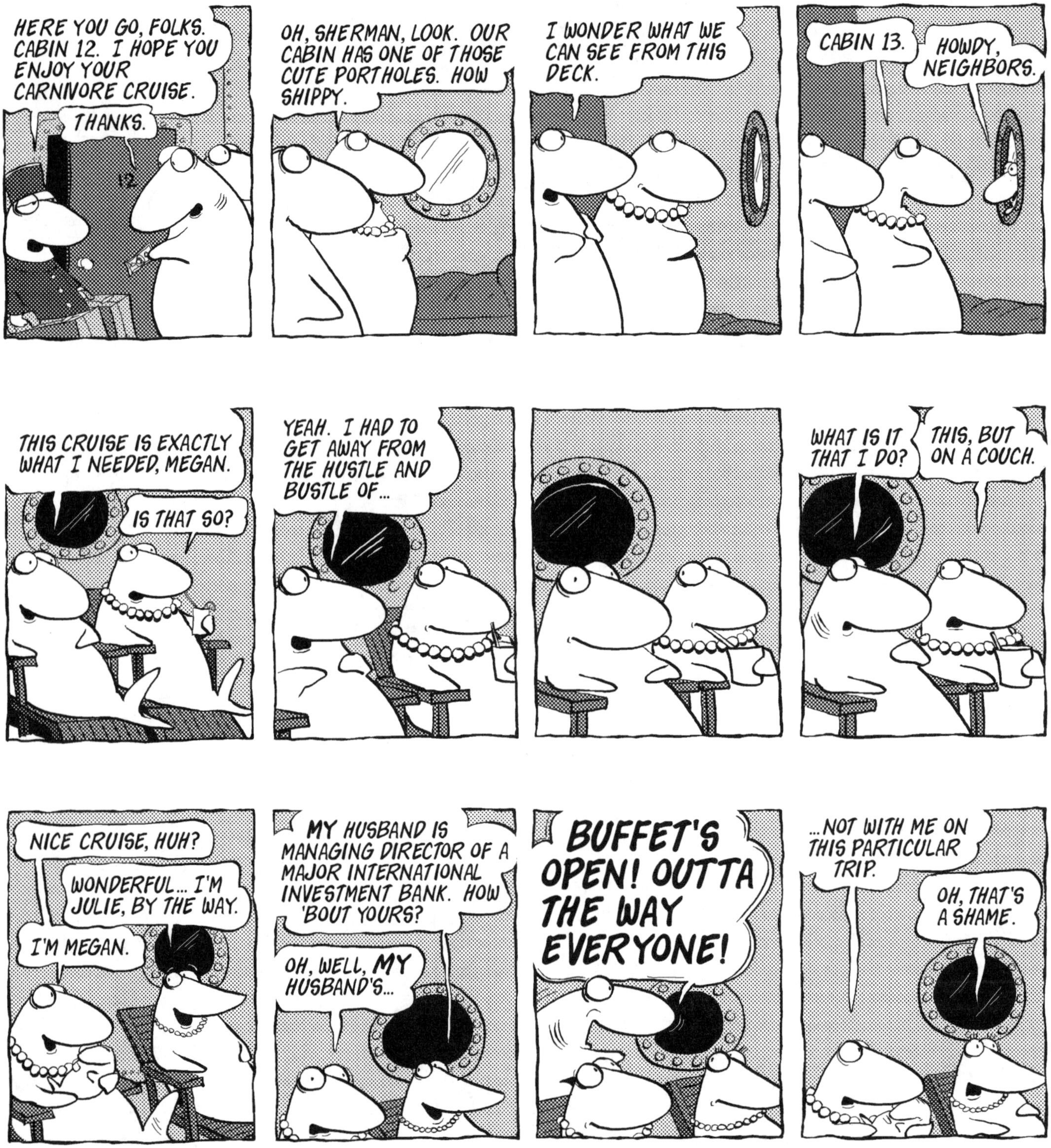
HERE YOU GO, FOLKS. CABIN 12. I HOPE YOU ENJOY YOUR CARNIVORE CRUISE.
THANKS.
12
OH, SHERMAN, LOOK. OUR CABIN HAS ONE OF THOSE CUTE PORTHOLES. HOW SHIPPY.
I WONDER WHAT WE CAN SEE FROM THIS DECK.
CABIN 13.
HOWDY, NEIGHBORS.
THIS CRUISE IS EXACTLY WHAT I NEEDED, MEGAN.
IS THAT SO?
YEAH. I HAD TO GET AWAY FROM THE HUSTLE AND BUSTLE OF...
WHAT IS IT THAT I DO?
THIS, BUT ON A COUCH.
NICE CRUISE, HUH?
WONDERFUL... I'M JULIE, BY THE WAY.
I'M MEGAN.
MY HUSBAND IS MANAGING DIRECTOR OF A MAJOR INTERNATIONAL INVESTMENT BANK. HOW 'BOUT YOURS?
OH, WELL, MY HUSBAND'S...
BUFFET'S OPEN! OUTTA THE WAY EVERYONE!
...NOT WITH ME ON THIS PARTICULAR TRIP.
OH, THAT'S A SHAME.

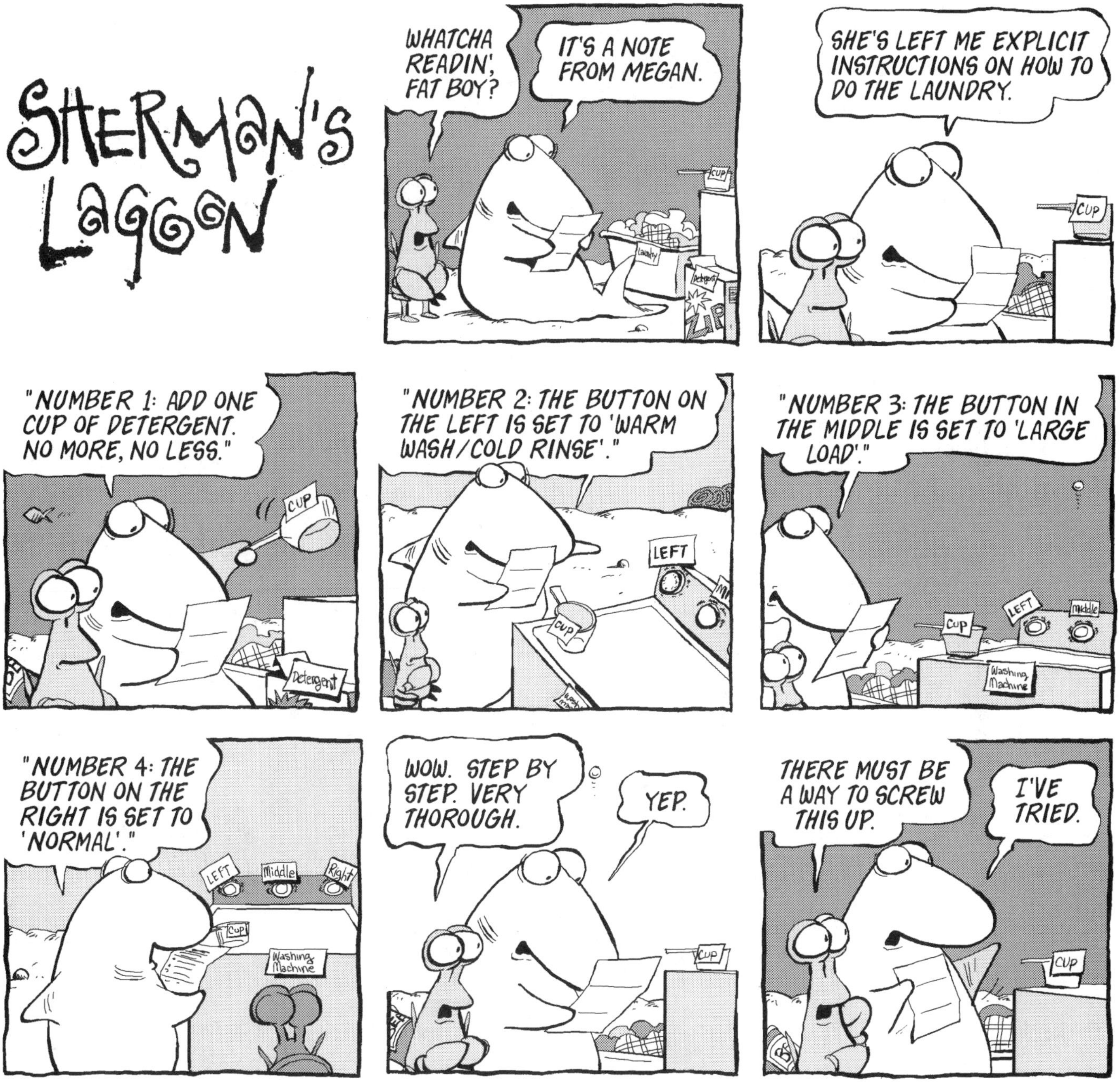
SHERMAN'S LAGOON
WHATCHA READIN', FAT BOY?
IT'S A NOTE FROM MEGAN.
CUP
SHE'S LEFT ME EXPLICIT INSTRUCTIONS ON HOW TO DO THE LAUNDRY.
CUP
"NUMBER 1: ADD ONE CUP OF DETERGENT. NO MORE, NO LESS."
CUP
Detergent
"NUMBER 2: THE BUTTON ON THE LEFT IS SET TO 'WARM WASH/COLD RINSE'."
LEFT
CUP
"NUMBER 3: THE BUTTON IN THE MIDDLE IS SET TO 'LARGE LOAD'."
CUP
LEFT
Middle
Washing Machine
"NUMBER 4: THE BUTTON ON THE RIGHT IS SET TO 'NORMAL'."
LEFT
Middle
Right
Cup
Washing Machine
WOW. STEP BY STEP. VERY THOROUGH.
YEP.
CUP
THERE MUST BE A WAY TO SCREW THIS UP.
I'VE TRIED.
CUP

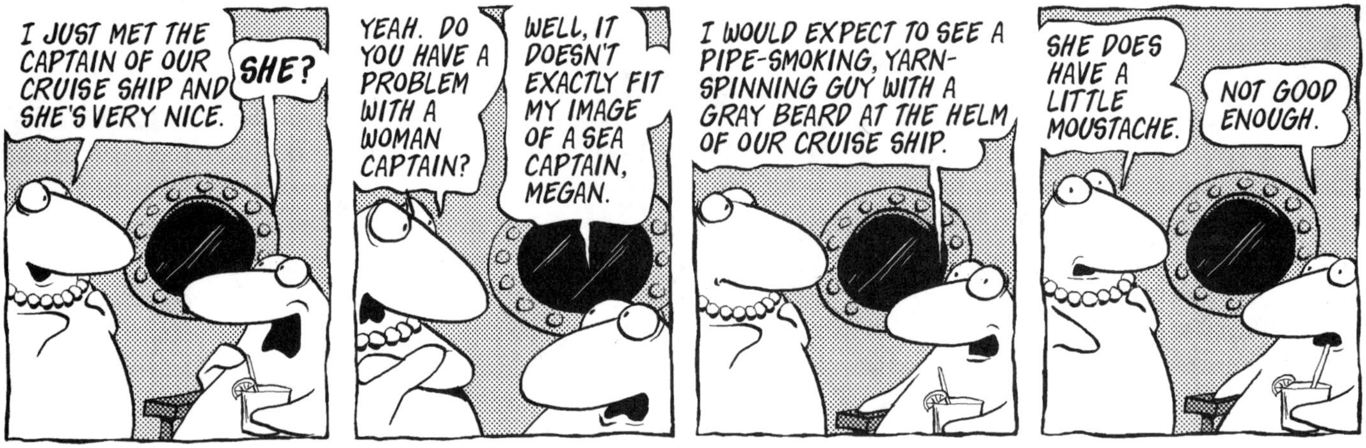
I JUST MET THE CAPTAIN OF OUR CRUISE SHIP AND SHE'S VERY NICE.
SHE?
YEAH. DO YOU HAVE A PROBLEM WITH A WOMAN CAPTAIN?
WELL, IT DOESN'T EXACTLY FIT MY IMAGE OF A SEA CAPTAIN, MEGAN.
I WOULD EXPECT TO SEE A PIPE-SMOKING, YARN-SPINNING GUY WITH A GRAY BEARD AT THE HELM OF OUR CRUISE SHIP.
SHE DOES HAVE A LITTLE MOUSTACHE.
NOT GOOD ENOUGH.

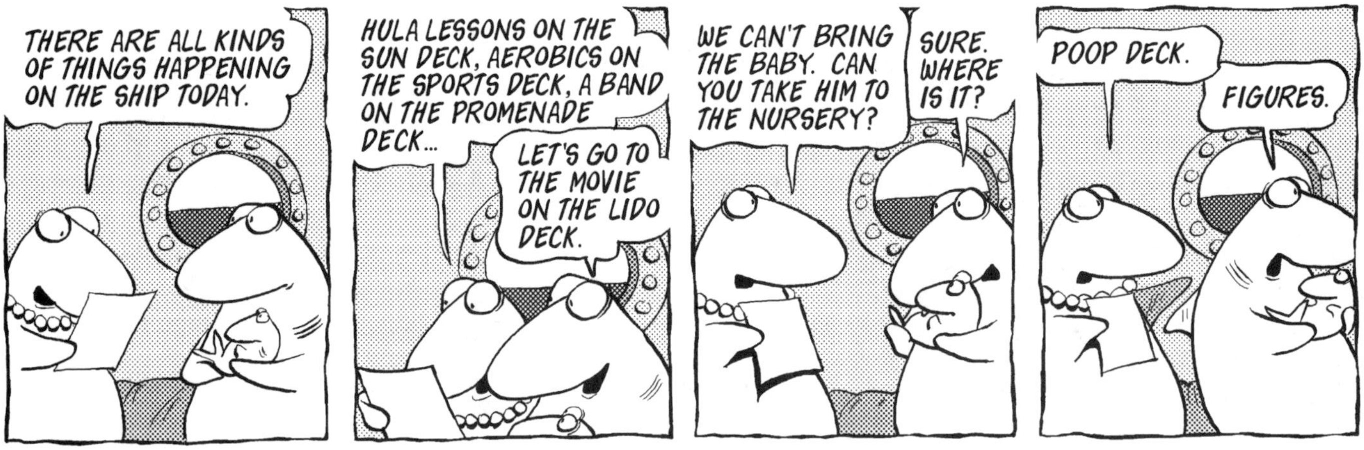
THERE ARE ALL KINDS OF THINGS HAPPENING ON THE SHIP TODAY.
HULA LESSONS ON THE SUN DECK, AEROBICS ON THE SPORTS DECK, A BAND ON THE PROMENADE DECK...
LET'S GO TO THE MOVIE ON THE LIDO DECK.
WE CAN'T BRING THE BABY. CAN YOU TAKE HIM TO THE NURSERY?
SURE. WHERE IS IT?
POOP DECK.
FIGURES.

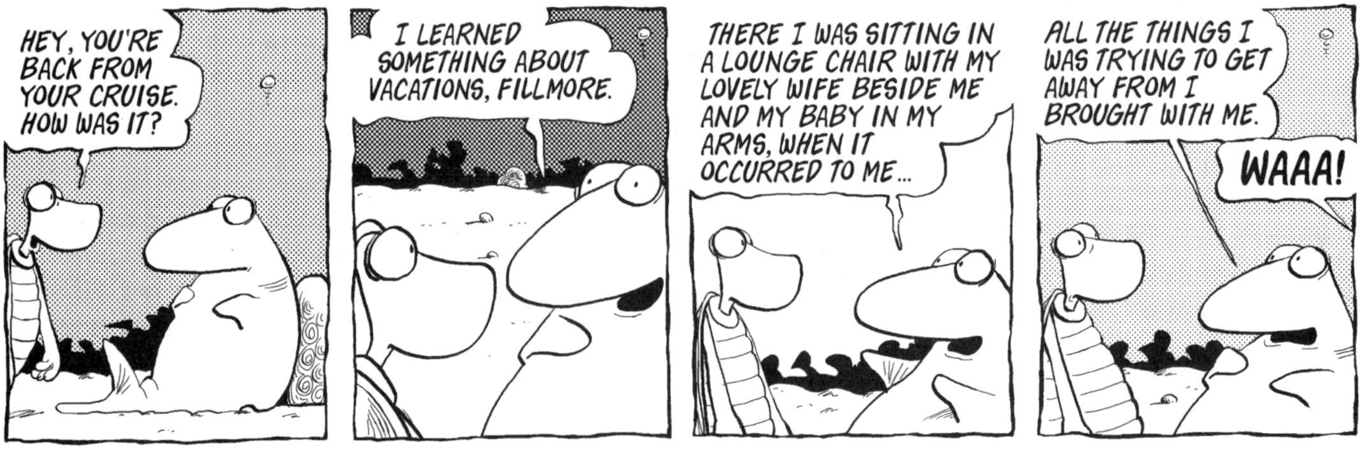
HEY, YOU'RE BACK FROM YOUR CRUISE. HOW WAS IT?
I LEARNED SOMETHING ABOUT VACATIONS, FILLMORE.
THERE I WAS SITTING IN A LOUNGE CHAIR WITH MY LOVELY WIFE BESIDE ME AND MY BABY IN MY ARMS, WHEN IT OCCURRED TO ME...
ALL THE THINGS I WAS TRYING TO GET AWAY FROM I BROUGHT WITH ME.
WAAA!

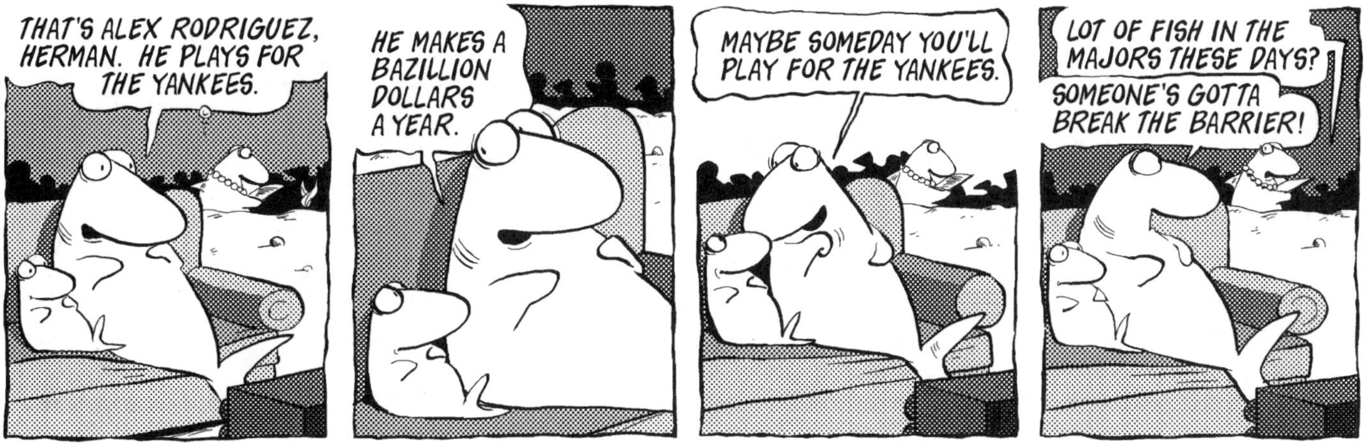
THAT'S ALEX RODRIGUEZ, HERMAN. HE PLAYS FOR THE YANKEES.
HE MAKES A BAZILLION DOLLARS A YEAR.
MAYBE SOMEDAY YOU'LL PLAY FOR THE YANKEES.
LOT OF FISH IN THE MAJORS THESE DAYS?
SOMEONE'S GOTTA BREAK THE BARRIER!

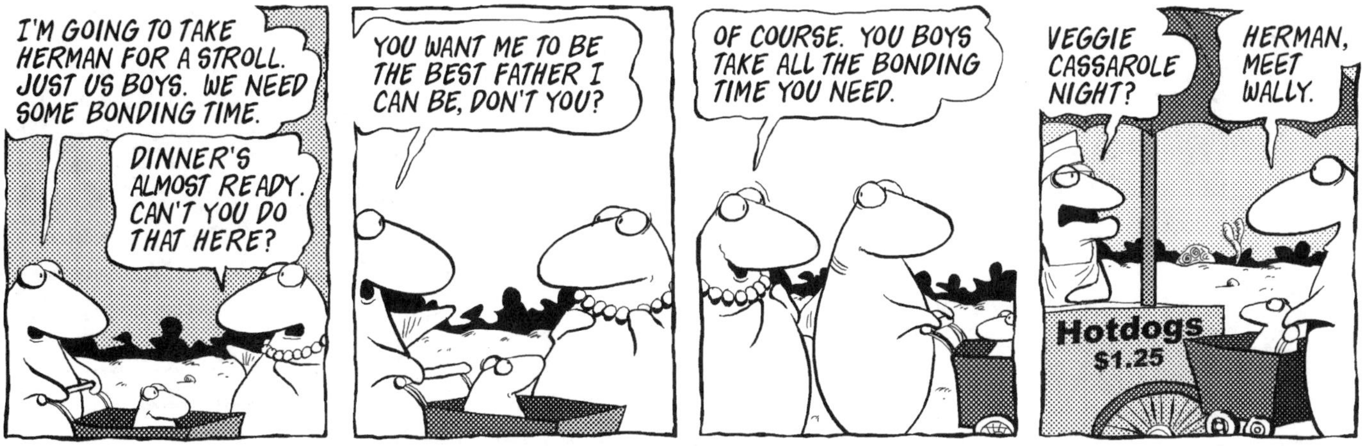
I'M GOING TO TAKE HERMAN FOR A STROLL. JUST US BOYS. WE NEED SOME BONDING TIME.
DINNER'S ALMOST READY. CAN'T YOU DO THAT HERE?
YOU WANT ME TO BE THE BEST FATHER I CAN BE, DON'T YOU?
OF COURSE. YOU BOYS TAKE ALL THE BONDING TIME YOU NEED.
VEGGIE CASSAROLE NIGHT?
HERMAN, MEET WALLY.
Hotdogs
$1.25

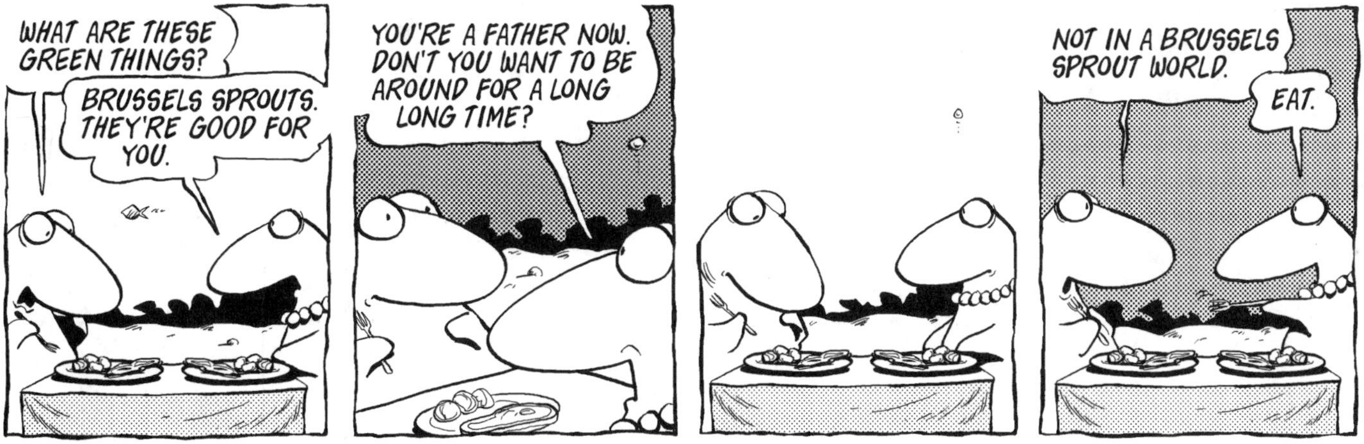
WHAT ARE THESE GREEN THINGS?
BRUSSELS SPROUTS. THEY'RE GOOD FOR YOU.
YOU'RE A FATHER NOW. DON'T YOU WANT TO BE AROUND FOR A LONG LONG TIME?
NOT IN A BRUSSELS SPROUT WORLD.
EAT.

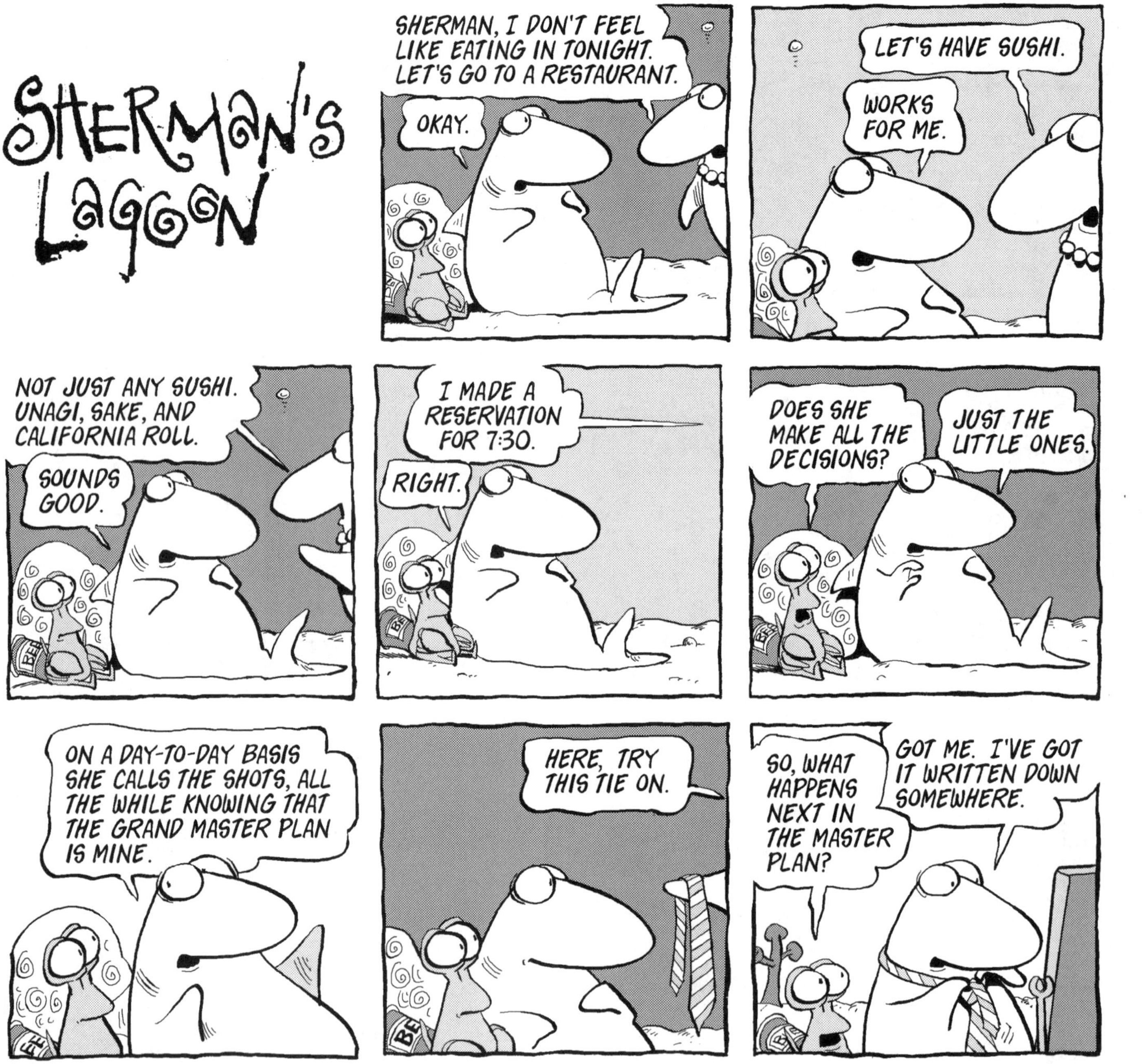
SHERMAN'S LAGOON
SHERMAN, I DON'T FEEL LIKE EATING IN TONIGHT. LET'S GO TO A RESTAURANT.
OKAY.
LET'S HAVE SUSHI.
WORKS FOR ME.
NOT JUST ANY SUSHI. UNAGI, SAKE, AND CALIFORNIA ROLL.
SOUNDS GOOD.
I MADE A RESERVATION FOR 7:30.
RIGHT.
DOES SHE MAKE ALL THE DECISIONS?
JUST THE LITTLE ONES.
ON A DAY-TO-DAY BASIS SHE CALLS THE SHOTS, ALL THE WHILE KNOWING THAT THE GRAND MASTER PLAN IS MINE.
HERE, TRY THIS TIE ON.
SO, WHAT HAPPENS NEXT IN THE MASTER PLAN?
GOT ME. I'VE GOT IT WRITTEN DOWN SOMEWHERE.

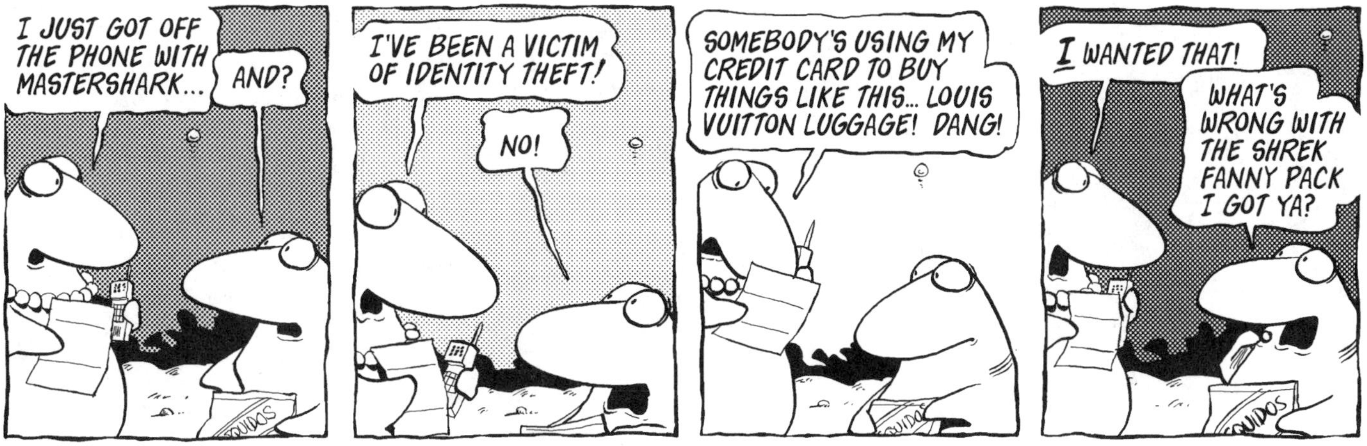
I JUST GOT OFF THE PHONE WITH MASTERSHARK...
AND?
I'VE BEEN A VICTIM OF IDENTITY THEFT!
NO!
SOMEBODY'S USING MY CREDIT CARD TO BUY THINGS LIKE THIS... LOUIS VUITTON LUGGAGE! DANG!
I WANTED THAT!
WHAT'S WRONG WITH THE SHREK FANNY PACK I GOT YA?

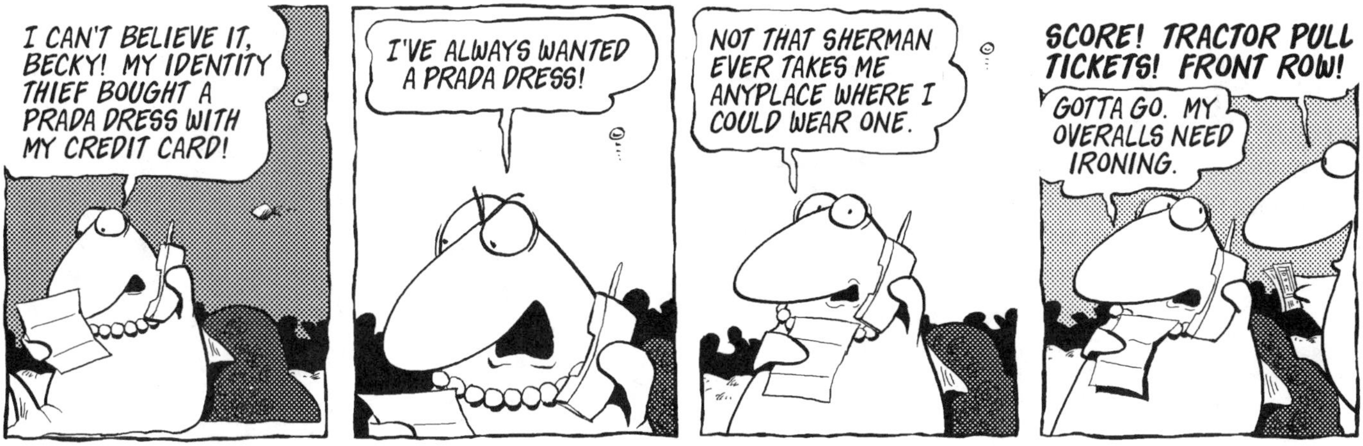
I CAN'T BELIEVE IT, BECKY! MY IDENTITY THIEF BOUGHT A PRADA DRESS WITH MY CREDIT CARD!
I'VE ALWAYS WANTED A PRADA DRESS!
NOT THAT SHERMAN EVER TAKES ME ANYPLACE WHERE I COULD WEAR ONE.
SCORE! TRACTOR PULL TICKETS! FRONT ROW!
GOTTA GO. MY OVERALLS NEED IRONING.

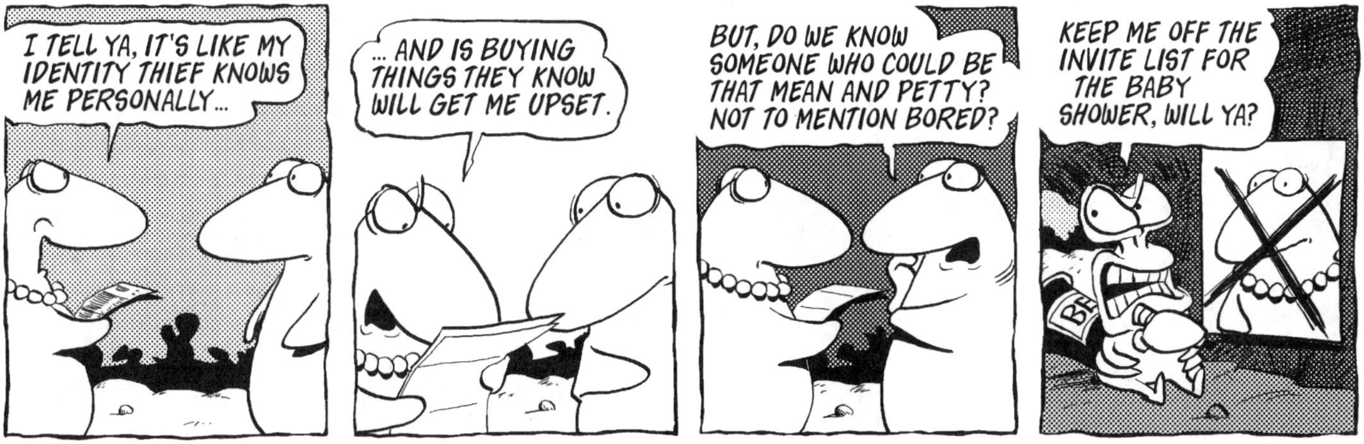
I TELL YA, IT'S LIKE MY IDENTITY THIEF KNOWS ME PERSONALLY...
... AND IS BUYING THINGS THEY KNOW WILL GET ME UPSET.
BUT, DO WE KNOW SOMEONE WHO COULD BE THAT MEAN AND PETTY? NOT TO MENTION BORED?
KEEP ME OFF THE INVITE LIST FOR THE BABY SHOWER, WILL YA?

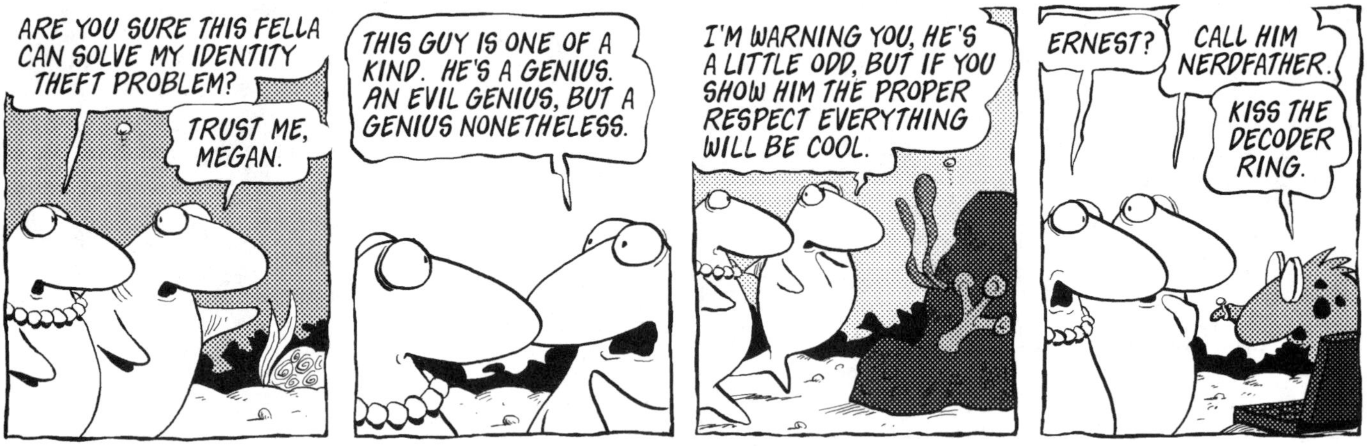
ARE YOU SURE THIS FELLA CAN SOLVE MY IDENTITY THEFT PROBLEM?
TRUST ME, MEGAN.
THIS GUY IS ONE OF A KIND. HE'S A GENIUS. AN EVIL GENIUS, BUT A GENIUS NONETHELESS.
I'M WARNING YOU, HE'S A LITTLE ODD, BUT IF YOU SHOW HIM THE PROPER RESPECT EVERYTHING WILL BE COOL.
ERNEST?
CALL HIM NERDFATHER.
KISS THE DECODER RING.

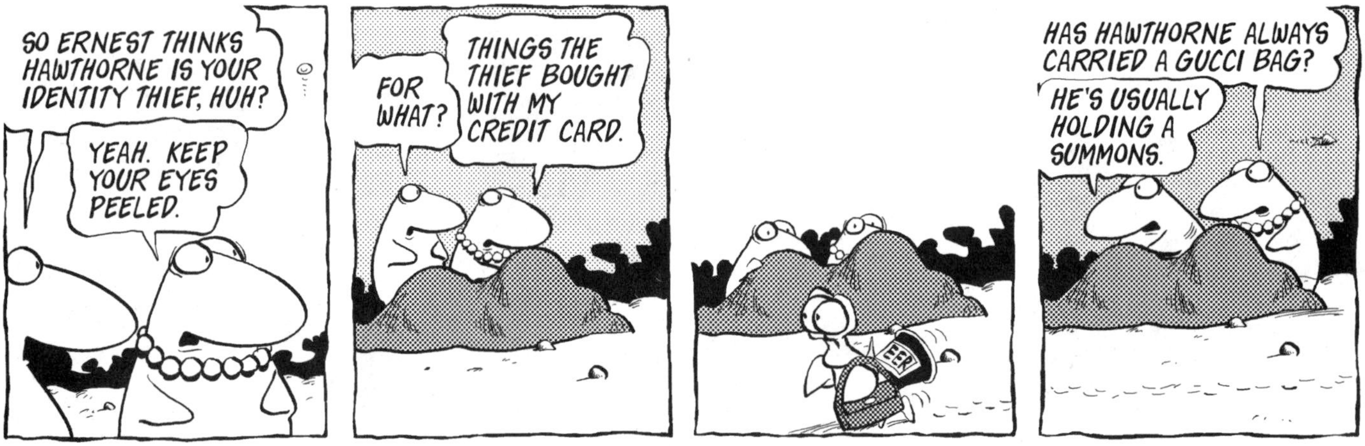
SO ERNEST THINKS HAWTHORNE IS YOUR IDENTITY THIEF, HUH?
YEAH. KEEP YOUR EYES PEELED.
FOR WHAT?
THINGS THE THIEF BOUGHT WITH MY CREDIT CARD.
EER
HAS HAWTHORNE ALWAYS CARRIED A GUCCI BAG?
HE'S USUALLY HOLDING A SUMMONS.

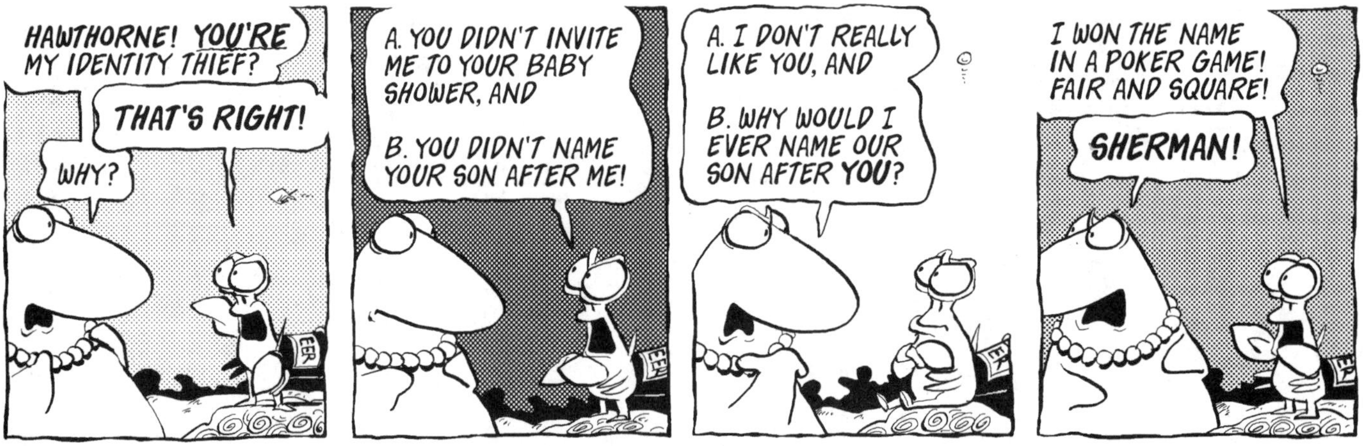
HAWTHORNE! YOU'RE MY IDENTITY THIEF?
THAT'S RIGHT!
WHY?
EER
A. YOU DIDN'T INVITE ME TO YOUR BABY SHOWER, AND
B. YOU DIDN'T NAME YOUR SON AFTER ME!
A. I DON'T REALLY LIKE YOU, AND
B. WHY WOULD I EVER NAME OUR SON AFTER YOU?
I WON THE NAME IN A POKER GAME! FAIR AND SQUARE!
SHERMAN!

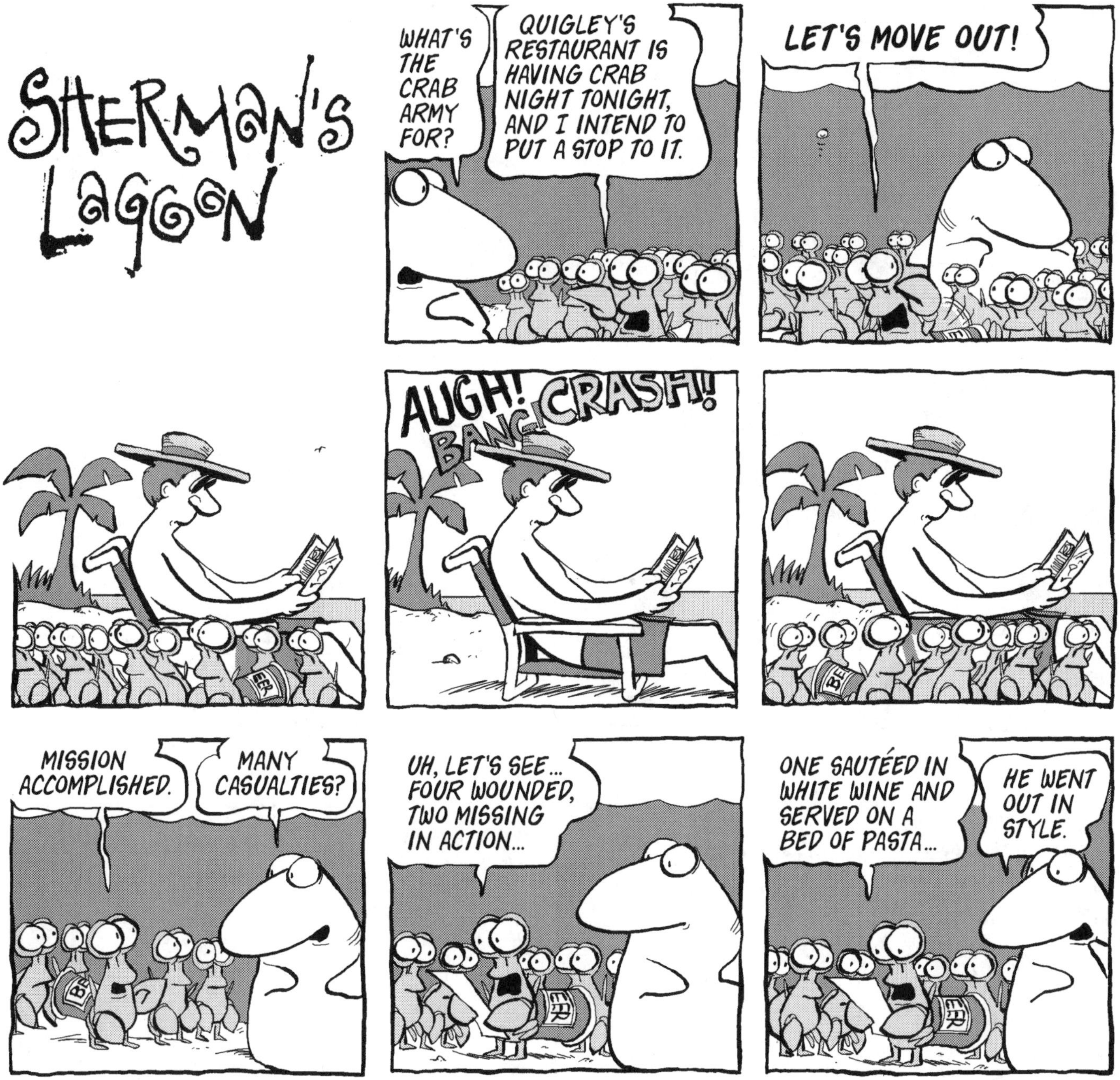
SHERMAN'S LAGOON
WHAT'S THE CRAB ARMY FOR?
QUIGLEY'S RESTAURANT IS HAVING CRAB NIGHT TONIGHT, AND I INTEND TO PUT A STOP TO IT.
LET'S MOVE OUT!
AUGH!
BANG!
CRASH!!
MISSION ACCOMPLISHED.
MANY CASUALTIES?
UH, LET'S SEE... FOUR WOUNDED, TWO MISSING IN ACTION...
ONE SAUTÉED IN WHITE WINE AND SERVED ON A BED OF PASTA...
HE WENT OUT IN STYLE.

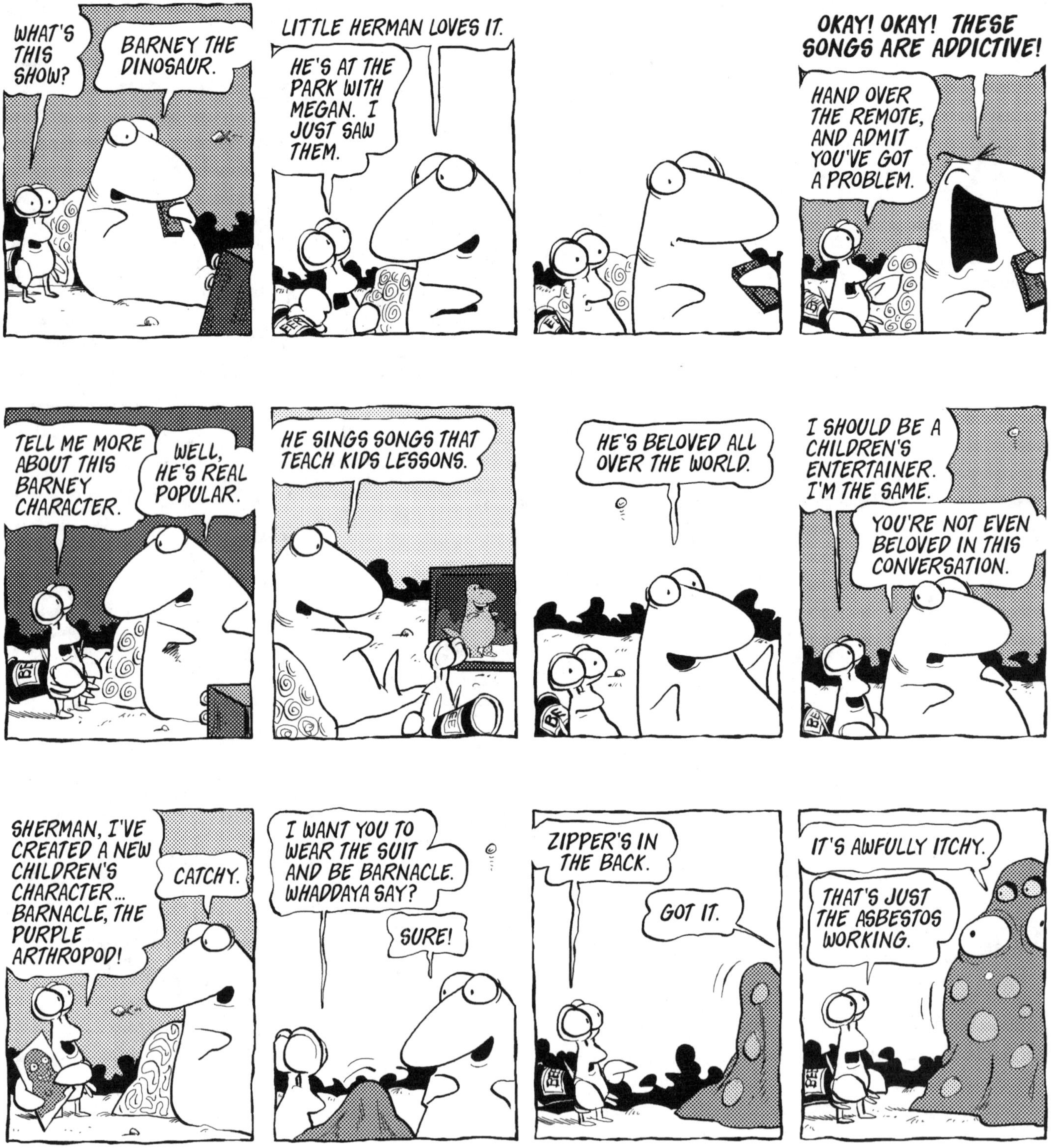
WHAT'S THIS SHOW?
BARNEY THE DINOSAUR.
LITTLE HERMAN LOVES IT.
HE'S AT THE PARK WITH MEGAN. I JUST SAW THEM.
OKAY! OKAY! THESE SONGS ARE ADDICTIVE!
HAND OVER THE REMOTE, AND ADMIT YOU'VE GOT A PROBLEM.
TELL ME MORE ABOUT THIS BARNEY CHARACTER.
WELL, HE'S REAL POPULAR.
HE SINGS SONGS THAT TEACH KIDS LESSONS.
HE'S BELOVED ALL OVER THE WORLD.
I SHOULD BE A CHILDREN'S ENTERTAINER. I'M THE SAME.
YOU'RE NOT EVEN BELOVED IN THIS CONVERSATION.
SHERMAN, I'VE CREATED A NEW CHILDREN'S CHARACTER... BARNACLE, THE PURPLE ARTHROPOD!
CATCHY.
I WANT YOU TO WEAR THE SUIT AND BE BARNACLE. WHADDAYA SAY?
SURE!
ZIPPER'S IN THE BACK.
GOT IT.
IT'S AWFULLY ITCHY.
THAT'S JUST THE ASBESTOS WORKING.

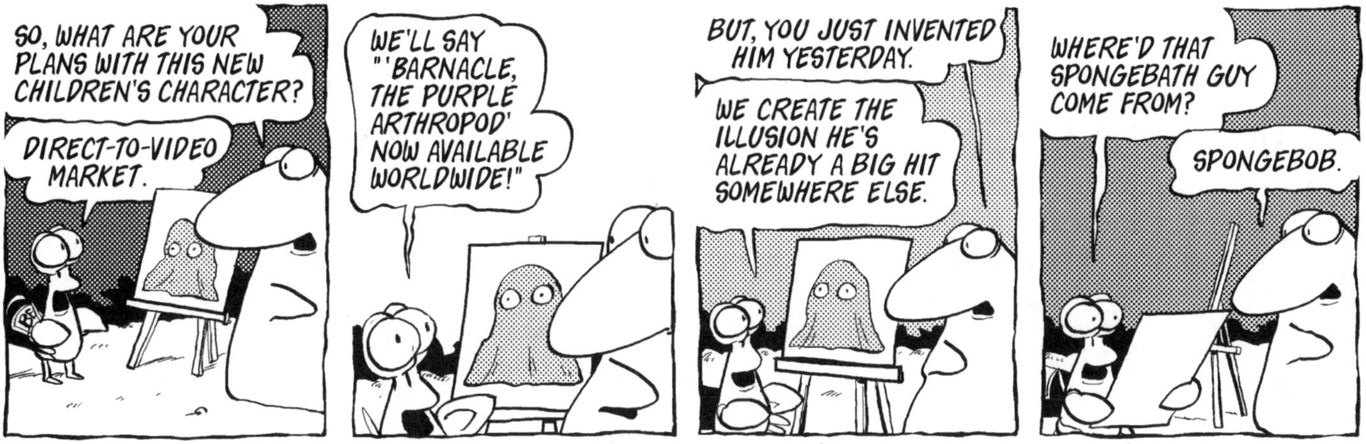
SO, WHAT ARE YOUR PLANS WITH THIS NEW CHILDREN'S CHARACTER?
DIRECT-TO-VIDEO MARKET.
WE'LL SAY "'BARNACLE, THE PURPLE ARTHROPOD' NOW AVAILABLE WORLDWIDE!"
BUT, YOU JUST INVENTED HIM YESTERDAY.
WE CREATE THE ILLUSION HE'S ALREADY A BIG HIT SOMEWHERE ELSE.
WHERE'D THAT SPONGEBATH GUY COME FROM?
SPONGEBOB.

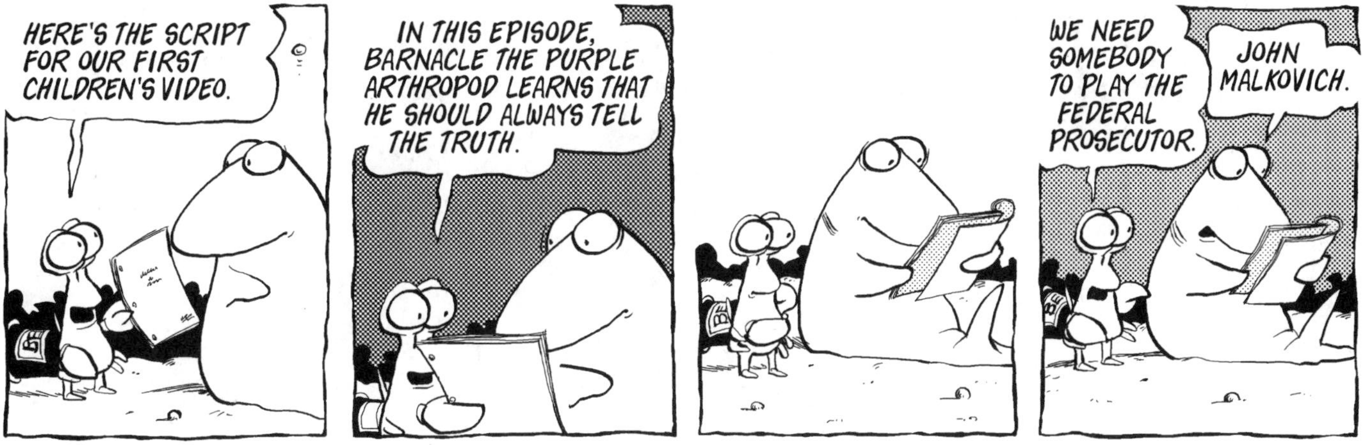
HERE'S THE SCRIPT FOR OUR FIRST CHILDREN'S VIDEO.
IN THIS EPISODE, BARNACLE THE PURPLE ARTHROPOD LEARNS THAT HE SHOULD ALWAYS TELL THE TRUTH.
WE NEED SOMEBODY TO PLAY THE FEDERAL PROSECUTOR.
JOHN MALKOVICH.

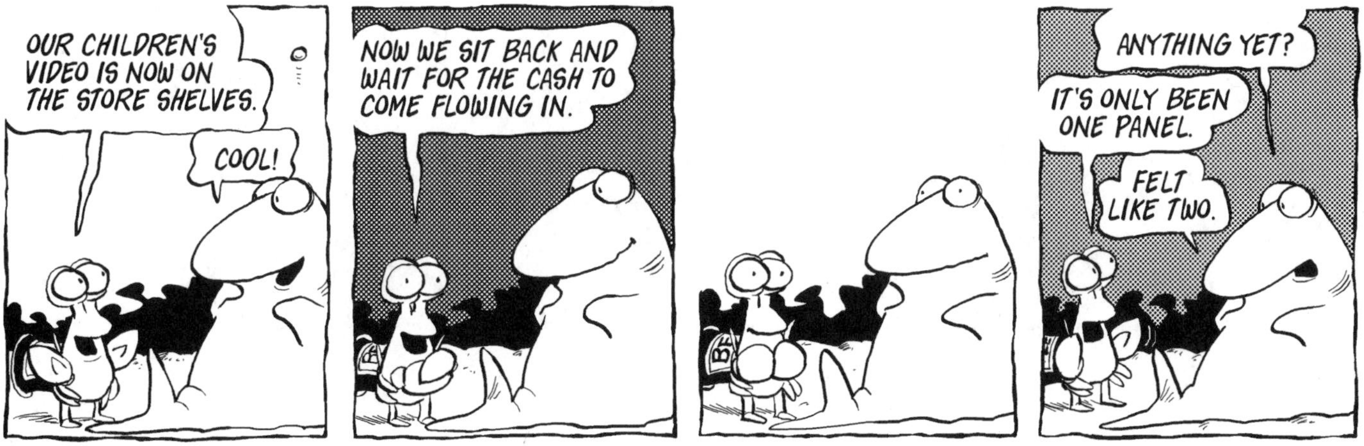
OUR CHILDREN'S VIDEO IS NOW ON THE STORE SHELVES.
COOL!
NOW WE SIT BACK AND WAIT FOR THE CASH TO COME FLOWING IN.
ANYTHING YET?
IT'S ONLY BEEN ONE PANEL.
FELT LIKE TWO.

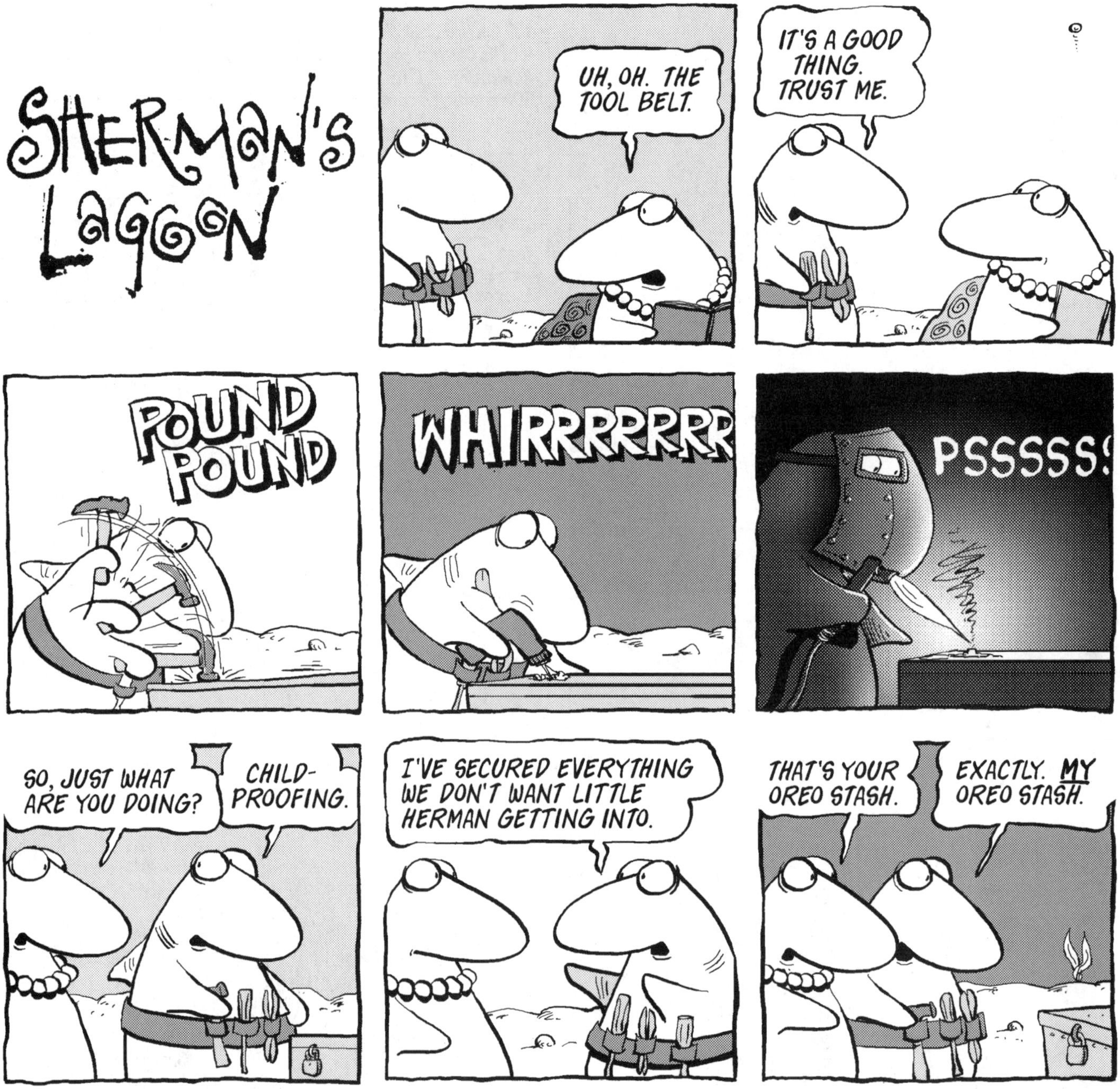
SHERMAN'S LAGOON
UH, OH. THE TOOL BELT.
IT'S A GOOD THING. TRUST ME.
POUND POUND
WHIRRRRRRR
PSSSSS
SO, JUST WHAT ARE YOU DOING?
CHILD-PROOFING.
I'VE SECURED EVERYTHING WE DON'T WANT LITTLE HERMAN GETTING INTO.
THAT'S YOUR OREO STASH.
EXACTLY. MY OREO STASH.

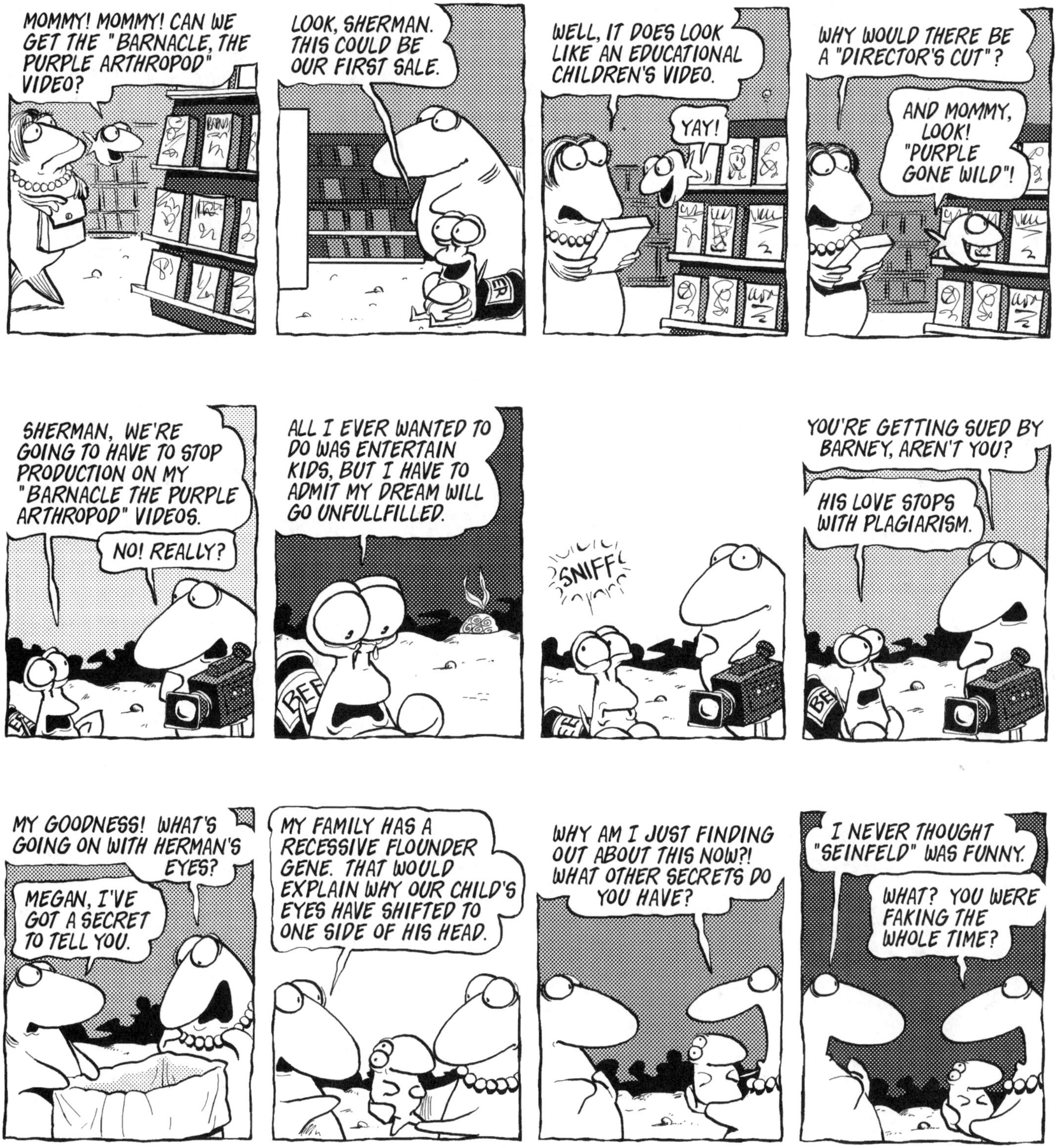
MOMMY! MOMMY! CAN WE GET THE "BARNACLE, THE PURPLE ARTHROPOD" VIDEO?
LOOK, SHERMAN. THIS COULD BE OUR FIRST SALE.
WELL, IT DOES LOOK LIKE AN EDUCATIONAL CHILDREN'S VIDEO.
YAY!
WHY WOULD THERE BE A "DIRECTOR'S CUT"?
AND MOMMY, LOOK! "PURPLE GONE WILD"!
SHERMAN, WE'RE GOING TO HAVE TO STOP PRODUCTION ON MY "BARNACLE THE PURPLE ARTHROPOD" VIDEOS.
NO! REALLY?
ALL I EVER WANTED TO DO WAS ENTERTAIN KIDS, BUT I HAVE TO ADMIT MY DREAM WILL GO UNFULLFILLED.
SNIFF
YOU'RE GETTING SUED BY BARNEY, AREN'T YOU?
HIS LOVE STOPS WITH PLAGIARISM.
MY GOODNESS! WHAT'S GOING ON WITH HERMAN'S EYES?
MEGAN, I'VE GOT A SECRET TO TELL YOU.
MY FAMILY HAS A RECESSIVE FLOUNDER GENE. THAT WOULD EXPLAIN WHY OUR CHILD'S EYES HAVE SHIFTED TO ONE SIDE OF HIS HEAD.
WHY AM I JUST FINDING OUT ABOUT THIS NOW?! WHAT OTHER SECRETS DO YOU HAVE?
I NEVER THOUGHT "SEINFELD" WAS FUNNY.
WHAT? YOU WERE FAKING THE WHOLE TIME?

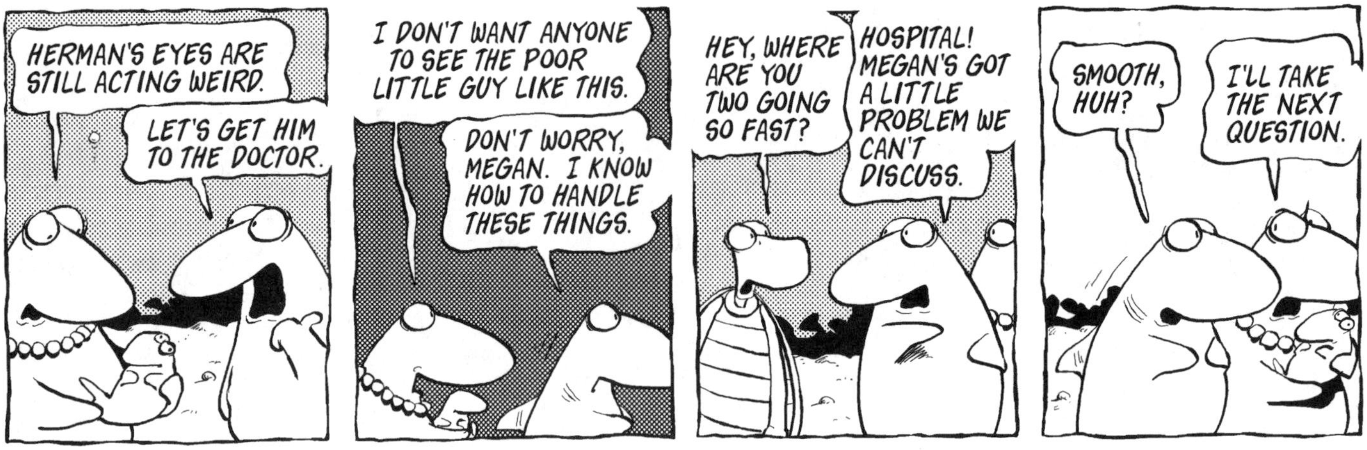
HERMAN'S EYES ARE STILL ACTING WEIRD.
LET'S GET HIM TO THE DOCTOR.
I DON'T WANT ANYONE TO SEE THE POOR LITTLE GUY LIKE THIS.
DON'T WORRY, MEGAN. I KNOW HOW TO HANDLE THESE THINGS.
HEY, WHERE ARE YOU TWO GOING SO FAST?
HOSPITAL! MEGAN'S GOT A LITTLE PROBLEM WE CAN'T DISCUSS.
SMOOTH, HUH?
I'LL TAKE THE NEXT QUESTION.

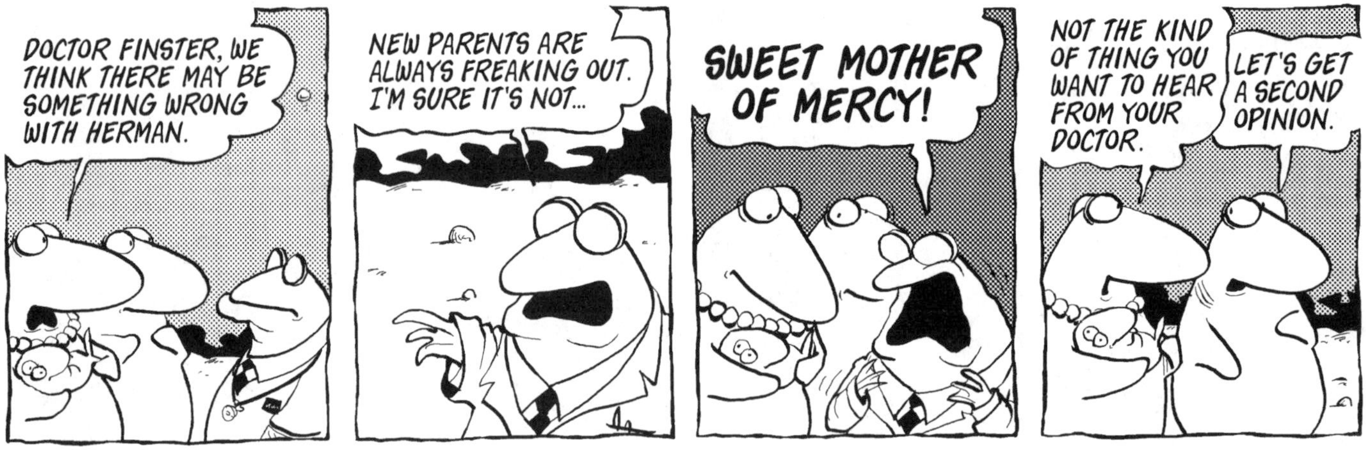
DOCTOR FINSTER, WE THINK THERE MAY BE SOMETHING WRONG WITH HERMAN.
NEW PARENTS ARE ALWAYS FREAKING OUT. I'M SURE IT'S NOT...
SWEET MOTHER OF MERCY!
NOT THE KIND OF THING YOU WANT TO HEAR FROM YOUR DOCTOR.
LET'S GET A SECOND OPINION.

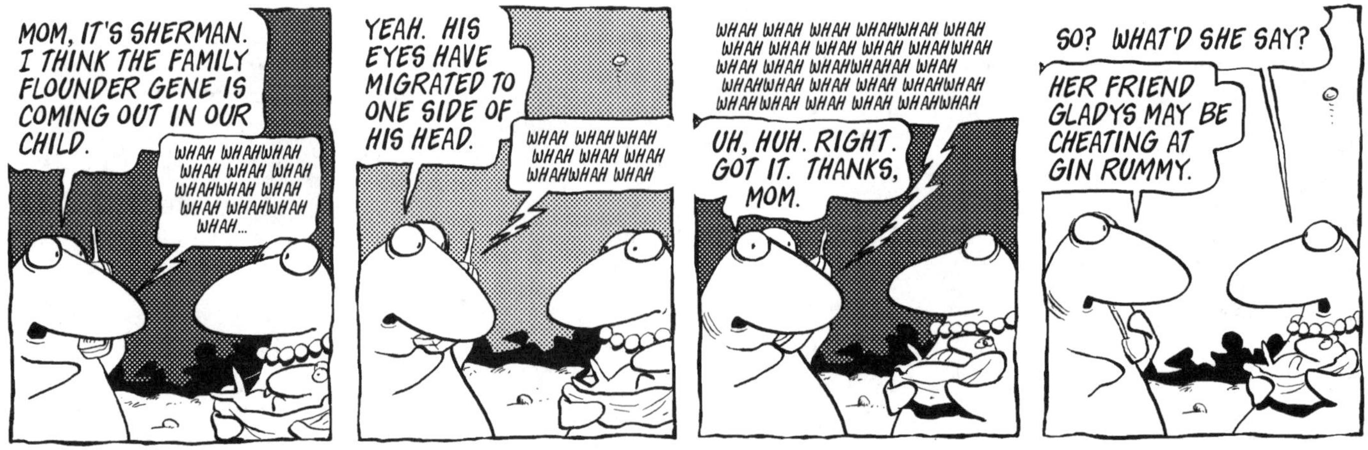
MOM, IT'S SHERMAN. I THINK THE FAMILY FLOUNDER GENE IS COMING OUT IN OUR CHILD.
WHAH WHAHWHAH WHAH WHAH WHAH WHAHWHAH WHAH WHAH WHAHWHAH WHAH...
YEAH. HIS EYES HAVE MIGRATED TO ONE SIDE OF HIS HEAD.
WHAH WHAHWHAH WHAH WHAH WHAH WHAHWHAH WHAH
WHAH WHAH WHAH WHAHWHAH WHAH WHAH WHAH WHAH WHAH WHAHWHAH WHAH WHAH WHAHWHAHAH WHAH WHAHWHAH WHAH WHAH WHAHWHAH WHAHWHAH WHAH WHAH WHAHWHAH
UH, HUH. RIGHT. GOT IT. THANKS, MOM.
SO? WHAT'D SHE SAY?
HER FRIEND GLADYS MAY BE CHEATING AT GIN RUMMY.

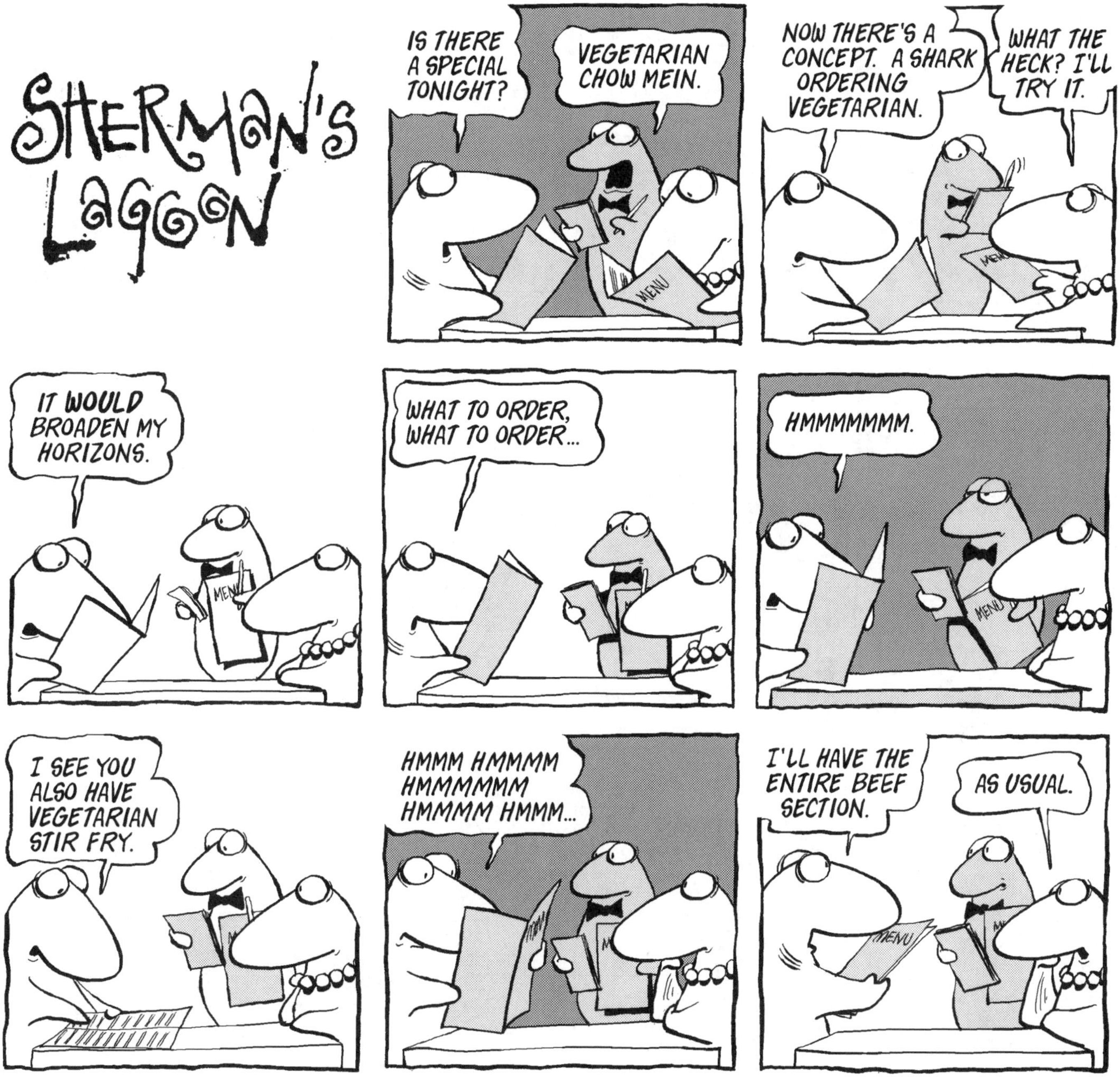
SHERMAN'S LAGOON
IS THERE A SPECIAL TONIGHT?
VEGETARIAN CHOW MEIN.
MENU
NOW THERE'S A CONCEPT. A SHARK ORDERING VEGETARIAN.
WHAT THE HECK? I'LL TRY IT.
MENU
IT WOULD BROADEN MY HORIZONS.
MENU
WHAT TO ORDER, WHAT TO ORDER...
HMMMMMMM.
MENU
I SEE YOU ALSO HAVE VEGETARIAN STIR FRY.
HMMM HMMMM HMMMMMM HMMMM HMMM...
I'LL HAVE THE ENTIRE BEEF SECTION.
AS USUAL.
MENU

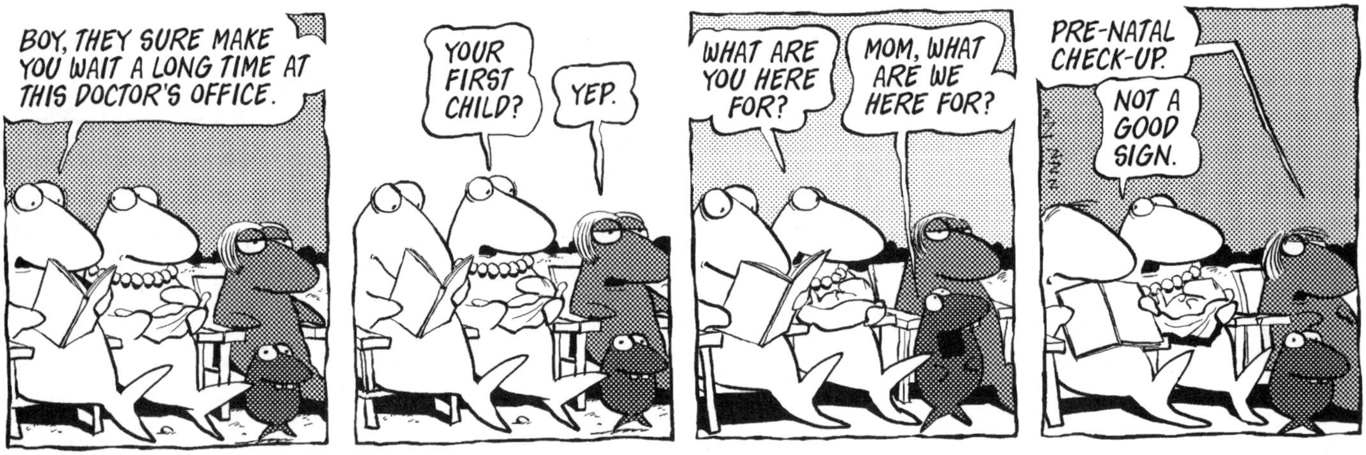

BOY, THEY SURE MAKE YOU WAIT A LONG TIME AT THIS DOCTOR'S OFFICE.
YOUR FIRST CHILD?
YEP.
WHAT ARE YOU HERE FOR?
MOM, WHAT ARE WE HERE FOR?
PRE-NATAL CHECK-UP.
NOT A GOOD SIGN.

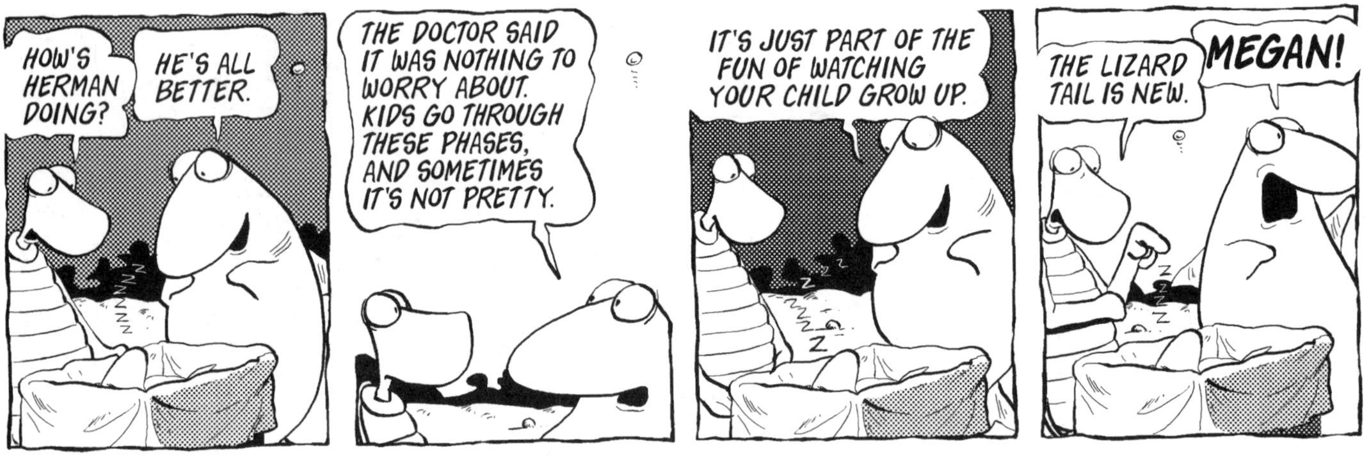

HOW'S HERMAN DOING?
HE'S ALL BETTER.
THE DOCTOR SAID IT WAS NOTHING TO WORRY ABOUT. KIDS GO THROUGH THESE PHASES, AND SOMETIMES IT'S NOT PRETTY.
IT'S JUST PART OF THE FUN OF WATCHING YOUR CHILD GROW UP.
THE LIZARD TAIL IS NEW.
MEGAN!

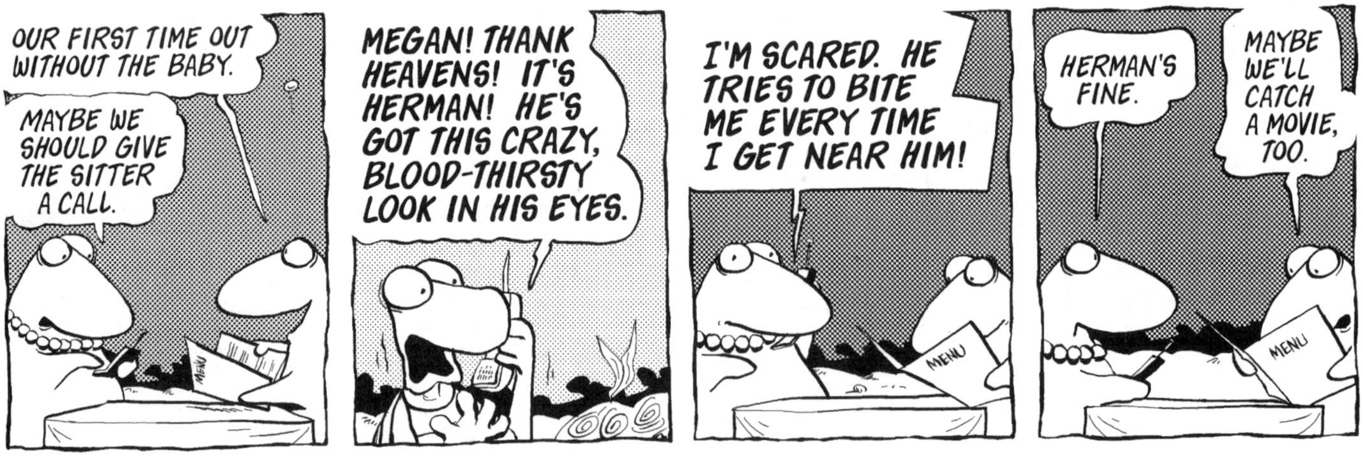

OUR FIRST TIME OUT WITHOUT THE BABY.
MAYBE WE SHOULD GIVE THE SITTER A CALL.
MENU
MEGAN! THANK HEAVENS! IT'S HERMAN! HE'S GOT THIS CRAZY, BLOOD-THIRSTY LOOK IN HIS EYES.
I'M SCARED. HE TRIES TO BITE ME EVERY TIME I GET NEAR HIM!
MENU
HERMAN'S FINE.
MAYBE WE'LL CATCH A MOVIE, TOO.
MENU

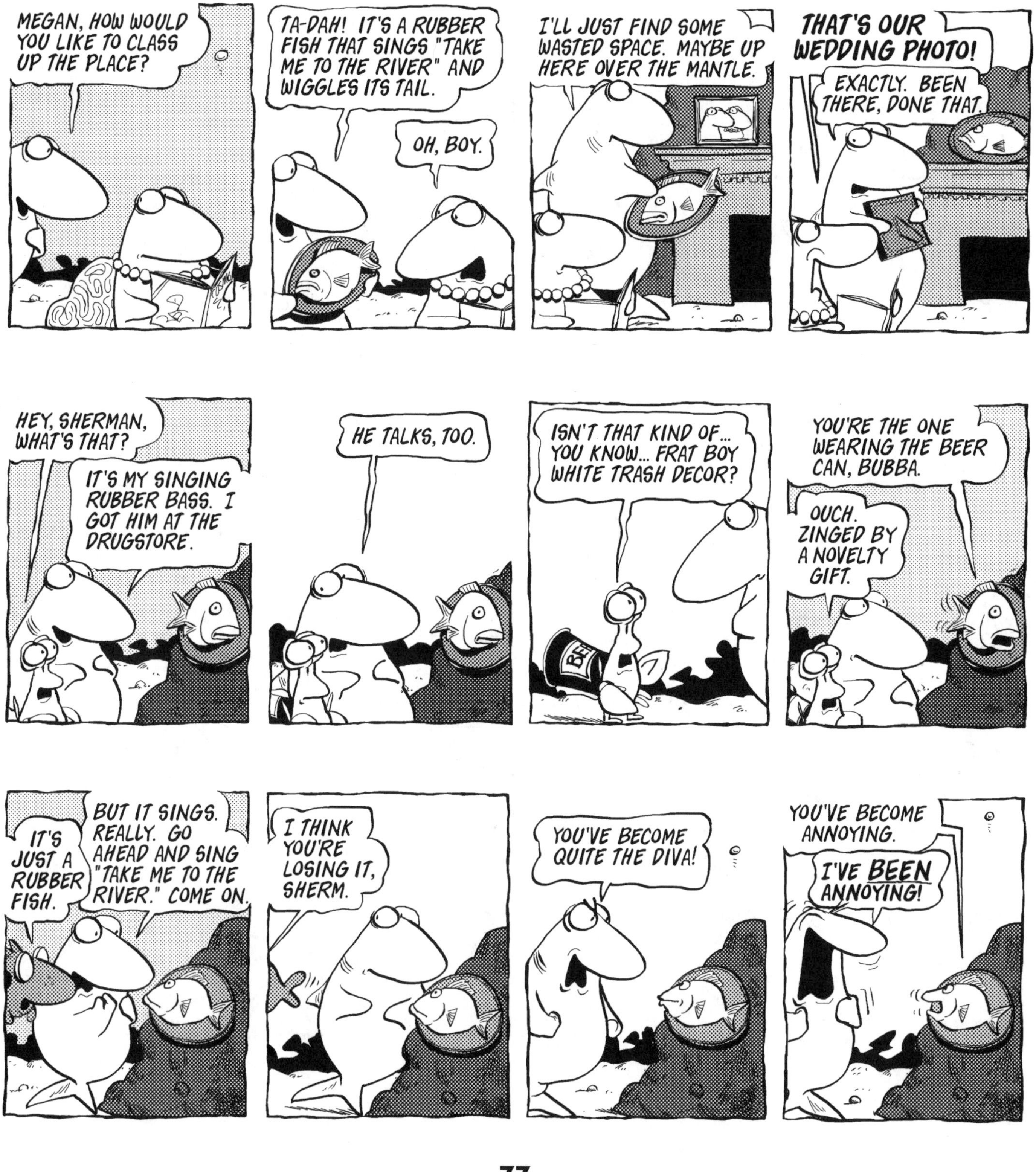
MEGAN, HOW WOULD YOU LIKE TO CLASS UP THE PLACE?
TA-DAH! IT'S A RUBBER FISH THAT SINGS "TAKE ME TO THE RIVER" AND WIGGLES ITS TAIL.
OH, BOY.
I'LL JUST FIND SOME WASTED SPACE. MAYBE UP HERE OVER THE MANTLE.
THAT'S OUR WEDDING PHOTO!
EXACTLY. BEEN THERE, DONE THAT.
HEY, SHERMAN, WHAT'S THAT?
IT'S MY SINGING RUBBER BASS. I GOT HIM AT THE DRUGSTORE.
HE TALKS, TOO.
ISN'T THAT KIND OF... YOU KNOW... FRAT BOY WHITE TRASH DECOR?
YOU'RE THE ONE WEARING THE BEER CAN, BUBBA.
OUCH. ZINGED BY A NOVELTY GIFT.
IT'S JUST A RUBBER FISH.
BUT IT SINGS. REALLY. GO AHEAD AND SING "TAKE ME TO THE RIVER." COME ON.
I THINK YOU'RE LOSING IT, SHERM.
YOU'VE BECOME QUITE THE DIVA!
YOU'VE BECOME ANNOYING.
I'VE BEEN ANNOYING!

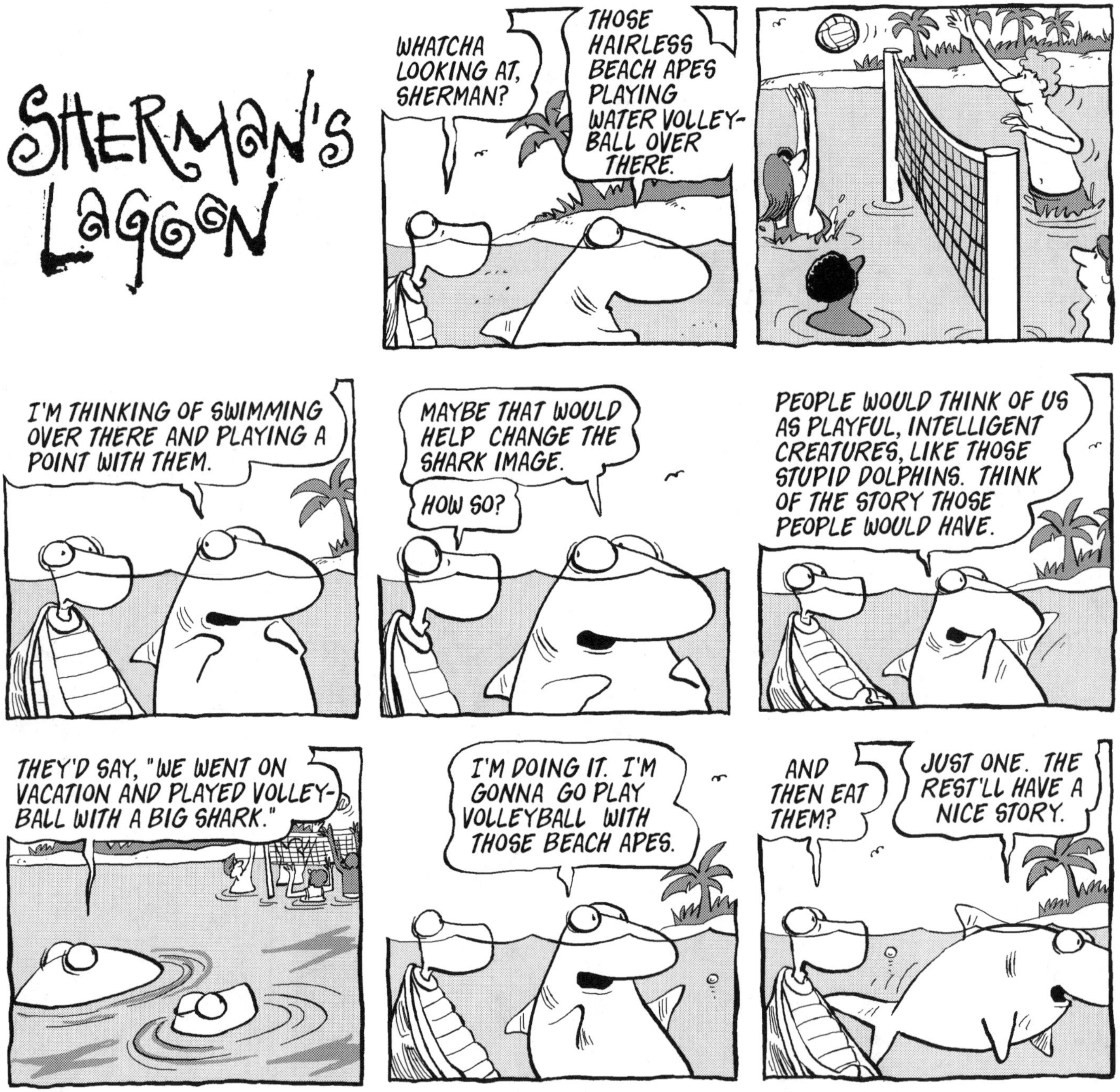
SHERMAN'S LAGOON
WHATCHA LOOKING AT, SHERMAN?
THOSE HAIRLESS BEACH APES PLAYING WATER VOLLEY-BALL OVER THERE.
I'M THINKING OF SWIMMING OVER THERE AND PLAYING A POINT WITH THEM.
MAYBE THAT WOULD HELP CHANGE THE SHARK IMAGE.
HOW SO?
PEOPLE WOULD THINK OF US AS PLAYFUL, INTELLIGENT CREATURES, LIKE THOSE STUPID DOLPHINS. THINK OF THE STORY THOSE PEOPLE WOULD HAVE.
THEY'D SAY, "WE WENT ON VACATION AND PLAYED VOLLEY-BALL WITH A BIG SHARK."
I'M DOING IT. I'M GONNA GO PLAY VOLLEYBALL WITH THOSE BEACH APES.
AND THEN EAT THEM?
JUST ONE. THE REST'LL HAVE A NICE STORY.

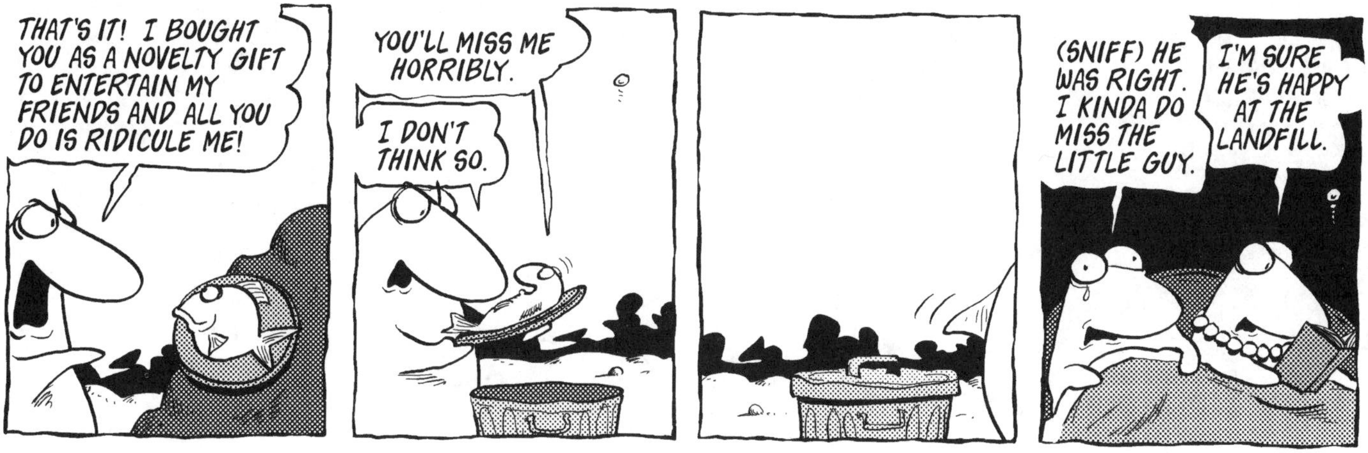
THAT'S IT! I BOUGHT YOU AS A NOVELTY GIFT TO ENTERTAIN MY FRIENDS AND ALL YOU DO IS RIDICULE ME!
YOU'LL MISS ME HORRIBLY.
I DON'T THINK SO.
(SNIFF) HE WAS RIGHT. I KINDA DO MISS THE LITTLE GUY.
I'M SURE HE'S HAPPY AT THE LANDFILL.

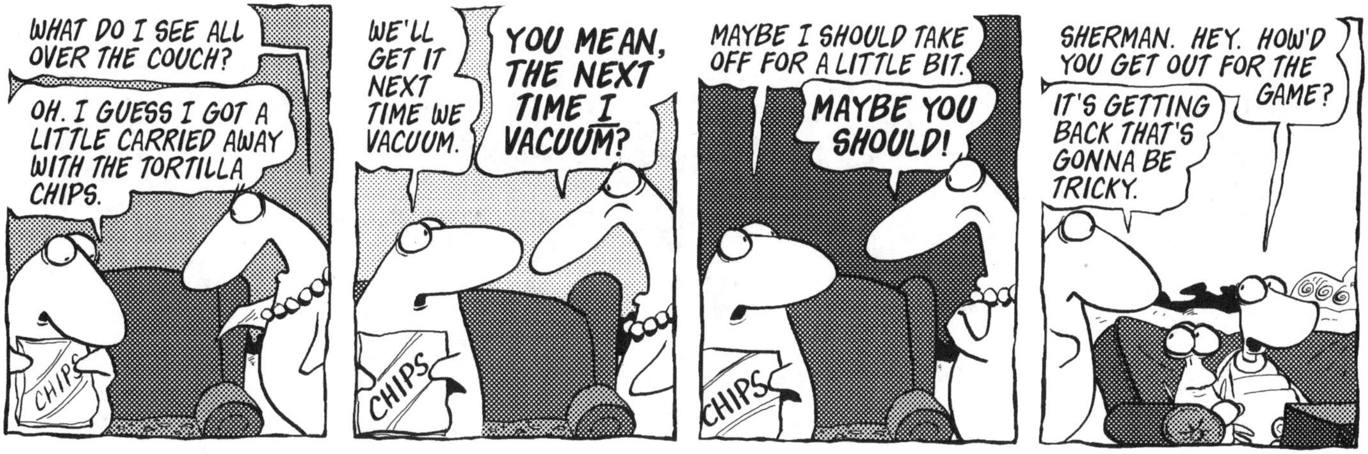
WHAT DO I SEE ALL OVER THE COUCH?
OH. I GUESS I GOT A LITTLE CARRIED AWAY WITH THE TORTILLA CHIPS.
CHIPS
WE'LL GET IT NEXT TIME WE VACUUM.
YOU MEAN, THE NEXT TIME I VACUUM?
CHIPS
MAYBE I SHOULD TAKE OFF FOR A LITTLE BIT.
MAYBE YOU SHOULD!
CHIPS
SHERMAN. HEY. HOW'D YOU GET OUT FOR THE GAME?
IT'S GETTING BACK THAT'S GONNA BE TRICKY.

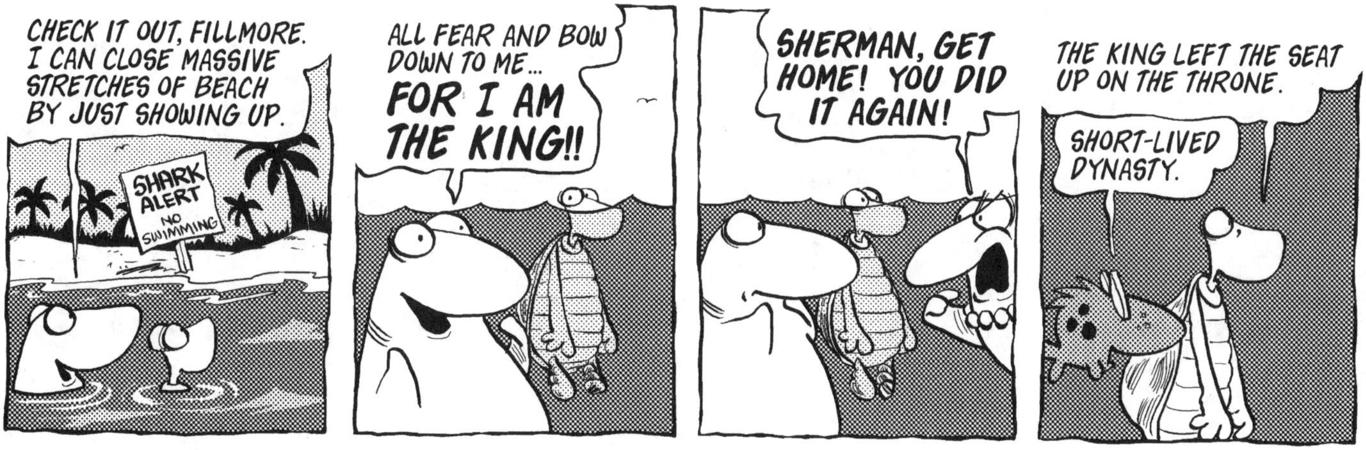
CHECK IT OUT, FILLMORE. I CAN CLOSE MASSIVE STRETCHES OF BEACH BY JUST SHOWING UP.
SHARK ALERT
NO SWIMMING
ALL FEAR AND BOW DOWN TO ME... FOR I AM THE KING!!
SHERMAN, GET HOME! YOU DID IT AGAIN!
THE KING LEFT THE SEAT UP ON THE THRONE.
SHORT-LIVED DYNASTY.

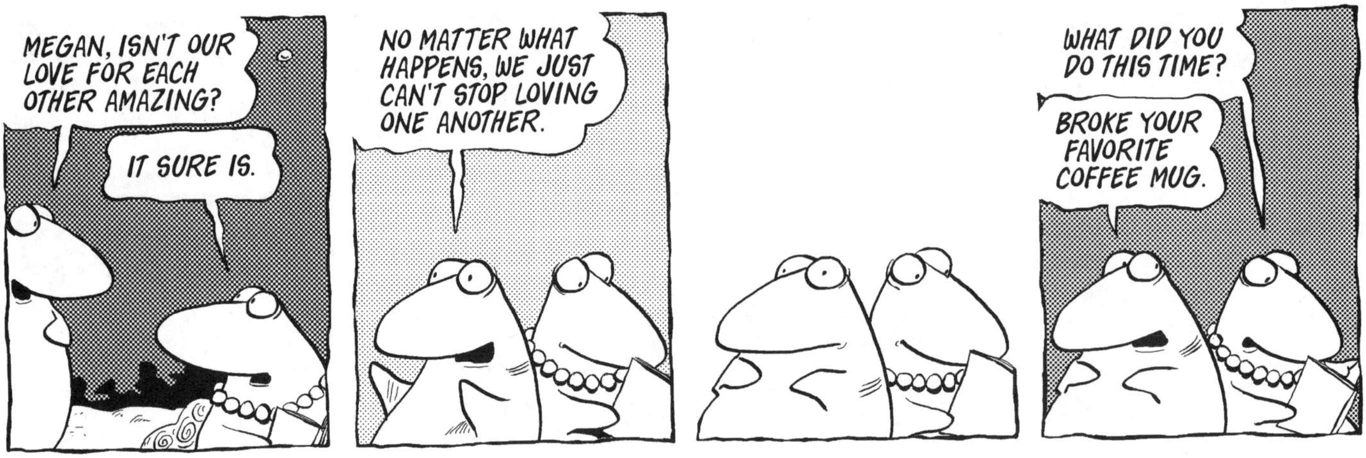
MEGAN, ISN'T OUR LOVE FOR EACH OTHER AMAZING?
IT SURE IS.
NO MATTER WHAT HAPPENS, WE JUST CAN'T STOP LOVING ONE ANOTHER.
WHAT DID YOU DO THIS TIME?
BROKE YOUR FAVORITE COFFEE MUG.

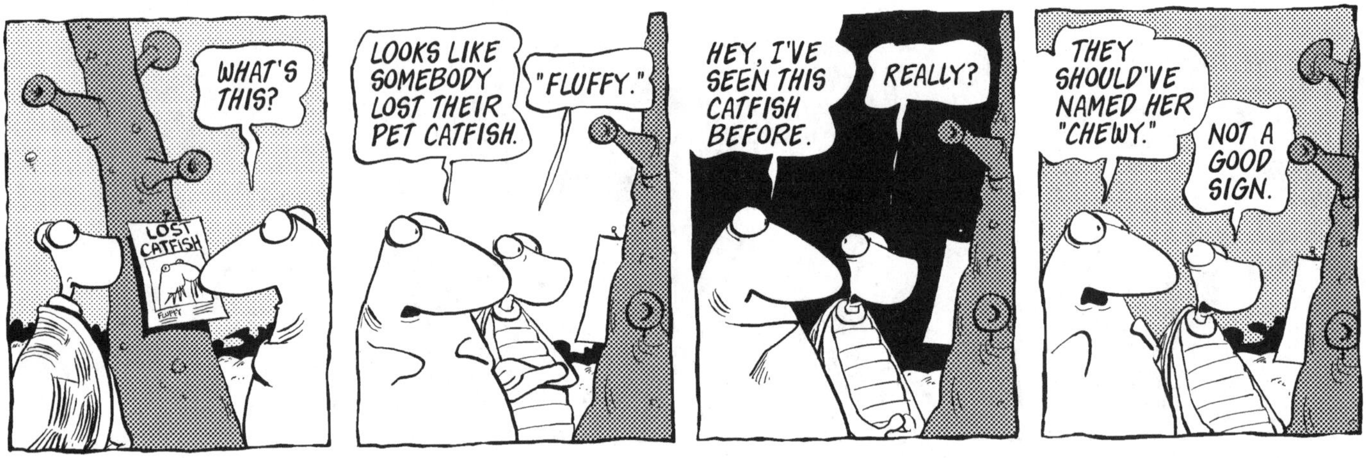
WHAT'S THIS?
LOST CATFISH
FLUFFY
LOOKS LIKE SOMEBODY LOST THEIR PET CATFISH.
"FLUFFY."
HEY, I'VE SEEN THIS CATFISH BEFORE.
REALLY?
THEY SHOULD'VE NAMED HER "CHEWY."
NOT A GOOD SIGN.

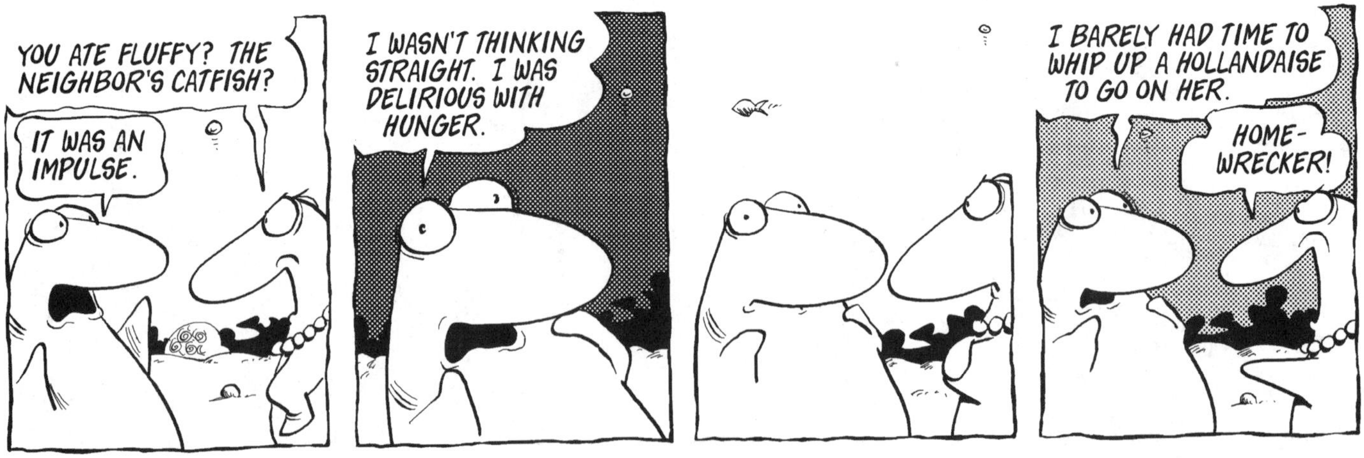
YOU ATE FLUFFY? THE NEIGHBOR'S CATFISH?
IT WAS AN IMPULSE.
I WASN'T THINKING STRAIGHT. I WAS DELIRIOUS WITH HUNGER.
I BARELY HAD TIME TO WHIP UP A HOLLANDAISE TO GO ON HER.
HOME-WRECKER!

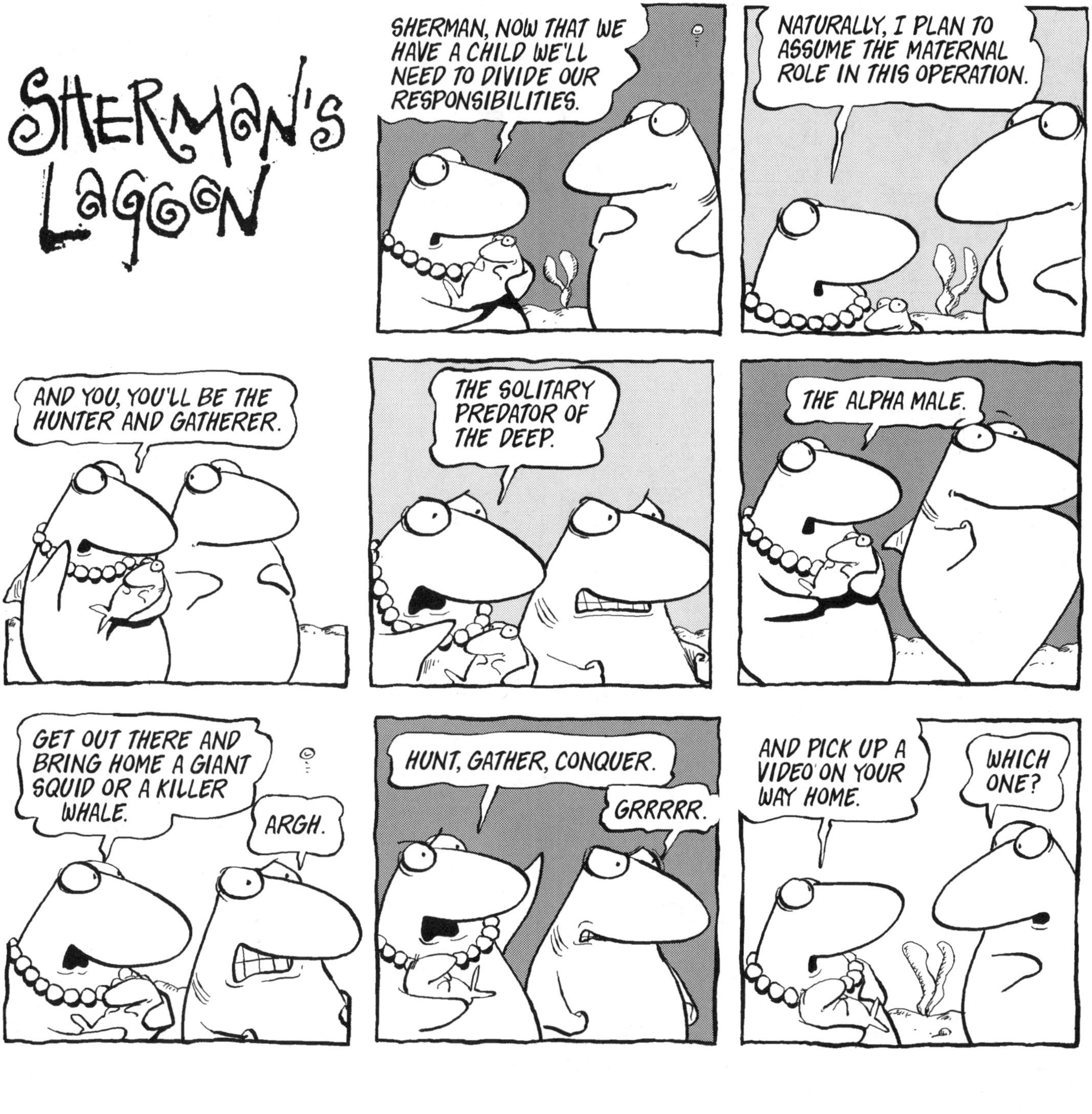
SHERMAN'S LAGOON
SHERMAN, NOW THAT WE HAVE A CHILD WE'LL NEED TO DIVIDE OUR RESPONSIBILITIES.
NATURALLY, I PLAN TO ASSUME THE MATERNAL ROLE IN THIS OPERATION.
AND YOU, YOU'LL BE THE HUNTER AND GATHERER.
THE SOLITARY PREDATOR OF THE DEEP.
THE ALPHA MALE.
GET OUT THERE AND BRING HOME A GIANT SQUID OR A KILLER WHALE.
ARGH.
HUNT, GATHER, CONQUER.
GRRRRR.
AND PICK UP A VIDEO ON YOUR WAY HOME.
WHICH ONE?

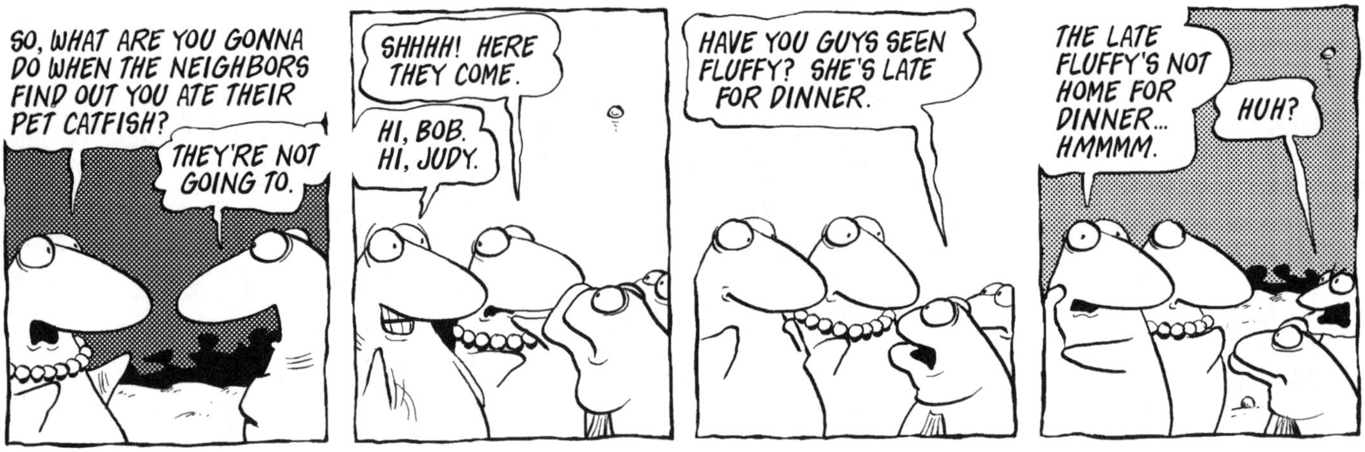
SO, WHAT ARE YOU GONNA DO WHEN THE NEIGHBORS FIND OUT YOU ATE THEIR PET CATFISH?
THEY'RE NOT GOING TO.
SHHHH! HERE THEY COME.
HI, BOB. HI, JUDY.
HAVE YOU GUYS SEEN FLUFFY? SHE'S LATE FOR DINNER.
THE LATE FLUFFY'S NOT HOME FOR DINNER... HMMMM.
HUH?

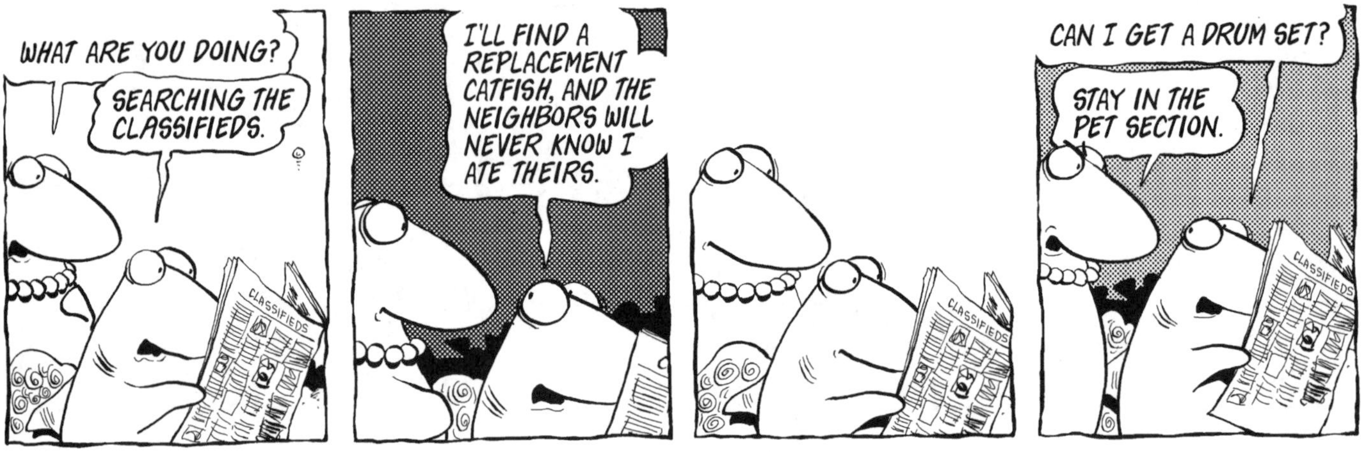
WHAT ARE YOU DOING?
SEARCHING THE CLASSIFIEDS.
I'LL FIND A REPLACEMENT CATFISH, AND THE NEIGHBORS WILL NEVER KNOW I ATE THEIRS.
CAN I GET A DRUM SET?
STAY IN THE PET SECTION.

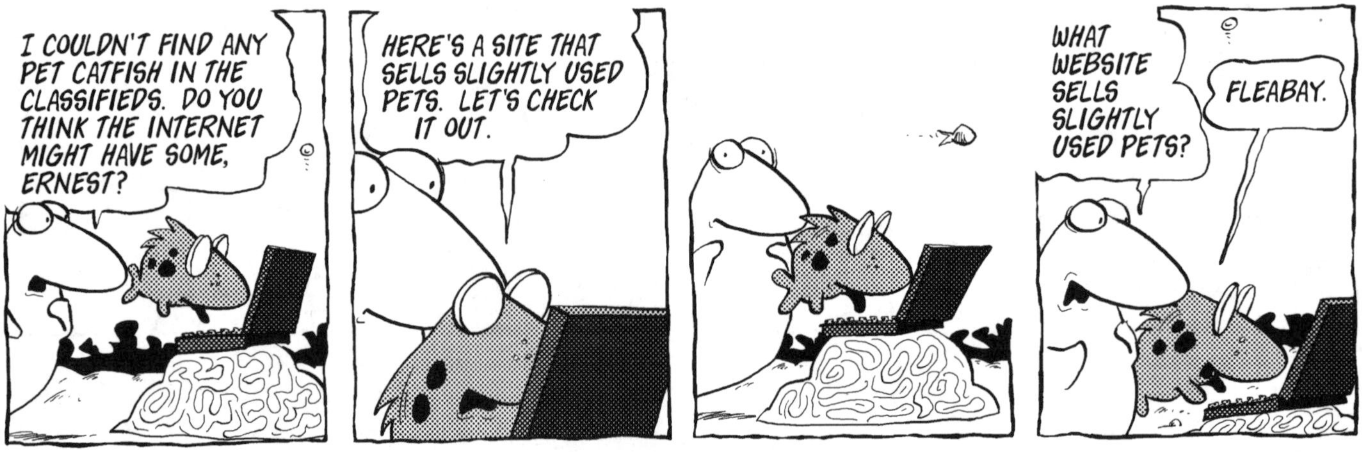
I COULDN'T FIND ANY PET CATFISH IN THE CLASSIFIEDS. DO YOU THINK THE INTERNET MIGHT HAVE SOME, ERNEST?
HERE'S A SITE THAT SELLS SLIGHTLY USED PETS. LET'S CHECK IT OUT.
WHAT WEBSITE SELLS SLIGHTLY USED PETS?
FLEABAY.

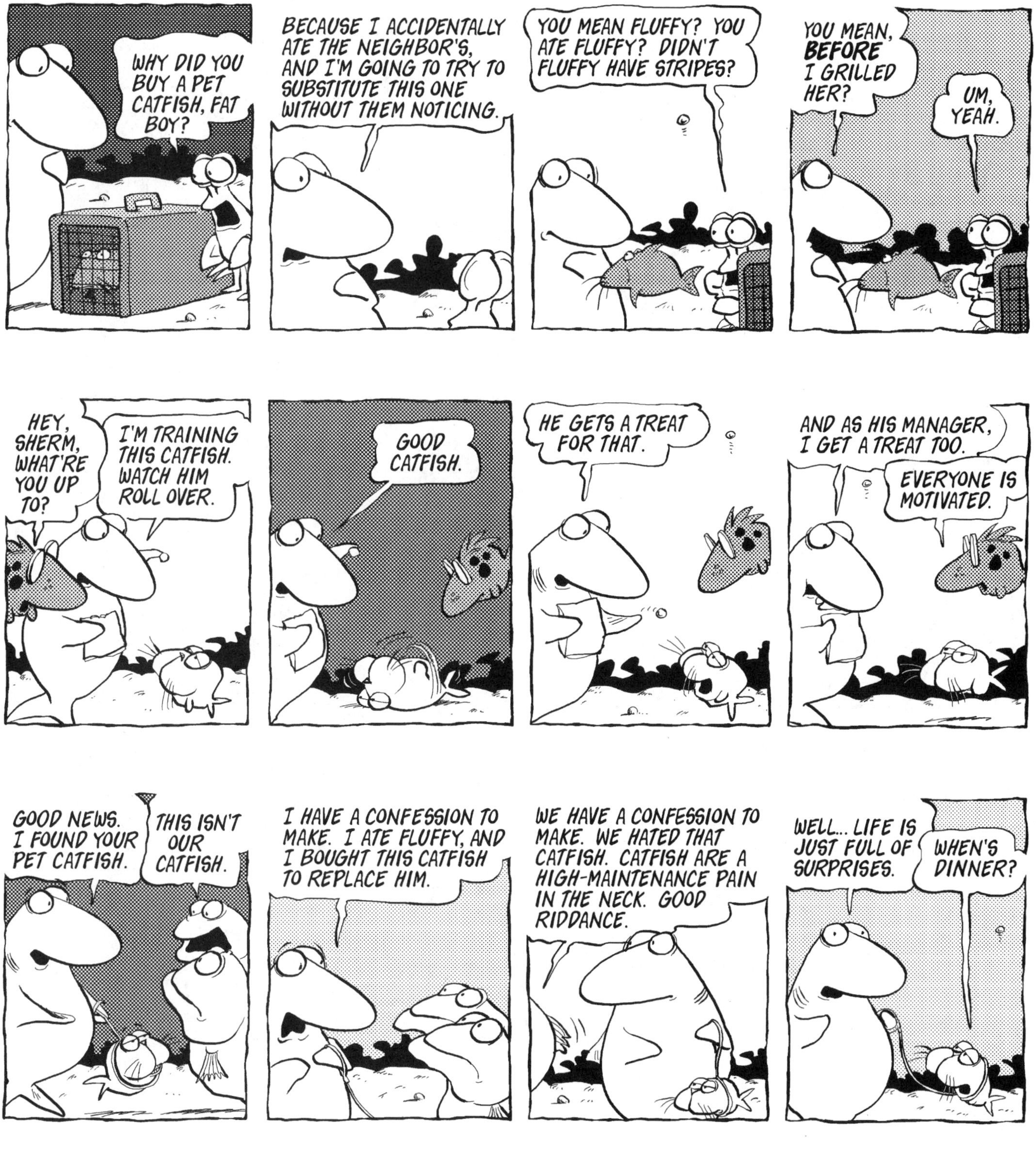
WHY DID YOU BUY A PET CATFISH, FAT BOY?
BECAUSE I ACCIDENTALLY ATE THE NEIGHBOR'S, AND I'M GOING TO TRY TO SUBSTITUTE THIS ONE WITHOUT THEM NOTICING.
YOU MEAN FLUFFY? YOU ATE FLUFFY? DIDN'T FLUFFY HAVE STRIPES?
YOU MEAN, BEFORE I GRILLED HER?
UM, YEAH.
HEY, SHERM, WHAT'RE YOU UP TO?
I'M TRAINING THIS CATFISH. WATCH HIM ROLL OVER.
GOOD CATFISH.
HE GETS A TREAT FOR THAT.
AND AS HIS MANAGER, I GET A TREAT TOO.
EVERYONE IS MOTIVATED.
GOOD NEWS. I FOUND YOUR PET CATFISH.
THIS ISN'T OUR CATFISH.
I HAVE A CONFESSION TO MAKE. I ATE FLUFFY, AND I BOUGHT THIS CATFISH TO REPLACE HIM.
WE HAVE A CONFESSION TO MAKE. WE HATED THAT CATFISH. CATFISH ARE A HIGH-MAINTENANCE PAIN IN THE NECK. GOOD RIDDANCE.
WELL... LIFE IS JUST FULL OF SURPRISES.
WHEN'S DINNER?

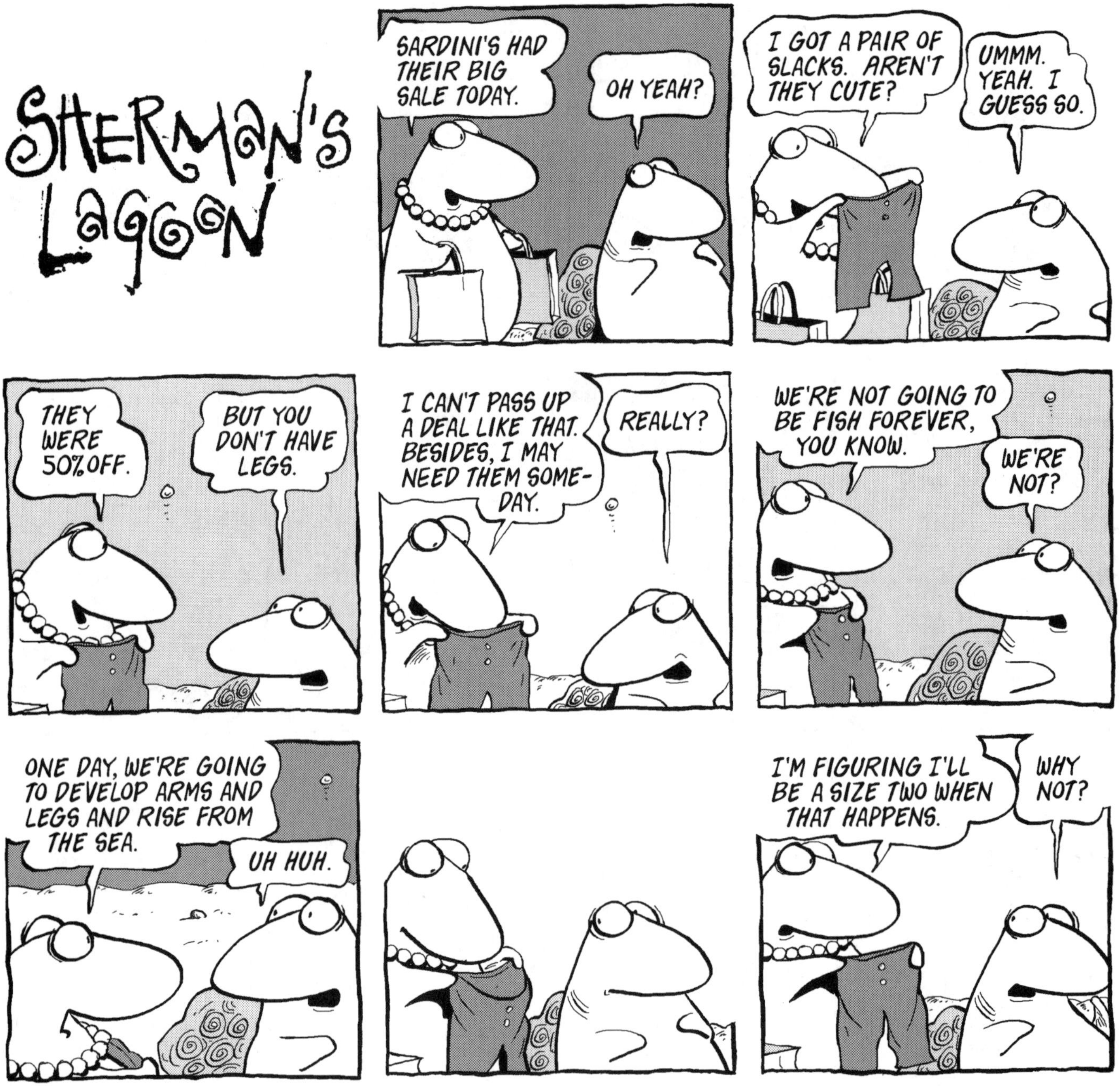
SHERMAN'S LAGOON
SARDINI'S HAD THEIR BIG SALE TODAY.
OH YEAH?
I GOT A PAIR OF SLACKS. AREN'T THEY CUTE?
UMMM. YEAH. I GUESS SO.
THEY WERE 50% OFF.
BUT YOU DON'T HAVE LEGS.
I CAN'T PASS UP A DEAL LIKE THAT. BESIDES, I MAY NEED THEM SOMEDAY.
REALLY?
WE'RE NOT GOING TO BE FISH FOREVER, YOU KNOW.
WE'RE NOT?
ONE DAY, WE'RE GOING TO DEVELOP ARMS AND LEGS AND RISE FROM THE SEA.
UH HUH.
I'M FIGURING I'LL BE A SIZE TWO WHEN THAT HAPPENS.
WHY NOT?

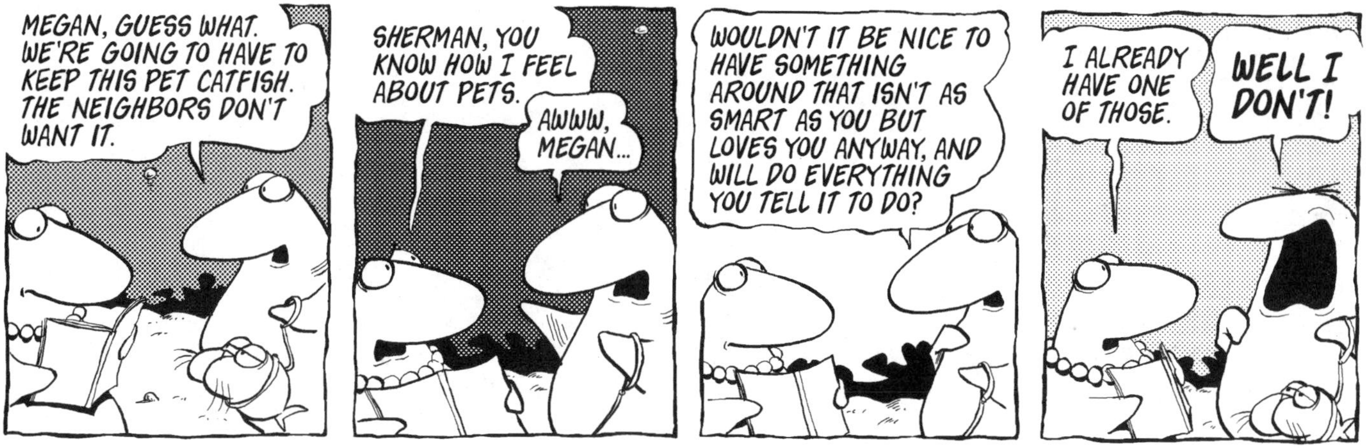
MEGAN, GUESS WHAT. WE'RE GOING TO HAVE TO KEEP THIS PET CATFISH. THE NEIGHBORS DON'T WANT IT.
SHERMAN, YOU KNOW HOW I FEEL ABOUT PETS.
AWWW, MEGAN...
WOULDN'T IT BE NICE TO HAVE SOMETHING AROUND THAT ISN'T AS SMART AS YOU BUT LOVES YOU ANYWAY, AND WILL DO EVERYTHING YOU TELL IT TO DO?
I ALREADY HAVE ONE OF THOSE.
WELL I DON'T!

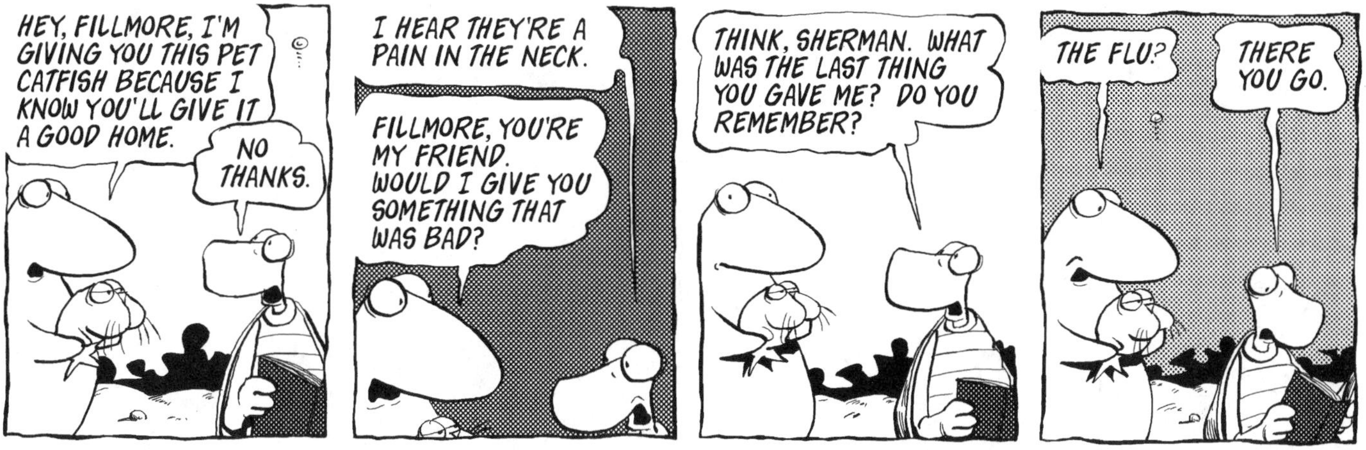
HEY, FILLMORE, I'M GIVING YOU THIS PET CATFISH BECAUSE I KNOW YOU'LL GIVE IT A GOOD HOME.
NO THANKS.
I HEAR THEY'RE A PAIN IN THE NECK.
FILLMORE, YOU'RE MY FRIEND. WOULD I GIVE YOU SOMETHING THAT WAS BAD?
THINK, SHERMAN. WHAT WAS THE LAST THING YOU GAVE ME? DO YOU REMEMBER?
THE FLU?
THERE YOU GO.

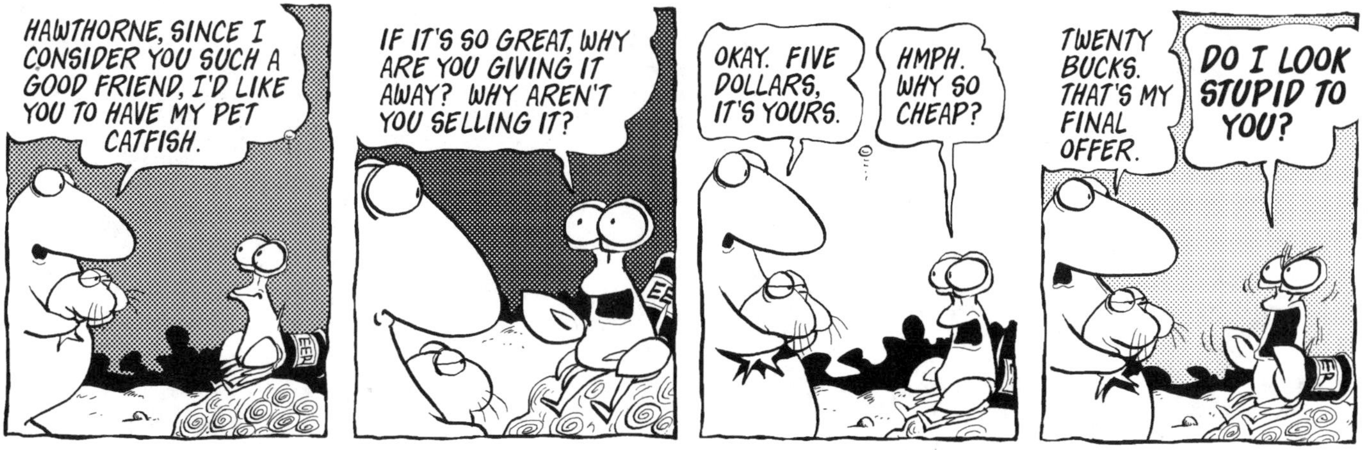
HAWTHORNE, SINCE I CONSIDER YOU SUCH A GOOD FRIEND, I'D LIKE YOU TO HAVE MY PET CATFISH.
IF IT'S SO GREAT, WHY ARE YOU GIVING IT AWAY? WHY AREN'T YOU SELLING IT?
OKAY. FIVE DOLLARS, IT'S YOURS.
HMPH. WHY SO CHEAP?
TWENTY BUCKS. THAT'S MY FINAL OFFER.
DO I LOOK STUPID TO YOU?

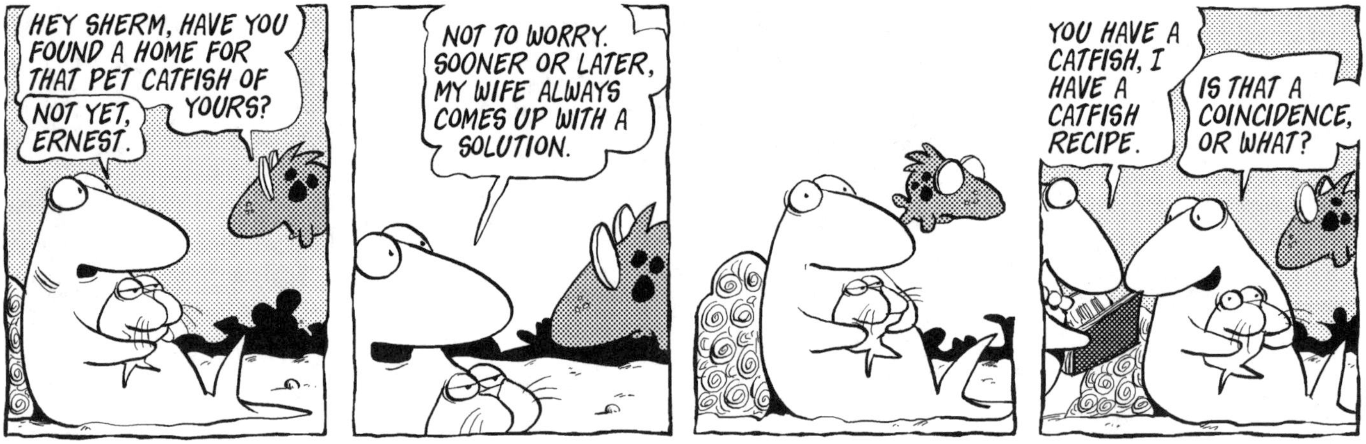
HEY SHERM, HAVE YOU FOUND A HOME FOR THAT PET CATFISH OF YOURS?
NOT YET, ERNEST.
NOT TO WORRY. SOONER OR LATER, MY WIFE ALWAYS COMES UP WITH A SOLUTION.
YOU HAVE A CATFISH, I HAVE A CATFISH RECIPE.
IS THAT A COINCIDENCE, OR WHAT?

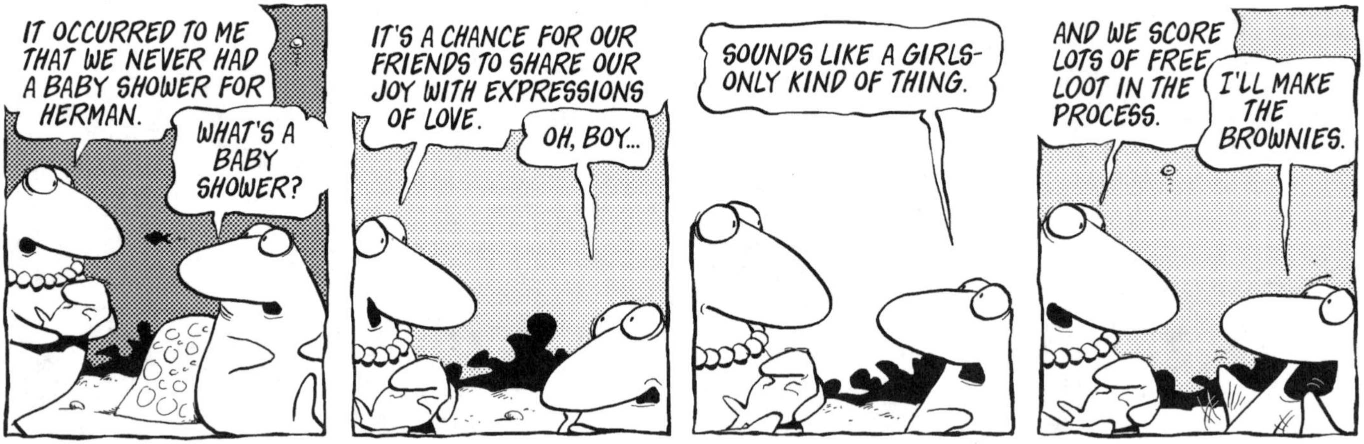
IT OCCURRED TO ME THAT WE NEVER HAD A BABY SHOWER FOR HERMAN.
WHAT'S A BABY SHOWER?
IT'S A CHANCE FOR OUR FRIENDS TO SHARE OUR JOY WITH EXPRESSIONS OF LOVE.
OH, BOY...
SOUNDS LIKE A GIRLS-ONLY KIND OF THING.
AND WE SCORE LOTS OF FREE LOOT IN THE PROCESS.
I'LL MAKE THE BROWNIES.

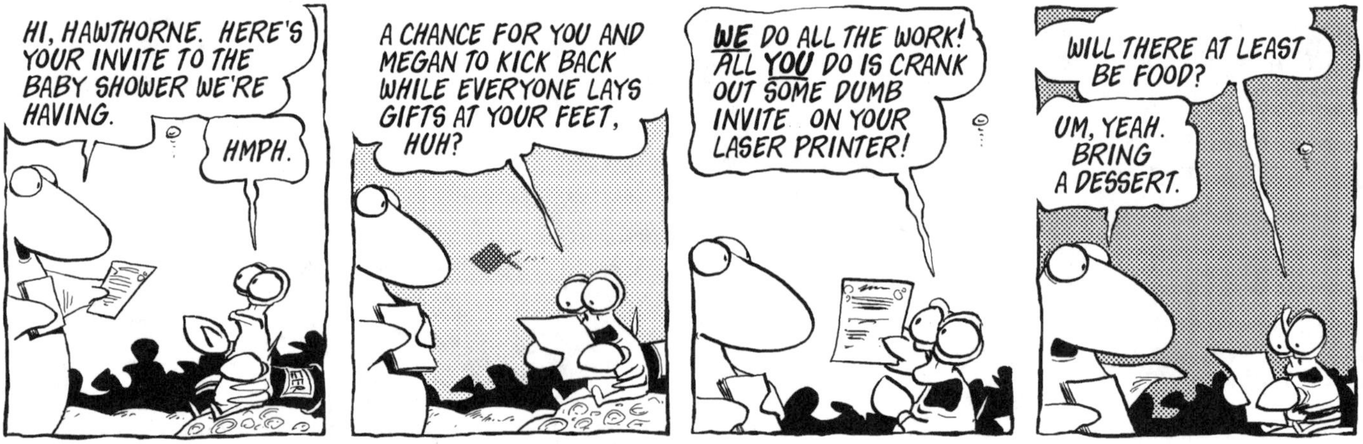
HI, HAWTHORNE. HERE'S YOUR INVITE TO THE BABY SHOWER WE'RE HAVING.
HMPH.
A CHANCE FOR YOU AND MEGAN TO KICK BACK WHILE EVERYONE LAYS GIFTS AT YOUR FEET, HUH?
WE DO ALL THE WORK! ALL YOU DO IS CRANK OUT SOME DUMB INVITE ON YOUR LASER PRINTER!
WILL THERE AT LEAST BE FOOD?
UM, YEAH. BRING A DESSERT.

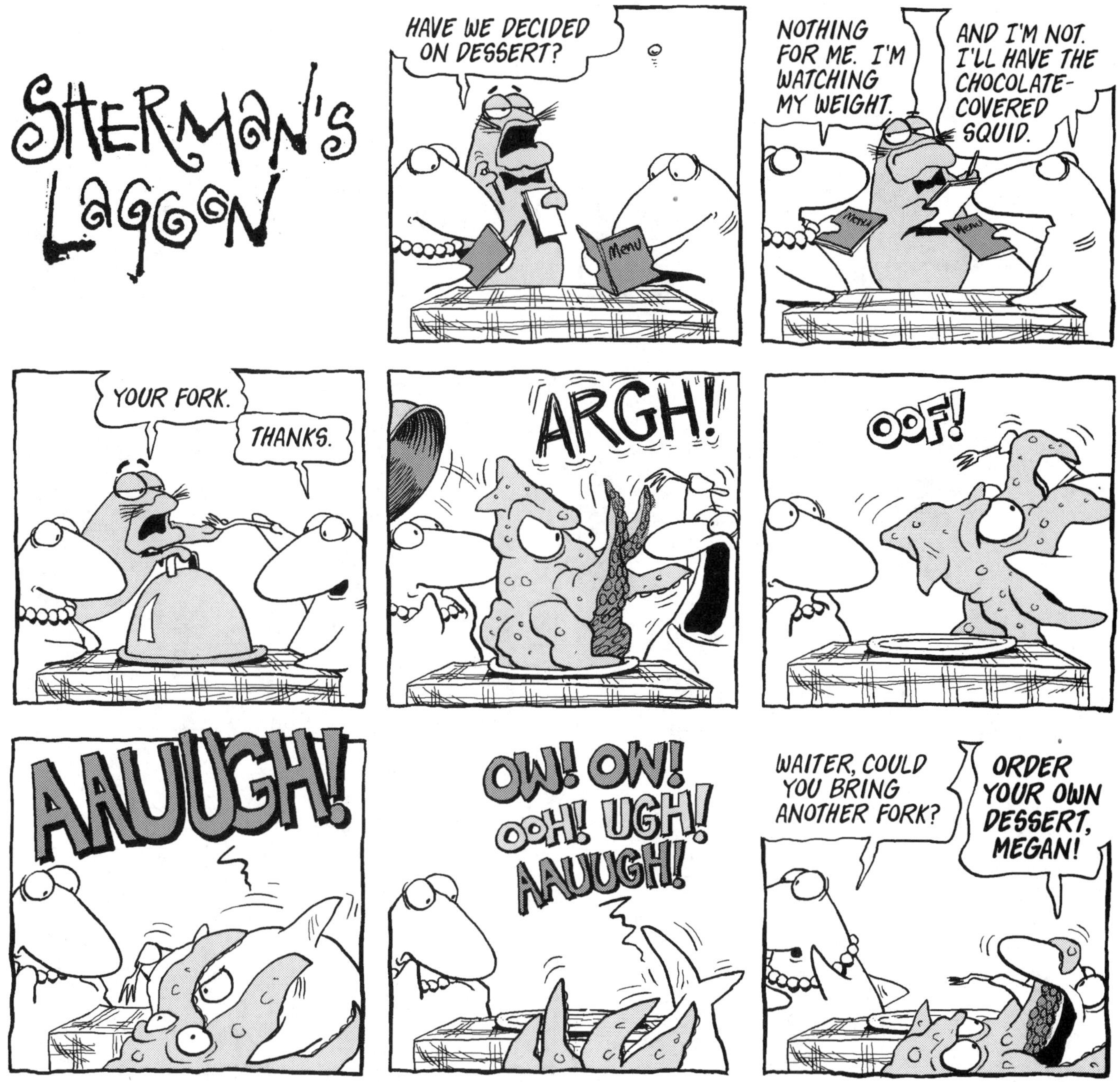
SHERMAN'S LAGOON
HAVE WE DECIDED ON DESSERT?
MENU
NOTHING FOR ME. I'M WATCHING MY WEIGHT.
AND I'M NOT. I'LL HAVE THE CHOCOLATE-COVERED SQUID.
YOUR FORK.
THANKS.
ARGH!
OOF!
AAUUGH!
OW! OW! OOH! UGH! AAUUGH!
WAITER, COULD YOU BRING ANOTHER FORK?
ORDER YOUR OWN DESSERT, MEGAN!

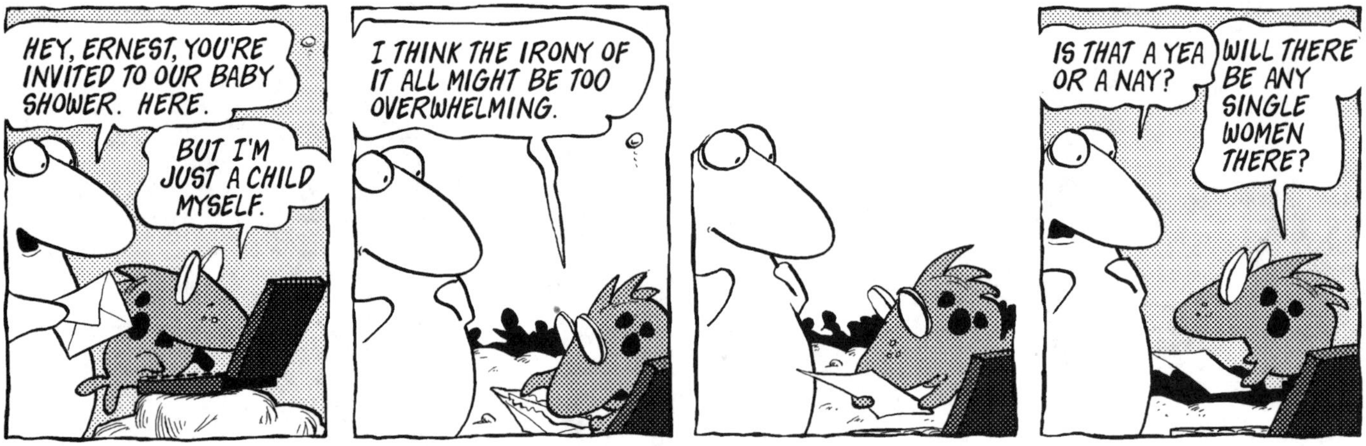
HEY, ERNEST, YOU'RE INVITED TO OUR BABY SHOWER. HERE.
BUT I'M JUST A CHILD MYSELF.
I THINK THE IRONY OF IT ALL MIGHT BE TOO OVERWHELMING.
IS THAT A YEA OR A NAY?
WILL THERE BE ANY SINGLE WOMEN THERE?

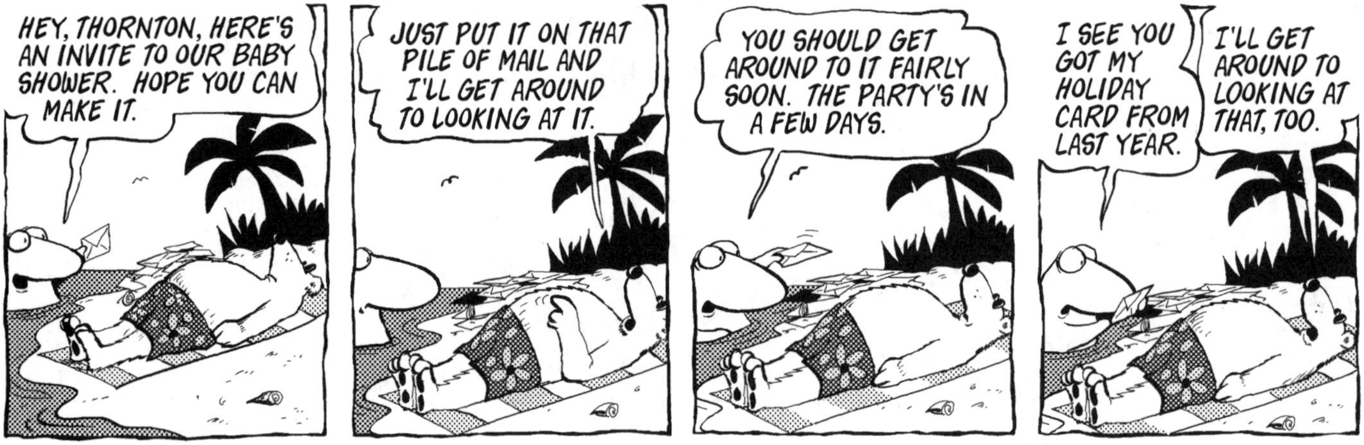
HEY, THORNTON, HERE'S AN INVITE TO OUR BABY SHOWER. HOPE YOU CAN MAKE IT.
JUST PUT IT ON THAT PILE OF MAIL AND I'LL GET AROUND TO LOOKING AT IT.
YOU SHOULD GET AROUND TO IT FAIRLY SOON. THE PARTY'S IN A FEW DAYS.
I SEE YOU GOT MY HOLIDAY CARD FROM LAST YEAR.
I'LL GET AROUND TO LOOKING AT THAT, TOO.

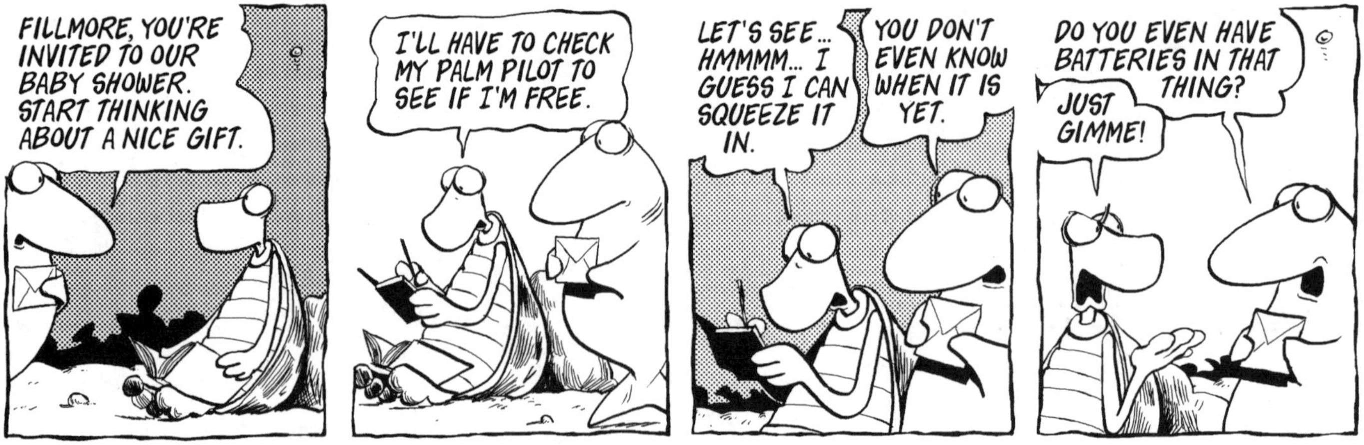
FILLMORE, YOU'RE INVITED TO OUR BABY SHOWER. START THINKING ABOUT A NICE GIFT.
I'LL HAVE TO CHECK MY PALM PILOT TO SEE IF I'M FREE.
LET'S SEE... HMMMM... I GUESS I CAN SQUEEZE IT IN.
YOU DON'T EVEN KNOW WHEN IT IS YET.
DO YOU EVEN HAVE BATTERIES IN THAT THING?
JUST GIMME!

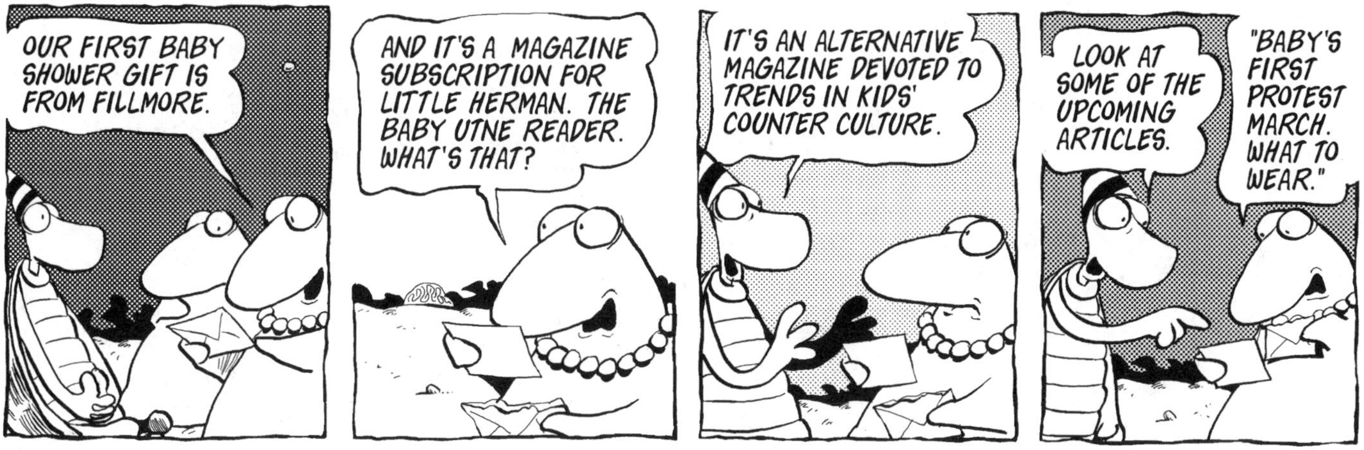
OUR FIRST BABY SHOWER GIFT IS FROM FILLMORE.
AND IT'S A MAGAZINE SUBSCRIPTION FOR LITTLE HERMAN. THE BABY UTNE READER. WHAT'S THAT?
IT'S AN ALTERNATIVE MAGAZINE DEVOTED TO TRENDS IN KIDS' COUNTER CULTURE.
LOOK AT SOME OF THE UPCOMING ARTICLES.
"BABY'S FIRST PROTEST MARCH. WHAT TO WEAR."

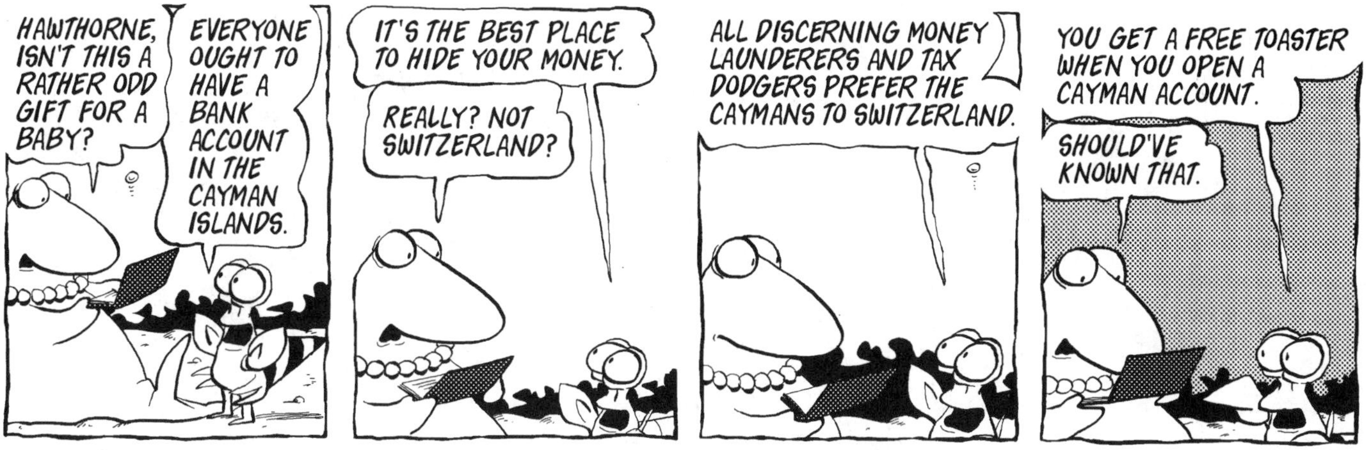
HAWTHORNE, ISN'T THIS A RATHER ODD GIFT FOR A BABY?
EVERYONE OUGHT TO HAVE A BANK ACCOUNT IN THE CAYMAN ISLANDS.
IT'S THE BEST PLACE TO HIDE YOUR MONEY.
REALLY? NOT SWITZERLAND?
ALL DISCERNING MONEY LAUNDERERS AND TAX DODGERS PREFER THE CAYMANS TO SWITZERLAND.
YOU GET A FREE TOASTER WHEN YOU OPEN A CAYMAN ACCOUNT.
SHOULD'VE KNOWN THAT.

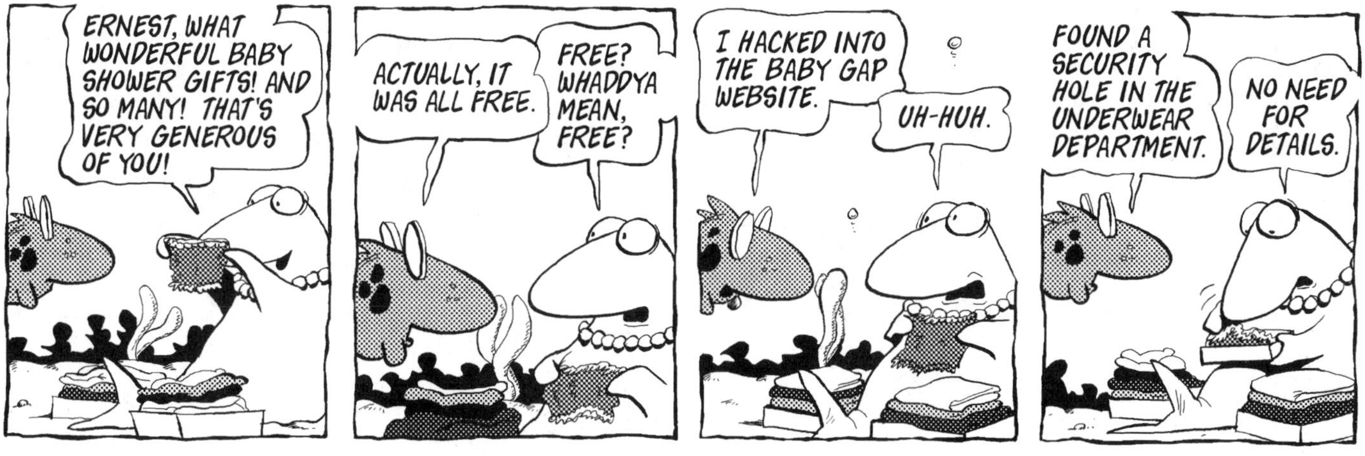
ERNEST, WHAT WONDERFUL BABY SHOWER GIFTS! AND SO MANY! THAT'S VERY GENEROUS OF YOU!
ACTUALLY, IT WAS ALL FREE.
FREE? WHADDYA MEAN, FREE?
I HACKED INTO THE BABY GAP WEBSITE.
UH-HUH.
FOUND A SECURITY HOLE IN THE UNDERWEAR DEPARTMENT.
NO NEED FOR DETAILS.

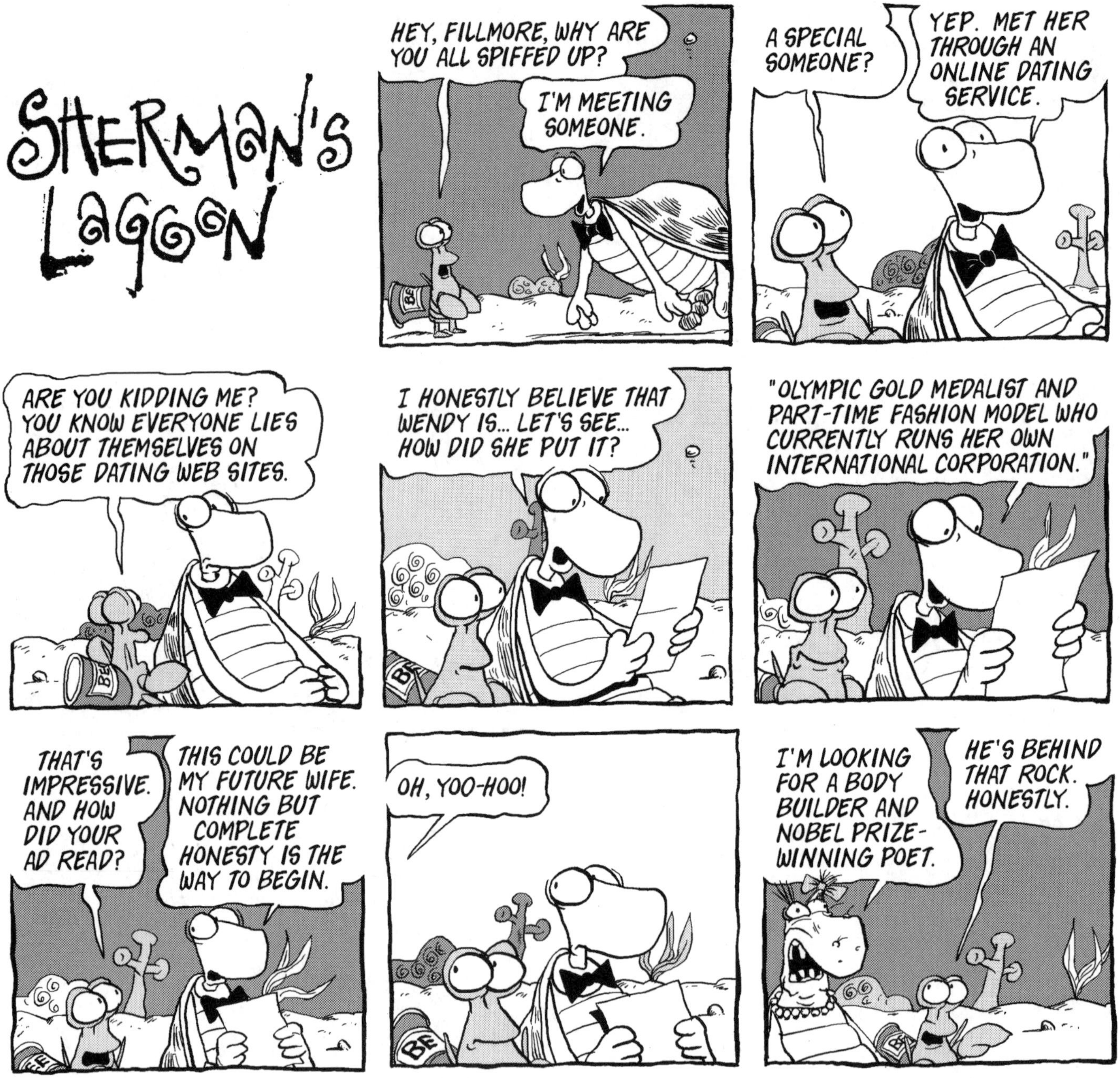
SHERMAN'S LAGOON
HEY, FILLMORE, WHY ARE YOU ALL SPIFFED UP?
I'M MEETING SOMEONE.
A SPECIAL SOMEONE?
YEP. MET HER THROUGH AN ONLINE DATING SERVICE.
ARE YOU KIDDING ME? YOU KNOW EVERYONE LIES ABOUT THEMSELVES ON THOSE DATING WEB SITES.
I HONESTLY BELIEVE THAT WENDY IS... LET'S SEE... HOW DID SHE PUT IT?
"OLYMPIC GOLD MEDALIST AND PART-TIME FASHION MODEL WHO CURRENTLY RUNS HER OWN INTERNATIONAL CORPORATION."
THAT'S IMPRESSIVE. AND HOW DID YOUR AD READ?
THIS COULD BE MY FUTURE WIFE. NOTHING BUT COMPLETE HONESTY IS THE WAY TO BEGIN.
OH, YOO-HOO!
I'M LOOKING FOR A BODY BUILDER AND NOBEL PRIZE-WINNING POET.
HE'S BEHIND THAT ROCK. HONESTLY.

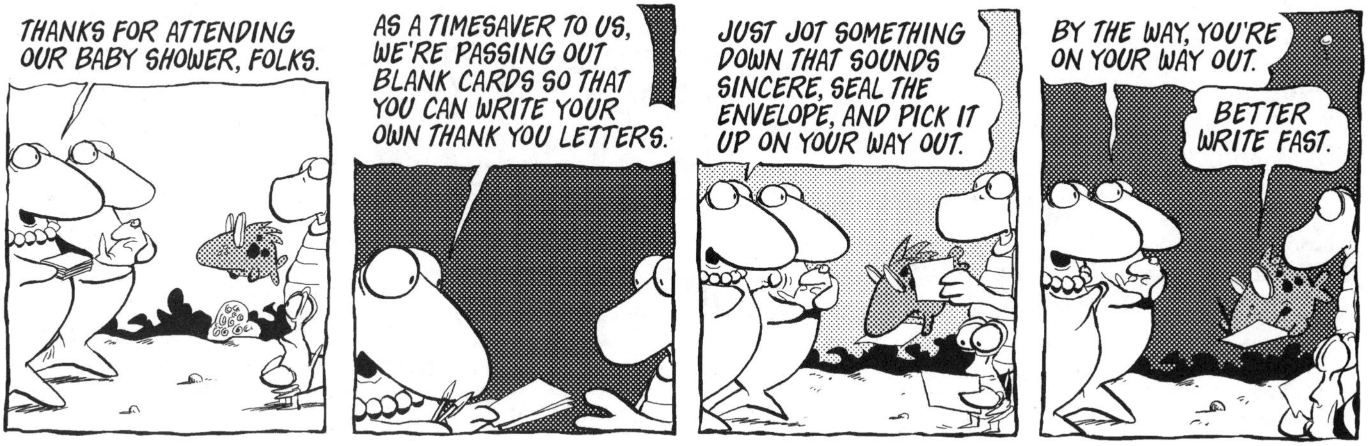
THANKS FOR ATTENDING OUR BABY SHOWER, FOLKS.
AS A TIMESAVER TO US, WE'RE PASSING OUT BLANK CARDS SO THAT YOU CAN WRITE YOUR OWN THANK YOU LETTERS.
JUST JOT SOMETHING DOWN THAT SOUNDS SINCERE, SEAL THE ENVELOPE, AND PICK IT UP ON YOUR WAY OUT.
BY THE WAY, YOU'RE ON YOUR WAY OUT.
BETTER WRITE FAST.

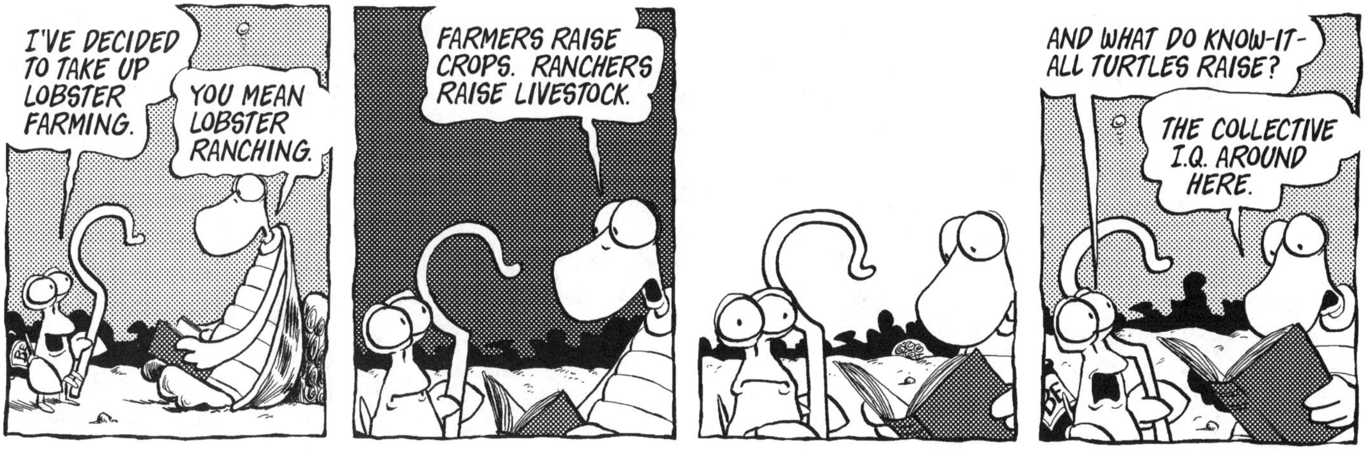
I'VE DECIDED TO TAKE UP LOBSTER FARMING.
YOU MEAN LOBSTER RANCHING.
FARMERS RAISE CROPS. RANCHERS RAISE LIVESTOCK.
AND WHAT DO KNOW-IT-ALL TURTLES RAISE?
THE COLLECTIVE I.Q. AROUND HERE.

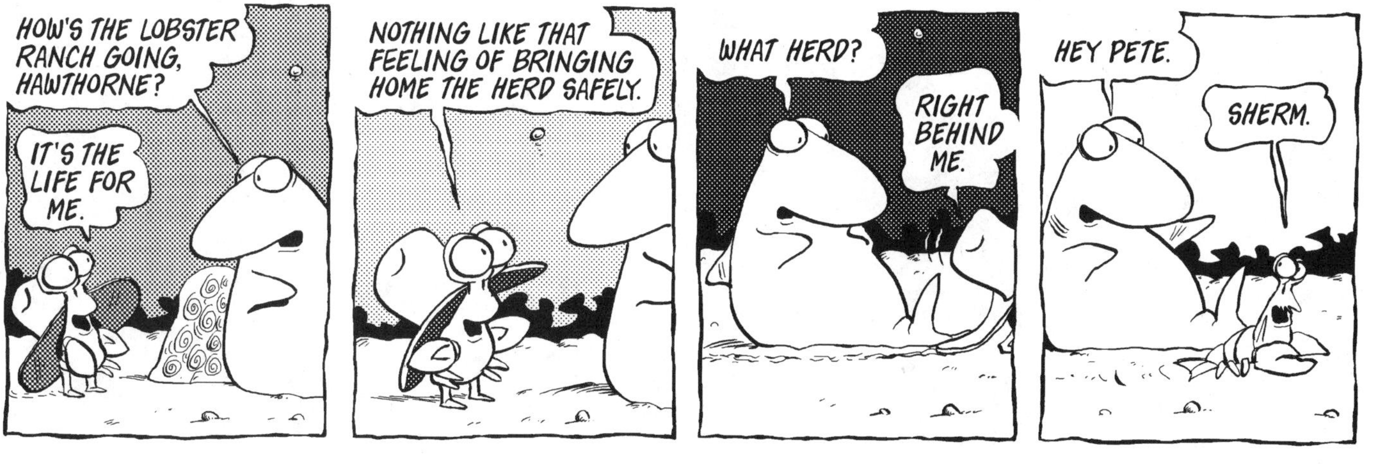
HOW'S THE LOBSTER RANCH GOING, HAWTHORNE?
IT'S THE LIFE FOR ME.
NOTHING LIKE THAT FEELING OF BRINGING HOME THE HERD SAFELY.
WHAT HERD?
RIGHT BEHIND ME.
HEY PETE.
SHERM.

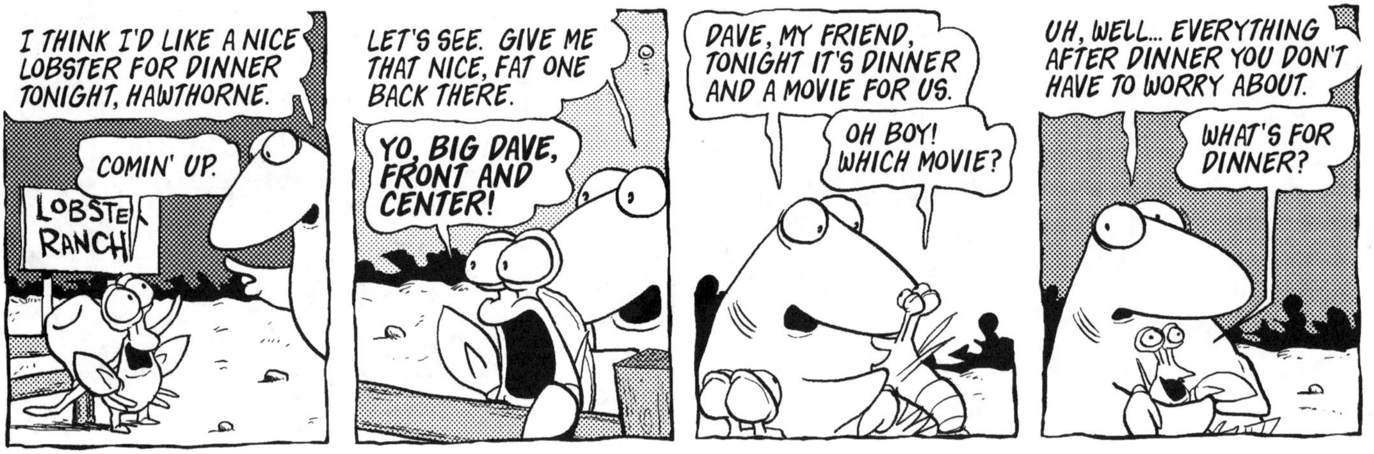
I THINK I'D LIKE A NICE LOBSTER FOR DINNER TONIGHT, HAWTHORNE.
COMIN' UP.
LOBSTER RANCH
LET'S SEE. GIVE ME THAT NICE, FAT ONE BACK THERE.
YO, BIG DAVE, FRONT AND CENTER!
DAVE, MY FRIEND, TONIGHT IT'S DINNER AND A MOVIE FOR US.
OH BOY! WHICH MOVIE?
UH, WELL... EVERYTHING AFTER DINNER YOU DON'T HAVE TO WORRY ABOUT.
WHAT'S FOR DINNER?

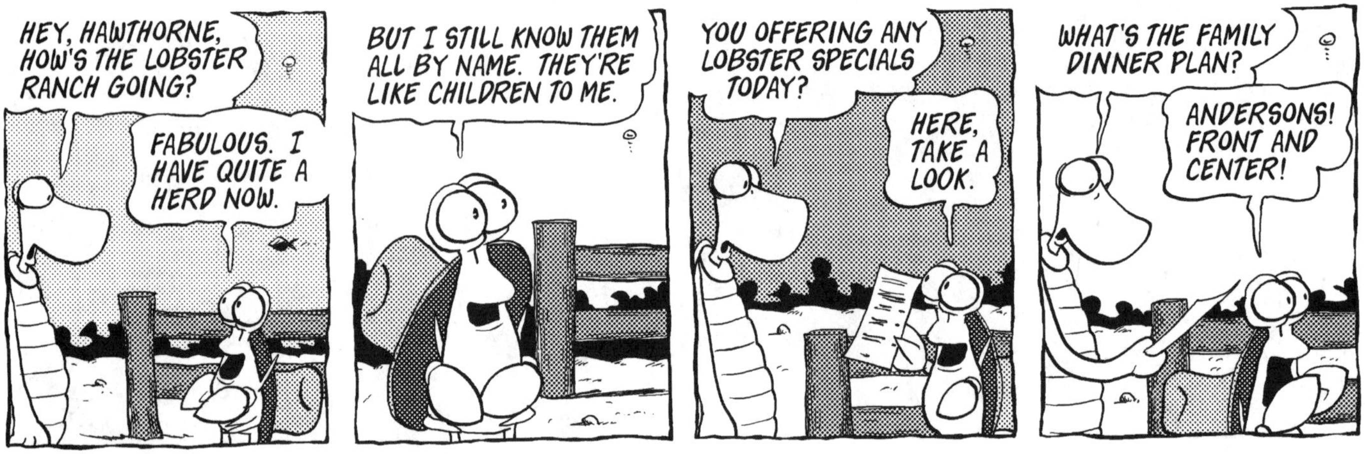
HEY, HAWTHORNE, HOW'S THE LOBSTER RANCH GOING?
FABULOUS. I HAVE QUITE A HERD NOW.
BUT I STILL KNOW THEM ALL BY NAME. THEY'RE LIKE CHILDREN TO ME.
YOU OFFERING ANY LOBSTER SPECIALS TODAY?
HERE, TAKE A LOOK.
WHAT'S THE FAMILY DINNER PLAN?
ANDERSONS! FRONT AND CENTER!

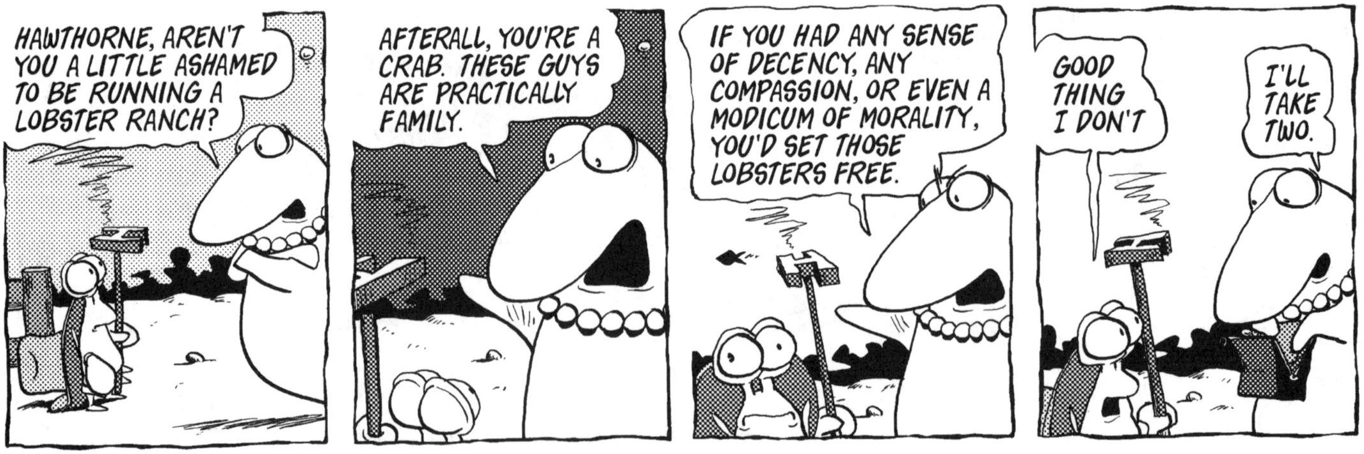
HAWTHORNE, AREN'T YOU A LITTLE ASHAMED TO BE RUNNING A LOBSTER RANCH?
AFTERALL, YOU'RE A CRAB. THESE GUYS ARE PRACTICALLY FAMILY.
IF YOU HAD ANY SENSE OF DECENCY, ANY COMPASSION, OR EVEN A MODICUM OF MORALITY, YOU'D SET THOSE LOBSTERS FREE.
GOOD THING I DON'T
I'LL TAKE TWO.

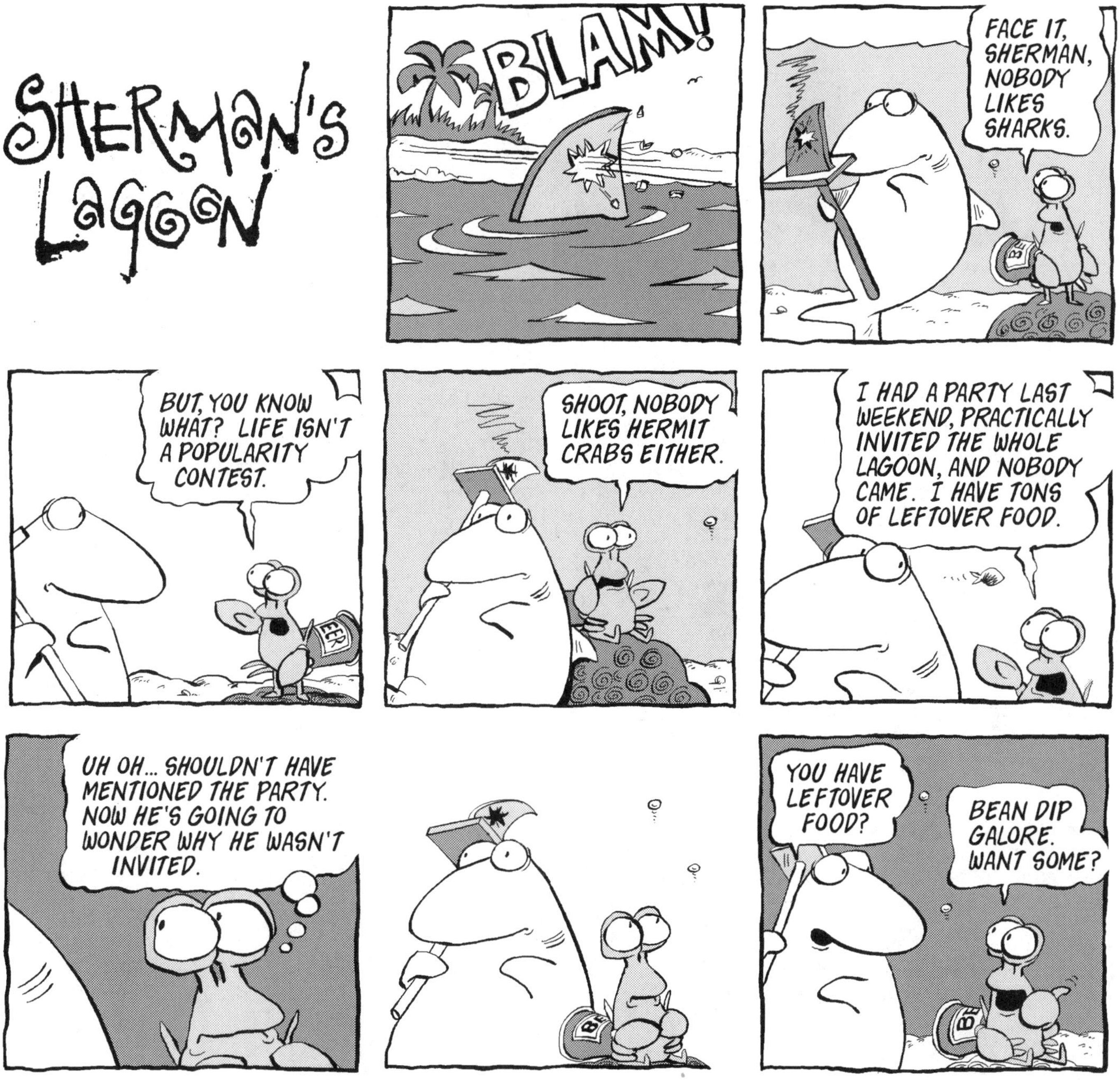
SHERMAN'S LAGOON
BLAM!
FACE IT, SHERMAN, NOBODY LIKES SHARKS.
BUT, YOU KNOW WHAT? LIFE ISN'T A POPULARITY CONTEST.
SHOOT, NOBODY LIKES HERMIT CRABS EITHER.
I HAD A PARTY LAST WEEKEND, PRACTICALLY INVITED THE WHOLE LAGOON, AND NOBODY CAME. I HAVE TONS OF LEFTOVER FOOD.
UH OH... SHOULDN'T HAVE MENTIONED THE PARTY. NOW HE'S GOING TO WONDER WHY HE WASN'T INVITED.
YOU HAVE LEFTOVER FOOD?
BEAN DIP GALORE. WANT SOME?

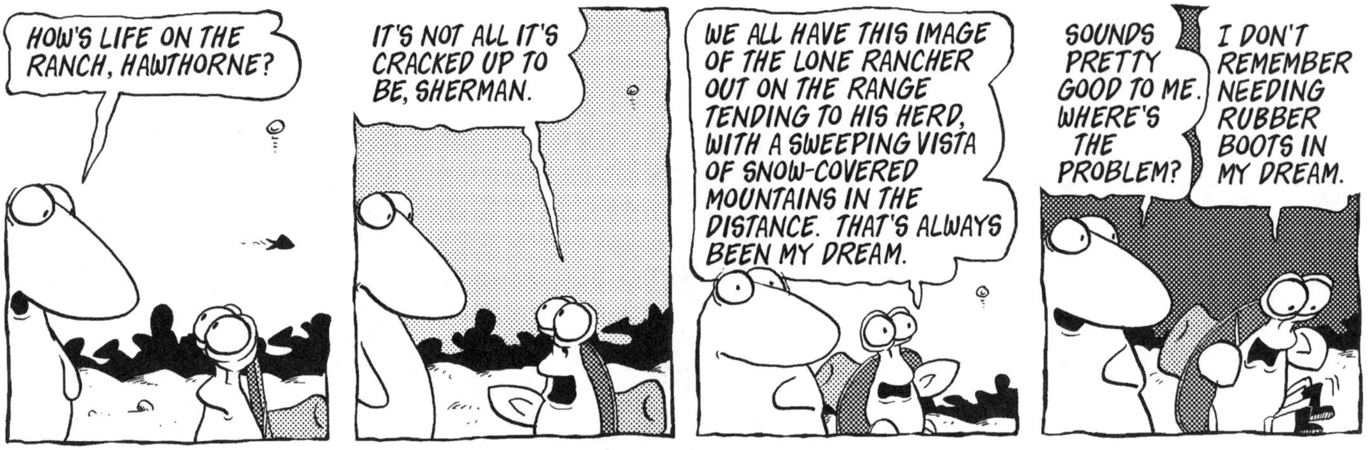
HOW'S LIFE ON THE RANCH, HAWTHORNE?
IT'S NOT ALL IT'S CRACKED UP TO BE, SHERMAN.
WE ALL HAVE THIS IMAGE OF THE LONE RANCHER OUT ON THE RANGE TENDING TO HIS HERD, WITH A SWEEPING VISTA OF SNOW-COVERED MOUNTAINS IN THE DISTANCE. THAT'S ALWAYS BEEN MY DREAM.
SOUNDS PRETTY GOOD TO ME. WHERE'S THE PROBLEM?
I DON'T REMEMBER NEEDING RUBBER BOOTS IN MY DREAM.

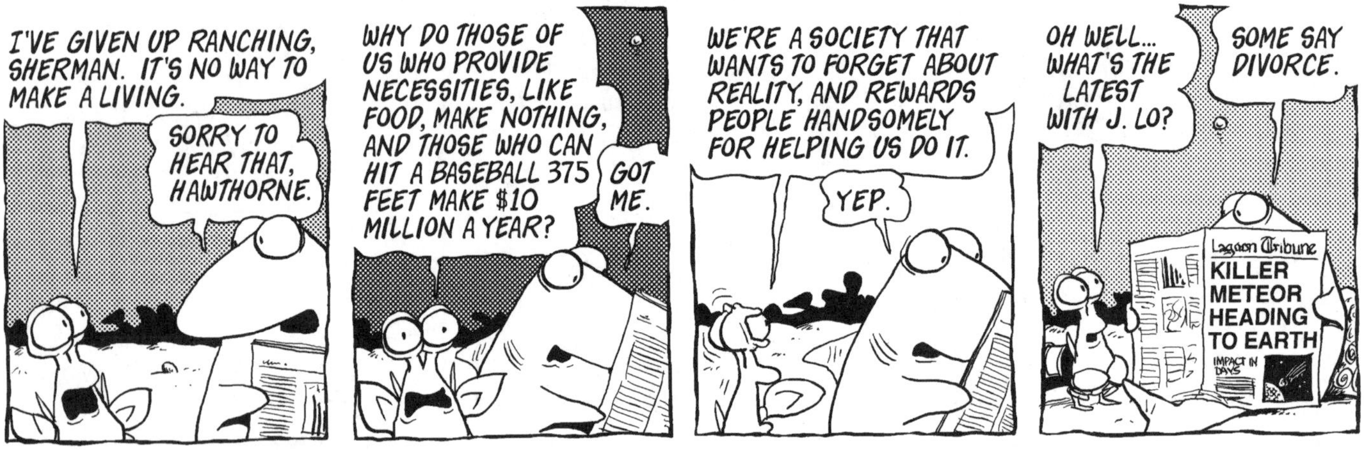
I'VE GIVEN UP RANCHING, SHERMAN. IT'S NO WAY TO MAKE A LIVING.
SORRY TO HEAR THAT, HAWTHORNE.
WHY DO THOSE OF US WHO PROVIDE NECESSITIES, LIKE FOOD, MAKE NOTHING, AND THOSE WHO CAN HIT A BASEBALL 375 FEET MAKE $10 MILLION A YEAR?
GOT ME.
WE'RE A SOCIETY THAT WANTS TO FORGET ABOUT REALITY, AND REWARDS PEOPLE HANDSOMELY FOR HELPING US DO IT.
YEP.
OH WELL... WHAT'S THE LATEST WITH J. LO?
SOME SAY DIVORCE.
Lagoon Tribune
KILLER METEOR HEADING TO EARTH
IMPACT IN DAYS

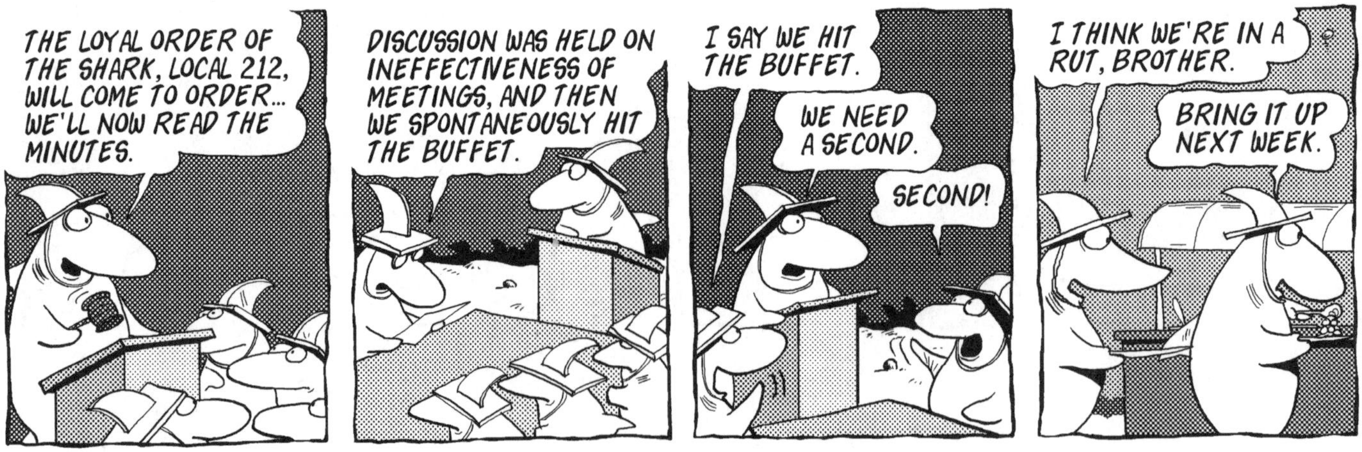
THE LOYAL ORDER OF THE SHARK, LOCAL 212, WILL COME TO ORDER... WE'LL NOW READ THE MINUTES.
DISCUSSION WAS HELD ON INEFFECTIVENESS OF MEETINGS, AND THEN WE SPONTANEOUSLY HIT THE BUFFET.
I SAY WE HIT THE BUFFET.
WE NEED A SECOND.
SECOND!
I THINK WE'RE IN A RUT, BROTHER.
BRING IT UP NEXT WEEK.

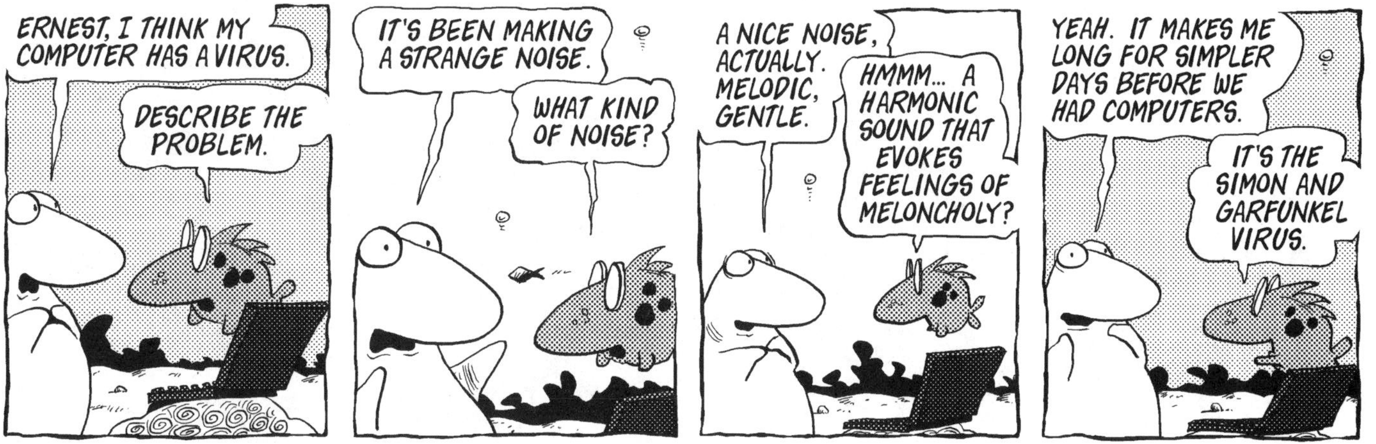
ERNEST, I THINK MY COMPUTER HAS A VIRUS.
DESCRIBE THE PROBLEM.
IT'S BEEN MAKING A STRANGE NOISE.
WHAT KIND OF NOISE?
A NICE NOISE, ACTUALLY. MELODIC, GENTLE.
HMMM... A HARMONIC SOUND THAT EVOKES FEELINGS OF MELONCHOLY?
YEAH. IT MAKES ME LONG FOR SIMPLER DAYS BEFORE WE HAD COMPUTERS.
IT'S THE SIMON AND GARFUNKEL VIRUS.

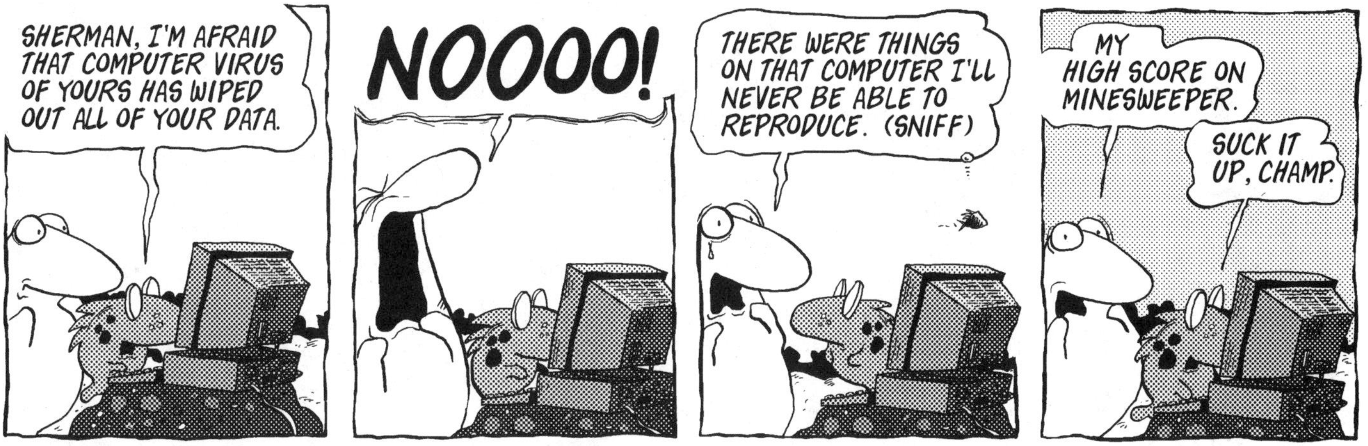
SHERMAN, I'M AFRAID THAT COMPUTER VIRUS OF YOURS HAS WIPED OUT ALL OF YOUR DATA.
NOOOO!
THERE WERE THINGS ON THAT COMPUTER I'LL NEVER BE ABLE TO REPRODUCE. (SNIFF)
MY HIGH SCORE ON MINESWEEPER.
SUCK IT UP, CHAMP.

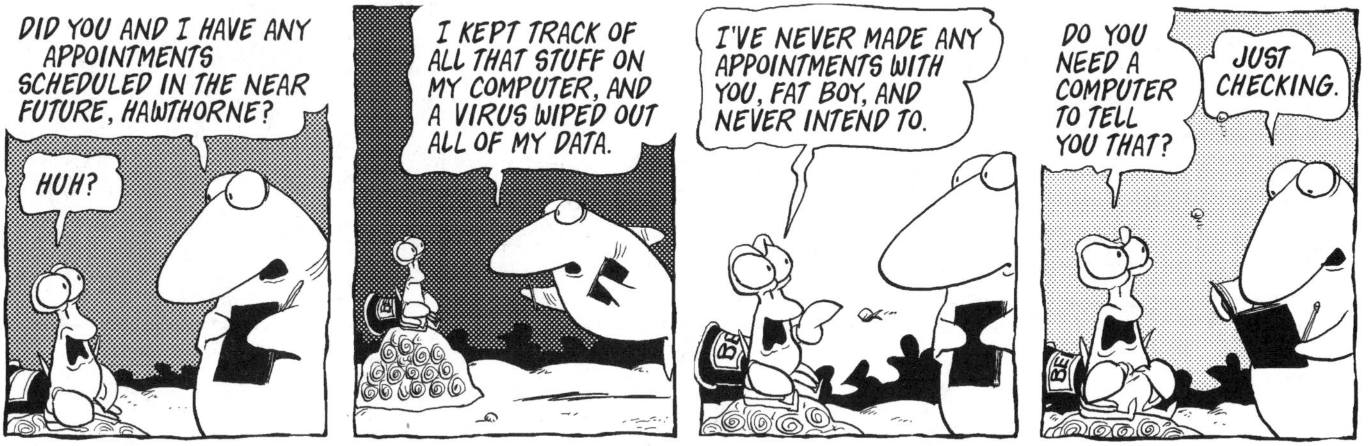
DID YOU AND I HAVE ANY APPOINTMENTS SCHEDULED IN THE NEAR FUTURE, HAWTHORNE?
HUH?
I KEPT TRACK OF ALL THAT STUFF ON MY COMPUTER, AND A VIRUS WIPED OUT ALL OF MY DATA.
I'VE NEVER MADE ANY APPOINTMENTS WITH YOU, FAT BOY, AND NEVER INTEND TO.
DO YOU NEED A COMPUTER TO TELL YOU THAT?
JUST CHECKING.

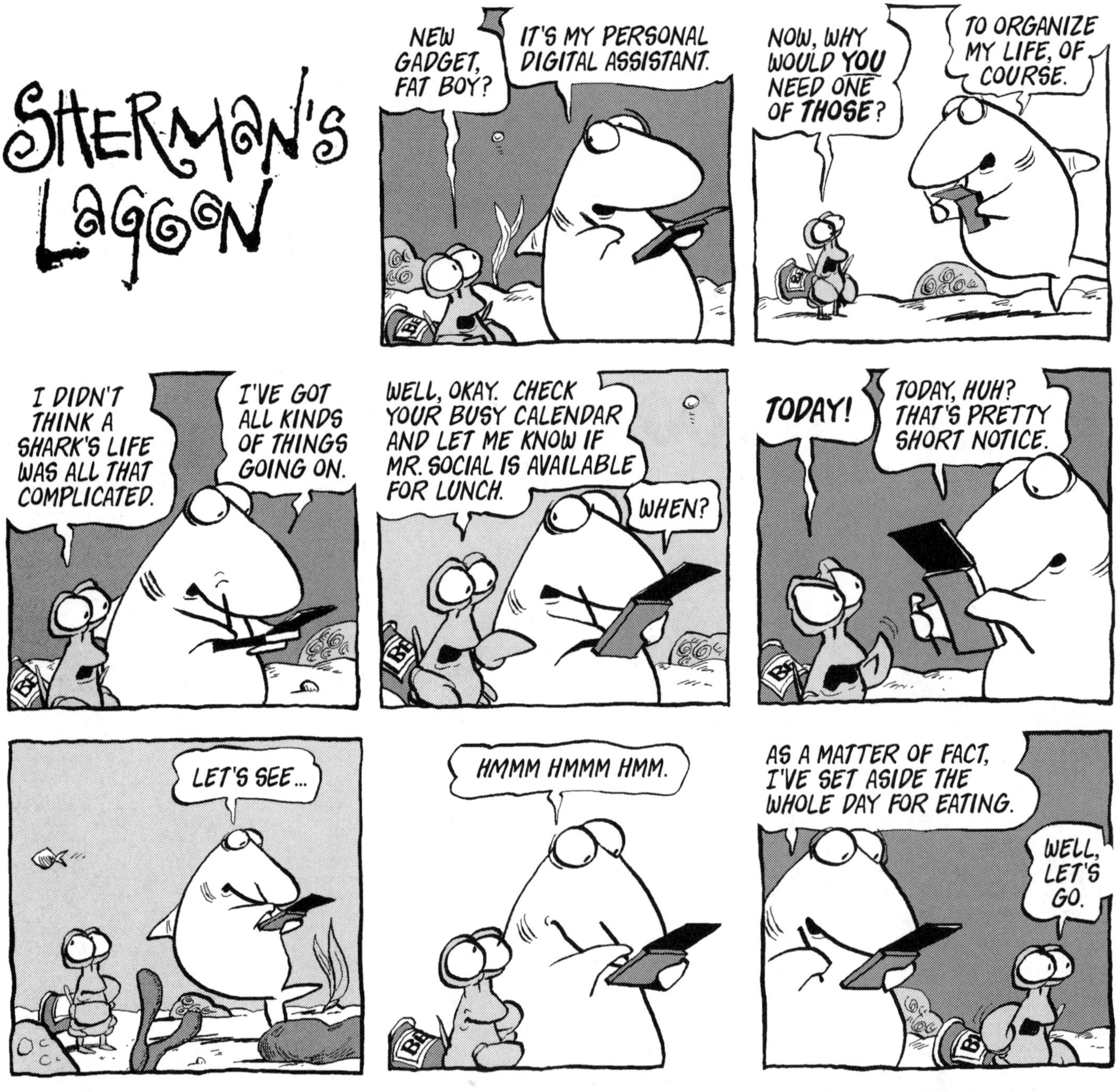
SHERMAN'S LAGOON
NEW GADGET, FAT BOY?
IT'S MY PERSONAL DIGITAL ASSISTANT.
NOW, WHY WOULD YOU NEED ONE OF THOSE?
TO ORGANIZE MY LIFE, OF COURSE.
I DIDN'T THINK A SHARK'S LIFE WAS ALL THAT COMPLICATED.
I'VE GOT ALL KINDS OF THINGS GOING ON.
WELL, OKAY. CHECK YOUR BUSY CALENDAR AND LET ME KNOW IF MR. SOCIAL IS AVAILABLE FOR LUNCH.
WHEN?
TODAY!
TODAY, HUH? THAT'S PRETTY SHORT NOTICE.
LET'S SEE...
HMMM HMMM HMM.
AS A MATTER OF FACT, I'VE SET ASIDE THE WHOLE DAY FOR EATING.
WELL, LET'S GO.

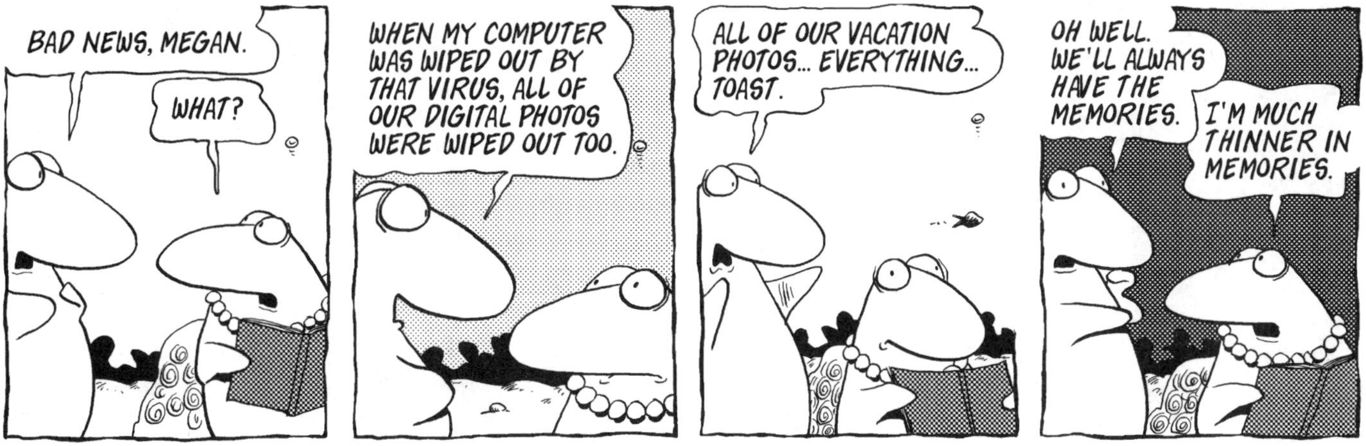
BAD NEWS, MEGAN.
WHAT?
WHEN MY COMPUTER WAS WIPED OUT BY THAT VIRUS, ALL OF OUR DIGITAL PHOTOS WERE WIPED OUT TOO.
ALL OF OUR VACATION PHOTOS... EVERYTHING... TOAST.
OH WELL. WE'LL ALWAYS HAVE THE MEMORIES.
I'M MUCH THINNER IN MEMORIES.

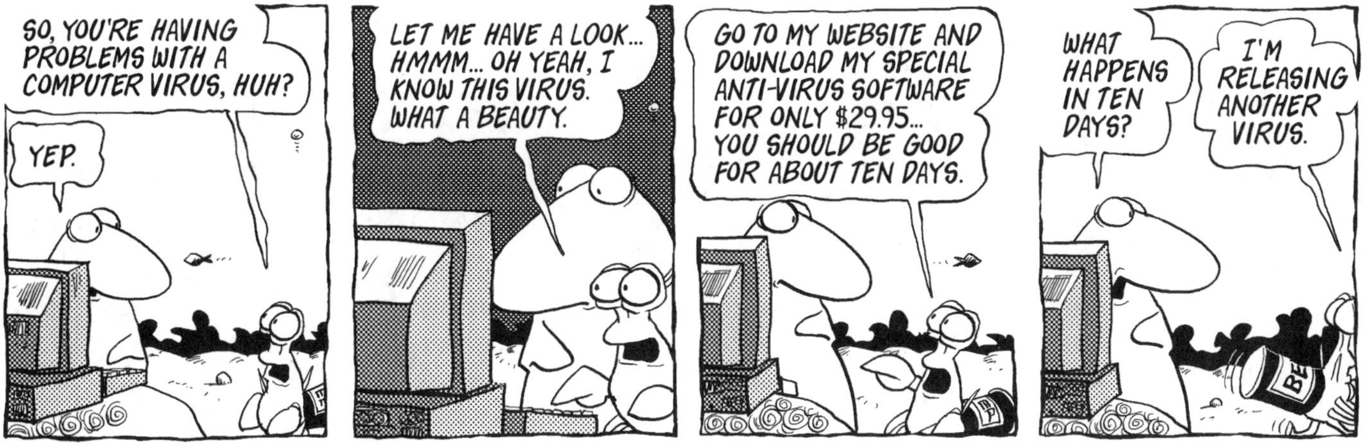
SO, YOU'RE HAVING PROBLEMS WITH A COMPUTER VIRUS, HUH?
YEP.
LET ME HAVE A LOOK... HMMM... OH YEAH, I KNOW THIS VIRUS. WHAT A BEAUTY.
GO TO MY WEBSITE AND DOWNLOAD MY SPECIAL ANTI-VIRUS SOFTWARE FOR ONLY $29.95... YOU SHOULD BE GOOD FOR ABOUT TEN DAYS.
WHAT HAPPENS IN TEN DAYS?
I'M RELEASING ANOTHER VIRUS.

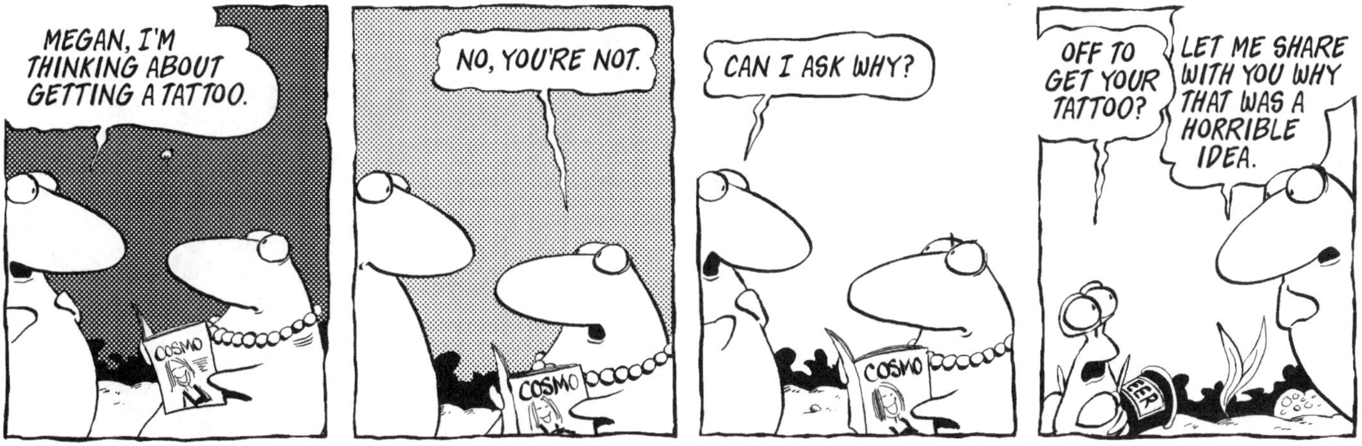
MEGAN, I'M THINKING ABOUT GETTING A TATTOO.
COSMO
NO, YOU'RE NOT.
COSMO
CAN I ASK WHY?
COSMO
OFF TO GET YOUR TATTOO?
LET ME SHARE WITH YOU WHY THAT WAS A HORRIBLE IDEA.

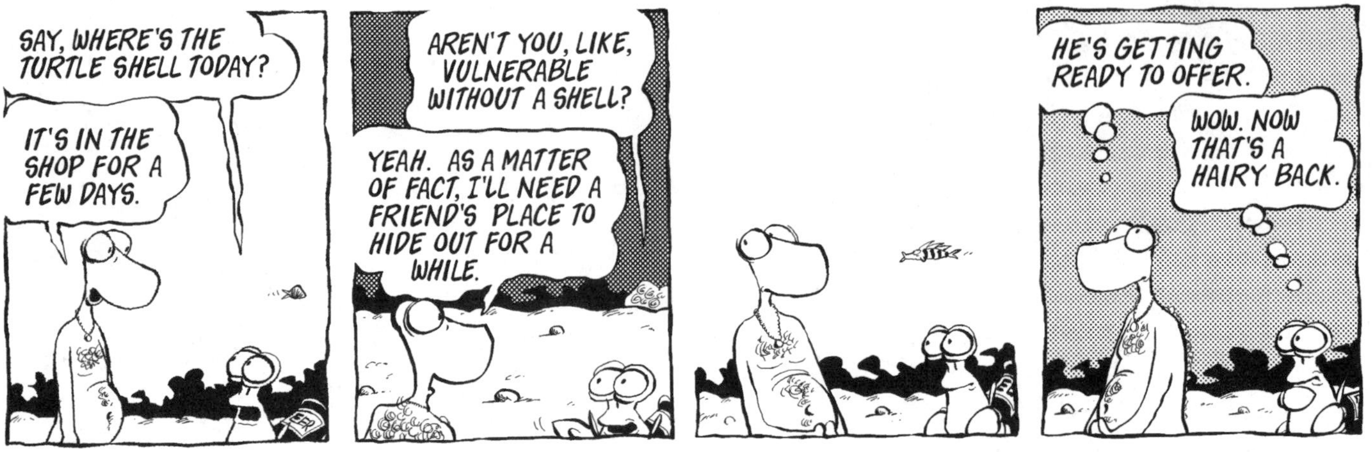
SAY, WHERE'S THE TURTLE SHELL TODAY?
IT'S IN THE SHOP FOR A FEW DAYS.
AREN'T YOU, LIKE, VULNERABLE WITHOUT A SHELL?
YEAH. AS A MATTER OF FACT, I'LL NEED A FRIEND'S PLACE TO HIDE OUT FOR A WHILE.
HE'S GETTING READY TO OFFER.
WOW. NOW THAT'S A HAIRY BACK.

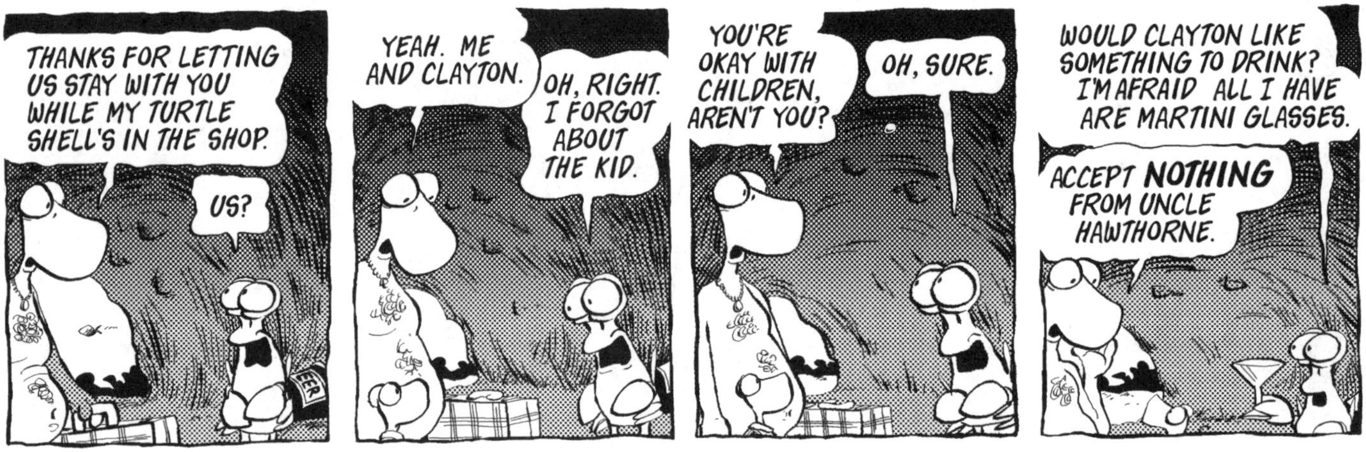
THANKS FOR LETTING US STAY WITH YOU WHILE MY TURTLE SHELL'S IN THE SHOP.
US?
YEAH. ME AND CLAYTON.
OH, RIGHT. I FORGOT ABOUT THE KID.
YOU'RE OKAY WITH CHILDREN, AREN'T YOU?
OH, SURE.
WOULD CLAYTON LIKE SOMETHING TO DRINK? I'M AFRAID ALL I HAVE ARE MARTINI GLASSES.
ACCEPT **NOTHING** FROM UNCLE HAWTHORNE.

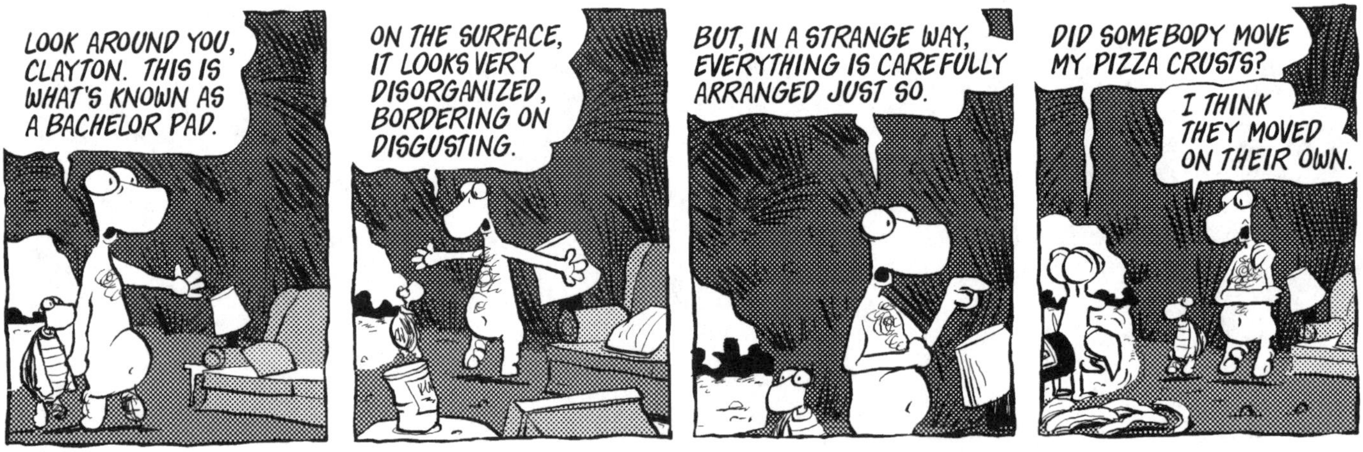
LOOK AROUND YOU, CLAYTON. THIS IS WHAT'S KNOWN AS A BACHELOR PAD.
ON THE SURFACE, IT LOOKS VERY DISORGANIZED, BORDERING ON DISGUSTING.
BUT, IN A STRANGE WAY, EVERYTHING IS CAREFULLY ARRANGED JUST SO.
DID SOMEBODY MOVE MY PIZZA CRUSTS?
I THINK THEY MOVED ON THEIR OWN.

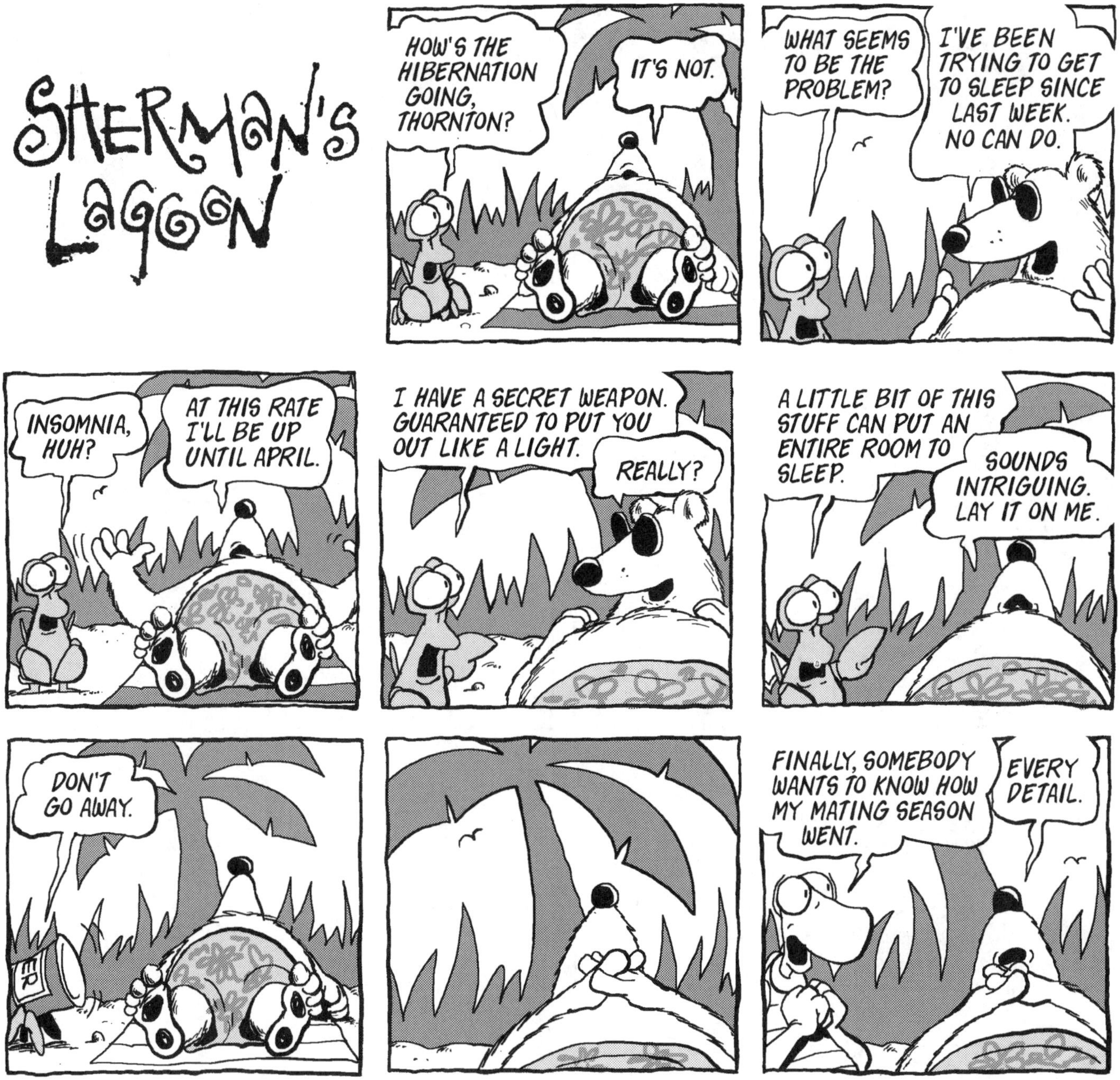
SHERMAN'S LAGOON
HOW'S THE HIBERNATION GOING, THORNTON?
IT'S NOT.
WHAT SEEMS TO BE THE PROBLEM?
I'VE BEEN TRYING TO GET TO SLEEP SINCE LAST WEEK. NO CAN DO.
INSOMNIA, HUH?
AT THIS RATE I'LL BE UP UNTIL APRIL.
I HAVE A SECRET WEAPON. GUARANTEED TO PUT YOU OUT LIKE A LIGHT.
REALLY?
A LITTLE BIT OF THIS STUFF CAN PUT AN ENTIRE ROOM TO SLEEP.
SOUNDS INTRIGUING. LAY IT ON ME.
DON'T GO AWAY.
FINALLY, SOMEBODY WANTS TO KNOW HOW MY MATING SEASON WENT.
EVERY DETAIL.

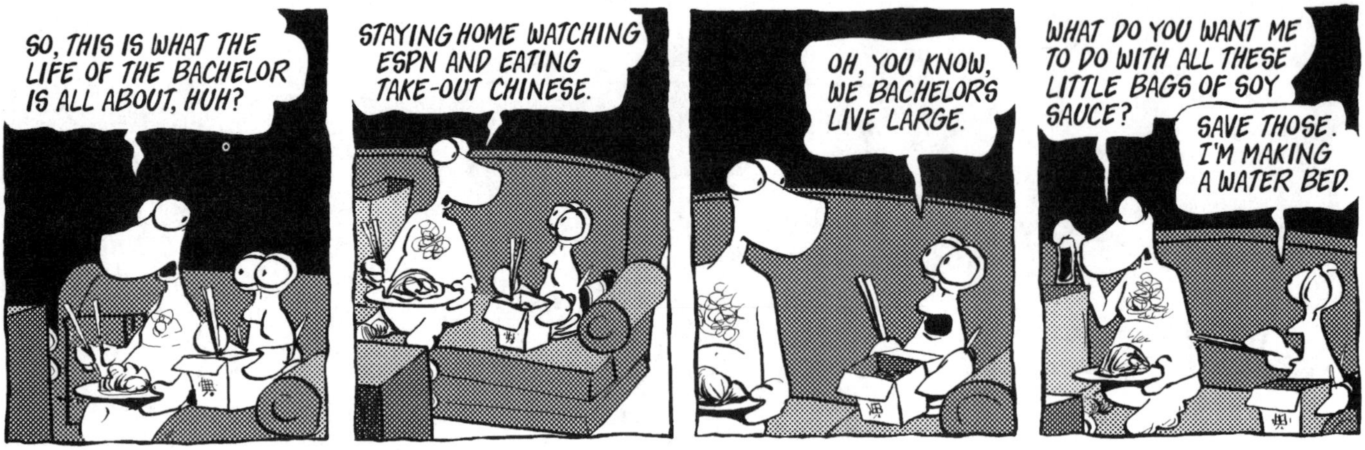
SO, THIS IS WHAT THE LIFE OF THE BACHELOR IS ALL ABOUT, HUH?
STAYING HOME WATCHING ESPN AND EATING TAKE-OUT CHINESE.
OH, YOU KNOW, WE BACHELORS LIVE LARGE.
WHAT DO YOU WANT ME TO DO WITH ALL THESE LITTLE BAGS OF SOY SAUCE?
SAVE THOSE. I'M MAKING A WATER BED.

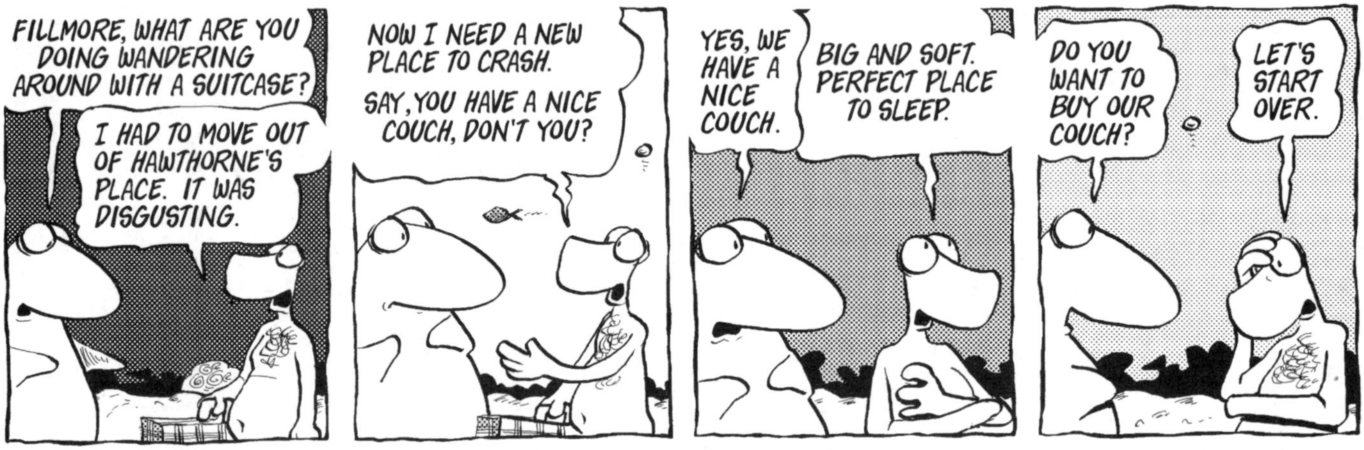
FILLMORE, WHAT ARE YOU DOING WANDERING AROUND WITH A SUITCASE?
I HAD TO MOVE OUT OF HAWTHORNE'S PLACE. IT WAS DISGUSTING.
NOW I NEED A NEW PLACE TO CRASH.
SAY, YOU HAVE A NICE COUCH, DON'T YOU?
YES, WE HAVE A NICE COUCH.
BIG AND SOFT. PERFECT PLACE TO SLEEP.
DO YOU WANT TO BUY OUR COUCH?
LET'S START OVER.

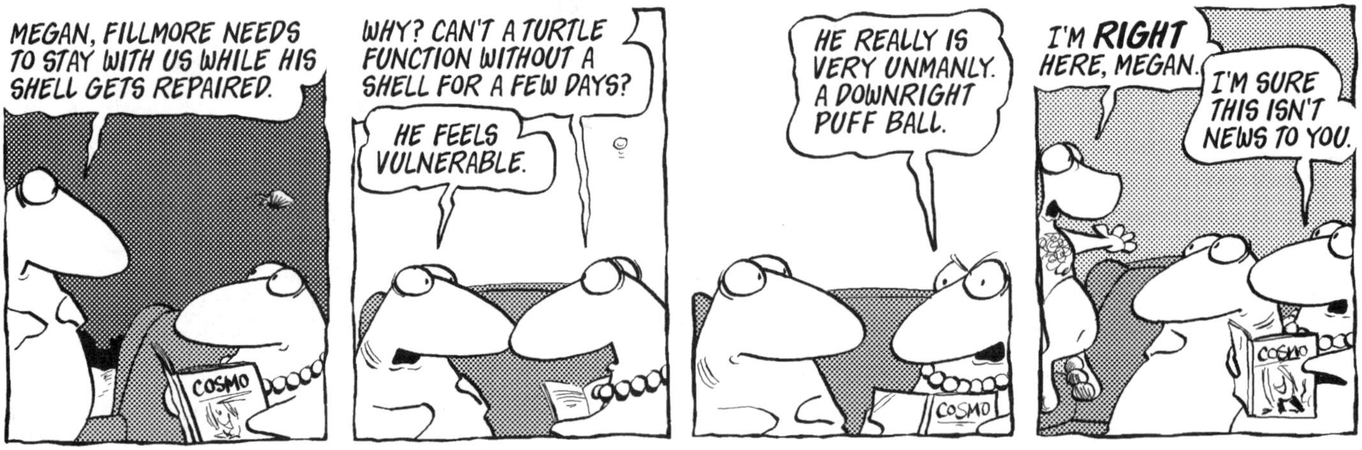
MEGAN, FILLMORE NEEDS TO STAY WITH US WHILE HIS SHELL GETS REPAIRED.
COSMO
WHY? CAN'T A TURTLE FUNCTION WITHOUT A SHELL FOR A FEW DAYS?
HE FEELS VULNERABLE.
HE REALLY IS VERY UNMANLY. A DOWNRIGHT PUFF BALL.
COSMO
I'M **RIGHT** HERE, MEGAN.
I'M SURE THIS ISN'T NEWS TO YOU.
COSMO

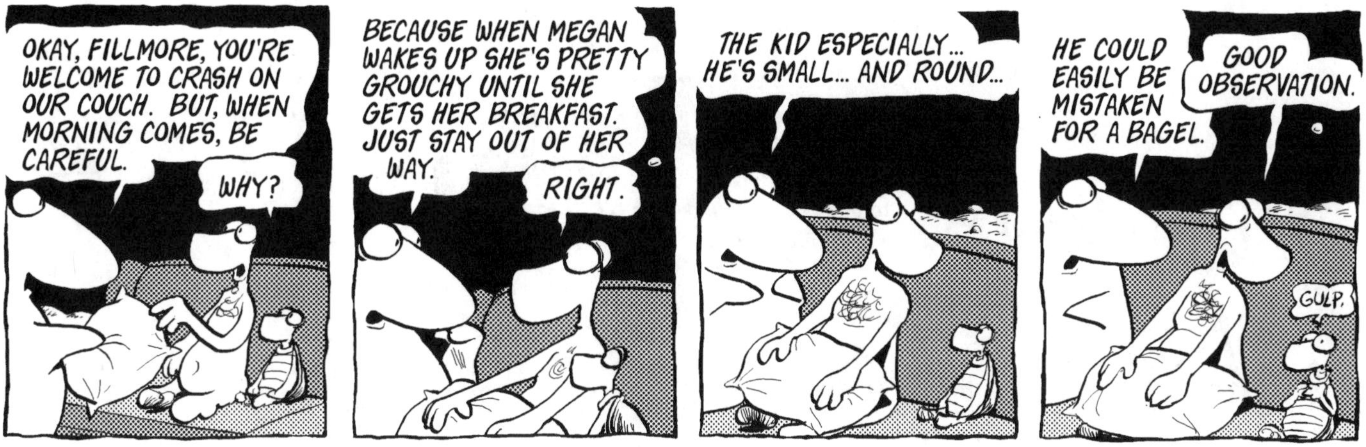
OKAY, FILLMORE, YOU'RE WELCOME TO CRASH ON OUR COUCH. BUT, WHEN MORNING COMES, BE CAREFUL.
WHY?
BECAUSE WHEN MEGAN WAKES UP SHE'S PRETTY GROUCHY UNTIL SHE GETS HER BREAKFAST. JUST STAY OUT OF HER WAY.
RIGHT.
THE KID ESPECIALLY... HE'S SMALL... AND ROUND...
HE COULD EASILY BE MISTAKEN FOR A BAGEL.
GOOD OBSERVATION.
GULP.

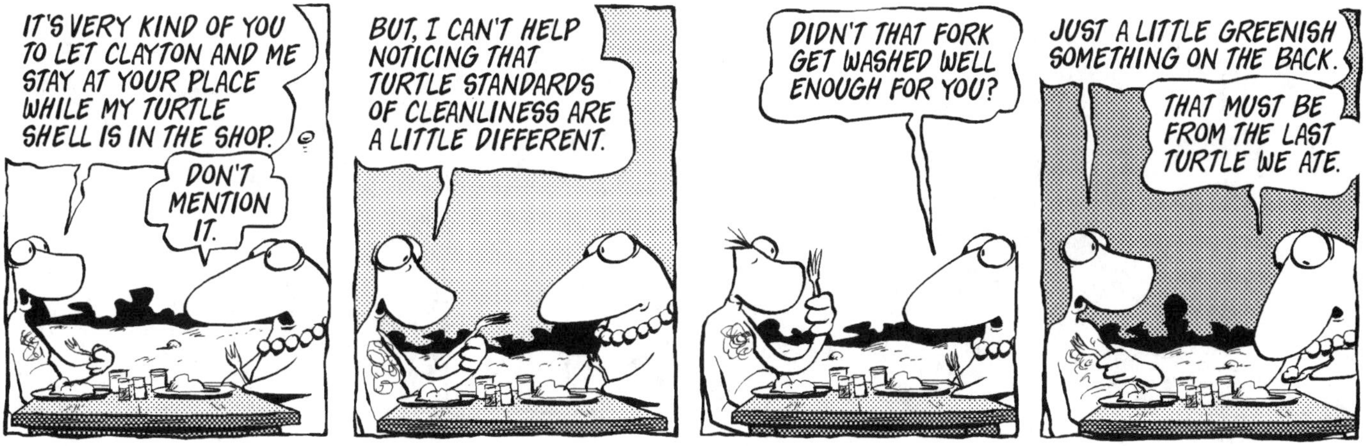
IT'S VERY KIND OF YOU TO LET CLAYTON AND ME STAY AT YOUR PLACE WHILE MY TURTLE SHELL IS IN THE SHOP.
DON'T MENTION IT.
BUT, I CAN'T HELP NOTICING THAT TURTLE STANDARDS OF CLEANLINESS ARE A LITTLE DIFFERENT.
DIDN'T THAT FORK GET WASHED WELL ENOUGH FOR YOU?
JUST A LITTLE GREENISH SOMETHING ON THE BACK.
THAT MUST BE FROM THE LAST TURTLE WE ATE.

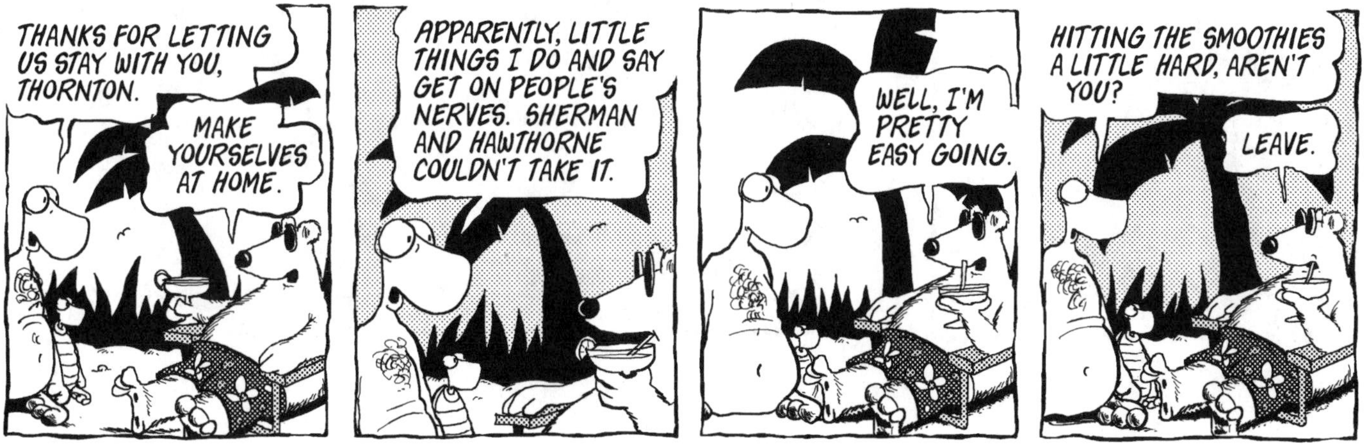
THANKS FOR LETTING US STAY WITH YOU, THORNTON.
MAKE YOURSELVES AT HOME.
APPARENTLY, LITTLE THINGS I DO AND SAY GET ON PEOPLE'S NERVES. SHERMAN AND HAWTHORNE COULDN'T TAKE IT.
WELL, I'M PRETTY EASY GOING.
HITTING THE SMOOTHIES A LITTLE HARD, AREN'T YOU?
LEAVE.

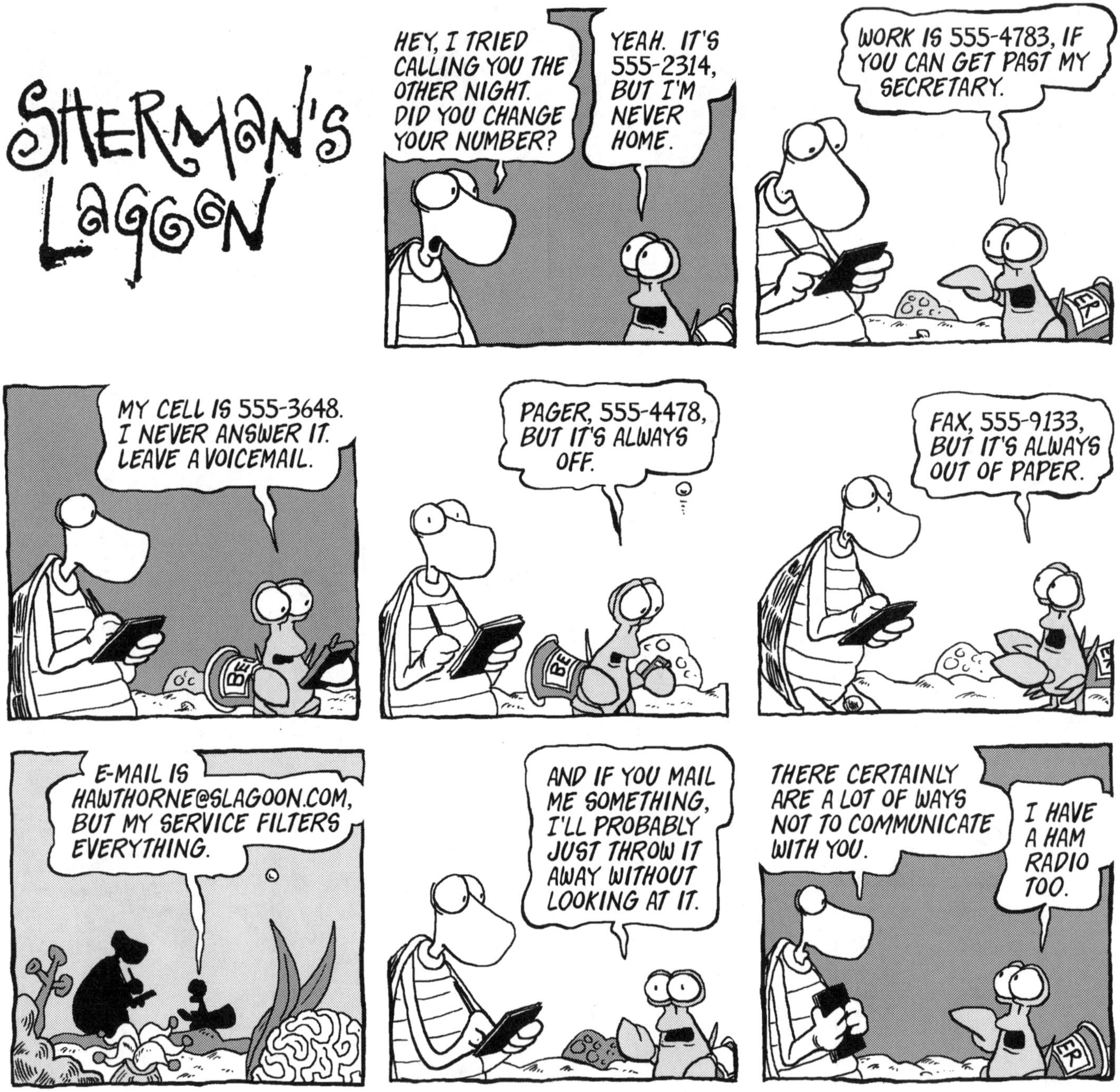
SHERMAN'S LAGOON
HEY, I TRIED CALLING YOU THE OTHER NIGHT. DID YOU CHANGE YOUR NUMBER?
YEAH. IT'S 555-2314, BUT I'M NEVER HOME.
WORK IS 555-4783, IF YOU CAN GET PAST MY SECRETARY.
MY CELL IS 555-3648. I NEVER ANSWER IT. LEAVE A VOICEMAIL.
PAGER, 555-4478, BUT IT'S ALWAYS OFF.
FAX, 555-9133, BUT IT'S ALWAYS OUT OF PAPER.
E-MAIL IS HAWTHORNE@SLAGOON.COM, BUT MY SERVICE FILTERS EVERYTHING.
AND IF YOU MAIL ME SOMETHING, I'LL PROBABLY JUST THROW IT AWAY WITHOUT LOOKING AT IT.
THERE CERTAINLY ARE A LOT OF WAYS NOT TO COMMUNICATE WITH YOU.
I HAVE A HAM RADIO TOO.

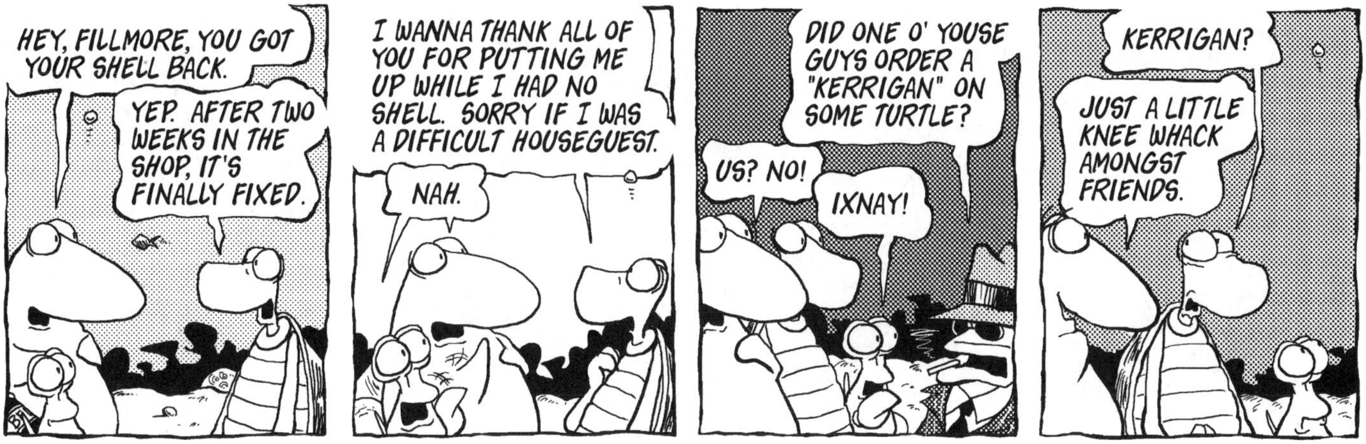
HEY, FILLMORE, YOU GOT YOUR SHELL BACK.
YEP. AFTER TWO WEEKS IN THE SHOP, IT'S FINALLY FIXED.
I WANNA THANK ALL OF YOU FOR PUTTING ME UP WHILE I HAD NO SHELL. SORRY IF I WAS A DIFFICULT HOUSEGUEST.
NAH.
DID ONE O' YOUSE GUYS ORDER A "KERRIGAN" ON SOME TURTLE?
US? NO!
IXNAY!
KERRIGAN?
JUST A LITTLE KNEE WHACK AMONGST FRIENDS.

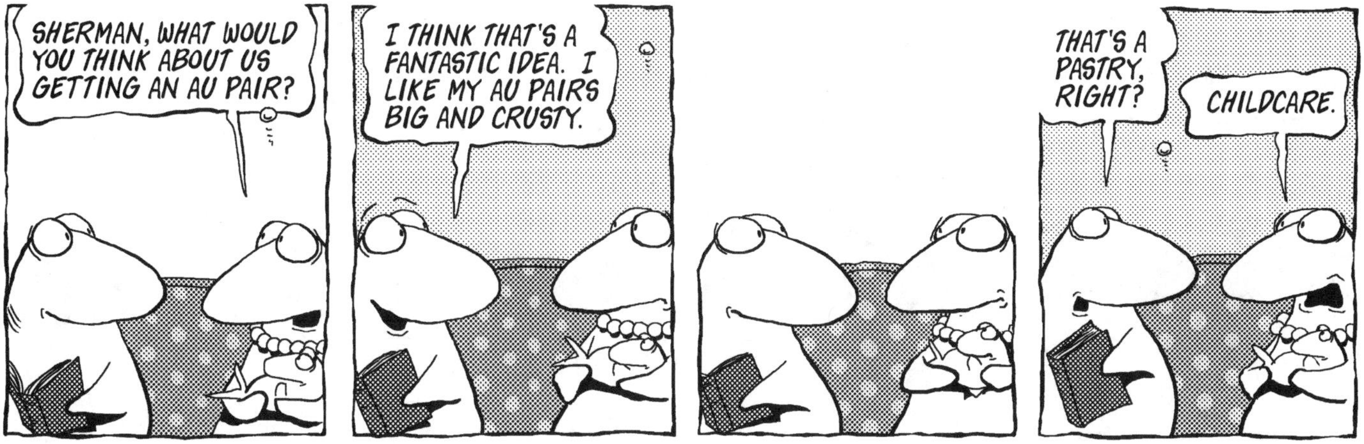
SHERMAN, WHAT WOULD YOU THINK ABOUT US GETTING AN AU PAIR?
I THINK THAT'S A FANTASTIC IDEA. I LIKE MY AU PAIRS BIG AND CRUSTY.
THAT'S A PASTRY, RIGHT?
CHILDCARE.

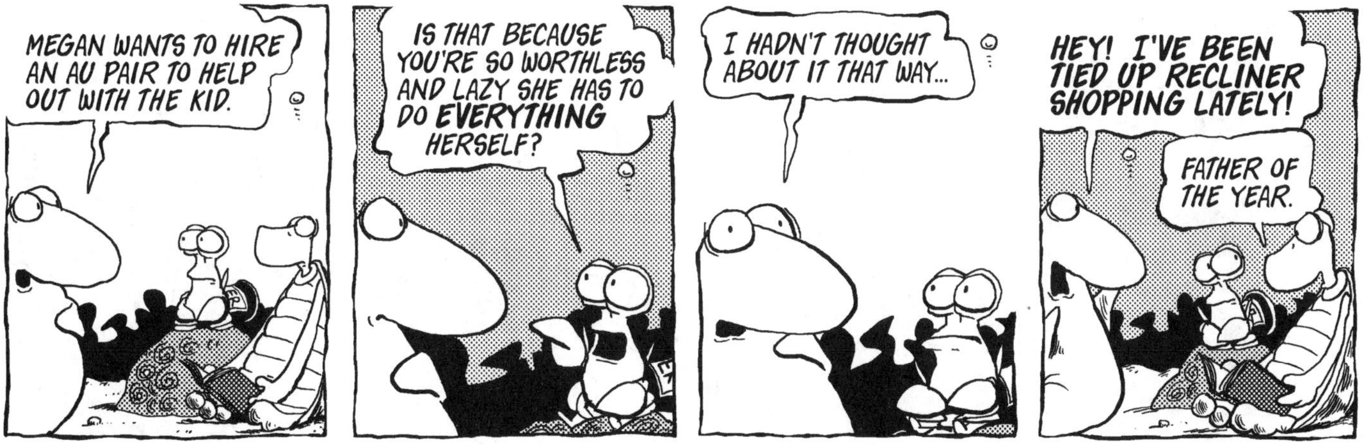
MEGAN WANTS TO HIRE AN AU PAIR TO HELP OUT WITH THE KID.
IS THAT BECAUSE YOU'RE SO WORTHLESS AND LAZY SHE HAS TO DO EVERYTHING HERSELF?
I HADN'T THOUGHT ABOUT IT THAT WAY...
HEY! I'VE BEEN TIED UP RECLINER SHOPPING LATELY!
FATHER OF THE YEAR.

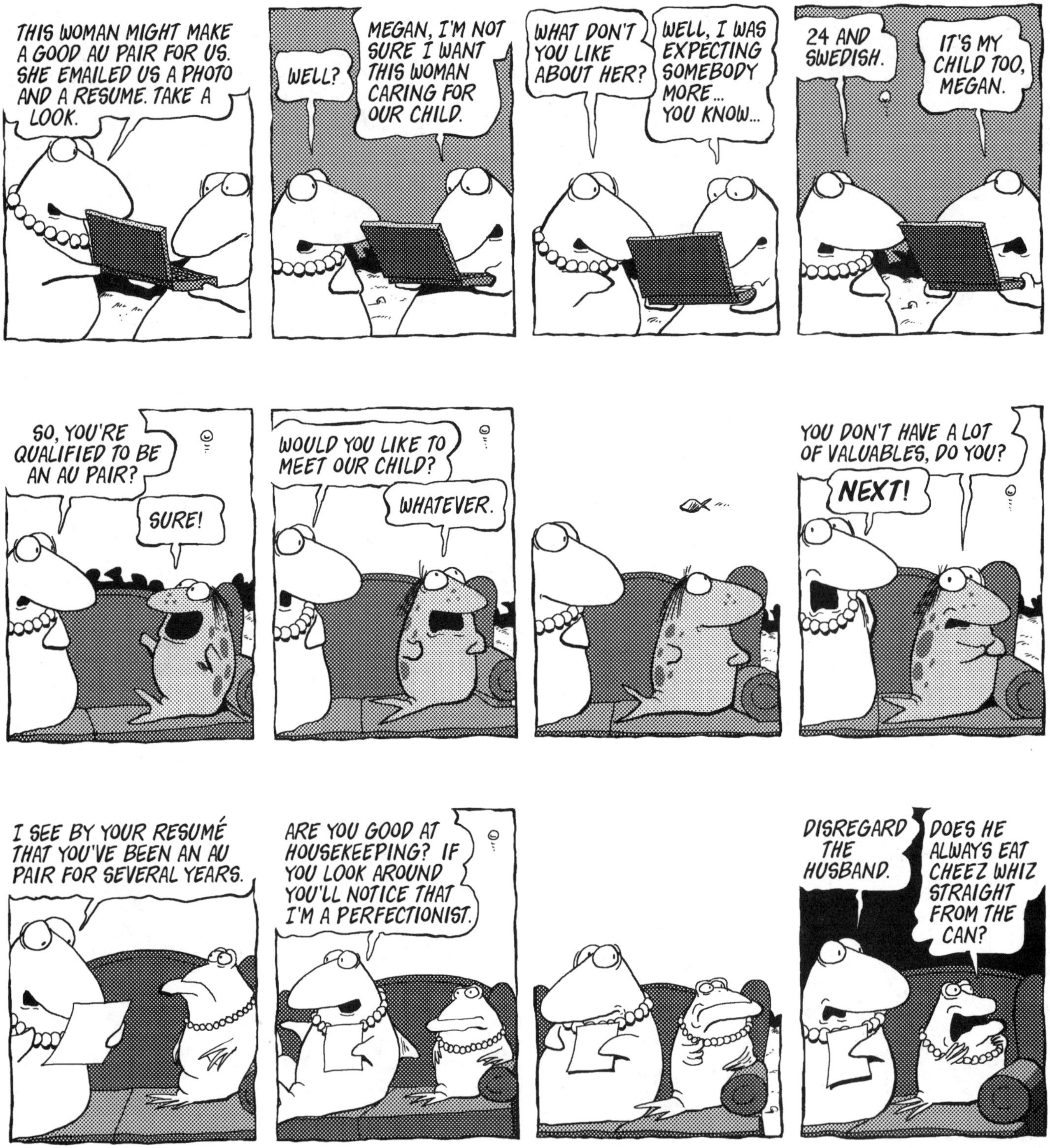
THIS WOMAN MIGHT MAKE A GOOD AU PAIR FOR US. SHE EMAILED US A PHOTO AND A RESUME. TAKE A LOOK.
WELL?
MEGAN, I'M NOT SURE I WANT THIS WOMAN CARING FOR OUR CHILD.
WHAT DON'T YOU LIKE ABOUT HER?
WELL, I WAS EXPECTING SOMEBODY MORE... YOU KNOW...
24 AND SWEDISH.
IT'S MY CHILD TOO, MEGAN.
SO, YOU'RE QUALIFIED TO BE AN AU PAIR?
SURE!
WOULD YOU LIKE TO MEET OUR CHILD?
WHATEVER.
YOU DON'T HAVE A LOT OF VALUABLES, DO YOU?
NEXT!
I SEE BY YOUR RESUMÉ THAT YOU'VE BEEN AN AU PAIR FOR SEVERAL YEARS.
ARE YOU GOOD AT HOUSEKEEPING? IF YOU LOOK AROUND YOU'LL NOTICE THAT I'M A PERFECTIONIST.
DISREGARD THE HUSBAND.
DOES HE ALWAYS EAT CHEEZ WHIZ STRAIGHT FROM THE CAN?

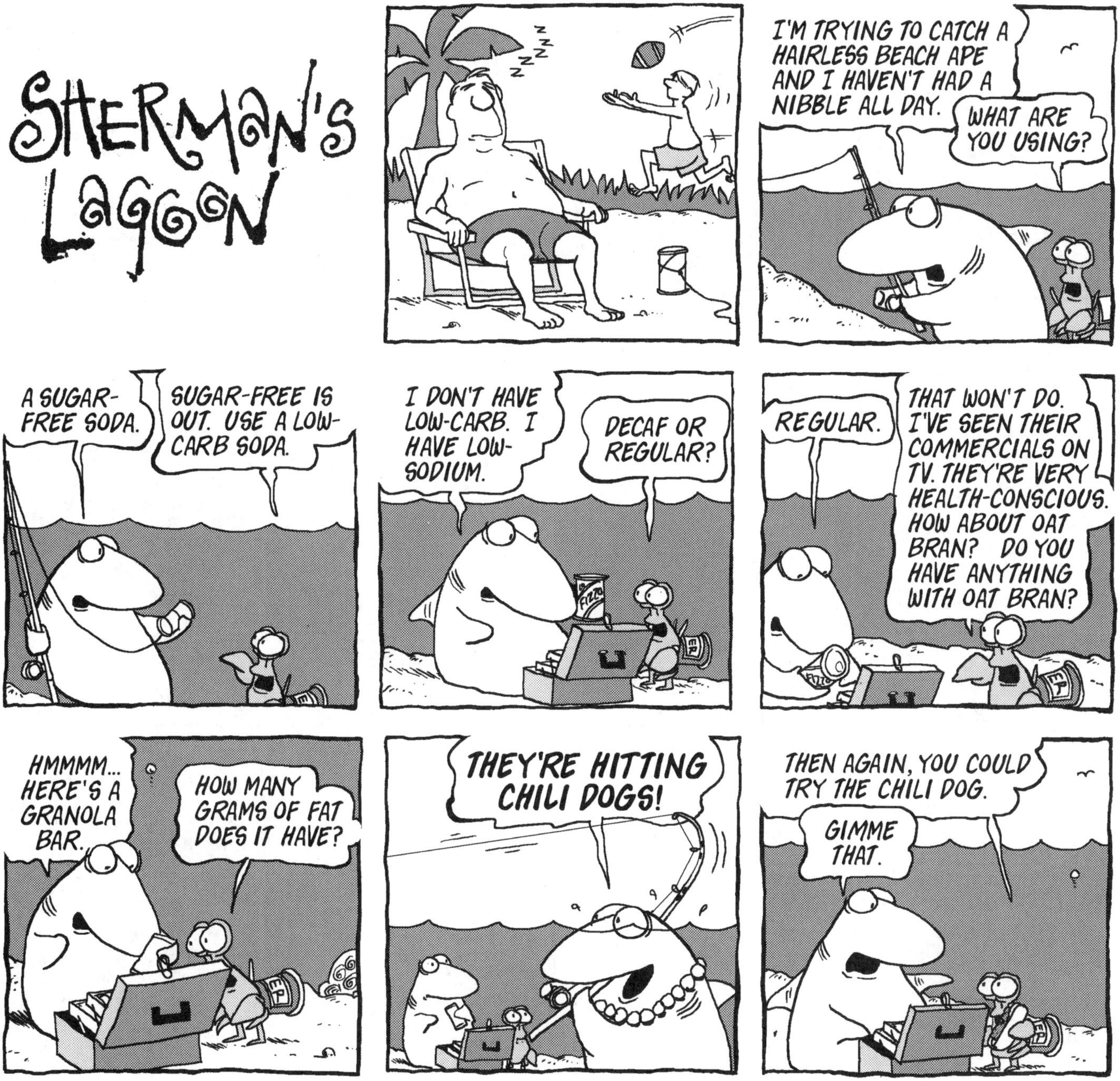
SHERMAN'S LAGOON
I'M TRYING TO CATCH A HAIRLESS BEACH APE AND I HAVEN'T HAD A NIBBLE ALL DAY.
WHAT ARE YOU USING?
A SUGAR-FREE SODA.
SUGAR-FREE IS OUT. USE A LOW-CARB SODA.
I DON'T HAVE LOW-CARB. I HAVE LOW-SODIUM.
DECAF OR REGULAR?
REGULAR.
THAT WON'T DO. I'VE SEEN THEIR COMMERCIALS ON TV. THEY'RE VERY HEALTH-CONSCIOUS. HOW ABOUT OAT BRAN? DO YOU HAVE ANYTHING WITH OAT BRAN?
HMMMM... HERE'S A GRANOLA BAR.
HOW MANY GRAMS OF FAT DOES IT HAVE?
THEY'RE HITTING CHILI DOGS!
THEN AGAIN, YOU COULD TRY THE CHILI DOG.
GIMME THAT.

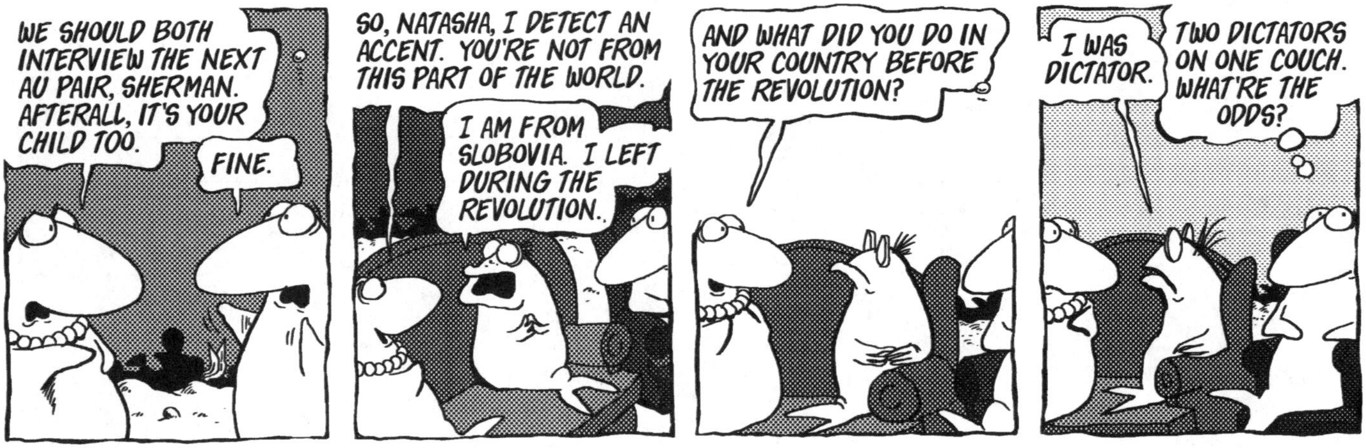
WE SHOULD BOTH INTERVIEW THE NEXT AU PAIR, SHERMAN. AFTERALL, IT'S YOUR CHILD TOO.
FINE.
SO, NATASHA, I DETECT AN ACCENT. YOU'RE NOT FROM THIS PART OF THE WORLD.
I AM FROM SLOBOVIA. I LEFT DURING THE REVOLUTION.
AND WHAT DID YOU DO IN YOUR COUNTRY BEFORE THE REVOLUTION?
I WAS DICTATOR.
TWO DICTATORS ON ONE COUCH. WHAT'RE THE ODDS?

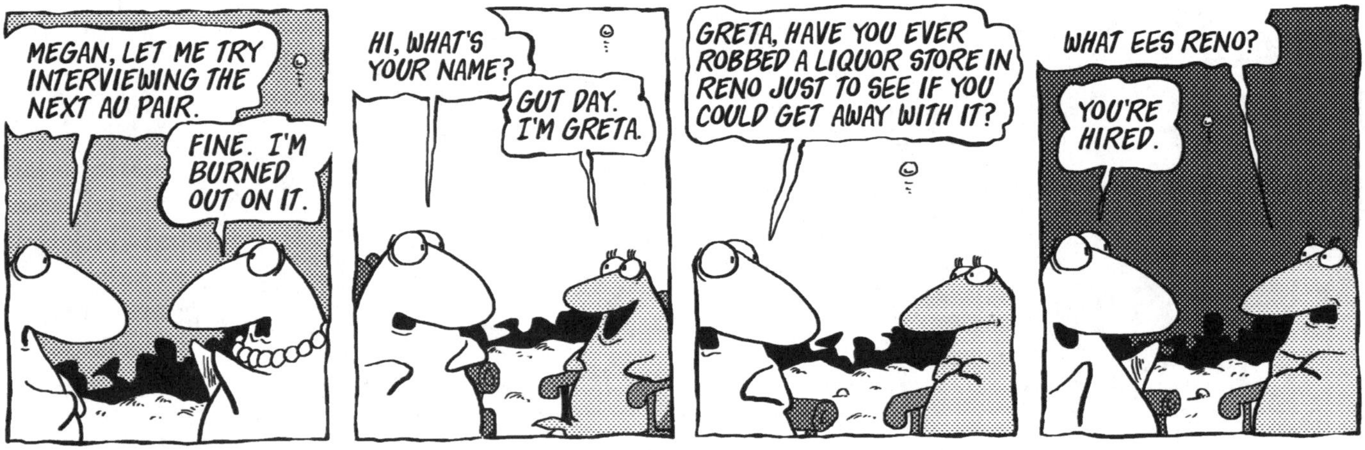
MEGAN, LET ME TRY INTERVIEWING THE NEXT AU PAIR.
FINE. I'M BURNED OUT ON IT.
HI, WHAT'S YOUR NAME?
GUT DAY. I'M GRETA.
GRETA, HAVE YOU EVER ROBBED A LIQUOR STORE IN RENO JUST TO SEE IF YOU COULD GET AWAY WITH IT?
WHAT EES RENO?
YOU'RE HIRED.

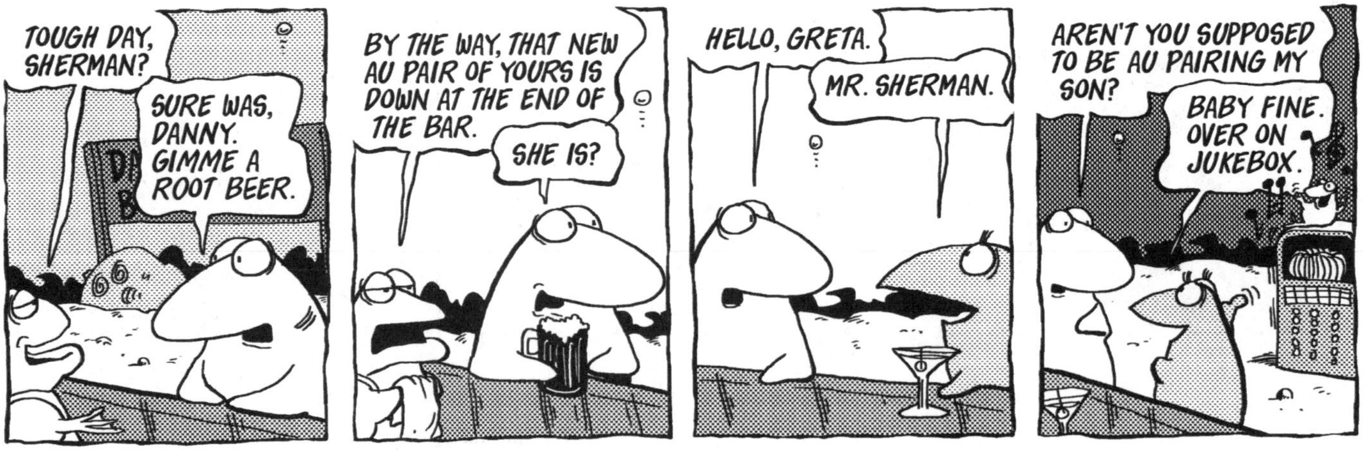
TOUGH DAY, SHERMAN?
SURE WAS, DANNY. GIMME A ROOT BEER.
BY THE WAY, THAT NEW AU PAIR OF YOURS IS DOWN AT THE END OF THE BAR.
SHE IS?
HELLO, GRETA.
MR. SHERMAN.
AREN'T YOU SUPPOSED TO BE AU PAIRING MY SON?
BABY FINE. OVER ON JUKEBOX.

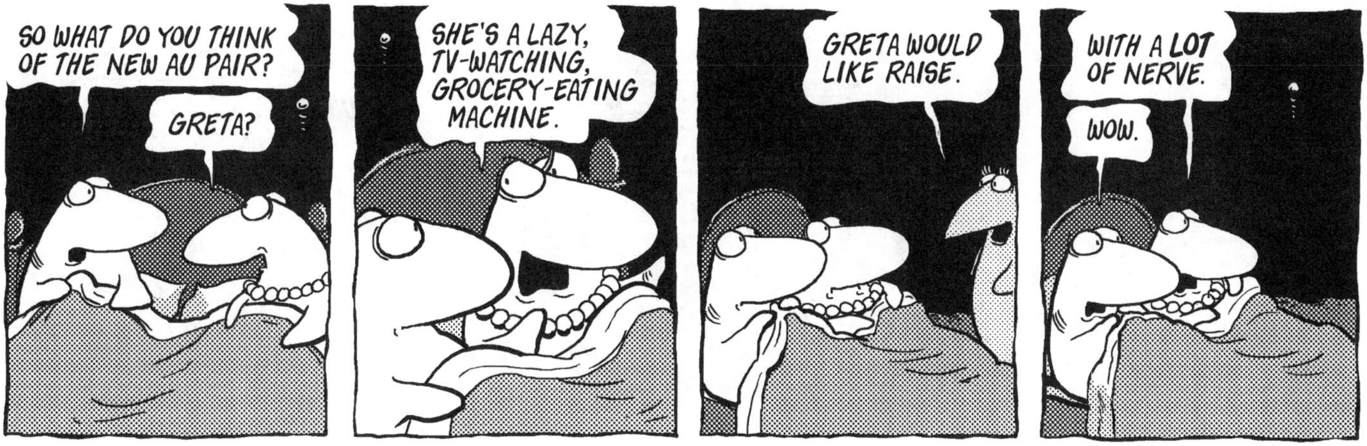
SO WHAT DO YOU THINK OF THE NEW AU PAIR?
GRETA?
SHE'S A LAZY, TV-WATCHING, GROCERY-EATING MACHINE.
GRETA WOULD LIKE RAISE.
WITH A LOT OF NERVE.
WOW.

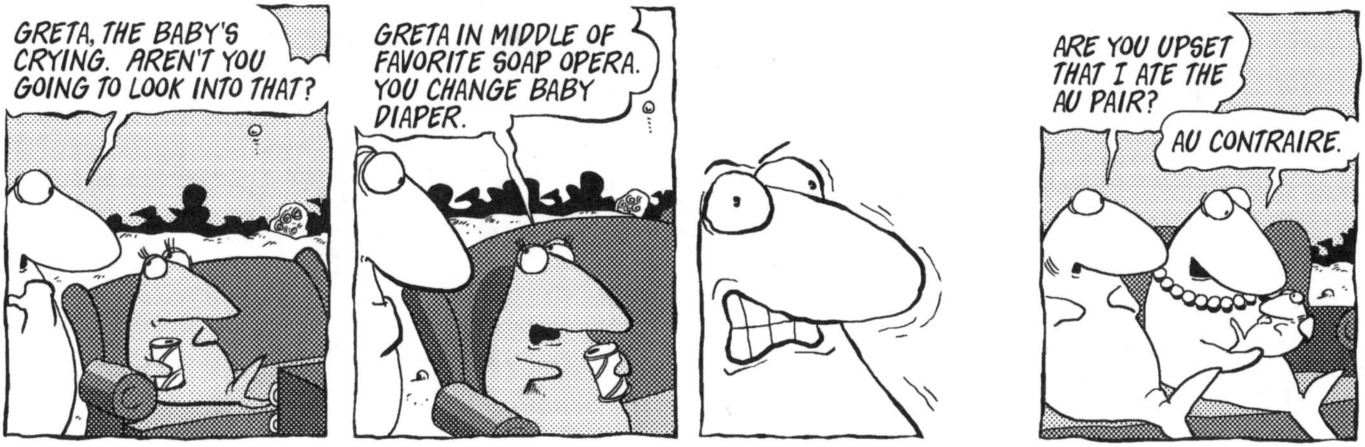
GRETA, THE BABY'S CRYING. AREN'T YOU GOING TO LOOK INTO THAT?
GRETA IN MIDDLE OF FAVORITE SOAP OPERA. YOU CHANGE BABY DIAPER.
ARE YOU UPSET THAT I ATE THE AU PAIR?
AU CONTRAIRE.

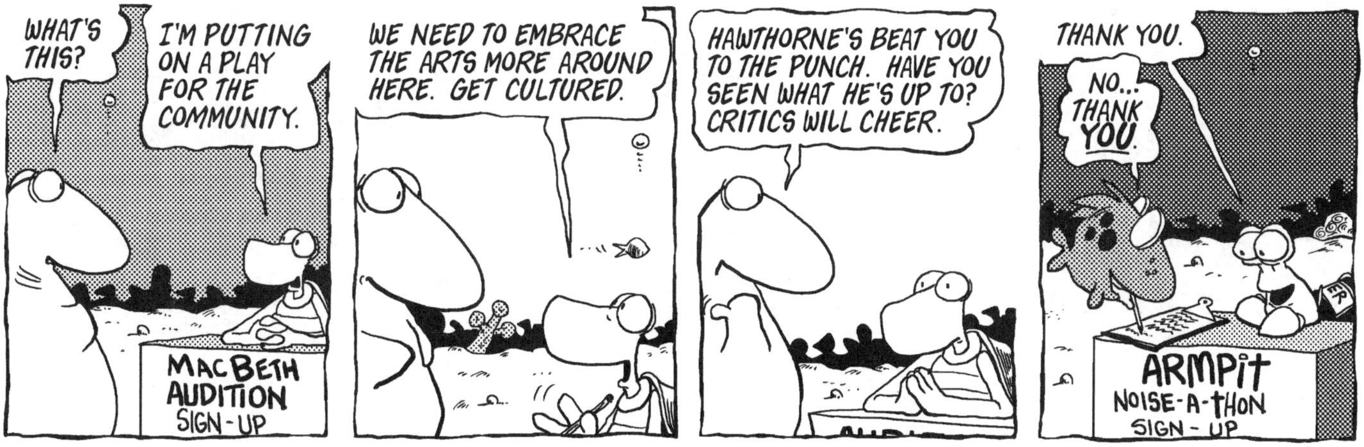
WHAT'S THIS?
I'M PUTTING ON A PLAY FOR THE COMMUNITY.
MACBETH AUDITION SIGN-UP
WE NEED TO EMBRACE THE ARTS MORE AROUND HERE. GET CULTURED.
HAWTHORNE'S BEAT YOU TO THE PUNCH. HAVE YOU SEEN WHAT HE'S UP TO? CRITICS WILL CHEER.
THANK YOU.
NO... THANK YOU.
ARMPIT NOISE-A-THON SIGN-UP

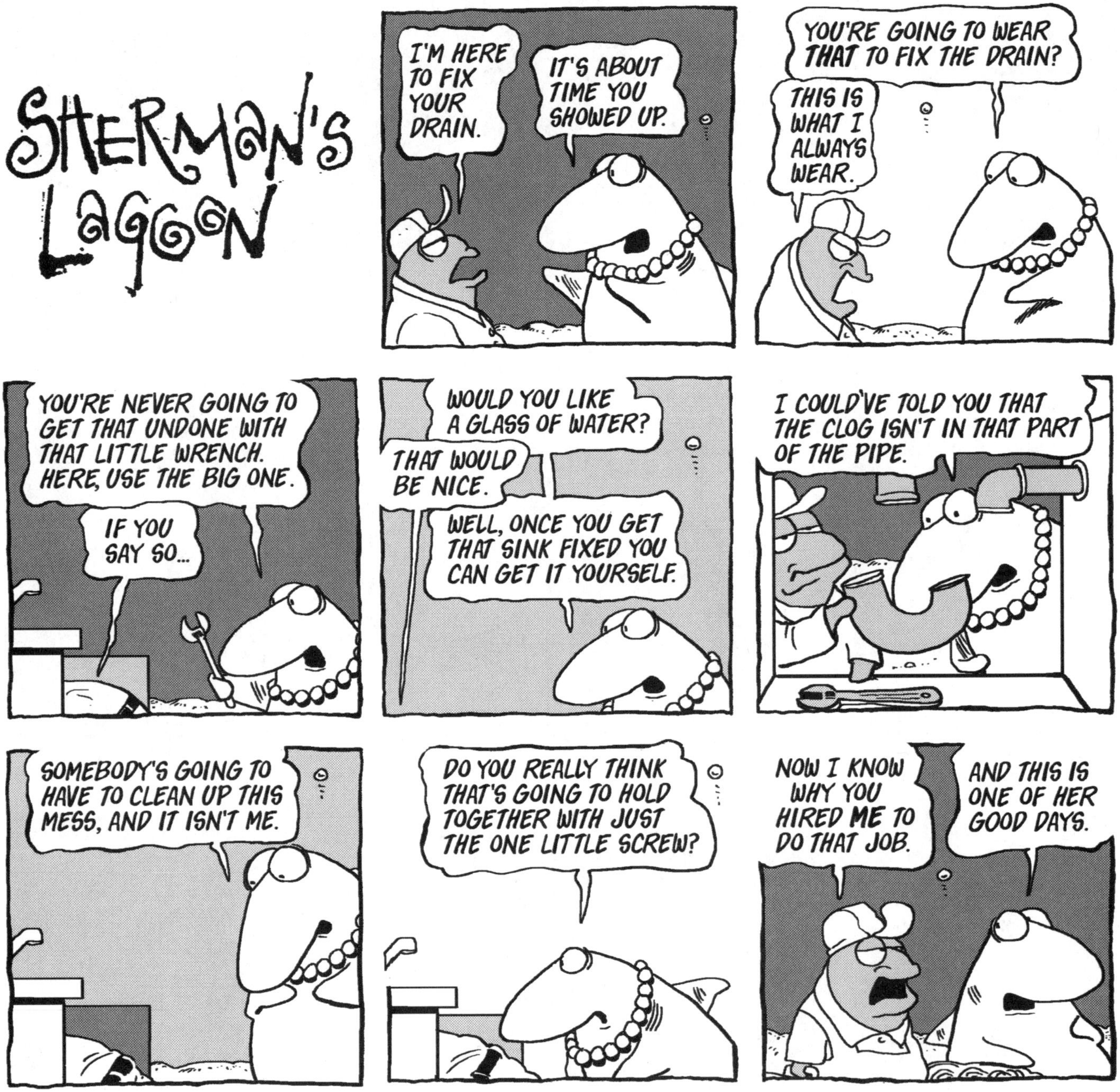
SHERMAN'S LAGOON
I'M HERE TO FIX YOUR DRAIN.
IT'S ABOUT TIME YOU SHOWED UP.
YOU'RE GOING TO WEAR THAT TO FIX THE DRAIN?
THIS IS WHAT I ALWAYS WEAR.
YOU'RE NEVER GOING TO GET THAT UNDONE WITH THAT LITTLE WRENCH. HERE, USE THE BIG ONE.
IF YOU SAY SO...
WOULD YOU LIKE A GLASS OF WATER?
THAT WOULD BE NICE.
WELL, ONCE YOU GET THAT SINK FIXED YOU CAN GET IT YOURSELF.
I COULD'VE TOLD YOU THAT THE CLOG ISN'T IN THAT PART OF THE PIPE.
SOMEBODY'S GOING TO HAVE TO CLEAN UP THIS MESS, AND IT ISN'T ME.
DO YOU REALLY THINK THAT'S GOING TO HOLD TOGETHER WITH JUST THE ONE LITTLE SCREW?
NOW I KNOW WHY YOU HIRED ME TO DO THAT JOB.
AND THIS IS ONE OF HER GOOD DAYS.

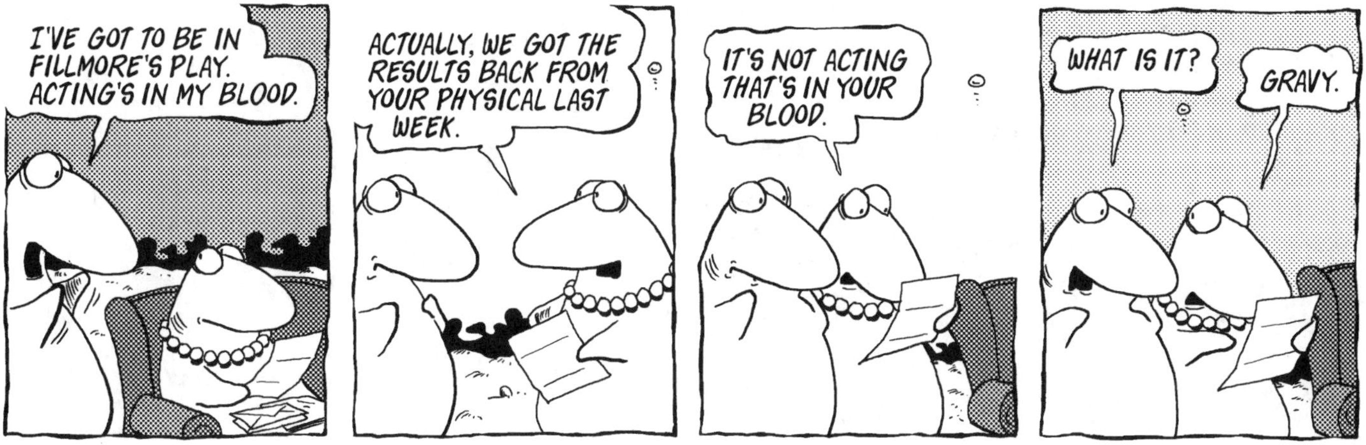
I'VE GOT TO BE IN FILLMORE'S PLAY. ACTING'S IN MY BLOOD.
ACTUALLY, WE GOT THE RESULTS BACK FROM YOUR PHYSICAL LAST WEEK.
IT'S NOT ACTING THAT'S IN YOUR BLOOD.
WHAT IS IT?
GRAVY.

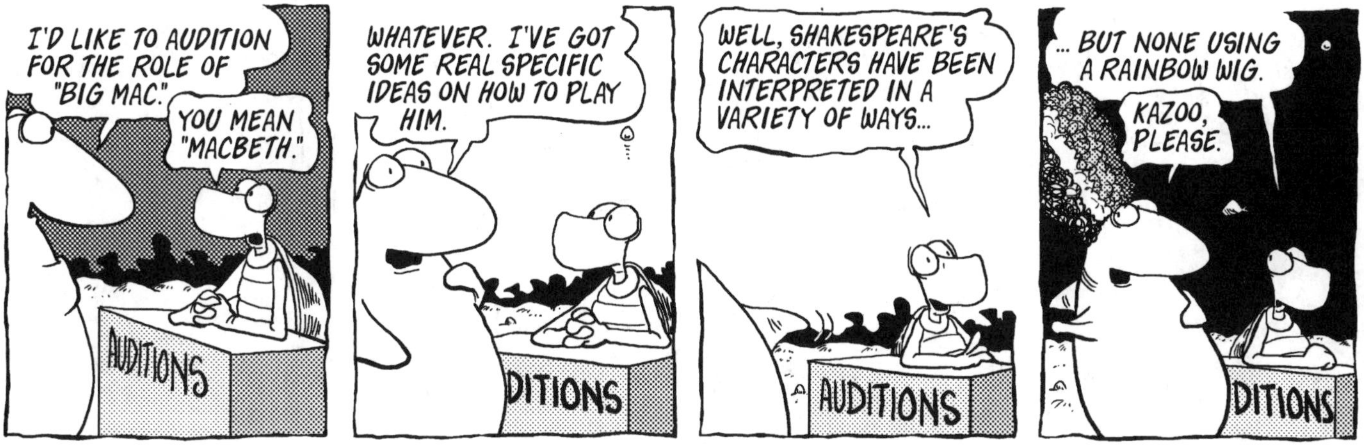
I'D LIKE TO AUDITION FOR THE ROLE OF "BIG MAC."
YOU MEAN "MACBETH."
AUDITIONS
WHATEVER. I'VE GOT SOME REAL SPECIFIC IDEAS ON HOW TO PLAY HIM.
DITIONS
WELL, SHAKESPEARE'S CHARACTERS HAVE BEEN INTERPRETED IN A VARIETY OF WAYS...
AUDITIONS
... BUT NONE USING A RAINBOW WIG.
KAZOO, PLEASE.
DITIONS

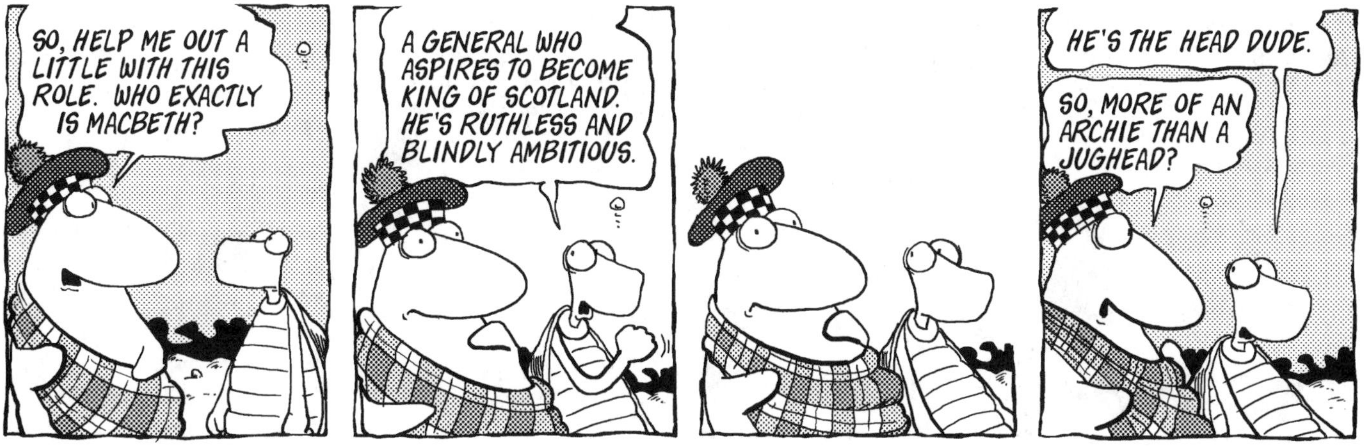
SO, HELP ME OUT A LITTLE WITH THIS ROLE. WHO EXACTLY IS MACBETH?
A GENERAL WHO ASPIRES TO BECOME KING OF SCOTLAND. HE'S RUTHLESS AND BLINDLY AMBITIOUS.
HE'S THE HEAD DUDE.
SO, MORE OF AN ARCHIE THAN A JUGHEAD?

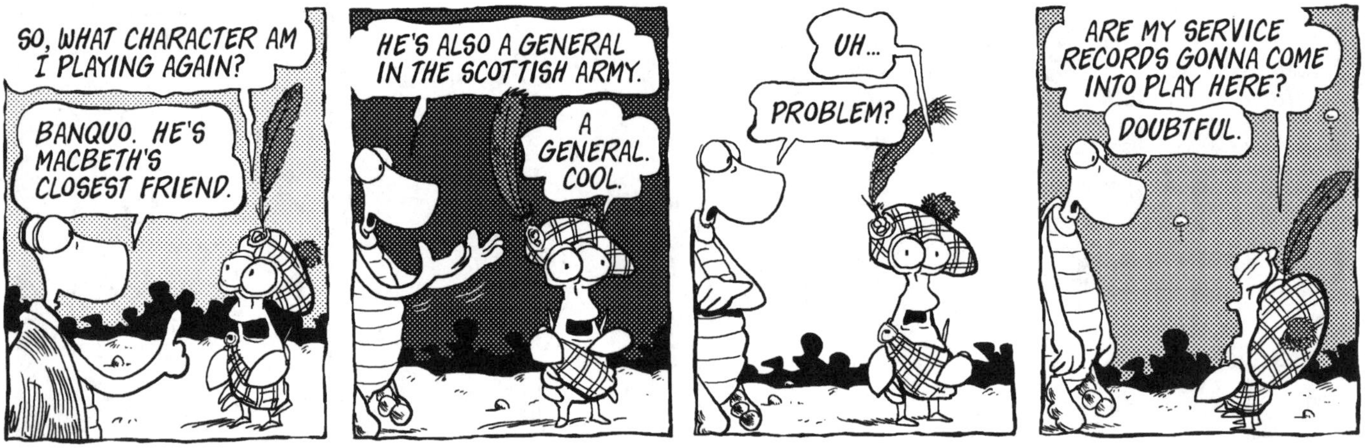
SO, WHAT CHARACTER AM I PLAYING AGAIN?
BANQUO. HE'S MACBETH'S CLOSEST FRIEND.
HE'S ALSO A GENERAL IN THE SCOTTISH ARMY.
A GENERAL. COOL.
UH...
PROBLEM?
ARE MY SERVICE RECORDS GONNA COME INTO PLAY HERE?
DOUBTFUL.

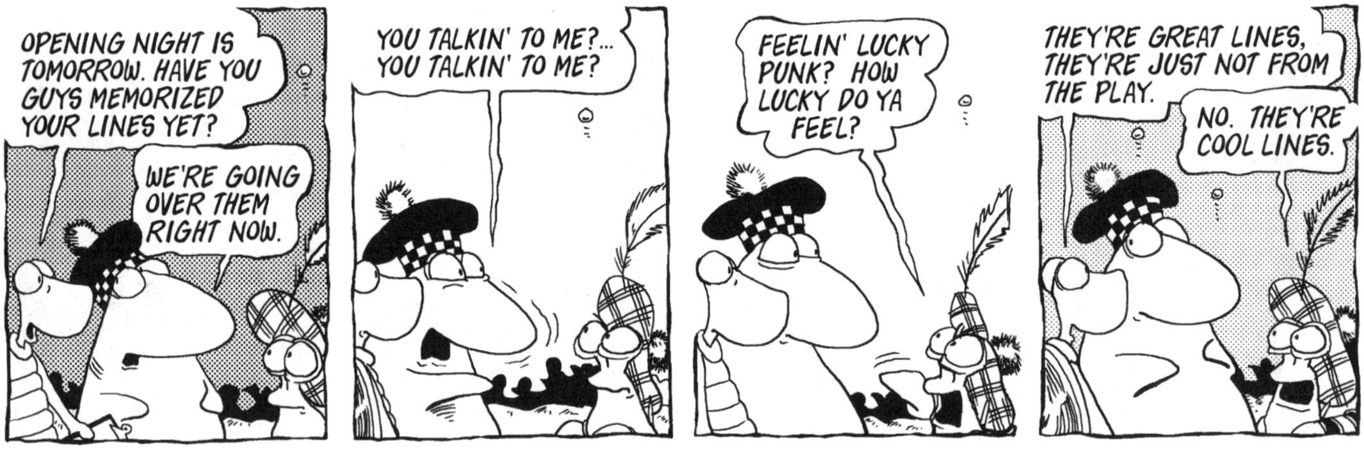
OPENING NIGHT IS TOMORROW. HAVE YOU GUYS MEMORIZED YOUR LINES YET?
WE'RE GOING OVER THEM RIGHT NOW.
YOU TALKIN' TO ME?... YOU TALKIN' TO ME?
FEELIN' LUCKY PUNK? HOW LUCKY DO YA FEEL?
THEY'RE GREAT LINES, THEY'RE JUST NOT FROM THE PLAY.
NO. THEY'RE COOL LINES.

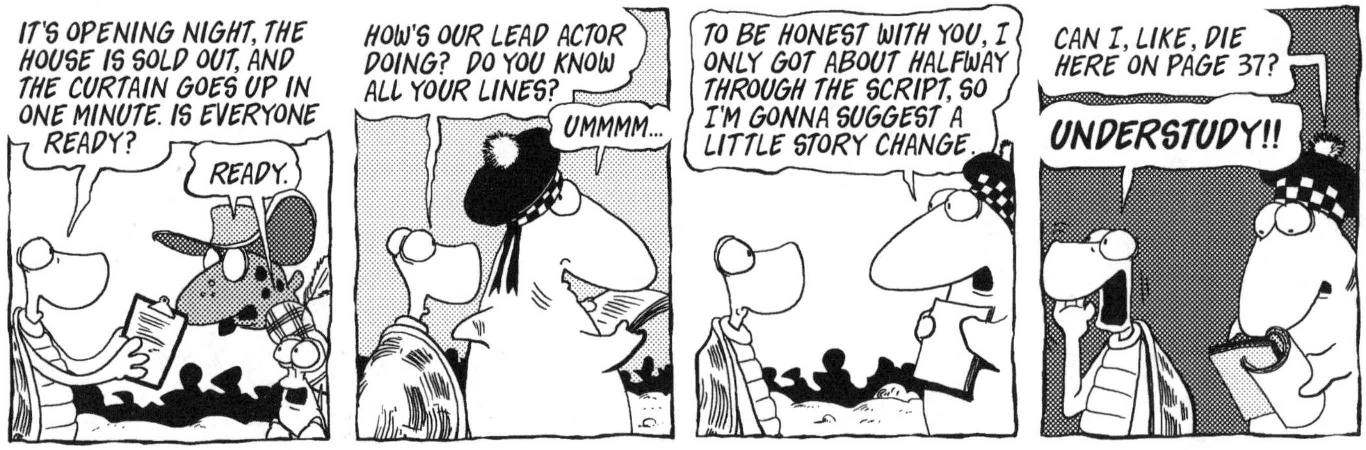
IT'S OPENING NIGHT, THE HOUSE IS SOLD OUT, AND THE CURTAIN GOES UP IN ONE MINUTE. IS EVERYONE READY?
READY.
HOW'S OUR LEAD ACTOR DOING? DO YOU KNOW ALL YOUR LINES?
UMMMM...
TO BE HONEST WITH YOU, I ONLY GOT ABOUT HALFWAY THROUGH THE SCRIPT, SO I'M GONNA SUGGEST A LITTLE STORY CHANGE.
CAN I, LIKE, DIE HERE ON PAGE 37?
UNDERSTUDY!!

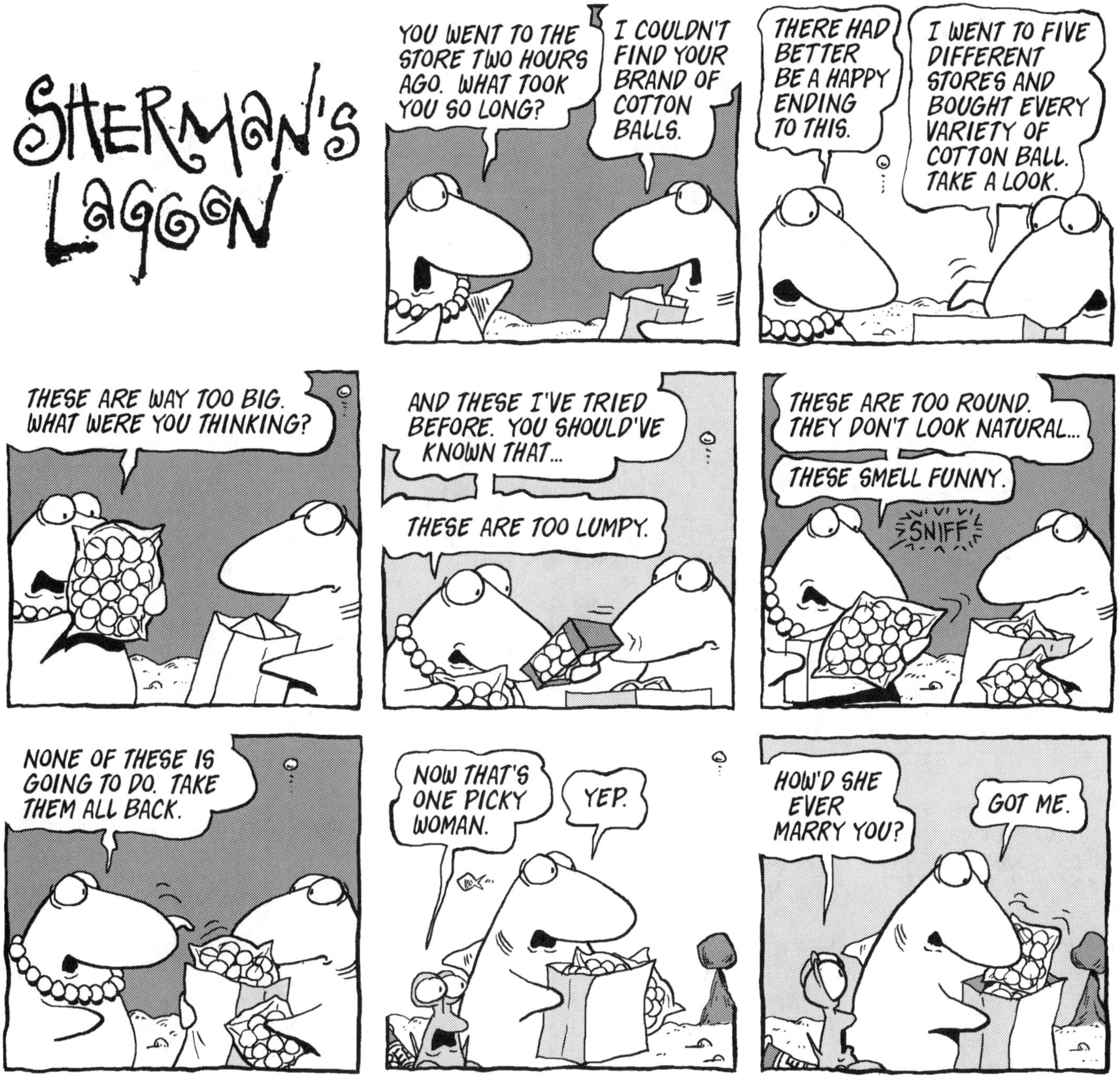
SHERMAN'S LAGOON
YOU WENT TO THE STORE TWO HOURS AGO. WHAT TOOK YOU SO LONG?
I COULDN'T FIND YOUR BRAND OF COTTON BALLS.
THERE HAD BETTER BE A HAPPY ENDING TO THIS.
I WENT TO FIVE DIFFERENT STORES AND BOUGHT EVERY VARIETY OF COTTON BALL. TAKE A LOOK.
THESE ARE WAY TOO BIG. WHAT WERE YOU THINKING?
AND THESE I'VE TRIED BEFORE. YOU SHOULD'VE KNOWN THAT...
THESE ARE TOO LUMPY.
THESE ARE TOO ROUND. THEY DON'T LOOK NATURAL...
THESE SMELL FUNNY.
SNIFF
NONE OF THESE IS GOING TO DO. TAKE THEM ALL BACK.
NOW THAT'S ONE PICKY WOMAN.
YEP.
HOW'D SHE EVER MARRY YOU?
GOT ME.

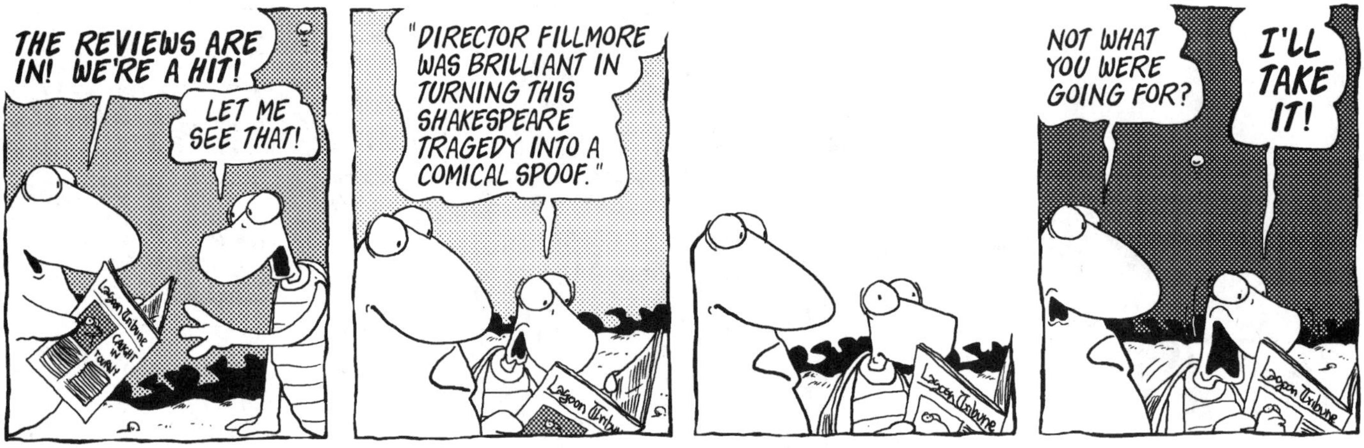
THE REVIEWS ARE IN! WE'RE A HIT!
LET ME SEE THAT!
"DIRECTOR FILLMORE WAS BRILLIANT IN TURNING THIS SHAKESPEARE TRAGEDY INTO A COMICAL SPOOF."
NOT WHAT YOU WERE GOING FOR?
I'LL TAKE IT!

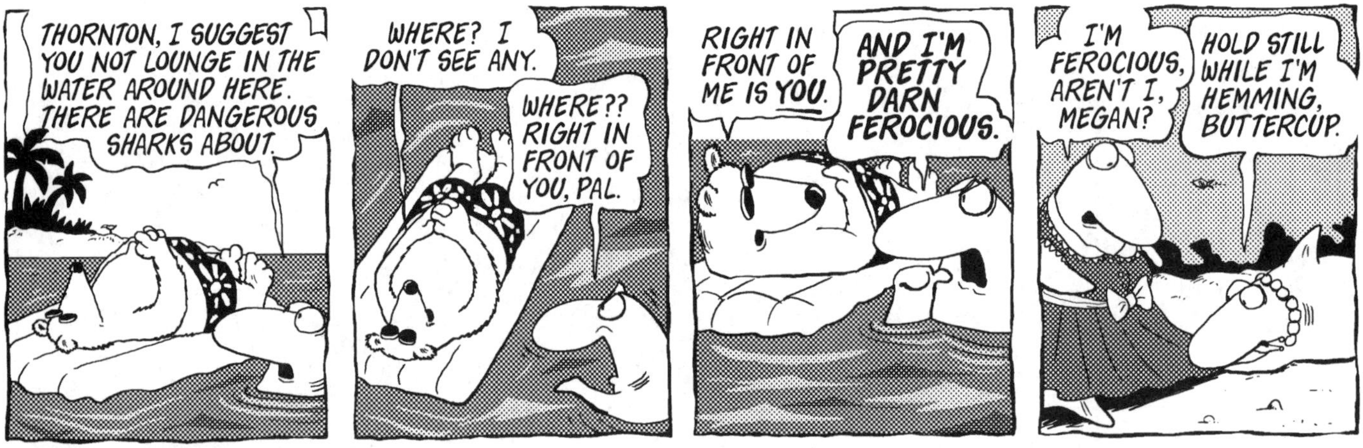
THORNTON, I SUGGEST YOU NOT LOUNGE IN THE WATER AROUND HERE. THERE ARE DANGEROUS SHARKS ABOUT.
WHERE? I DON'T SEE ANY.
WHERE?? RIGHT IN FRONT OF YOU, PAL.
RIGHT IN FRONT OF ME IS YOU.
AND I'M PRETTY DARN FEROCIOUS.
I'M FEROCIOUS, AREN'T I, MEGAN?
HOLD STILL WHILE I'M HEMMING, BUTTERCUP.

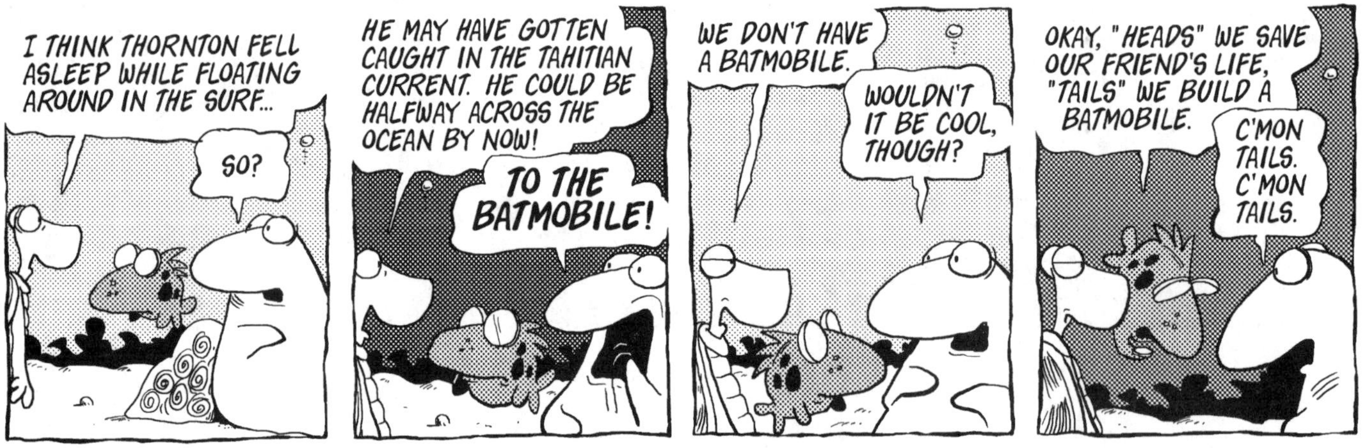
I THINK THORNTON FELL ASLEEP WHILE FLOATING AROUND IN THE SURF...
SO?
HE MAY HAVE GOTTEN CAUGHT IN THE TAHITIAN CURRENT. HE COULD BE HALFWAY ACROSS THE OCEAN BY NOW!
TO THE BATMOBILE!
WE DON'T HAVE A BATMOBILE.
WOULDN'T IT BE COOL, THOUGH?
OKAY, "HEADS" WE SAVE OUR FRIEND'S LIFE, "TAILS" WE BUILD A BATMOBILE.
C'MON TAILS. C'MON TAILS.

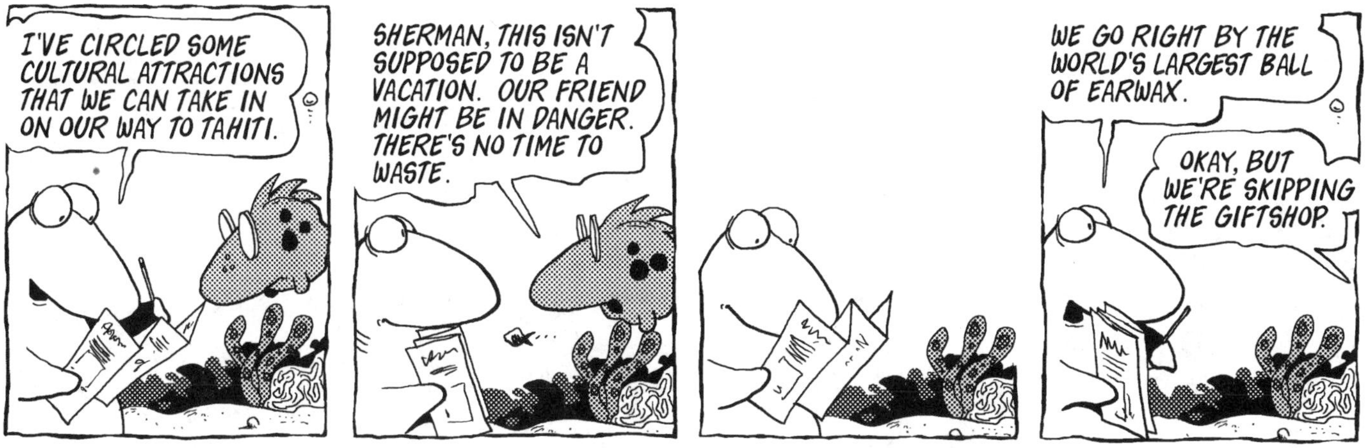
I'VE CIRCLED SOME CULTURAL ATTRACTIONS THAT WE CAN TAKE IN ON OUR WAY TO TAHITI.
SHERMAN, THIS ISN'T SUPPOSED TO BE A VACATION. OUR FRIEND MIGHT BE IN DANGER. THERE'S NO TIME TO WASTE.
WE GO RIGHT BY THE WORLD'S LARGEST BALL OF EARWAX.
OKAY, BUT WE'RE SKIPPING THE GIFTSHOP.

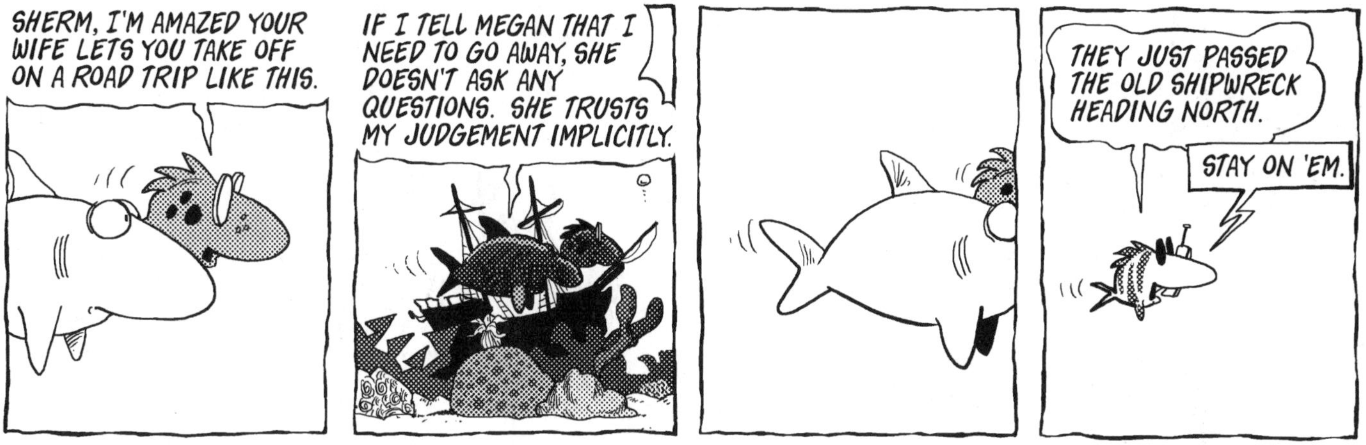
SHERM, I'M AMAZED YOUR WIFE LETS YOU TAKE OFF ON A ROAD TRIP LIKE THIS.
IF I TELL MEGAN THAT I NEED TO GO AWAY, SHE DOESN'T ASK ANY QUESTIONS. SHE TRUSTS MY JUDGEMENT IMPLICITLY.
THEY JUST PASSED THE OLD SHIPWRECK HEADING NORTH.
STAY ON 'EM.

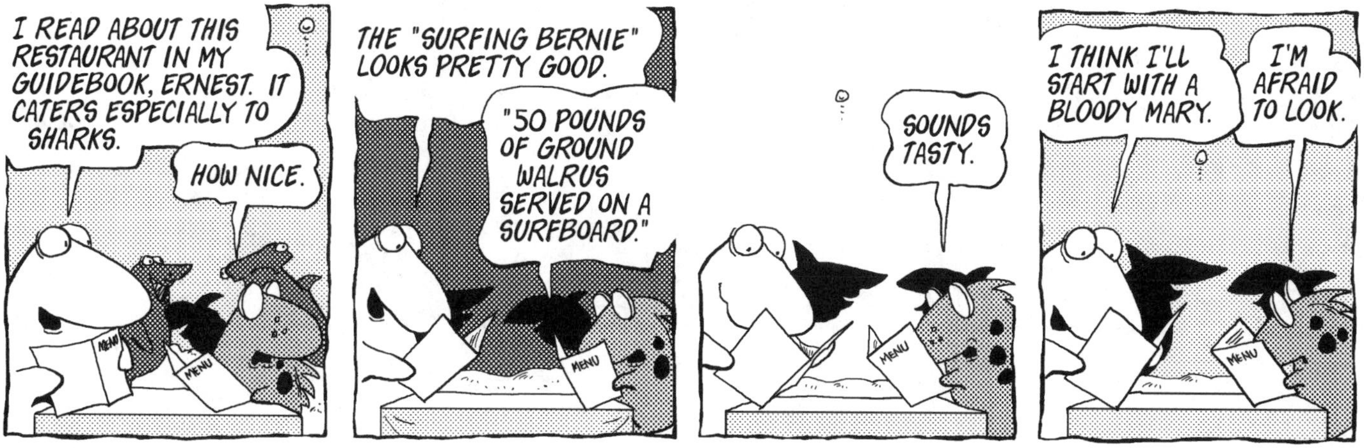
I READ ABOUT THIS RESTAURANT IN MY GUIDEBOOK, ERNEST. IT CATERS ESPECIALLY TO SHARKS.
HOW NICE.
MENU
MENU
THE "SURFING BERNIE" LOOKS PRETTY GOOD.
"50 POUNDS OF GROUND WALRUS SERVED ON A SURFBOARD."
MENU
SOUNDS TASTY.
MENU
I THINK I'LL START WITH A BLOODY MARY.
I'M AFRAID TO LOOK.
MENU

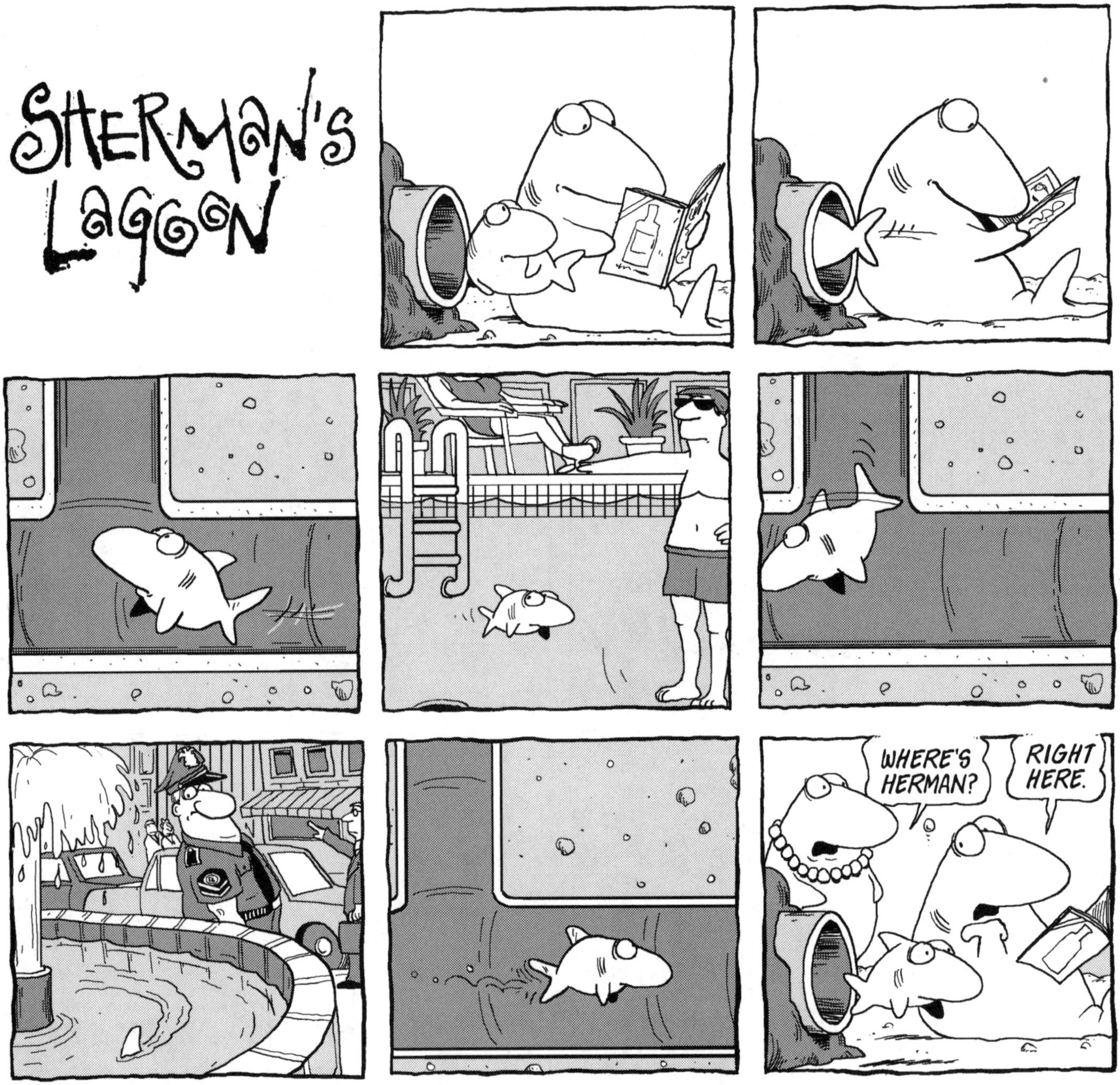
SHERMAN'S LAGOON
WHERE'S HERMAN?
RIGHT HERE.

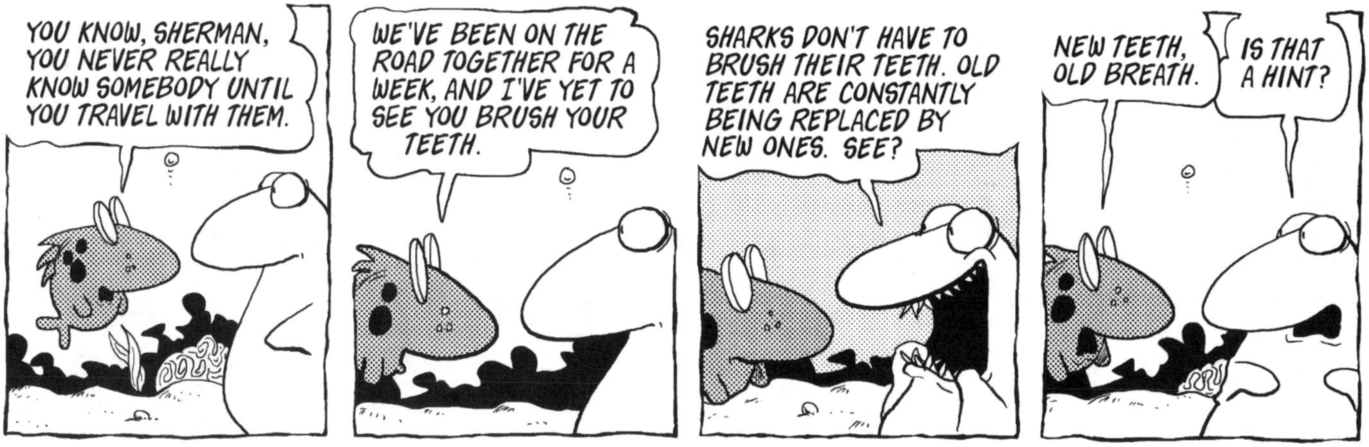
YOU KNOW, SHERMAN, YOU NEVER REALLY KNOW SOMEBODY UNTIL YOU TRAVEL WITH THEM.
WE'VE BEEN ON THE ROAD TOGETHER FOR A WEEK, AND I'VE YET TO SEE YOU BRUSH YOUR TEETH.
SHARKS DON'T HAVE TO BRUSH THEIR TEETH. OLD TEETH ARE CONSTANTLY BEING REPLACED BY NEW ONES. SEE?
NEW TEETH, OLD BREATH.
IS THAT A HINT?

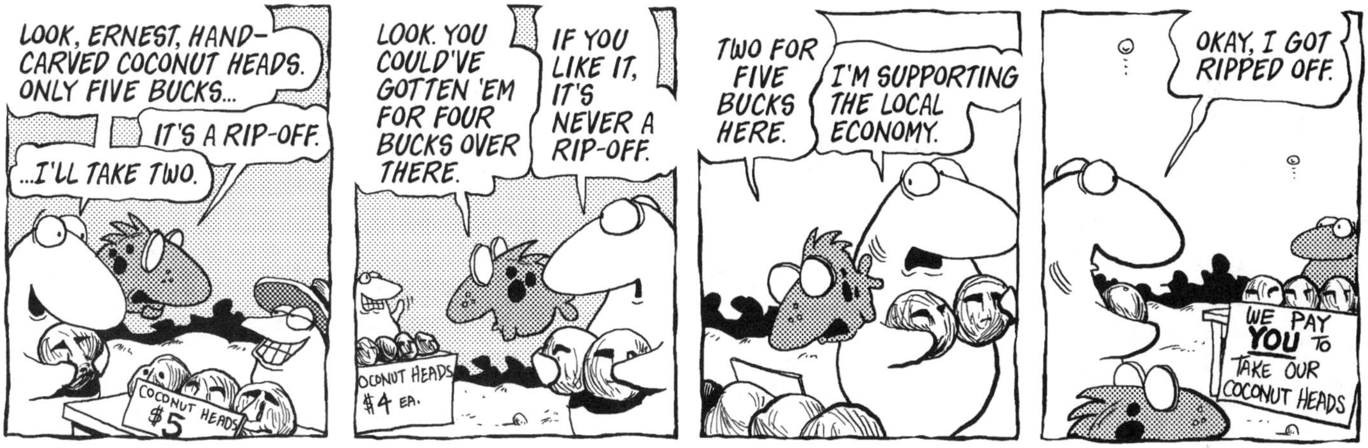
LOOK, ERNEST, HAND-CARVED COCONUT HEADS. ONLY FIVE BUCKS...
IT'S A RIP-OFF.
...I'LL TAKE TWO.
COCONUT HEADS $5
LOOK. YOU COULD'VE GOTTEN 'EM FOR FOUR BUCKS OVER THERE.
IF YOU LIKE IT, IT'S NEVER A RIP-OFF.
COCONUT HEADS $4 EA.
TWO FOR FIVE BUCKS HERE.
I'M SUPPORTING THE LOCAL ECONOMY.
OKAY, I GOT RIPPED OFF.
WE PAY YOU TO TAKE OUR COCONUT HEADS

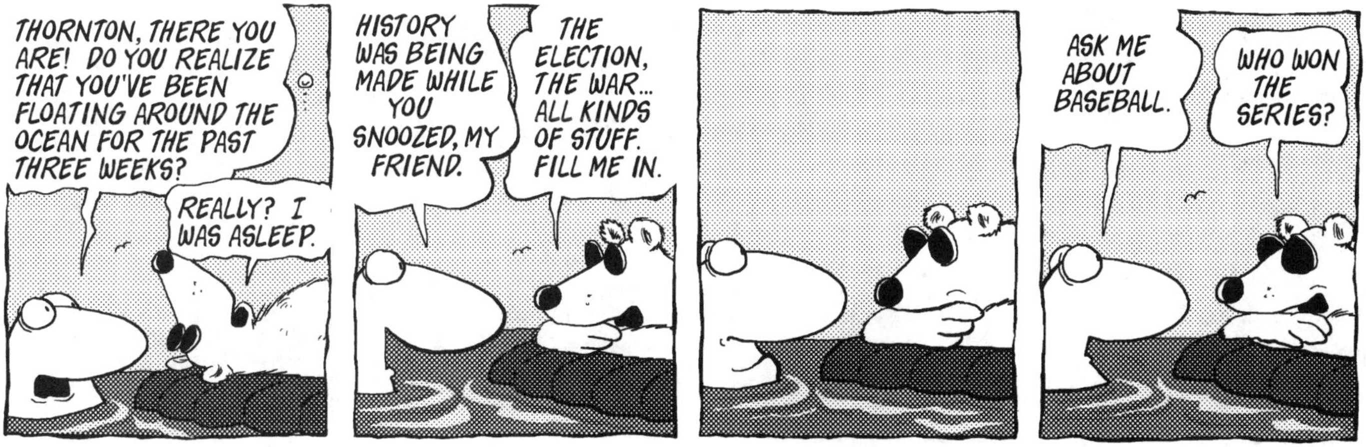
THORNTON, THERE YOU ARE! DO YOU REALIZE THAT YOU'VE BEEN FLOATING AROUND THE OCEAN FOR THE PAST THREE WEEKS?
REALLY? I WAS ASLEEP.
HISTORY WAS BEING MADE WHILE YOU SNOOZED, MY FRIEND.
THE ELECTION, THE WAR... ALL KINDS OF STUFF. FILL ME IN.
ASK ME ABOUT BASEBALL.
WHO WON THE SERIES?

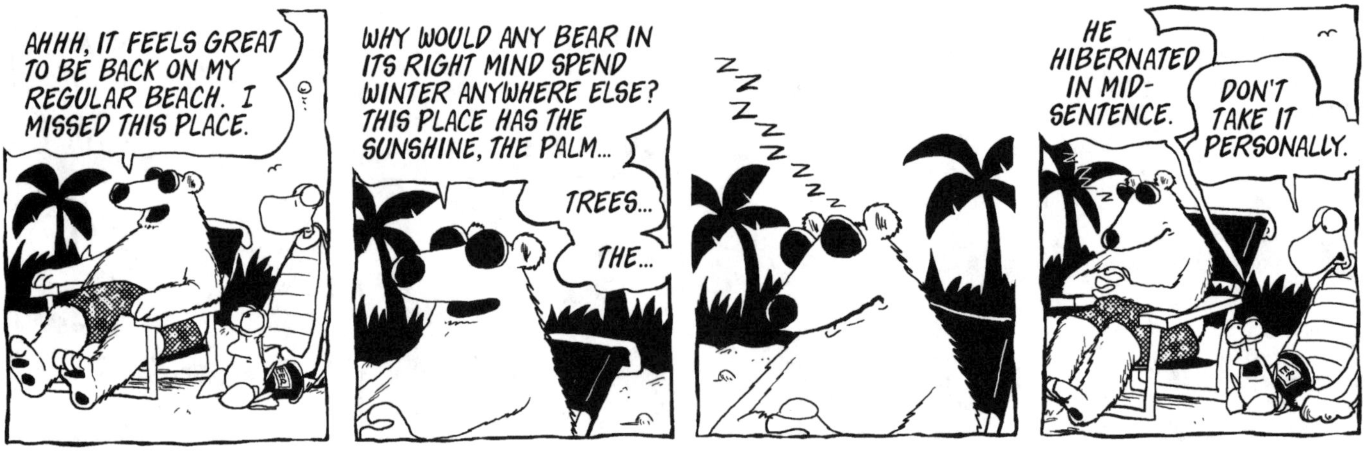
AHHH, IT FEELS GREAT TO BE BACK ON MY REGULAR BEACH. I MISSED THIS PLACE.
WHY WOULD ANY BEAR IN ITS RIGHT MIND SPEND WINTER ANYWHERE ELSE? THIS PLACE HAS THE SUNSHINE, THE PALM...
TREES...
THE...
ZZZZZZZZ
HE HIBERNATED IN MID-SENTENCE.
DON'T TAKE IT PERSONALLY.

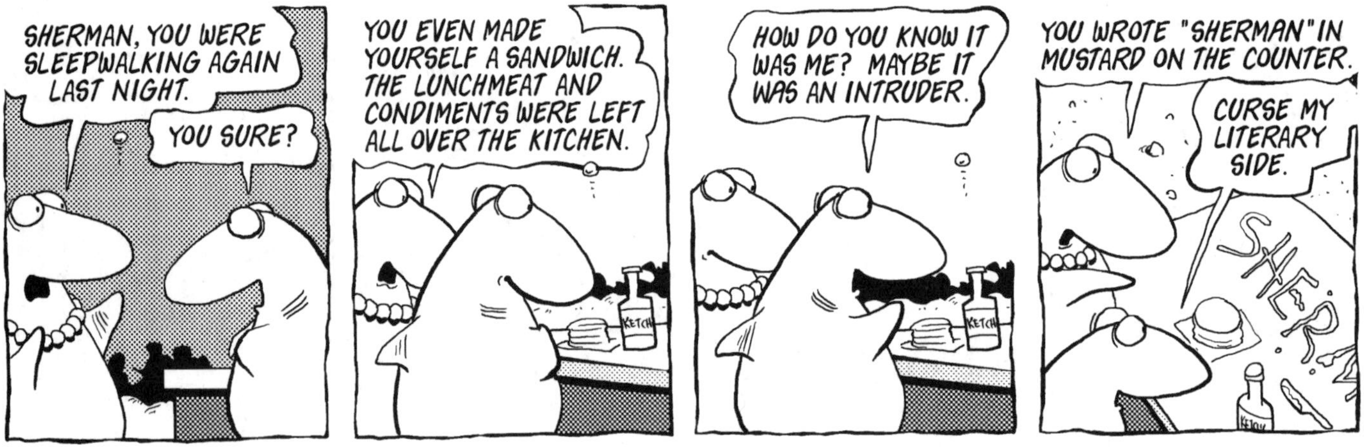
SHERMAN, YOU WERE SLEEPWALKING AGAIN LAST NIGHT.
YOU SURE?
YOU EVEN MADE YOURSELF A SANDWICH. THE LUNCHMEAT AND CONDIMENTS WERE LEFT ALL OVER THE KITCHEN.
KETCH
HOW DO YOU KNOW IT WAS ME? MAYBE IT WAS AN INTRUDER.
KETCH
YOU WROTE "SHERMAN" IN MUSTARD ON THE COUNTER.
CURSE MY LITERARY SIDE.
SHER

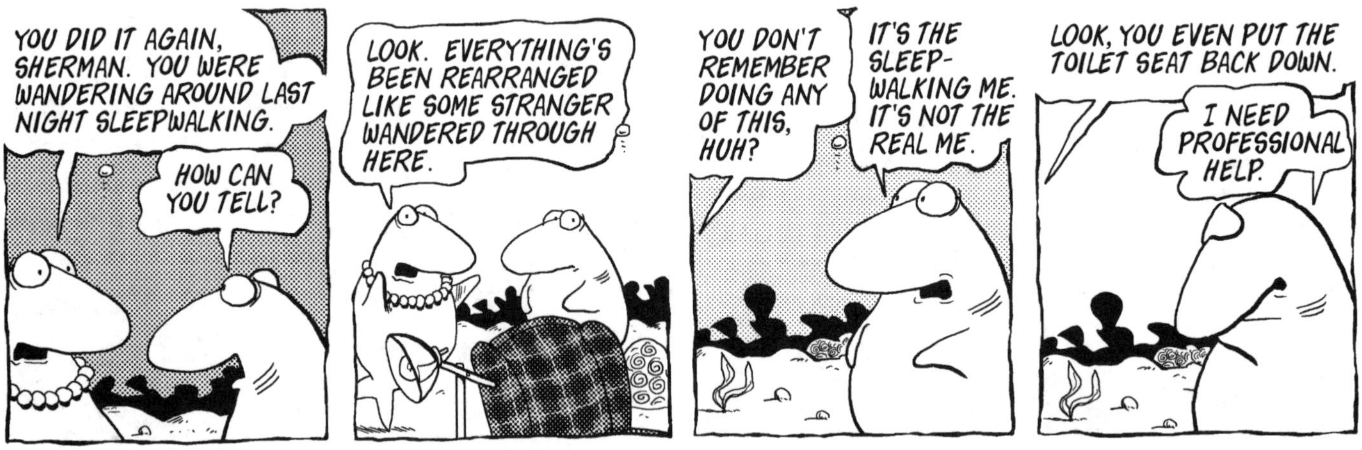
YOU DID IT AGAIN, SHERMAN. YOU WERE WANDERING AROUND LAST NIGHT SLEEPWALKING.
HOW CAN YOU TELL?
LOOK. EVERYTHING'S BEEN REARRANGED LIKE SOME STRANGER WANDERED THROUGH HERE.
YOU DON'T REMEMBER DOING ANY OF THIS, HUH?
IT'S THE SLEEP-WALKING ME. IT'S NOT THE REAL ME.
LOOK, YOU EVEN PUT THE TOILET SEAT BACK DOWN.
I NEED PROFESSIONAL HELP.

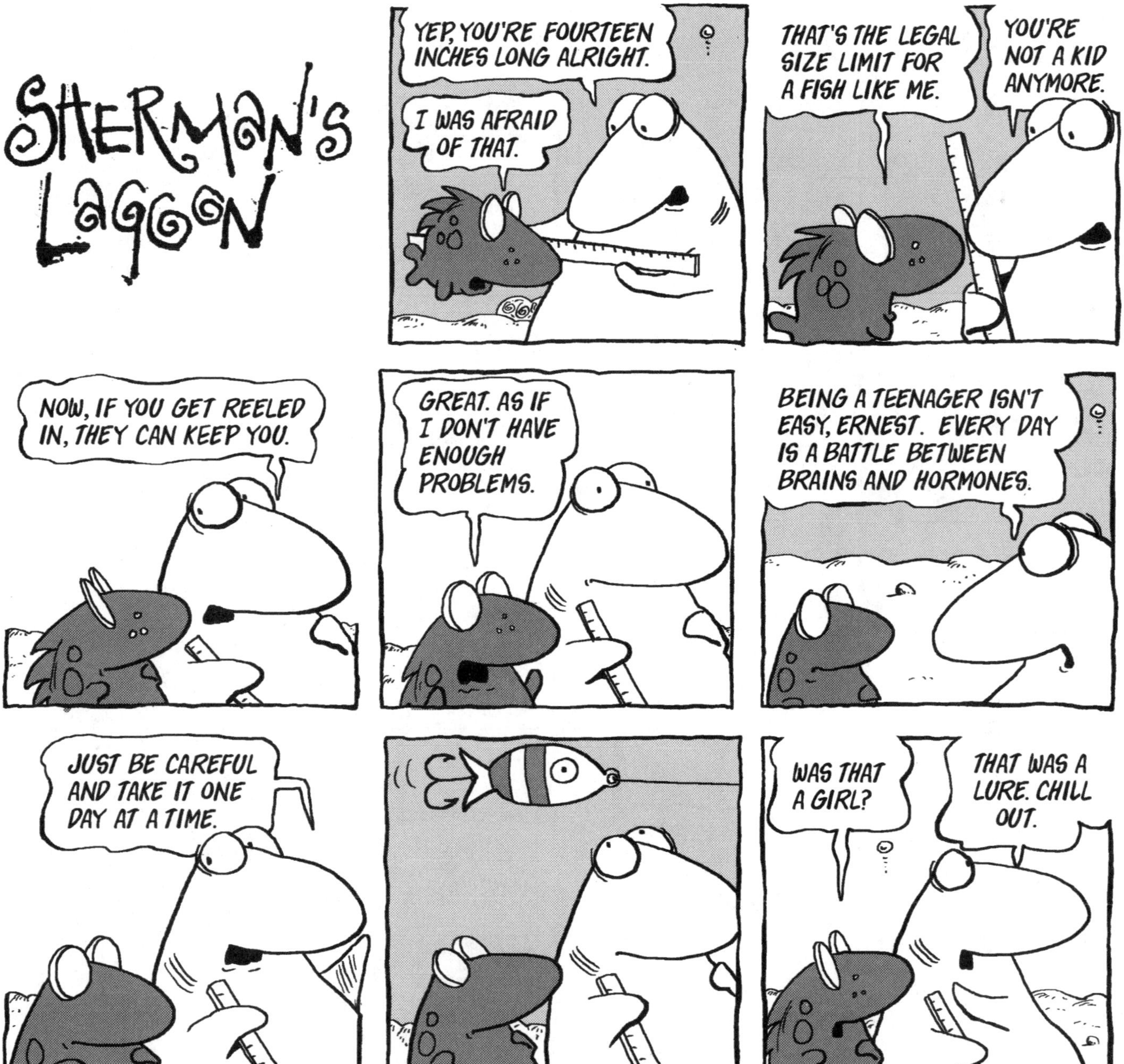
SHERMAN'S LAGOON
YEP, YOU'RE FOURTEEN INCHES LONG ALRIGHT.
I WAS AFRAID OF THAT.
THAT'S THE LEGAL SIZE LIMIT FOR A FISH LIKE ME.
YOU'RE NOT A KID ANYMORE.
NOW, IF YOU GET REELED IN, THEY CAN KEEP YOU.
GREAT. AS IF I DON'T HAVE ENOUGH PROBLEMS.
BEING A TEENAGER ISN'T EASY, ERNEST. EVERY DAY IS A BATTLE BETWEEN BRAINS AND HORMONES.
JUST BE CAREFUL AND TAKE IT ONE DAY AT A TIME.
WAS THAT A GIRL?
THAT WAS A LURE. CHILL OUT.

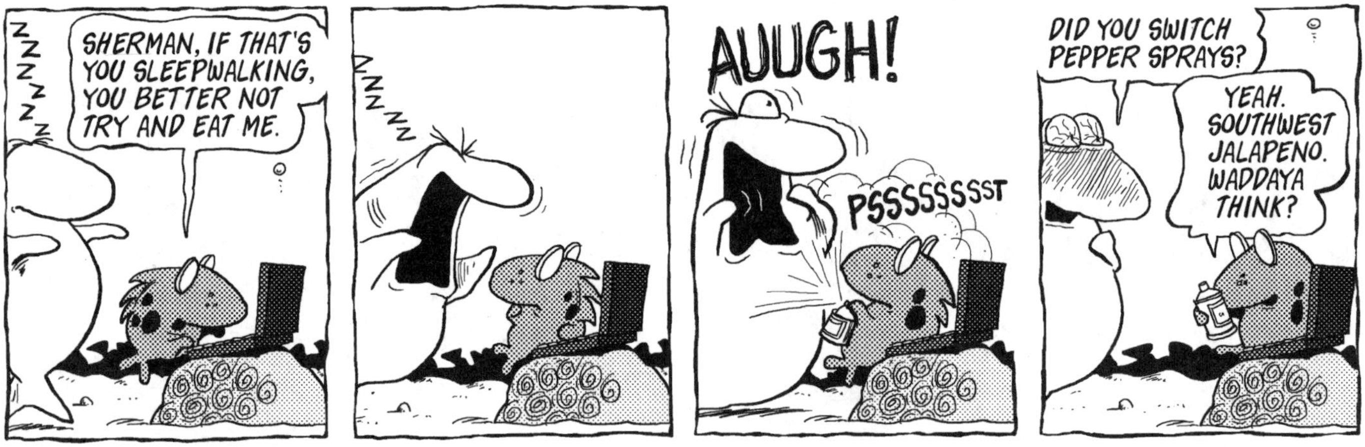
Z Z Z Z Z
SHERMAN, IF THAT'S YOU SLEEPWALKING, YOU BETTER NOT TRY AND EAT ME.
Z Z Z Z
AUUGH!
PSSSSSSSST
DID YOU SWITCH PEPPER SPRAYS?
YEAH. SOUTHWEST JALAPENO. WADDAYA THINK?

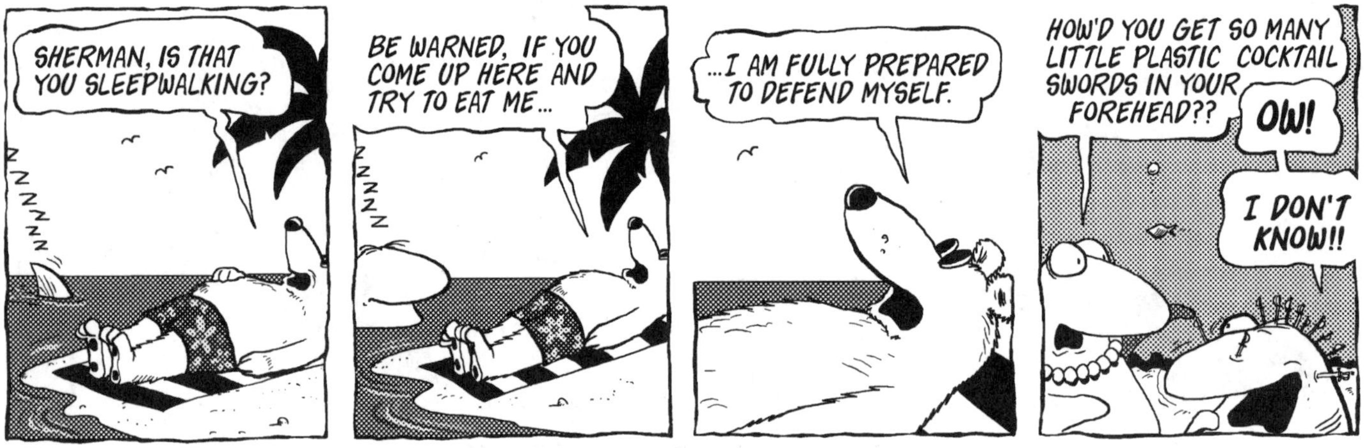
SHERMAN, IS THAT YOU SLEEPWALKING?
Z Z Z Z Z Z
BE WARNED, IF YOU COME UP HERE AND TRY TO EAT ME...
Z Z Z Z
...I AM FULLY PREPARED TO DEFEND MYSELF.
HOW'D YOU GET SO MANY LITTLE PLASTIC COCKTAIL SWORDS IN YOUR FOREHEAD??
OW!
I DON'T KNOW!!

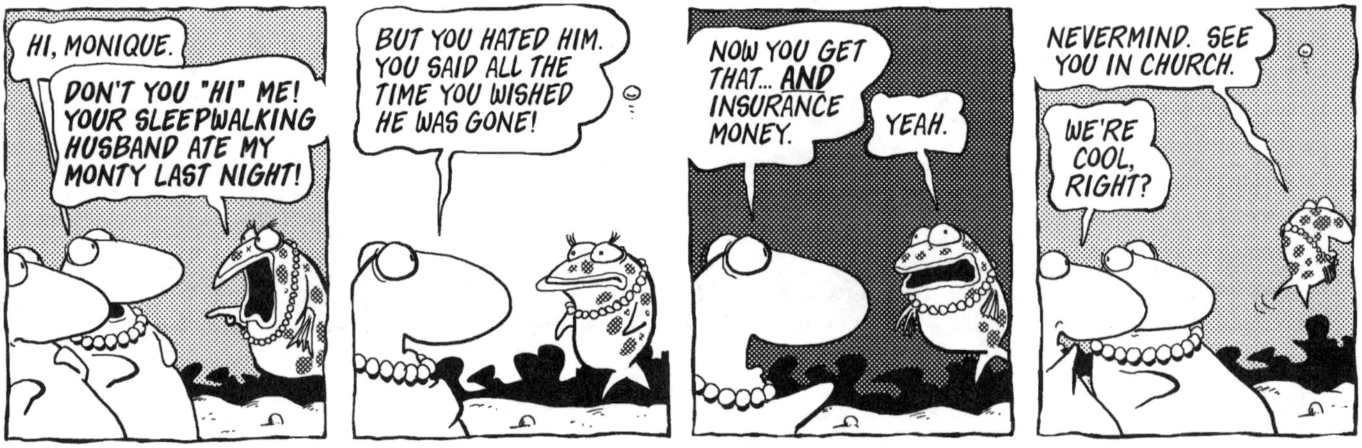
HI, MONIQUE.
DON'T YOU "HI" ME! YOUR SLEEPWALKING HUSBAND ATE MY MONTY LAST NIGHT!
BUT YOU HATED HIM. YOU SAID ALL THE TIME YOU WISHED HE WAS GONE!
NOW YOU GET THAT... AND INSURANCE MONEY.
YEAH.
NEVERMIND. SEE YOU IN CHURCH.
WE'RE COOL, RIGHT?

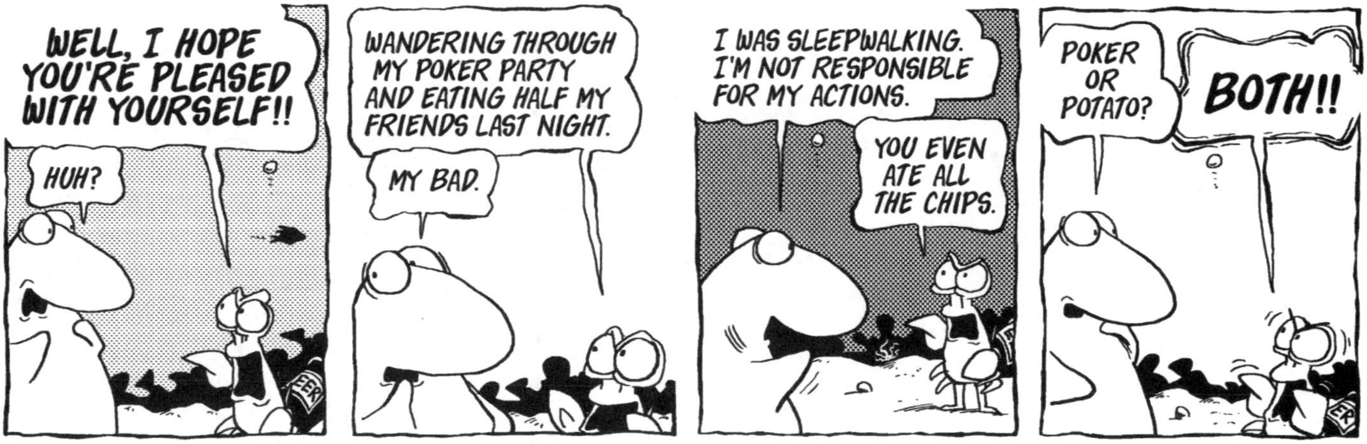
WELL, I HOPE YOU'RE PLEASED WITH YOURSELF!!
HUH?
WANDERING THROUGH MY POKER PARTY AND EATING HALF MY FRIENDS LAST NIGHT.
MY BAD.
I WAS SLEEPWALKING. I'M NOT RESPONSIBLE FOR MY ACTIONS.
YOU EVEN ATE ALL THE CHIPS.
POKER OR POTATO?
BOTH!!

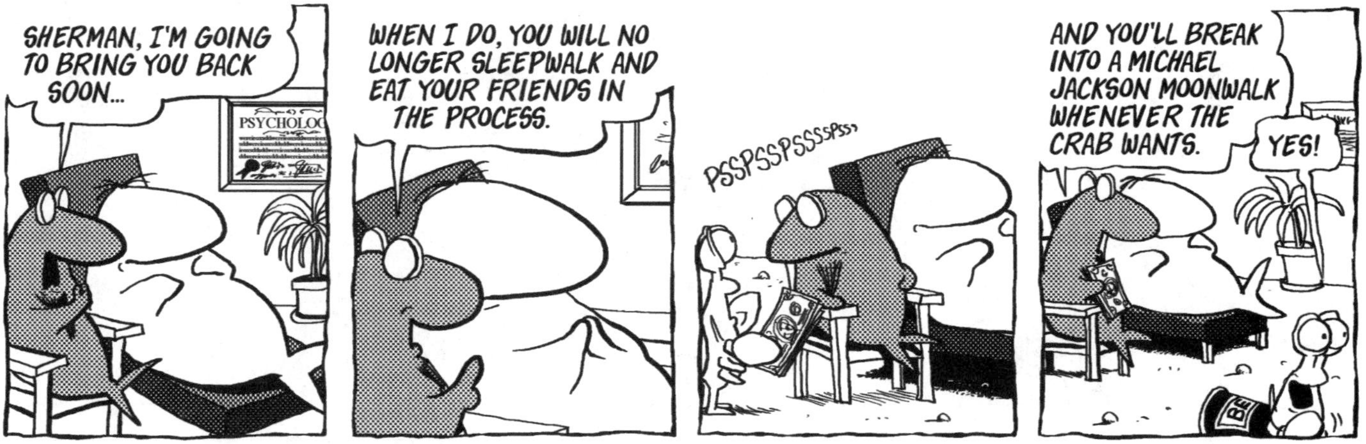
SHERMAN, I'M GOING TO BRING YOU BACK SOON...
PSYCHOLOG
WHEN I DO, YOU WILL NO LONGER SLEEPWALK AND EAT YOUR FRIENDS IN THE PROCESS.
PSSPSSPSSSSPSSS
AND YOU'LL BREAK INTO A MICHAEL JACKSON MOONWALK WHENEVER THE CRAB WANTS.
YES!

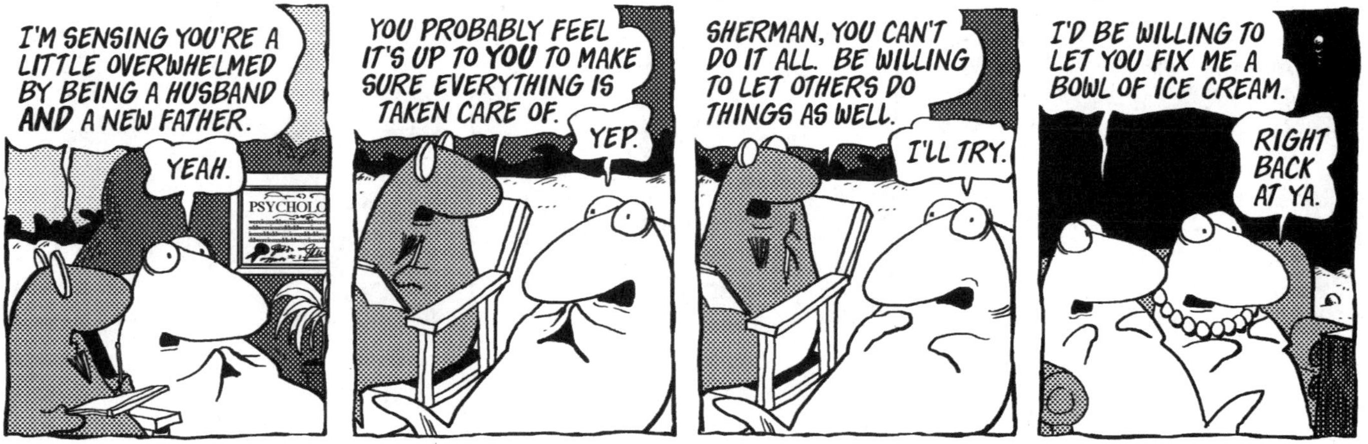
I'M SENSING YOU'RE A LITTLE OVERWHELMED BY BEING A HUSBAND AND A NEW FATHER.
YEAH.
PSYCHOLO
YOU PROBABLY FEEL IT'S UP TO YOU TO MAKE SURE EVERYTHING IS TAKEN CARE OF.
YEP.
SHERMAN, YOU CAN'T DO IT ALL. BE WILLING TO LET OTHERS DO THINGS AS WELL.
I'LL TRY.
I'D BE WILLING TO LET YOU FIX ME A BOWL OF ICE CREAM.
RIGHT BACK AT YA.

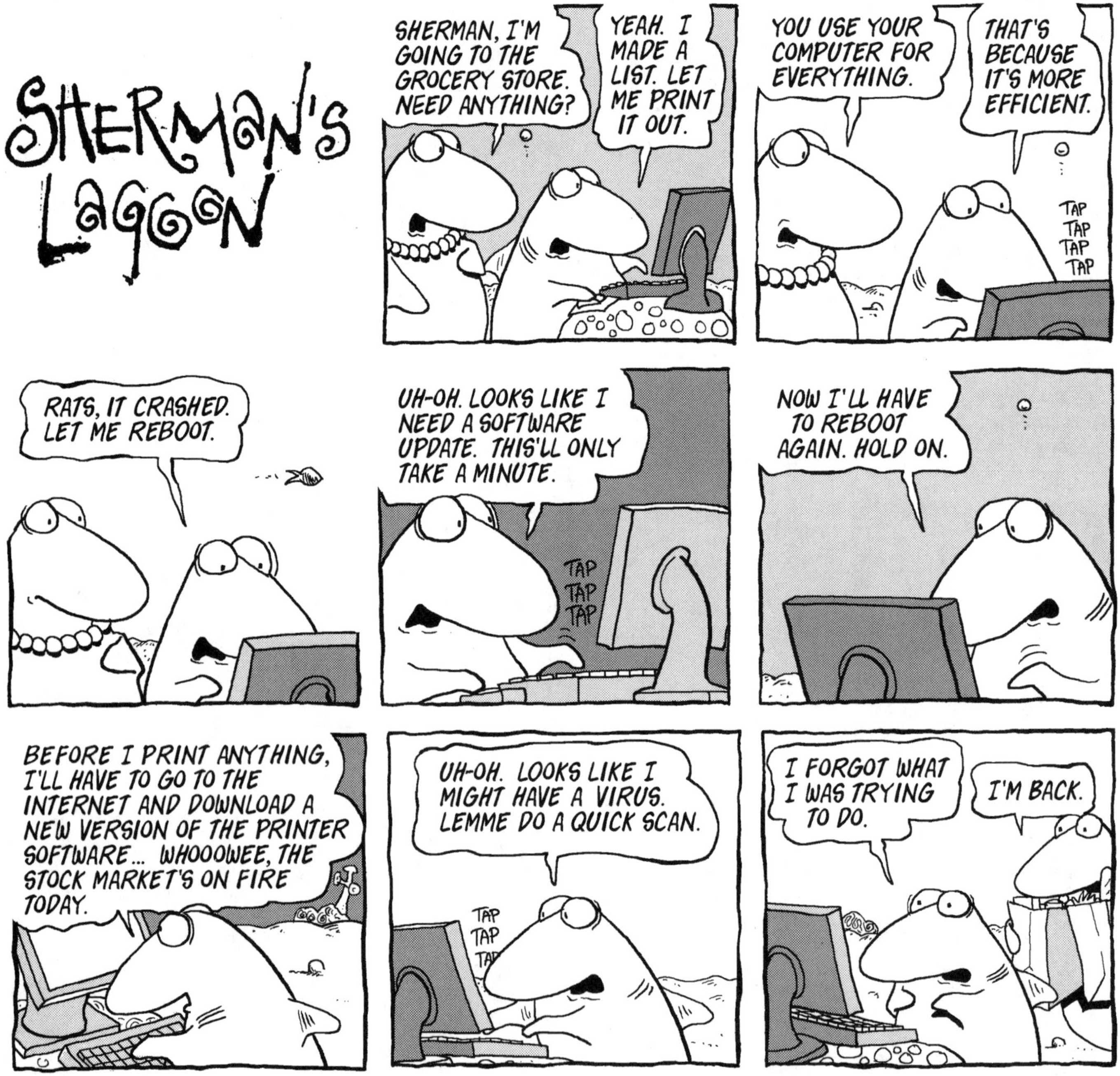
SHERMAN'S LAGOON
SHERMAN, I'M GOING TO THE GROCERY STORE. NEED ANYTHING?
YEAH. I MADE A LIST. LET ME PRINT IT OUT.
YOU USE YOUR COMPUTER FOR EVERYTHING.
THAT'S BECAUSE IT'S MORE EFFICIENT.
TAP TAP TAP TAP
RATS, IT CRASHED. LET ME REBOOT.
UH-OH. LOOKS LIKE I NEED A SOFTWARE UPDATE. THIS'LL ONLY TAKE A MINUTE.
TAP TAP TAP
NOW I'LL HAVE TO REBOOT AGAIN. HOLD ON.
BEFORE I PRINT ANYTHING, I'LL HAVE TO GO TO THE INTERNET AND DOWNLOAD A NEW VERSION OF THE PRINTER SOFTWARE... WHOOOWEE, THE STOCK MARKET'S ON FIRE TODAY.
UH-OH. LOOKS LIKE I MIGHT HAVE A VIRUS. LEMME DO A QUICK SCAN.
TAP TAP
I FORGOT WHAT I WAS TRYING TO DO.
I'M BACK.

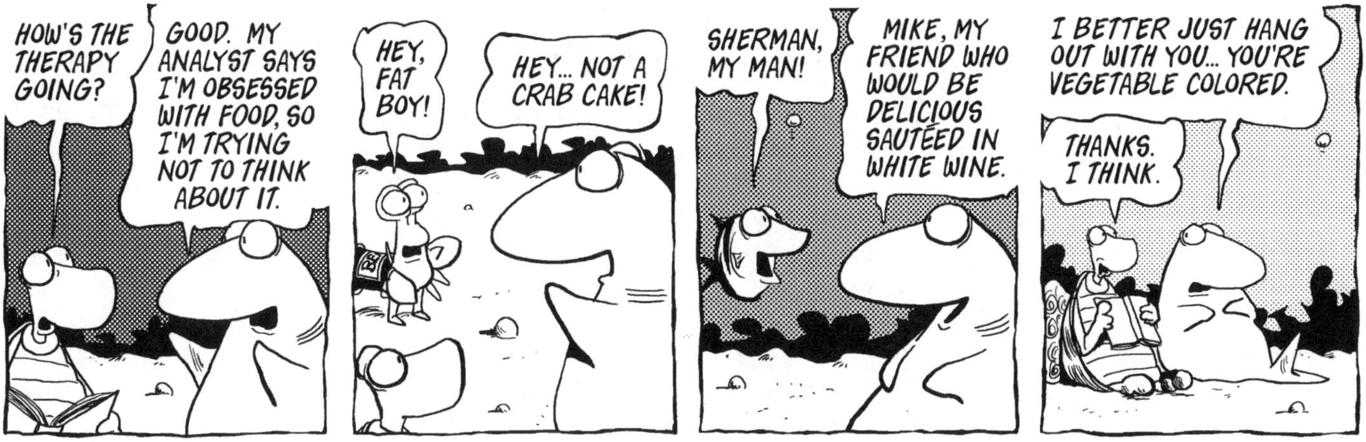
HOW'S THE THERAPY GOING?
GOOD. MY ANALYST SAYS I'M OBSESSED WITH FOOD, SO I'M TRYING NOT TO THINK ABOUT IT.
HEY, FAT BOY!
HEY... NOT A CRAB CAKE!
SHERMAN, MY MAN!
MIKE, MY FRIEND WHO WOULD BE DELICIOUS SAUTÉED IN WHITE WINE.
I BETTER JUST HANG OUT WITH YOU... YOU'RE VEGETABLE COLORED.
THANKS. I THINK.

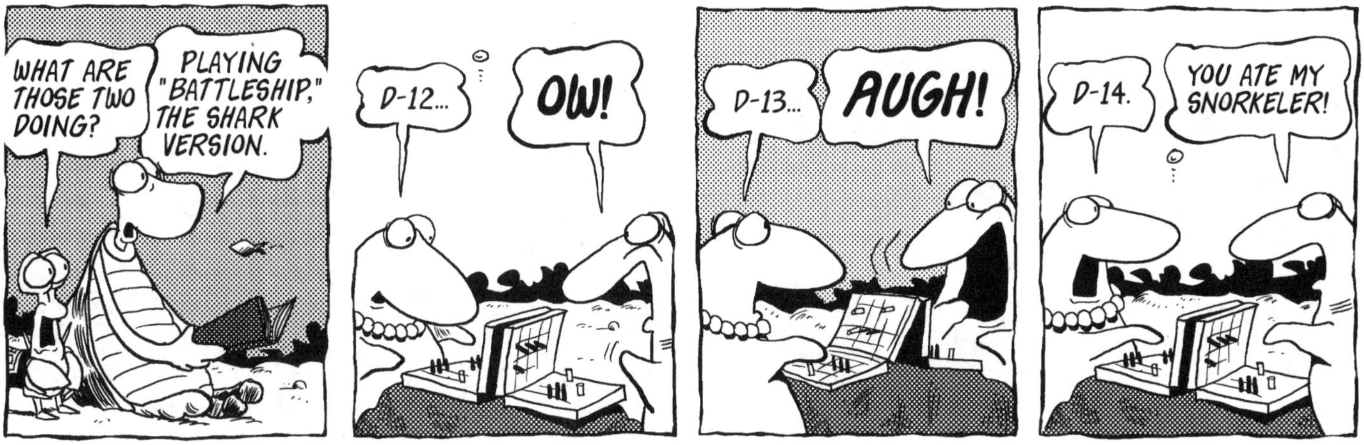
WHAT ARE THOSE TWO DOING?
PLAYING "BATTLESHIP," THE SHARK VERSION.
D-12...
OW!
D-13...
AUGH!
D-14.
YOU ATE MY SNORKELER!

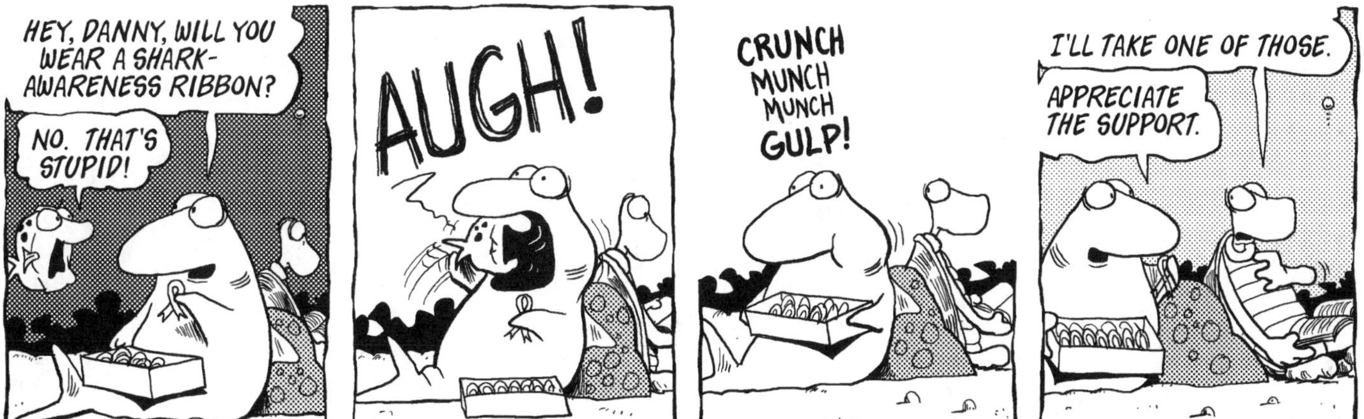
HEY, DANNY, WILL YOU WEAR A SHARK-AWARENESS RIBBON?
NO. THAT'S STUPID!
AUGH!
CRUNCH
MUNCH
MUNCH
GULP!
I'LL TAKE ONE OF THOSE.
APPRECIATE THE SUPPORT.

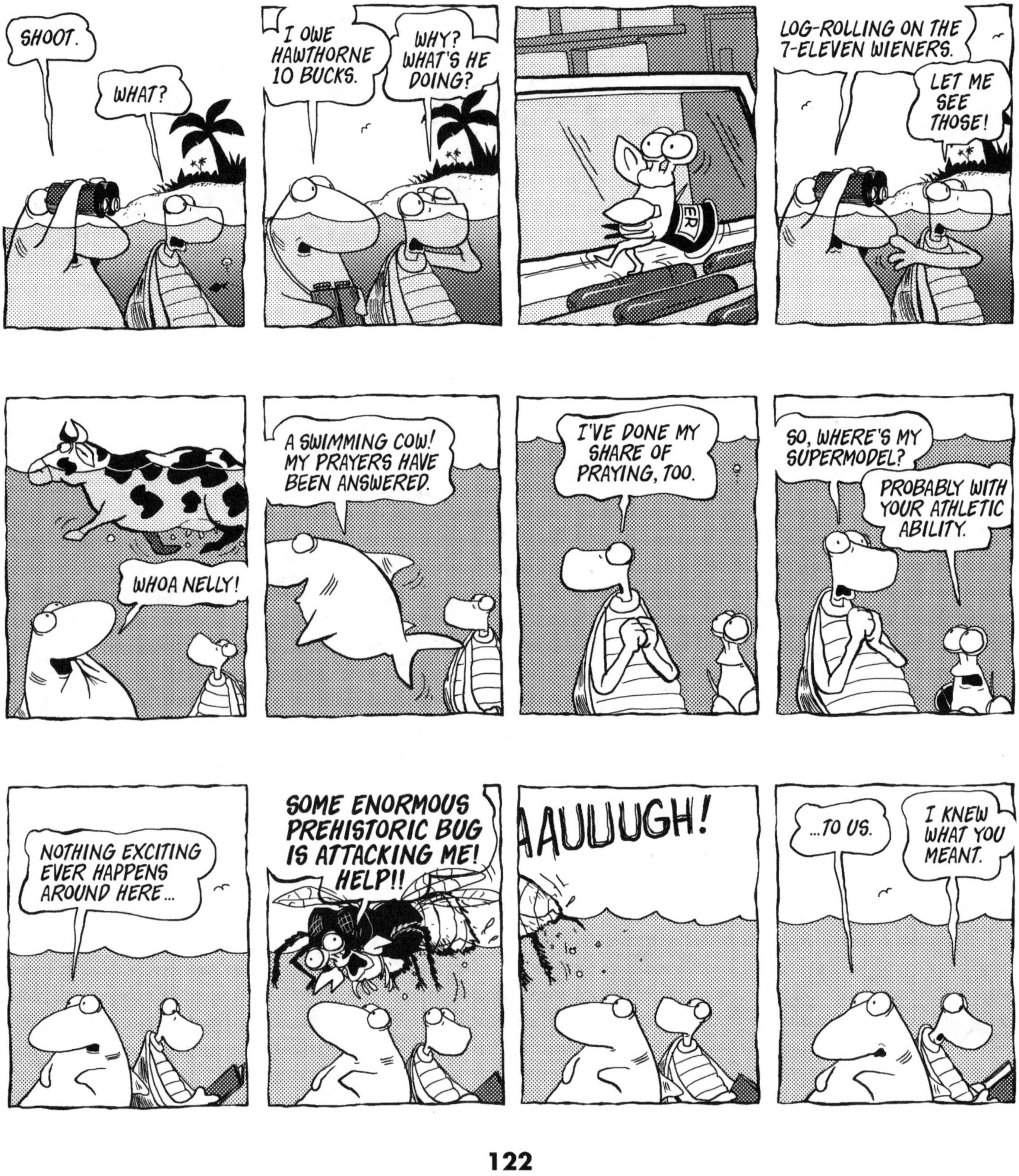
SHOOT.
WHAT?
I OWE HAWTHORNE 10 BUCKS.
WHY? WHAT'S HE DOING?
LOG-ROLLING ON THE 7-ELEVEN WIENERS.
LET ME SEE THOSE!
WHOA NELLY!
A SWIMMING COW! MY PRAYERS HAVE BEEN ANSWERED.
I'VE DONE MY SHARE OF PRAYING, TOO.
SO, WHERE'S MY SUPERMODEL?
PROBABLY WITH YOUR ATHLETIC ABILITY.
NOTHING EXCITING EVER HAPPENS AROUND HERE...
SOME ENORMOUS PREHISTORIC BUG IS ATTACKING ME! HELP!!
AAUUUGH!
...TO US.
I KNEW WHAT YOU MEANT.

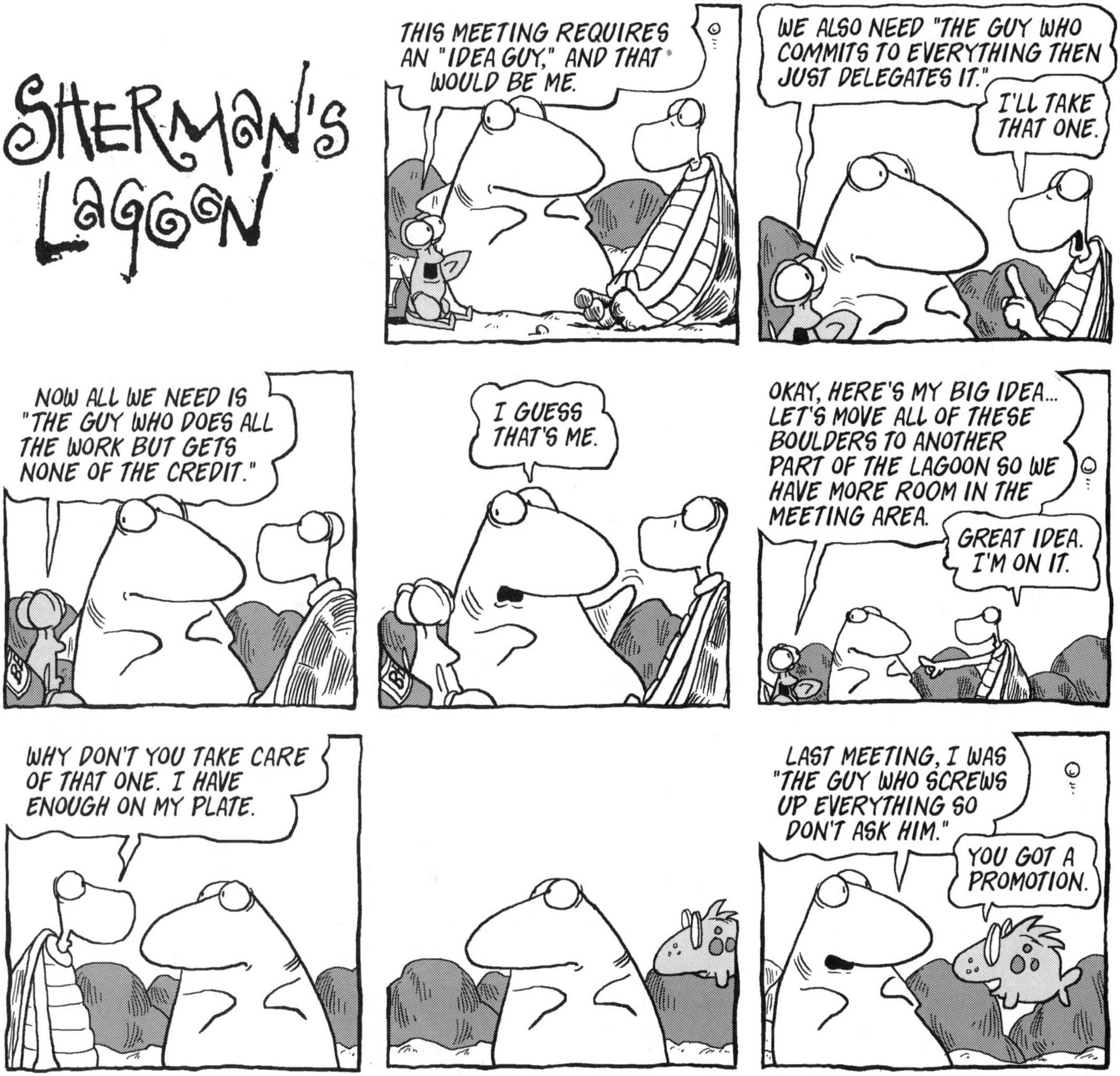
SHERMAN'S LAGOON
THIS MEETING REQUIRES AN "IDEA GUY," AND THAT WOULD BE ME.
WE ALSO NEED "THE GUY WHO COMMITS TO EVERYTHING THEN JUST DELEGATES IT."
I'LL TAKE THAT ONE.
NOW ALL WE NEED IS "THE GUY WHO DOES ALL THE WORK BUT GETS NONE OF THE CREDIT."
I GUESS THAT'S ME.
OKAY, HERE'S MY BIG IDEA... LET'S MOVE ALL OF THESE BOULDERS TO ANOTHER PART OF THE LAGOON SO WE HAVE MORE ROOM IN THE MEETING AREA.
GREAT IDEA. I'M ON IT.
WHY DON'T YOU TAKE CARE OF THAT ONE. I HAVE ENOUGH ON MY PLATE.
LAST MEETING, I WAS "THE GUY WHO SCREWS UP EVERYTHING SO DON'T ASK HIM."
YOU GOT A PROMOTION.

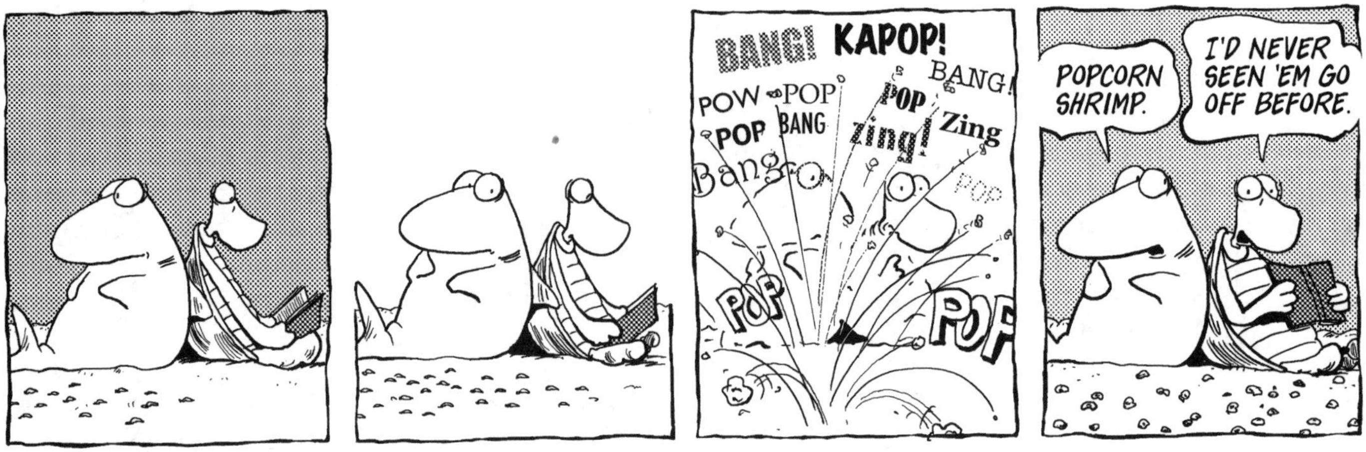
BANG! KAPOP!
BANG!
POW POP
POP
POP BANG
zing!
Zing
Bang
POP
POP
POP
POPCORN SHRIMP.
I'D NEVER SEEN 'EM GO OFF BEFORE.

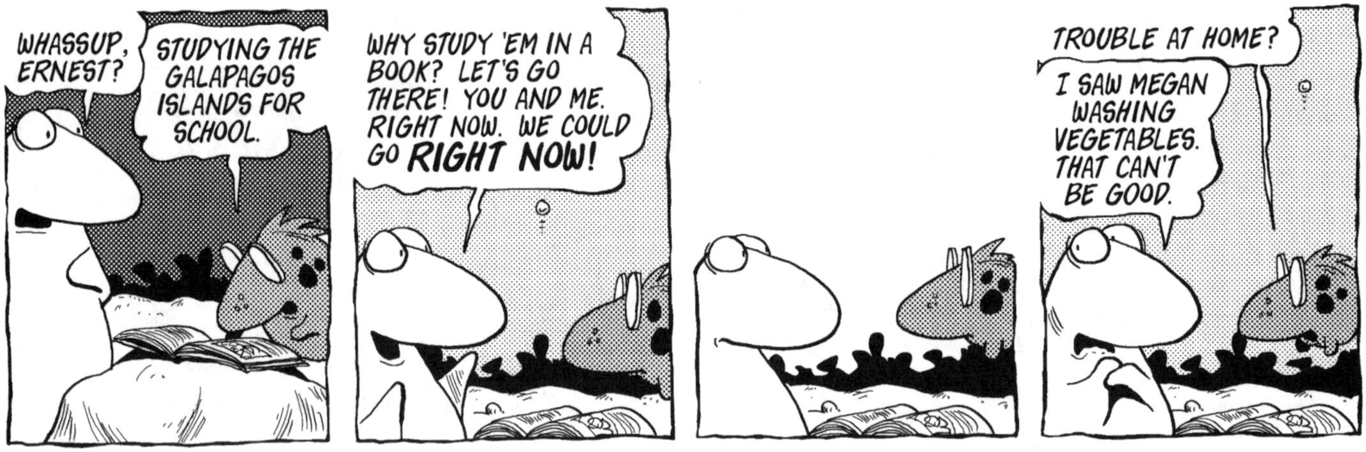
WHASSUP, ERNEST?
STUDYING THE GALAPAGOS ISLANDS FOR SCHOOL.
WHY STUDY 'EM IN A BOOK? LET'S GO THERE! YOU AND ME. RIGHT NOW. WE COULD GO RIGHT NOW!
TROUBLE AT HOME?
I SAW MEGAN WASHING VEGETABLES. THAT CAN'T BE GOOD.

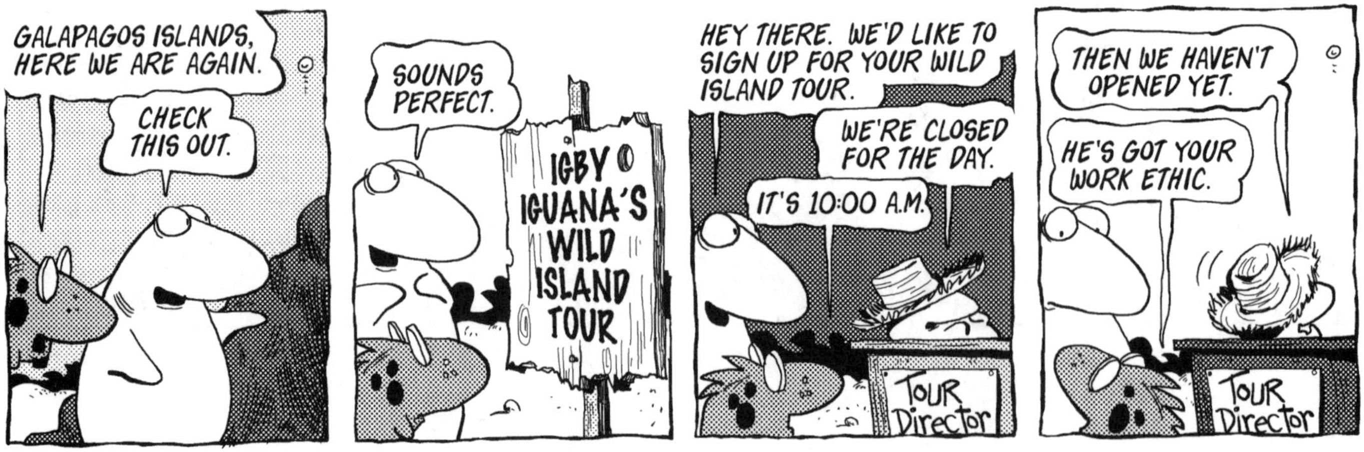
GALAPAGOS ISLANDS, HERE WE ARE AGAIN.
CHECK THIS OUT.
SOUNDS PERFECT.
IGBY IGUANA'S WILD ISLAND TOUR
HEY THERE. WE'D LIKE TO SIGN UP FOR YOUR WILD ISLAND TOUR.
WE'RE CLOSED FOR THE DAY.
IT'S 10:00 A.M.
TOUR Director
THEN WE HAVEN'T OPENED YET.
HE'S GOT YOUR WORK ETHIC.
TOUR Director

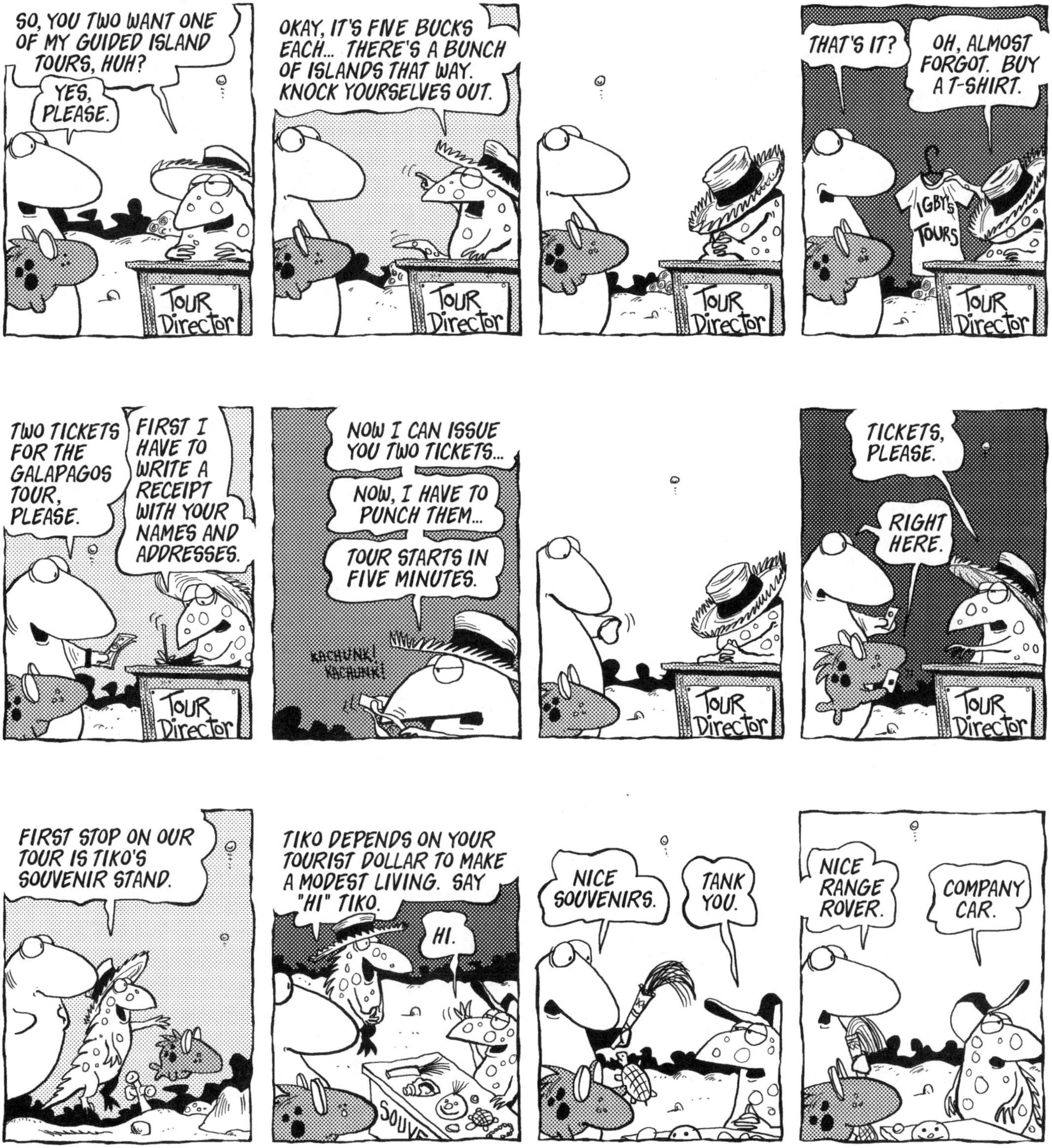
SO, YOU TWO WANT ONE OF MY GUIDED ISLAND TOURS, HUH?
YES, PLEASE.
TOUR Director
OKAY, IT'S FIVE BUCKS EACH... THERE'S A BUNCH OF ISLANDS THAT WAY. KNOCK YOURSELVES OUT.
TOUR Director
TOUR Director
THAT'S IT?
OH, ALMOST FORGOT. BUY A T-SHIRT.
IGBY'S TOURS
TOUR Director
TWO TICKETS FOR THE GALAPAGOS TOUR, PLEASE.
FIRST I HAVE TO WRITE A RECEIPT WITH YOUR NAMES AND ADDRESSES.
TOUR Director
NOW I CAN ISSUE YOU TWO TICKETS...
NOW, I HAVE TO PUNCH THEM...
TOUR STARTS IN FIVE MINUTES.
KACHUNK! KACHUNK!
TOUR Director
TICKETS, PLEASE.
RIGHT HERE.
TOUR Director
FIRST STOP ON OUR TOUR IS TIKO'S SOUVENIR STAND.
TIKO DEPENDS ON YOUR TOURIST DOLLAR TO MAKE A MODEST LIVING. SAY "HI" TIKO.
HI.
SOUV
NICE SOUVENIRS.
TANK YOU.
NICE RANGE ROVER.
COMPANY CAR.

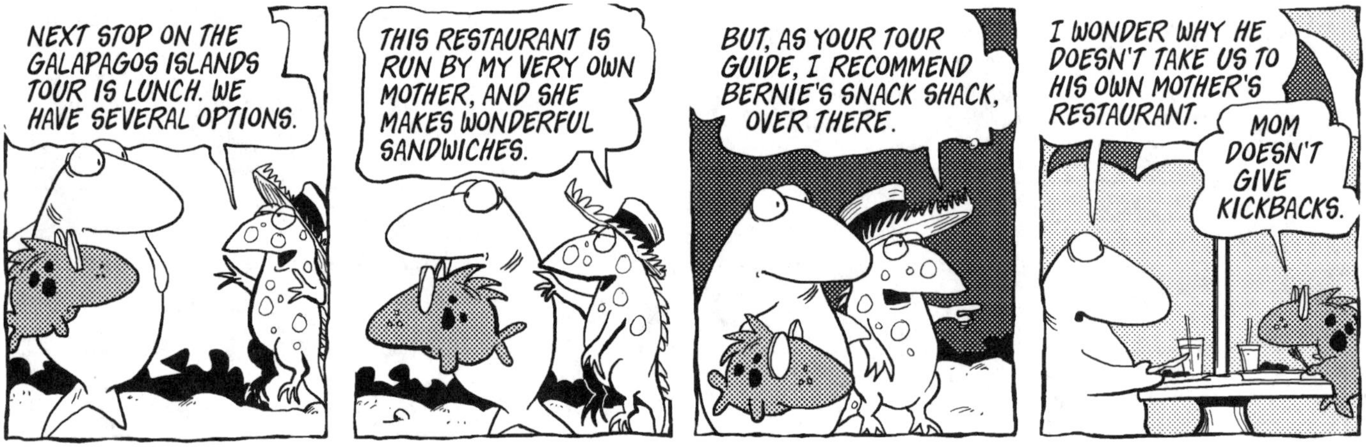
NEXT STOP ON THE GALAPAGOS ISLANDS TOUR IS LUNCH. WE HAVE SEVERAL OPTIONS.
THIS RESTAURANT IS RUN BY MY VERY OWN MOTHER, AND SHE MAKES WONDERFUL SANDWICHES.
BUT, AS YOUR TOUR GUIDE, I RECOMMEND BERNIE'S SNACK SHACK, OVER THERE.
I WONDER WHY HE DOESN'T TAKE US TO HIS OWN MOTHER'S RESTAURANT.
MOM DOESN'T GIVE KICKBACKS.

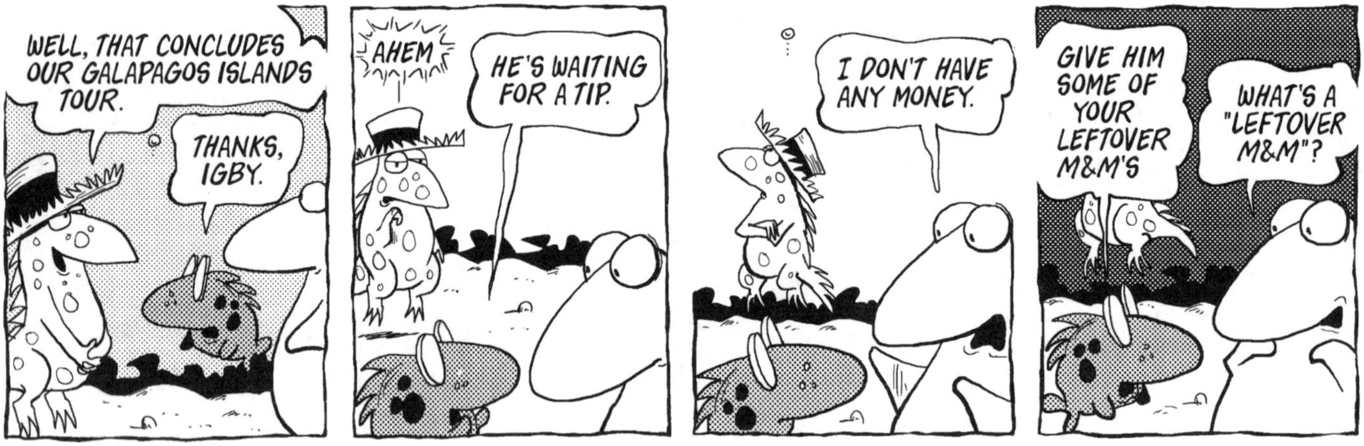
WELL, THAT CONCLUDES OUR GALAPAGOS ISLANDS TOUR.
THANKS, IGBY.
AHEM
HE'S WAITING FOR A TIP.
I DON'T HAVE ANY MONEY.
GIVE HIM SOME OF YOUR LEFTOVER M&M'S
WHAT'S A "LEFTOVER M&M"?

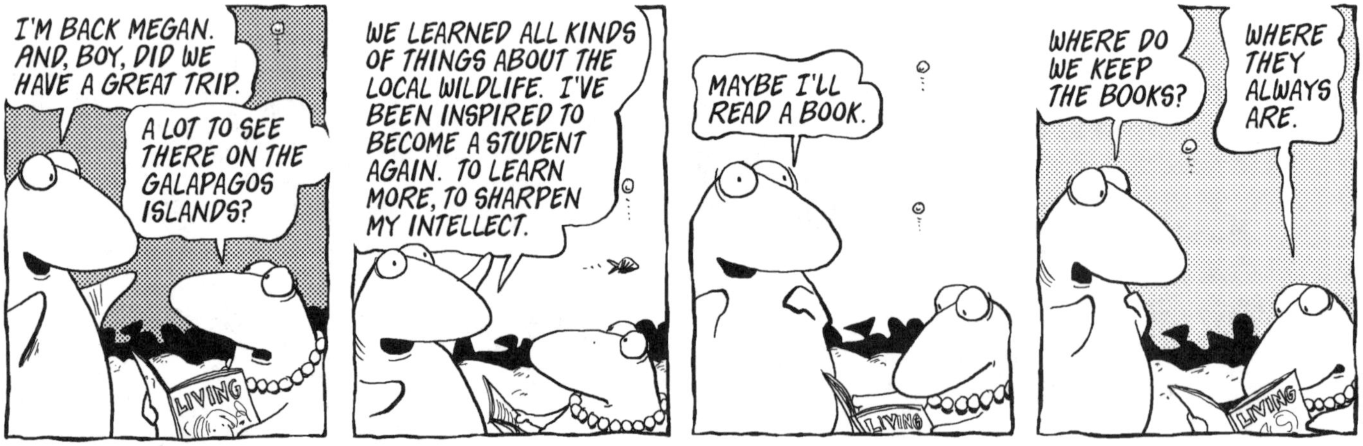
I'M BACK MEGAN. AND, BOY, DID WE HAVE A GREAT TRIP.
A LOT TO SEE THERE ON THE GALAPAGOS ISLANDS?
LIVING
WE LEARNED ALL KINDS OF THINGS ABOUT THE LOCAL WILDLIFE. I'VE BEEN INSPIRED TO BECOME A STUDENT AGAIN. TO LEARN MORE, TO SHARPEN MY INTELLECT.
MAYBE I'LL READ A BOOK.
LIVING
WHERE DO WE KEEP THE BOOKS?
WHERE THEY ALWAYS ARE.
LIVING

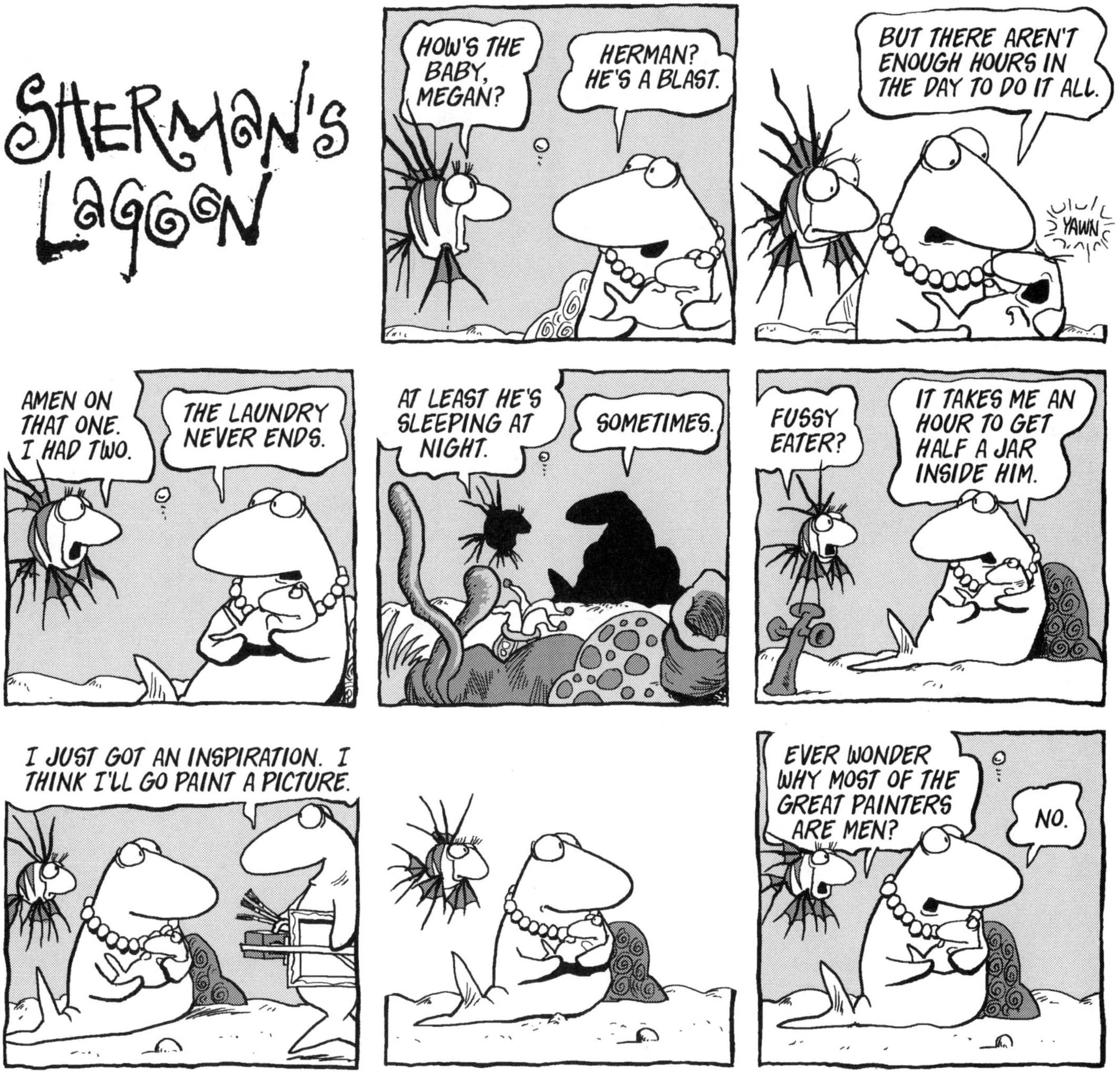
SHERMAN'S LAGOON
HOW'S THE BABY, MEGAN?
HERMAN? HE'S A BLAST.
BUT THERE AREN'T ENOUGH HOURS IN THE DAY TO DO IT ALL.
YAWN
AMEN ON THAT ONE. I HAD TWO.
THE LAUNDRY NEVER ENDS.
AT LEAST HE'S SLEEPING AT NIGHT.
SOMETIMES.
FUSSY EATER?
IT TAKES ME AN HOUR TO GET HALF A JAR INSIDE HIM.
I JUST GOT AN INSPIRATION. I THINK I'LL GO PAINT A PICTURE.
EVER WONDER WHY MOST OF THE GREAT PAINTERS ARE MEN?
NO.